K

SACRED PROFANITY

SACRED PROFANITY

Spirituality at the Movies

Aubrey Malone

PRAEGER

AN IMPRINT OF ABC-CLIO, LLC
Santa Barbara, California • Denver, Colorado • Oxford, England

Library of Congress Cataloging-in-Publication Data
Dillon-Malone, A. (Aubrey)
    Sacred Profanity: Spirituality at the movies / Aubrey Malone.
        p. cm.
    Includes bibliographical references and index.
    ISBN 978-0-313-37922-2 (hard copy : alk. paper)—ISBN 978-0-313-37923-9 (ebook)
1. Christianity in motion pictures. 2. Christians in motion pictures.
3. Motion pictures—Religious aspects. I. Title.
    PN1995.9.C49D55 2010
    791.43'652827—dc22   2009048543

ISBN: 978-0-313-37922-2
EISBN: 978-0-313-37923-9

14   13   12   11   10   1   2   3   4   5

This book is also available on the World Wide Web as an eBook.
Visit www.abc-clio.com for details.

Praeger
An Imprint of ABC-CLIO, LLC

ABC-CLIO, LLC
130 Cremona Drive, P.O. Box 1911
Santa Barbara, California 93116-1911

This book is printed on acid-free paper (∞)

Manufactured in the United States of America

Contents

Photo essay follows page 177

Acknowledgments

Thanks to Daniel Harmon for taking up this project. To Robert Dudley for suggesting it. To Mary for all her help in putting it together. To Keith for countless numbers of old movies and books. To the good people at Photofest for their advice. To the editors who published my film-based articles over the years. To Denise for her computer expertise. To all the librarians who sourced rare research material for me.

—— 1 ——

Quoting Scripture for One's Purpose

In the beginning was the epic, and the epic was with DeMille and the epic *was* DeMille. . . . Films about the early days of Christianity came about for reasons that were far from Christian. The motive was more likely a five-letter word beginning with "m" and ending with "y." The jury is still out on exactly how committed to his art Cecil B. DeMille was when it came to directing Biblical movies. Was he motivated by genuine spiritual feeling or the profits generated by this genre?

Norman Bel Geddes said, "Never have I seen a man with so prominent a position splash so fondly about in mediocrity, and, like a child building a sandcastle, so serenely convinced that he was producing works of art."[1]

Or was he? He once confessed, "Every time I make a picture, the critics' estimation of public taste goes down 10 percent."[2] Howard Hawks was similarly disparaging, claiming that he learned a lot from him "by doing the opposite."[3] Richard Walsh's view was that his admixture of "sex, spectacle and sentiment" was primarily targeted towards Protestant audiences.[4]

It would be easy to condemn DeMille out of hand as a cynical exploiter of all things Biblical for profit. This is far from the truth. The son of a lay minister, he was weaned on the Bible with his mother's milk, and most of it stuck. He saw himself in a missionary, nay, messianic role when it came to transmitting the message of God to his flock of cineastes. A frugal workaholic, while filming *The Ten Commandments* DeMille issued an eleventh commandment: all cast members were to keep a copy of the Bible with them and read it on a daily basis. He meant it to be like a second script to them.

He didn't suffer fools gladly. His themes may have been sacred but there was nothing sacred about his temper tantrums. He was a vicious reader of scripts, refusing to spare any author's blush. He famously replied to one aspiring screenwriter with the words, "I have crossed out the parts of your script that I did not like. What I haven't crossed out I'm not happy with."[5]

On set he scolded actors if they weren't behaving as he wanted, and frequently reduced actresses to tears. He never improvised, and expected actors to hit the marks with clockwork precision. "If someone didn't do their job right," according to Michael Munn, "he'd chew them out there and then."[6]

On the set of *Samson and Delilah*, when Victor Mature appeared too nervous, DeMille told him he had met many men in his life who were afraid of various things like water, fire or closed spaces, or even open spaces, but never someone who was as utterly cowardly as Mature in over three decades as a director. Mature was 100% yellow in his view.

He accepted the fact that he was a tough taskmaster. "I have been called a tyrant, a despot and a martinet," he conceded, but felt he was entitled to lose his temper "when I have somebody playing checkers on a set that costs $40,000 a day when he should be paying attention to his job."[7] He even told extras he expected just as much from them as he did from actors. Indeed, he drew little distinction between the two. If an extra misbehaved on set rather than in character or at some activity, he would be fired.

Few denied his inimitable mastery when it came to orchestrating crowd scenes. The common belief was that he could have coordinated mice at a crossroads. He was less talented in nuanced intimacies. He never considered failure an option. He often said to his crew, "Gentlemen, I know you'll give me 1000 reasons why this can't be done. Now let's forget that and see how it *can* be done."[8]

Ray Milland once commented, "He didn't know much about acting. He couldn't tell you the first word about how to play a scene. He set it up camera-wise and you just read your lines."[9] Gloria Swanson, one of his favorite actresses, said she remembered a young actor asking him if he would tell him how to play a scene in the film *Don't Change Your Husband*. "Certainly not!" DeMille roared, "This is not an acting school. When you do something wrong, *that* is when I will talk to you!"[10] Charlton Heston believed he adhered to the old Spencer Tracy dictum of "Come on time, know your lines, and don't bump into the furniture."[11]

"He was the Spielberg of his day," Heston contended.[12] When it came to pomp and ceremony, however, his eye for pageantry took over, and in an age of blockbusters, this was a very enviable talent.

His father, a Dutch Episcopalian, wanted him to be a lay reader in his church, but a colleague persuaded him that he could "preach" to a larger audience through the medium of film.

He directed his first film, *The Squaw Man* (1913), in a barn.[13] He made many comedies in his early years but it was in 1923, with the making of *The Ten Commandments* that he really came of age. This started when Al Winkie, his press agent, organized a national contest with a prize of $1000 to anyone who suggested the best idea for a film. Letters poured in on a multitude of topics, eight of them advancing the Ten Commandments as a possibility. DeMille was captivated by the idea of making a film about the Ten Commandments, so he gave all eight of the entrants $1000 each instead of splitting the prize money among them. Already his profligacy was evident.

Spending money was easier than getting the studio moguls to share his enthusiasm. "Old men wearing tablecloths and beards?" Adolph Zukor hissed, "What budget would you be thinking of?" "One million dollars," DeMille replied.[14]

Zukor eventually came around to DeMille's way of thinking and DeMille sprang into action. The film ended up costing $1,500,000 to make but took in almost three times that amount at the box office. "I believe it will be the biggest picture ever made," DeMille boasted, "not only from the standpoint of spectacle but from the point of humanness, dramatic power, and the great good it will do."[15]

It contained the largest exterior set of its time, its construction requiring 550,000 feet of timber, 300 tons of plaster, 25,000 pounds of nails and 75 miles of cable and wire. The set was so elaborate that after the film was completed it was buried on location in Guadalupe, California to save money rather than being sent back to Hollywood. Over 33,000 yards of cloth were used for the costumes. That comes to almost 19 miles of cloth, a staggering length. Not even today's computer-generated effects could emulate it.

DeMille's next film was *Joan the Woman* (1916), the story of Joan of Arc. Jeanie McPherson played her as "a vulnerable woman, longing for sexual fulfilment from the soldier she loves, but deliberately rejecting him in favour of serving Christ."[16]

After the film was previewed in New York, a member of the censor board objected to Joan of Arc's line "My God, my God, why hast thou forsaken me?" DeMille asked her if she knew who had first spoken these words. "It doesn't make any difference," she bristled, "It means that God would forsake someone and it has to come out." She only relented when she was informed that it was Christ himself who coined the phrase.[17]

This anecdote points to the fact that DeMille was better versed in the Bible than many of his detractors—not that this was necessarily saying much. But he did seem to have a genuine piety about him which is attested to by everyone from Gloria Swanson to Henry Wilcoxon, two stars who knew him better than most. Wilcoxon said he was a "painfully honourable man who never did anything that was underhanded or sneaky. Further, the gates of Paramount wouldn't be open today if he hadn't been there."[18] Bob Hope echoed this when he said "DeMille's films have brought something new to the theatres. They call them customers."[19]

In 1921 DeMille made *Queen of Sheba*, a film full of flimsily-attired ladies. As Betty Blythe, who played the lead role, deadpanned, "I wear twenty-eight costumes in the movie. If I put them all on at once, I still wouldn't be warm."[20]

He directed *The King of Kings*, the story of the life of Christ, in 1927. A silent movie, it was elegant and reverential. The Resurrection scene in particular stood out. The evangelist Billy Graham said the film taught him "more about the life of Christ than did a great deal of the Sunday School training [he] had as a boy."[21] In the view of Ronald Fraser, however, DeMille "capitalized" Jesus, making him not so much a peasant as "an icon of the American middle class."[22]

DeMille sent a copy of the Bible to every member of the cast during the shooting of the film, ordering them to memorize every word of the gospels, just as he had during *The Ten Commandments*, and calling them in every day for a lesson on what they'd learned. In some ways it was like being back at school. He donated all profits from the film, as he also did with *The Ten Commandments*, to charity.[23]

On the second day of shooting, he convened a throng of august religious figures and proceeded to lecture them on the gospels, a classic case of over-elaboration. Such was his commanding presence, however, that nobody saw fit to interrupt his diatribes. He had the people standing in semi-circles while he addressed them from a pulpit. The location for this homily was a delicious example of his wicked wit: Mary Magdalene's brothel. The final print was 1,500,000 feet, which was 300 miles of celluloid—the distance from Los Angeles to San Diego. It was eventually whittled down to 14,000 feet.

The film opens with a lavish party thrown by Mary Magdalene, a rich courtesan who utters lines like "harness my zebras—gifts of the Nubian king!" Magdalene is outraged that Judas—her lover—has left her to follow a humble Nazarene preacher. This melodramatically kitschy scene swiftly segues into a reverential one. In one author's view it was as if DeMille "suddenly realised his error."[24] Derek Elley writes about his "artistic schizophrenia."[25] He loved to shock—and then inspire. If a scene went well he was reputed to go down on his knees and thank God.

Jesus is played by a 50-year-old H.B. Warner. When we first see Jesus he performs a miracle, giving a blind girl back her sight. Thus we go from the ridiculous to the sublime without a by-your-leave. DeMille doesn't seem to have seen any disjunction in this collusion of poignancy and eroticism. Magdalene finally falls under Jesus' spell herself, which isn't the way the Bible tells the story of her conversion, but DeMille allowed himself this kind of leverage.

DeMille's brother William quipped, "Cecil always bites off more than he can chew—and then chews it."[26] John Gilbert added, "He was no director. He didn't know what to tell us. I think the only man he ever envied was Hitler."[27] Pauline Kael captured his paradox when she said, "He made small-minded pictures on a big scale."[28]

His life, like his films, was a bundle of contradictions. He was a devout Christian but openly maintained relationships with two mistresses, Jeanie MacPherson and Julia Faye, for many years. He was also a foot fetishist.

He said in his defense, "I'm sometimes accused of gingering up the Bible with lavish infusions of sex and violence, but I wish that my accusers would read their Bibles more closely, for in those pages are more sex and violence than I could ever portray on the screen."[29]

DeMille directed from a platform, transmitting instructions to his crew and stars by means of a megaphone. This gave him a kind of messianic bearing even in his working methods. Sometimes he even used a radio telephone to give orders. Ken Brownslow remarked, "He directed as though chosen by God for this one task."[30] Barry Norman believed his so-called "All Star" pictures "actually meant no stars at all except the flamboyant director himself."[31] He even resided on DeMille Drive. Evelyn Keyes said, "He lived like an emperor. If he entered the commissary it was always with a retinue following him. *Nobody* walked alongside."[32]

His films have orgiastic delights but also deep religious fervour. He directed *The Sign of the Cross* in 1932. This also mixed sensuality with religious zeal. Such was his high reputation with church authorities that they all but turned a blind eye to the dizzy delights on display. With the Bible, one could get away with murder. Or, even worse, sex.

"An audience of churchgoers," he once remarked, "can enjoy having their libido stimulated so long as the sinners are punished in the final reel by an avenging God"[33] David Thomson believes he found "unexpected showbiz rewards when he realized that Biblical subjects necessarily involved original sin, dancing girls, and a good deal of skin."[34] Hedy Lamarr emoted, "When it comes to sex and spectacle, no one can tear down a temple or tear off a piece of clothing at one and the same time like he can. When he sells sex, sister, people buy it because he wraps it in fancy paper and pink ribbons."[35]

How did he get away with this double standard? Frank Miller opined that the authorities of the time allowed it because of the reputation he had built up with such "high moral works" as *The King of Kings* and *The Ten Commandments*.[36]

This meant that he could have his celluloid cake and eat it too, but his comments displayed an avowed cynicism towards the churchgoing audience, and a theological assumption that sinners were most likely to suffer their hell in this life rather than the next. One scene featured a near-naked woman tied to a stake, about to be ravaged by a gorilla. Was this "sinner" going to be punished by an "avenging God" as well? Another has Claudette Colbert washing herself in a bath filled with asses' milk, displaying more flesh than moralists were happy with.

First filmed in 1914, *The Sign of the Cross* basically deals with the attempts of the scheming Poppeia (Colbert) to win the heart of Marcus (Frederic March). Marcus is more attracted to the virginal Mercia (Elissa Landi). One commentator suggests there's an anachronism in the title of the film, since, in his view, the cross didn't become a Christian symbol until six centuries after Nero's time "when it was authorized by the Quinsexte Council."[37]

Though Marcus is a Roman soldier and Mercia a Christian, he wants to marry her. This will mean her giving up silly habits like chastity, so he brings her to an orgy to try and knock some sense into her Christian head about the joys of hedonism. During the orgy, Marcus has one of his female friends perform an erotic dance around Mercia which also involves her kissing and caressing her. One can only assume Marcus feels chastity has to be renounced gradually through same-sex overtures. But Mercia resists, so she's thrown to the lions along with the other "deluded" Christians.

As she waits for her horrific fate to unfold in the amphitheatre she watches decapitations, death by elephant trampling and even hungry crocodiles getting their "Christian" dinner as Nero casually oversees it all, chomping on the inevitable grapes while the macabre slaughter takes place.

One of the other prisoners wonders "Where is God?" and she answers blithely, having no doubt read her Catechism assiduously, "He is closer to us now than he has ever been."

One more surprise is in store for us because Marcus now approaches Nero, Poppeia's husband, to spare Mercia. Poppeia prevails upon the emperor not to accede to Marcus' wish because, of course, she wants Marcus for herself. Marcus then makes the gallant decision to accompany Mercia into the arena. Obviously orgies are fun, but not half as enjoyable as being gobbled up by lions when one feels sure immortality awaits. "I'm full of strange hope," he tells Mercia as they march together to embrace their destiny. Strange indeed.

Poor Poppeia is left alone and bereft, her wicked plan to snare Marcus backfiring on her. While she can still have her milk baths, they won't be half as much fun with Nero, a portly Charles Laughton, as they would have been with the dashing Frederic March.

It's easy for us to chortle today but in 1932 this kind of bombastic depravity was taken very seriously. Nobody even laughed at the fact that the characters spoke in tones that more resembled late Brooklynese ("Look out, will ya?") than early Christian, though George MacDonald Fraser commented that his history teacher was reluctant to see the film "because he feared he might be offended by the sight of gladiators who chewed gum and talked like gangsters."[38] John Baxter felt its cocktail of sex and violence, played out against ornate backgrounds, embodied "under a veil of gimcrack Christian propaganda, a celebration of paganism."[39]

DeMille wanted Laughton to play Nero as a chilling villain but Laughton was historically well versed enough to know that Nero was more of a camp figure and insisted on playing him as such. The homophobia in DeMille balked at this but Laughton was resolute. Laughton's standing up to DeMille took guts, considering he was a gay man himself at a time when actors would do anything to avoid attracting attention to such a fact in their performances. Laughton, in fact, revelled in it: supervising his own make-up as he rouged his cheeks, plucked his eyebrows and even applied lipstick. He also spoke in a lisp to complete the package. As we watch Nero/Laughton plucking his harp, munching grapes and having his fingernails manicured, we're left in little doubt about his sexual orientation, much to the chagrin of the director.

DeMille never seemed bothered by trifling details like period authenticity. All he needed was for the overall plan to work, and audiences to pour in. "I make my pictures for people," he bragged, "not the critics."[40] His colleague Jesse Lasky Jr knew that "[i]t didn't concern him in the least that in the opinion of serious film-makers his works were considered as artistically significant as Barnum & Bailey's circus. He feared only one thing—that an audience might be bored."[41] John Naughton credited him with the gift of "knowing what the public wanted before they knew themselves."[42] Neal Gabler felt he "wrapped moralism in sensualism, thereby mediating between the genteel and the Jazz Age."[43]

The Sign of the Cross had a $650,000 budget, which allowed DeMille to fully indulge his penchant tor the spectacular. He hired 4000 extras and recreated Rome almost brick by brick. He threw himself into it 110 percent, as always. To "persuade" the lions to attack the Christians, he half-starved them and then stuffed lamb's carcasses under the Christians' costumes.[44] To get the lions to climb the stairs to the main arena he chased them with an axe in one hand and the arm of a chair in the other. He knew no fear. As a result, the take was everything. In an age before special effects, it had to be done the hard way. But he loved a challenge.

Daniel Lord, a Jesuit who loved movies, had been appointed as an advisor on the moral aspect of scenes in the film. Gregory Black says Lord begged DeMille not to make his pagans "attractive, warm-blooded, alive human beings" and his Christians "plaster saints" but DeMille ignored him.[45] Black adds that Ms Colbert, and the imperial women of Rome, "were not shy about wearing flimsy gowns, backless and cut to the waist in the front, and slit to the thigh on each leg. Whenever they moved, the dresses gaped openly, the camera lingering lovingly over their exposed flesh." In contrast, Christian women wore plain homespun clothes that covered them from neck to toe. DeMille's explanation was that this was "good versus evil." His critics alleged that it was more likely hypocrisy, designed to show "as much female flesh as possible."[46]

Lord told DeMille that he liked the overall concept of the film but that the pagans looked "nightclubish" while the Christians were "dull, plodding and uninspiring."[47] "You can't show triumph over sin unless you show the temptation," he told Lord. And boy did he show it.

D.W. Griffith, in a denunciation of DeMille's tactics, remarked, "I'll never use the Bible as a chance to undress a woman." DeMille didn't have any such compunctions. Gloria Swanson said his films had an air of "delicate, authentic decadence about them, like the smell of cut gardenias at the end of a party."[48]

Lord disagreed with DeMille on many occasions during the shoot. DeMille lost his temper with him once and told him to go to hell. Lord replied casually, "I can't. I already have a reservation elsewhere."[49]

After their argument, DeMille agreed to tone down some scenes, but the so-called "lesbian" dance stayed in, as did Colbert bathing nude in the tub, and even entreating her voluptuous handmaiden to "[t]ake off your clothes and get in here." Joseph Scrembs, a Cleveland bishop, went so far as to condemn the film in his New Year's Eve homily, which was transcribed by the Catholic News Service and transmitted across America.

But still the audiences turned out in droves to see DeMille's films. What made this even more surprising was that there was so little money floating around the American economy at the time. Many people gained admission to the film with IOUs. According to DeMille, most of these were redeemed when the economy picked up again.

Martin Quigley, who helped draft the 1930 Production Code, of which more anon, conveyed his chagrin to DeMille in a caustic letter. DeMille defended himself by replying, "I seem to remember certain inhabitants of two towns in the Bible, Sodom and Gomorrah," but Quigley wasn't impressed. "So do I," Quigley wrote back to him, "and I also seem to remember they got hell, and lots of it."[50] Quigley was pitching the ball back in the punishment court and also implying that one could suggest debauchery without actually depicting it. But depicting debauchery was half the fun for the duplicitous DeMille.

After viewing the explicit orgy scene, Will Hays, the chief administrator of Hollywood's self-censorship body, called DeMille to ask him what he planned to do about the aforementioned controversial scene to render it more edifying for the public. DeMille replied, "Not a damn thing." Few in the industry could stand up to Hays like that but DeMille did and he got away with it. The film proved to be a huge success and reinvigorated DeMille's career, paving the way for his lavish *Cleopatra* in 1934. It earned so much money for Paramount, in fact, that it all but rescued the company from bankruptcy.

DeMille was an *auteur* before the term was invented, which meant he had dictatorial control over his material. He ran a tight ship but also a limited one. He painted in large brushstrokes that militated against subtlety. Since he wasn't a subtle man there was little chance that any abstruse message would be constrained by his crowd-pleasing format.

Gloria Swanson remarked: "Working for him was like playing house in the world's most expensive department store."[51]

His general status in the film trade was conveyed in an anecdote related during the making of *The Ten Commandments*. Theodore Roberts and James Neil, who played Moses and Aaron, respectively, were in costume and waiting outside DeMille's office to see him about the interpretation of a particular scene. When he didn't appear after an inordinate amount of time they asked his secretary to "[j]ust say that Moses and Aaron are waiting to see God."[52] A more irreverent gag tells of a psychiatrist who was needed in heaven "because God thought he was Cecil B. DeMille."[53]

He directed *Samson and Delilah* in 1949, making a return to Biblical material after various other projects. It was unintentionally laughable, a run-of-de-Mille effort that owed less to God than Mammon. In many ways the costumes were the best part of the performances. Victor Mature who played Samson had little chance of winning an Oscar. "I'm no actor," he once said with commendable frankness, "and I've got sixty-four pictures to prove it."[54] Hedy Lamarr wasn't much better as the lady who clipped his locks in a "hell hath no fury like a woman scorned" vein.

DeMille said he planned to market the film as a story of faith to satisfy the censors but inside this format there was a torrid romance. Such doublespeak was part and parcel of DeMille's whole career, and much of the reason behind his enormous box office success. He always saw his saints as profits more than prophets.

Theresa Sanders stated that in interviews DeMille claimed he included sensual scenes of the Roman Empire "only in order to highlight the Christians' purity and moral superiority"—the angle he pedalled to Lord & Co.[55] Even if DeMille's claims were true, and I doubt it, it backfired on him because after *The Sign of the Cross* was released, the same Christians "responded to his film with outrage." Indeed, their anger was one of the factors that led to the founding of the Catholic Legion of Decency in 1934.[56]

Groucho Marx famously declined to see the film noting that "I never go to a film where the hero's bust is bigger than the heroine's."[57] Neither Mr Mature nor Ms Lamarr was impressed with the comment. Pauline Kael echoed Marx when she said Mature was so flaccid he looked as if he couldn't even tear down a papier-mâché temple, never mind a real one. And yet the film has him wrestling a lion to death with his bare hands in one scene. "But you might have been hurt!" Lamarr exclaimed, to which Mature replied, "It was nothing. It was only a young lion." Thereafter, the exchanges got even worse, if that's possible.

This kind of sackcloth-and-ashes nonsense always made money, though. America was on the verge of the television revolution, and Hollywood had to up the ante. What better way to do this than with epics? It was all very well to look down on "the eternal rectangle" as the poor relation of movies art-wise, but the threat was real. In 1946 only one home in every 5000 in the United States had a television set. Two years later, however, one in 250 homes had a television set—an increase of a staggering 2000 percent.[58] Television was instant and affordable and, as Alfred Hitchcock remarked, you didn't need to pay for a babysitter. Billy Wilder put it a different way. After decades of being sneered at by intellectuals, he remarked, film-makers finally had a medium they could look down on.[59]

But that little box sitting in the corner of Joe Blow's living-room was powerful; so powerful that if the moguls didn't do something, and fast, they were in danger of being blown out of the water financially speaking. Many people thought, "Why pay to see a bad movie when you can stay home and see a bad TV programme for nothing?"

By this time, weekly sales of movie tickets had plummeted from sixty million to forty million, while the number of TV sets had inversely jumped from a million to eleven million in just two years. So the studio heads put on their thinking caps and decided to pump up the celluloid volume with a string of quasi-Biblical epics that would prioritize their visual impact. In this department, for obvious reasons, the "goggle box" couldn't compete.

Henry King directed *David and Bathsheba* in 1951. This film was a better than average depiction of the Judaean king seizing Jerusalem and then being followed by the wife of one of his officers. Gregory Peck and Susan Hayward essayed the main roles. Screenwriter Philip Dunne, a non-believer, kept the use of miracles to a minimum in an effort to avoid what he called "DeMillisms." He also took care to make sure there were "no heavenly choirs" and no actors "making with the holy look."[60] Monsignor Devlin, previewing the film for Joe Breen's censorship office, and being aware that Dunne was: "a backslidden Catholic," said to him one day on the set, "Have you forgotten that David is a Catholic saint?" Dunne replied that seeing as the Pope who canonized him was willing to forgive his sins, so also should audiences.[61]

Quo Vadis?, directed by Mervyn LeRoy, was released in 1951 as well. The film was a typical example of tacky commercialism. In many ways this returns us to a *Sign of the Cross*–style plot, with Christians being liberally thrown to the lions while a Roman soldier, the ever-wooden Robert Taylor, becomes converted by a female Christian of this particular species, Deborah Kerr. Calling the film a biblical epic is really a misnomer. The apostle Peter appears in the film as an old man, the film being set many years after Jesus' crucifixion. He reminisces on his life with Jesus in a series of flashbacks but these bear little or no relation to the main business of the film and their insertion is both distracting and unnecessary. It falls to a delightfully camp Peter Ustinov to rescue matters as Nero in the performance of his career.

When he gives the thumbs down to Taylor in the arena you almost find yourself cheering. His interpretation has obviously been influenced by that of Charles Laughton, a similarly leering Nero in *The Sign of the Cross*, as we saw, but he still steals the show. Not that he has much opposition. Taylor mouths his lines as if he's in a particular hurry to get off the set. His "conversion" to Christianity is difficult to accept. It's a case of "religion gets you the doll" or as DeMille might have said, "It gets you the dollar."

William Dieterle's *Salome* in 1953 was also farcical. Derek Elley rightly said that the film was "less important for its preposterous plot than for its portrait of a bad woman rescued by a good religion."[62] Rita Hayworth starred as Salome in the film. Salome dances for Herod, played by Charles Laughton, to try and entice him to spare John the Baptist's life rather than to demand his head on a plate. This was about the only innovative thing about the film. In other adaptations of the tale, Salome is the demon of the piece. Here it's her mother who asks Laughton for the prophet's head.

Jesus' preaching, like that of John the Baptist, resounds from a hilltop at the end of the movie, which incidentally doesn't finish with "The End" but rather "This Was the Beginning."

Such a melodramatic endline is fairly typical of the film itself. John the Baptist rants about the evil of the Roman Empire with its "iniquitous" rulers. The "king of kings," he informs us, will overthrow the house of Herod "as certainly as all rivers rush to the ocean."

Laughton is willing to spare John the Baptist's life to gain Hayworth's love but her mother has different ideas. Stewart Granger is the token romantic lead, and he and Hayworth finish by converting to Christianity. Their love scenes, according to one writer, are "so lacking in excitement they wouldn't have caused a ripple in a Sunday school."[63]

The Dance of the Seven Veils, the axis around which the film revolves, is hardly erotic. Hayworth whirls about the place like a spinning top gone out of control, prostrating herself at Laughton's feet as she finally shows a flash of thigh. But it's all, alas, for nothing as her mother has already forced Laughton's hand.

Granger has to struggle with lines like, "I've found a far greater loyalty than Rome—eternity," but the star turn is John the Baptist, who speaks with such passion he makes the Nazarene carpenter look like a tame sideshow. The prophet imagines he'll make Caesar and his soldiers tremble with his apocalyptic bleating but he hasn't bargained on their cynicism. As one of the soldiers deadpans, "I hear this man from Nazareth turned water into wine at a wedding. Imagine the money he could save us." George MacDonald Fraser remarked witheringly that the reason for making the film was probably nothing more profound than "to give Rita Hayworth the chance to undress to music in the presence of Charles Laughton."[64]

The New York Times called it "a lush conglomeration of historical pretences, make-believe pseudo-religious ostentation and just plain insinuated sex," adding "the billboard appearances of Miss Hayworth in various attitudes of repose, gowned in diaphanous garments and making come-hither looks, suggest more profound enthusiasm for the delights of theatrical couture and the well-advertised allurements of a famous glamour queen."[65]

20th Century Fox released *The Robe* in the same year, 1953, with high hopes. Darryl F. Zanuck told *Variety* magazine that Hollywood would "rise or fall" on how the film fared. It was to be a "spiritual *Ben-Hur*, Christianity in Cinemascope."[66] Based on a novel by Lloyd Douglas, *The Robe* deals with Roman soldiers casting lots at the foot of Jesus' cross for the right to wear his crucifixion garment. Douglas wrote over 500 pages on the implications of this Biblical fragment.

His main character, Marcellus, wins the robe but the moment he tries it on he finds himself beset by pangs of remorse for what he's done. Marcellus throws the robe off, believing it has put a curse on his life. Afterward he travels through Galilee learning all about Jesus before eventually converting to Christianity and becoming a martyr himself at the hands of the Roman emperor Caligula. Hollywood newcomer Richard Burton won an Oscar nomination for playing Marcellus, though his performance seems stilted according to today's standards. Henry Koster's direction is also rather leaden-footed.

The Robe made Burton an instant star, which probably worked against him. Huge things were predicted for him on the basis of his chocolate box good looks and a sepulchral voice that seemed tailor-made for ventures of this nature. In subsequent years, sadly, he became typecast in a raft of forgettable features. He went for the dollar, and also fell prey to alcoholism, which robbed him of whatever limited talent he had. He ended up doing, on his own admission, "unutterable rubbish" just to have somewhere to go in the mornings.

Burton, who referred to himself as "the poor man's Olivier," was delighted to have scooped the role. When an emissary from the Vatican called to bless the set Burton told him that playing Marcellus was "like playing Hamlet."[67]

The script of *The Robe* has lines like "We gotta find out where he holes up at night"—the "he" being Jesus. Such phraseology would have been more suited to a Dead End Kids drama than a Biblical epic but Hollywood didn't seem to care about such details. Its priority was always in making a film that looked good rather than the script being properly written. Indeed, Hollywood regarded the screenwriters as the Cinderellas of the industry. As long as one dressed in a toga, one was allowed to speak like Damon Runyon.

Koster directs the film in a lacklustre style. I'm inclined to agree with the renowned British critic Dilys Powell, who wrote of it, "Few of us will want to defend Caligula, but I'm sorry to see yet another film fostering the popular notion that Rome was little more than a collection of Nazis in short skirts."[68]

Jesus' face wasn't shown in the movie as the producers were reluctant to re-cut the film for release in England, which at that time forbade films that showed the Messiah's image. When Jesus' name is spoken, the camera pans to the crowd for a reaction, and only shows him vaguely in long shot. As he walks towards Golgotha with the cross on his back, only the cross's beams are shown. When he falls, the camera only shows his legs. As he hangs on the cross, only his feet are shown as he says, "Forgive them, for they know not what they do." These are the most restrained scenes in the film, and the most effective, even if such an effect was gained as a result of censorial necessity rather than inspiration.

The film hasn't weathered the test of time well, largely due to the fact that, as Derek Elley wrote, there are "insufficient treats to sustain almost two and a half hours of ponderous storytelling, especially when the first real action doesn't occur until some hundred minutes in."[69]

In the film, Victor Mature played a Greek slave named Demetrius who helped Marcellus. Fox began filming the sequel, *Demetrius and the Gladiators* even before *The Robe* wrapped up. The cash registers were ringing and Hollywood was happy. Philip Dunne said the film had been cobbled together from the narrative leftovers of *The Robe*. He described it as "a corny exercise in adventure and romance" which reversed the plot of the former film by having a Christian "deconverted" instead of a pagan converted.[70] It was to be the first of many such gimmicky contrivances in the years to come.

Paul Newman made an inauspicious screen debut in *The Silver Chalice* in 1954. Playing a sculptor who designs the chalice used by Christ at the Last Supper, he vies between loyalty to his Christian wife (Pier Angeli) and a pagan seductress (Virginia Mayo).

Newman wanted the role of Cal Trask in *East of Eden*, which was being shot at the same time on an adjoining lot, but it went to James Dean instead—Angeli's boyfriend. This was a double thorn in the side for Newman, who was shortlisted for the role of Trask before Elia Kazan presented it to Dean, thereby giving the screen its first talkie legend. A lesser actor's career would have been irrevocably stunted by this achingly amateurish effort, and it wasn't until two years after the release of *The Silver Chalice* that Newman mustered up the courage to make another film. Awash with corny dialogue, cardboard characters and a plot that went nowhere after 144 tortuous minutes, Newman described it as "the worst film of the 1950s."[71] He was embarrassed by the way his "supposedly bony legs" showed up in the "knee-revealing tunics" he had to wear, and also by the dire nature of the script.[72] The film was so bad he told an interviewer on the set that he was seriously considering going back to the family business selling sporting goods.[73]

A review in the *New Yorker* noted that "Paul Newman delivers his lines with the emotional fervour of a Putnam Division conductor announcing local stops."[74] When the movie was shown on late-night TV many decades later, Newman went so far as to take out an ad in *The New York Times*, framed in a "funereal black border" that said "Paul Newman Apologizes Every Night This Week—Channel 9."[75] The ad, ironically, had the effect of making thousands tune in, turning it into something of a cult classic of Biblical banality, which proved the truth of the old adage that there's no such thing as bad publicity. Newman even showed a print of the ad in his home to gatherings of his friends. This, he found, was "fun for the first reel, but then the awfulness of the thing took over."[76]

Richard Thorpe directed (or rather misdirected) *The Prodigal* in 1955 in which Hebrew farmer Edmund Purdum falls into the clutches of pagan-temptress Lana Turner. Unfortunately, Turner as a *femme fatale* never ignited and the film flopped. Dore Schary, the producer, pined. He believed the film suffered because DeMille had "an exclusive" on the Bible!

In 1956 DeMille was at it again, re-making *The Ten Commandments.* No matter what other genres he tried, DeMille always seemed to come back to the Bible. He admitted himself, "What else has 2000 years of advance publicity?"[77] Elsewhere he said, "Creation is a drug I can't do without."[78] His use of language is significant—he didn't say "creativity."

The crowd scenes were indeed astounding but by now people were beginning to suspect his motive for such magnificent special effects might be mercenary. One wag remarked, "It makes you realize what God could have done if he'd had the money."[79] Another contended that it was the Bible for the TV generation.

The parting of the Red Sea was achieved by using a bent steel tray, which was painted and used as a landscape. Three hundred thousand gallons of water were poured into the tray. The water seemed to part when the film was shown in reverse. The use of the steel tray was a simple but clever device in an age that didn't have the luxury of computer-generated special effects.

Around this time Nicholas Bentley coined a famous clerihew about DeMille:

> Cecil B. DeMille
> Much against his will
> Was persuaded to leave Moses
> Out of the War of the Roses.

DeMille himself said, "Give me any two pages of the Bible and I'll give you a picture."[80] He also said, "The best way to make a hit is to start with an earthquake and work up to a climax."[81] The film was a huge hit, bringing in over $50 million at the box office, having only cost $13.5 million to make.

In 1951 a journalist asked DeMille to list his ten favorite films of all time. His choices were political: *Cabiria, The Birth of a Nation, Ben-Hur, The Ten Commandments, The King of Kings, The Big Parade, The Sign of the Cross, Gone with the Wind, Going My Way* and *Samson and Delilah.* DeMille had made four of the ten films on his list and only one wasn't an epic: *Going My Way.* The fact that it had a priest in the lead role was apt compensation, one imagines, for the kind of God-fearing people he was targeting with his list. The idea of representing himself four times in a "Best of" list of ten was typical of his almost unconscious messianic sense.

DeMille insisted that his motives in remaking the film were religious. At a Manhattan meeting with clergy, he announced that the profits from the remake would be used to create a charitable trust. He urged the congregation to use the film for the good of the world–as God himself would have.

He always seemed to have the capacity of serving both God and Mammon simultaneously. He had the ability to convince himself that what he wanted to do was what the Lord wanted to do—if not Daniel Lord. He never saw himself as exploiting the Bible, but merely as its spokesman. William Goldman opined that DeMille's main talent was "wizardry at personal publicity."[82] DeMille's daughter Agnes accurately noted that he kept "sex, sadism, patriotism, real estate, religion and public relations dancing in mid-air like jugglers' balls for fifty years."[83]

DeMille said he remade the film partly for religious reasons and partly for political ones. "The horrors of World War II," he proclaimed, "and our awful experiences of totalitarianism, both fascist and communist, has made many thoughtful people realize anew that the law of God is the essential bedrock of human freedom."[84] Such a rationalization sounds more like a clever marketing strategy than words from the heart, as if he were exploiting the excesses of the Holocaust to drive people back to God—and his films.

Charlton Heston played Moses in the remake and took the role seriously, reading no less than twenty-two volumes on Moses' life and learning large chunks of the Old Testament by heart. According to Heston's biographer Michael Munn, he drove his wife Lydia "half crazy each breakfast, dinner and supper with talk of nothing but the Dead Sea scrolls."[85]

Heston decided to portray Moses as "a man much scarred by the stress of being the instrument of God's will, [and] lacking Christ's serene certainty of the divinity of his mission." DeMille chose Heston for an unusual reason. "My choice was strikingly confirmed," he said, "when I had a sketch made of [Heston] in a white beard and happened to set it beside a photograph of Michelangelo's famous statue of Moses. The resemblance was amazing."[86]

DeMille shot the scene of Moses wandering in the desert near St Catherine's monastery, the oldest monastery in the world, founded in 339 AD on the site of the Burning Bush. Heston was inspired by the location, as he was by the nearby Mount Sinai musing, "If Moses could find God on that mountain, I should be able to find Moses there."[87]

The dialogue is stilted, the characters little more than cardboard cut-outs, and the acting is at best, serviceable. However, on its own terms of barnstorming spectacle the film does what it says on the box. A "prophet and lust" parable was a fitting swansong for the man who almost single-handedly made religion into a multi-million-dollar industry. The film was Grade-A kitsch but with a curious persuasiveness. DeMille's large brushstrokes are enigmatically alluring, even if the sight of Edward G. Robinson in period garb looks faintly ridiculous. As Moses, Heston acts as the oracular axis around which everything else revolves, and because his Moses works we accept the package, garish and all as it is. But this was really the last death-rattle of the sand-and-sex mini-genre.

It was hard to take some of the film seriously, as for instance when Anne Baxter says to Heston in her boudoir, "They may be your people, but do you have to *smell* like them?" It isn't long before The Bearded One disengages himself from her to embrace his destiny. "Let my people go!" he barks at his half-brother Ramses, played by Yul Brynner, more than once.

Another risible piece of dialogue occurs when a travelling Hebrew pipes to no one in particular, "We're going to the land of milk and honey. Anybody know the way?"

Before the first scene, DeMille gave an introduction in which he promised to fill in the thirty years of Moses' life that the Bible had omitted. At the end of the film, one finds oneself severely doubting that Moses spent those thirty years in the manner that DeMille would have us believe. Dilys Powell said she was so bored by its four-hour duration that long before the end she was "silently imploring" Mr DeMille to "let his people go."[88]

Religious leaders were kinder to the film than the critics, and it made a fortune at the box office. DeMille suffered a heart attack on a Friday during the shoot but continued unabated, reporting back to work the following Monday. He didn't take a personal salary for his work. He regarded the film as his finest achievement. Heston was also highly impressed, saying that the film "will have been seen by more people than any other [film] I have ever made, or probably ever will make. If you can't make a career out of two DeMille pictures, I guess you'll never make it."[89]

John May aptly pointed out that despite the film's literal fidelity to the Book of Exodus, it "does little more than create the impression that God is the Divine Impressario."[90] I'm not at all sure that DeMille would have been insulted by this estimation of his work. He quite liked the idea of the Prime Mover pulling invisible strings, with himself as the obliging middleman. The Bible was his nickelodeon. It was "The Book" by which means he would make "The Film", or films. It was quite literally an organ grinder for him, a veritable license to print money. In making *The Ten Commandments*, John Naughton wrote, "he obeyed Hollywood's first [rule], make money."[91] In the words of the screenwriter Philip Dunne, "[i]n the motion picture industry, blessed are the money-makers, for theirs is the kingdom of heaven."[92] The irony of money being the root of all evil as its central message seemed to escape him.

On the other hand, DeMille was always his own man. When he was chastised by Adolph Zukor for being over budget on the film due to his perfectionism, he responded with the witty barb, "What do you want me to do—stop shooting now and release it as *The Five Commandments*?"[93]

The *New Yorker* said he always handled Biblical scripts "with the proprietary air of a gentleman fondling old love letters." When God sent a hurricane, the joke went, DeMille directed its course. His peremptory air also had something to do with it. He exuded an enormous sense of self-belief. Gloria Swanson even said of his baldness, "[H]e wore it like an expensive hat, as if it were out of the question for him to have hair like other men."[94] Charles Bronson saw him as an American Benito Mussolini. Norah Alexander suggested that the B in his name could stand for anything from Ballyhoo to Box Office to Baloney to Billion Dollars.[95]

DeMille died in 1959, his passing re-igniting the old debates of whether he was a maestro or fraud. Maybe he was both. Fellow director George Cukor put it well, "He was preposterous, illiterate and ludicrous—but what a storyteller."[96]

Perhaps fittingly, *Ben-Hur* was re-made in the same year. It had originally been filmed in 1926 with Ramon Novarro as the Jewish galley slave who finally gains his freedom. The 1956 version made a star and an Oscar winner of the oracular, square-jawed Charlton Heston.

The early sea battle was impressive, as was the climactic chariot race, with the crucifixion sandwiched in between in somewhat perfunctory and jagged fashion. But the film is still one of the few epics that has stood the test of time with its personal drama of the treachery of Messala (Stephen Boyd) set against the backdrop of momentous events like the crucifixion of Jesus.

In his memoirs Heston said he was deeply moved by the crucifixion scene. He said he tried his utmost to act "without visible emotion" in the scene because Ben-Hur had seen many people die: "Christ was simply a criminal condemned to the cross." But when the camera focused on him, Heston was crying.[97]

There's no gainsaying the power of Heston's acting but there was also something of a one-note performer about him, attested to by this waspish jibe from Dwight MacDonald apropos of his performance: "Heston throws all his punches in the first ten minutes, three grimaces and two intonations so that he has nothing left long before he stumbles to the end, four hours later, and has to react to the crucifixion. He does make it clear, though, that he disapproves of it."[98]

MacDonald's statement was unfair, but Heston left himself open to abrasive comments from critics not only because of his work in *Ben-Hur*, but throughout his epic career. Perhaps the critics were so used to seeing him in historical roles they found it hard to accept him in contemporary ones with the same degree of mystique, or at least suspension of disbelief.

Heston was so ubiquitous in Biblical roles that George Burns claimed that some of his favorite characters in the Bible were King David, Delilah . . . and Heston. Heston himself said the same thing slightly differently, "If you need a chariot race run, a city besieged or the Red Sea parted, you think of me."[99]

The acknowledged cinematic equivalent of Mount Rushmore, Heston believed he was an egotist as a result of being frequently cast as presidents, saints, and geniuses. Not everybody agreed he was justified in having an ego problem. Rex Reed said he was good at being arrogant in the same way as a dwarf was good at being small. Hugh Leonard thought of him as Lon Chaney minus 999 faces.

The film was directed by William Wyler, who had actually worked on the original DeMille version in 1925 as one of sixty assistant directors. DeMille, as we know, was never a man to do things half-heartedly.

The book upon which the film was based was written by Lew Wallace and was subtitled *A Tale of the Christ*. This is a misnomer really because the focal point of the story is the friendship between Judah Ben-Hur and Messala neither of whom appear in the Bible.

The plot begins with Messala, a Roman soldier returning to his homeland of Judea to ask his old friend Ben-Hur—now a leader of the Jewish ruling class—to give him the names of any local troublemakers threatening to defy Rome. When Ben-Hur refuses this request he's sold as a galley slave. He escapes from captivity after rescuing the life of an admiral during a shipwreck and returns to Jerusalem years later to exact revenge in the much-hyped chariot race. Afterward, in a kind of subplot, he finds his mother and sister suffering from leprosy. This is where Jesus—who has made a brief appearance earlier on in the film—returns to work some miracles before his crucifixion. After Jesus dies it starts to rain. Ben-Hur's mother and his dying sister are cured of leprosy, the healing waters of the rain purifying them. Ben-Hur realizes that God's forgiveness, added to his own for Messala, has expedited the catharsis.

Water is a symbol of purification in the film. In an early scene, Jesus offers Ben-Hur a glass of water to quench his thirst. Ben-Hur returns the favor just before Jesus is crucified on the Hill of Calvary. Toward the end of the film, Jesus' blood is "gradually dispersed by the rain, heralding a new beginning."[100]

At the end of the day the film is an adventure story. Tacking on the religious conversion of its main character, especially in what amounts to an extended epilogue, betrays the foregoing. When Esther tells Ben-Hur, "Blood begets blood as dog begets dog," we don't really hear her. Likewise when she speaks of the Nazarene on the hill who exhorts people to love their enemies we don't hear her. The point is that Ben-Hur has attained his freedom through violence, not loving his enemies, so the "peace and love to all men" message is misdirected. The film should have ended when Messala died. Heston's "I know this man" as he espies Jesus, and Esther's "[I]n his pain is the look of peace," seem like lines from another movie. The final scenes of purification, grounded firmly in a previous era, demeaned the gallant efforts the film has already made to break through the sackcloth-and-ashes milieu with many choreographed action sequences, and of course Heston's dynamism.

The screenplay has an interesting anecdotal backdrop. Christopher Fry wrote the lion's share of it with the uncredited help of Gore Vidal. Vidal started with what he called "a silent movie with miles of windy dialogue."[101] He said he fashioned the script into a story of unrequited homosexual love between Heston, whom he accused of having "all the charm of a wooden Indian," and Boyd. According to Vidal, Wyler panicked at the idea of including such inflammatory material in a Biblical film until Vidal promised to make "the love that dared not screech its name" very latent.[102]

Although Vidal's statement has been hotly disputed, Vidal stated that Wyler was coming around to the idea that he might risk it provided Heston wasn't informed, Heston being decidedly nervous about anything smacking of homosexuality. Vidal claims Boyd believed the homosexual love storyline made his betrayal of his old friend more believable.

According to Vidal, Boyd believed that "hell hath no fury like an old lover scorned," was a believable working principle behind the fractured friendship.

Vidal wrote in his memoirs that he envisioned the relationship between Ben-Hur and Messala as "boyhood lovers. But Ben-Hur, under the fierce Palestinian sun and its jealous god, had turned straight as a die while Messala, the decadent gentile, had remained in love with Ben and wanted to take up where they had left off." When Hur rebuffs Messala's advances, a "deep and abiding" hatred fills Messala to the brim, resulting in Messala literally selling Hur down the river.

Wyler was terrified that Vidal would make the homosexual element blatant but Vidal assured him he knew how to make dialogue "sound like one thing and mean another" from his work in television. The undertone was to be conveyed by glances and inflections. If Heston himself didn't pick them up, it was unlikely the censors would.

When Wyler told Vidal he couldn't be overt, Vidal alleges that he replied, "I can write it in such a way that the audience is going to feel there's something emotional between them which blows the fuse in Messala. He's spurned, so it's a love scene gone wrong." Wyler always denied this conversation took place.

I met Heston when he was promoting his autobiography and asked him about the incident. "It never happened" he said in the kind of voice that makes you not want to argue. "Vidal has been on a mission about this for years but it was a non-event. The story doesn't even need it. Willy understood that. They're putting homosexuality into things nowadays for reasons that are beyond me. It seems modish. But it wouldn't have worked in *Ben-Hur*. If that view makes me sound old-fashioned, so be it. It was a great story of a broken bond and you don't need any subtext to bolster it up. Vidal can't accept that because he has a tendency to write most things with a particular edge. It's no secret to him that I disapprove of that. So did Willy and so did our main writer Christopher Fry. Vidal was one against many, but he likes to single me out as the prude in the whole affair."

No matter whom you believe regarding this vexed issue, the final cut seems to have little or no homo-erotic content to speak of. The question is why did Vidal spend so many years suggesting that he was the guiding force behind the *Ben-Hur* script? Heston told me, "I don't know. Maybe because that's what Vidal does. It seems to be important to him to perpetuate these kinds of myths even when the facts flagrantly contradict him. Everybody knows Christopher Fry's fingerprints are all over *Ben-Hur*.

Anyone who's in the least bit familiar with Fry's work can see that. And anyone who's in the least bit familiar with Vidal's work can see that his fingerprints *aren't* on the finished script. The bottom line was that Willy gave him his marching papers in Rome." Quite apart from this debate, most viewers would agree that the relationship between Ben-Hur and Esther isn't half as interesting as the one between Hur and Messala.

Even Fry, an avowed enemy of Vidal, admitted that "the only relationship that counts is the one between Ben-Hur and Messala. You can't make the audience care about the love story." Fry was reiterating Vidal's point, but without acknowledging the potential homosexual relationship between Hur and Messala, even covertly. Undoubtedly, the situation would be different if the film was to be made a third time today where even a gay Jesus would be a distinct possibility.

The film won eleven Oscars and made so much money it saved MGM from financial ruin. The epic was back and bigger, if not better, than ever. It was the only re-make in Hollywood's history to win a Best Picture award. Significantly, the only Oscar it didn't win for was the rocky screenplay. This was eventually credited to Karl Tunberg. Fry's name had been removed from it along with Vidal's, and Maxwell Anderson and S.N. Behrman, two others who had worked on it at one point or another. According to an old Hollywood saying, the more people who work on a script, the lousier it turns out. The unevenness of this script didn't show up too badly in the final cut, but it lacked an individual style. Looking at it now, it's the work of an unhappy committee. As they finished making the movie, Wyler joked to Heston, "Thanks a lot, Chuck. I'll try to give you a better part next time."[103] The truth of the matter was that Heston was in every other frame.

When I asked Heston about his general feelings on the film, he admitted he was happy with it but noted that he didn't like to be viewed as a "Biblical" actor at the expense of all his other work. "I'm proud of all my films in different ways," he said. "The Biblical ones have been more high-profiled. That doesn't necessarily mean they represent my best work." What did represent your best work, I asked. He paused. "I like what I did in *Will Penny*," he said, "that's my *Shane*. I enjoyed *The Big Country* too, even though it was only a supporting role. *Dark City* was a good challenge too. That was my first film. You always have a special feeling for the first one, despite your faults, or even because of them. I look at it now and smile. Maybe it's like a mother with a handicapped child. But I'm not embarrassed by it. There are a lot of things I'd change, but then there are a lot of things I'd change with everything I've done.

William Dieterle, the director, threw me in at the deep end. I struggled, but I think I rose to the challenge. Does that sound arrogant?" How does one tell Moses he sounds arrogant? I thought. "There are other films I like too. *Touch of Evil*—mainly because I was working with Orson Welles. He was a genius. Some films you do for special reasons. The money. Because the timing is right. As a career move. Most actors start out like that. But then you change. You become choosy. Modern audiences associate me primarily with *Planet of the Apes*. I could be snobbish about that but I choose not to be. It was work. I'll say no more."

When I suggested he might be protesting too much about his high-profile films, he became agitated. "I'm not trying to diss *Ben-Hur* or any of the other ones I'm best known for but they've been monkeys on my back in some ways. They've pigeonholed me. Directors look at me as a package. They don't think I can be stretched. As a result, I haven't done enough emotional vulnerability. That makes me something of an anachronism in today's films." Was it why he was reduced to appearing in cameos? I asked. He refused to answer the question, suddenly looking like Moses after having had one of his tablets broken. "Let's just say I'm only 90 percent happy with what I've done." I got the feeling that nothing less than 100 percent would have satisfied him. In the chariot race of life he also liked to be the winner.

When I asked him about DeMille, he replied: "Well what can you say about that man? It's fashionable to debunk him today in this age of psychological realism but nobody loved movies like he did. He got a heart attack on *The Ten Commandments* but still wouldn't stop. He was 74—and a workaholic. You can't not respect that." When I asked him whether DeMille was genuinely religious or a dollars man, Heston replied "I don't like to make those cosy distinctions. Nobody is simple. He went in the devil's door, if you like, to come out God's side. He was the most fulfilled man I've ever met. He took no stick from anyone because he was—can I say he was God? He certainly acted like it. But a benign God. He knew what he was doing and that made him arrogant."

Heston noted "Yes, I'm arrogant too. I don't suffer fools. I work hard and I expect other people to know their jobs. I'm impatient. I've had problems with a lot of actors—your own Richard Harris, for instance, and some others. Usually for professional reasons. But when a film wraps I don't hold grudges. In this business you can't. It comes back to haunt you." I asked Heston whether he believed the old adage about the importance of being nice to people on the way up because you'll meet them on the way down again. He said "That sounds cynical and thought-out. I've never consciously sucked up to anyone to get a part. Having said that, you have to let people know you're around, and what you can do. Before DeMille offered me the part of Moses he played his cards close to his chest and so did I. I didn't want to appear too eager but I researched the background to the film and I let him know that. I think that might have swung it for me. Or maybe he had his mind made up anyway. I don't know."

In response to my inquiry as to whether he saw Moses as his break-through character, he replied "Both of my biggest Biblical films I got from working in non-Biblical roles. I worked with DeMille on *The Greatest Show on Earth* before he gave me *The Ten Commandments* and Willy (Wyler) on *The Big Country* before he gave me *Ben-Hur*. What goes around comes around. I didn't want to take *The Big Country* at first. I thought it was a step down, playing second banana to Greg Peck. But Herman Citron, my agent, told me Wyler was the man to be with, and he was right. I came away from those two movies feeling that if Willy called me and asked me to read the telephone directory, I'd do it."

Spartacus, made the following year by Stanley Kubrick, was equally effective and similarly themed, dealing with the revolt of a slave played by Kirk Douglas against the Romans. Douglas invested the same visceral energy into the role as Heston did the previous year, and Kubrick's direction had his trademark punctiliousness. The film had less of a spiritual impulse than *Ben-Hur* but shared its sense of gritty determination as a muscular individual struggled to stay alive under fierce pressure from the slave-masters.

In 1963 the Italian-financed *Sodom and Gomorrah* was filmed. It was a rather overacted confection memorable mostly for wicked queen Anouk Aimee's classic line as her palace was about to be razed by fire and brimstone: "It's just a summer storm. Nothing to worry about." This was a lavish spectacle with, on paper, a strong theme, but somehow you felt a nostalgia for somebody like DeMille pulling the scriptural strings as he chronicled the decline of two of Christendom's most notorious cities.

George Stevens made *The Greatest Story Ever Told* in 1965. The film was a noble attempt to chronicle the life of Christ but it was defeated in the end by some hammy scenes and a melodramatic, over-inflated atmosphere that was perhaps inevitable considering the scope of the project. The film's original running time was a staggering 260 minutes. In the end, it was whittled down to 196 minutes but it's still pedestrian.

Stevens plays around with certain Biblical staples. Judas for instance, doesn't hang himself but commits suicide by falling into a fire instead. In addition, Pontius Pilate doesn't wash his hands. Stevens filmed in Utah and Colorado but as Bryan Stone notes, the strategy backfired "as movie-goers were apparently all too familiar with the canyons, cliffs, mountains and rivers of the great American South-West."[104] Stone wasn't impressed by the filming of the Sea of Galilee against the backdrop of "the majestic, snow capped Rocky mountains."[105] Stone stated that the film basically demonstrates "how inadequate, tiresome and silly Holly-wood clichés can be when attempting to signal religious faith and devo-tion, or the presence of the divine. These are notoriously difficult to depict through dialogue alone, so Stevens adds trumpets, violins and choirs of angels, with perhaps a pained expression or two to depict intense piety."[106]

Heston played John the Baptist in the film. It was a small but signifi-cant role. He told his biographer Michael Munn that he mainly took the part to work with Stevens, but also because it was a great role. "I think out of all these parts, Jesus aside—and Jesus is really unplayable—the Baptist was really the best."[107]

Heston played the part well. However, critic Glenn Hopp observed that when we see Heston "one might wonder if he will baptise people in the Jordan River or part it and lead them across."[108] Unfortunately, Heston came to every film with his "Biblical baggage," which was often a double-edged sword for him.

Off-set, Heston found time to adopt a whimsical view of the baptism scene. When Stevens asked him how he felt as he stood knee-deep in the water, he replied, "I'm okay, George, but I'll tell you this. If the Jordan had been as cold as the Colorado, Christianity would've never gotten off the ground!"[109]

In 1966 John Huston used Italian funding for his overblown epic *The Bible*, which covered the first twenty-one chapters of Genesis. The film portrayed Adam and Eve, Cain and Abel, an outraged Abraham and Huston himself as Noah, acquitting himself admirably in the flood scene.

As was the case with *The Greatest Story Ever Told*, too many recog-nizable faces were in the cast. George C. Scott, Richard Harris, Peter O'Toole, Ava Gardner and others warred against period authenticity. It was more like a Who's Who of Hollywood, despite Huston's best efforts to be majestic.

Huston admitted that the film was always going to be episodic—if not unfilmable.[110] Though it was called *The Bible*, the film really only dealt with half of the book of Genesis, ending with the story of Abraham. To be fair, it was subtitled "In the Beginning" but not many people seemed to notice that or take it in if they did.

Huston asked his friend and sometime idol Charlie Chaplin to play Noah but he demurred. Alec Guinness also passed, so Huston played the role himself. He probably looked the part more than Chaplin or Guinness and, as he said in his memoirs, he had the added advantage of being familiar with the animals. He was proud of the fact that after much planning and training, he managed to get all of the animals to enter the ark two by two. Huston complained that nobody who saw the film seemed to think this was a big deal but in an age before computer-generated special effects it was phenomenal. As for the creation scene he joked, "I don't know how God managed. I'm having a terrible time."[111] God also rested on the Sabbath; no such luxury was available to this workaholic.

The film was marred by an off-screen relationship between Scott and Gardner that veered from idolatry on his part to outright derision. Gardner rebuffed Scott's advances and he couldn't take this so he turned his ire on her with full force, particularly when he drank. On one particular night during the shooting of the film, Huston had to climb on Scott's back to stop him from physically harming Gardner. In the months afterward, Frank Sinatra became Gardner's bodyguard.

The film was originally intended to be a fourteen-hour epic spanning both the Old and New Testaments and co-directed by Huston, Fellini and Orson Welles. One can only wonder how much more exciting it would have been had that venture become a reality. Of course, it could also have been a disaster with so many eclectic talents locking horns on matters of such importance.

In the end, the film was almost three hours long, causing one author to remark: "[It] got no farther than Genesis 22, which . . . suggests that a film of the entire Holy Writ would last the better part of a week."[112] Jerzy Toeplitz accused it of being in the DeMille era, stating that "[v]aseline generously coated over the lens gave the images of Paradise with its golden trees a 'poetic' aura."[113]

The one blatant anachronism in the film is the sight of Adam's navel. (Compare this with a vaccination mark on Kirk Douglas' arm in Stanley Kubrick's *Spartacus*, and a label on the robe of the Messiah in Martin Scorsese's *The Last Temptation of Christ*.)

One came away from the film feeling the Old Testament had been tabloidized. It would be difficult to point to any one scene and say it was done badly. However, the effrontery was in the ambition rather than the film itself. Perhaps it was doomed to fail even before Huston shouted "Action!" for the first time.

Hollywood learned from the experience of the filming of *The Bible* and stayed away from big-budget movies for a long time afterward. In the 70s, the trend was to turn to subjects like devil possession in films like *The Exorcist* and *The Omen* when Tinseltown felt itself nudged towards religion. This trend continues today.

Is this trend for the better or worse? Perhaps diabolism and Biblical epics are equally exploitative in their own way. Diabolism is exploitative for obvious reasons. Biblical epics, on the other hand, are exploitative because, as Philip Dunne points out, they were often awash with superstition and also used religion as a cloak for sex while oversimplifying religious conflict into "Christians Always the Good Guys, Pagans the Bad Guys."[114] Dunne said he didn't begrudge DeMille the millions of dollars he made for his distortions of the Holy Writ, but resented his success in creating "an image of himself as a prophet of the Lord" when in fact he was an extremely shrewd film-maker "tailored to the least common denominator in the public's taste."[115]

— 2 —

The Changing Face of Jesus

Portrayals of the Messiah in movies have been many and varied. In the old days, directors of sackcloth-and-ashes epics tended to go for a standard, picture-book approach. The result was often a perfunctory re-tread of stale dialogue and melodramatic camerawork. Jesus might make his first appearance as a shadow across an arid landscape, accompanied by a foreboding music score. The accents of the casts in such movies were also questionable—more Bel Air than Israel—or an even more embarrassing hybrid of both.

Early religious epics tended to portray Jesus as both timid and terrifying. This isn't as contradictory as it sounds. It means that he didn't have to earn his sacred status; it was taken for granted. They portrayed no anguish; that would come later with *Jesus Christ Superstar* and *The Last Temptation of Christ*. The films simply showed a quiet figure, often bathed in light or maybe not even seen at all but indicated by people's reaction to him. Jesus had a huge presence in these films based merely on his "being there."

In 1927, in Cecil B. DeMille's original version of *The King of Kings*, Jesus was a remote, standard figure. During the making of the movie, DeMille prevailed upon H.B. Warner, the actor who played Jesus, to stay alone in his trailer between takes so his concentration wouldn't be disrupted by the "mere mortals" who were his co-stars.

Only DeMille spoke to him when he was in costume "to maintain the spirit of reverence."[1] DeMille had a curtain draped over the cross so that no one could see Warner get up or down from it. Warner was also transported from his dressing-room to the set in a closed car and he wasn't allowed to smile. Warner and the cast had to sign agreements that "they would behave themselves for the next year, and not get divorced or cut up in a nightclub."[2]

Director Jens Jorgen tried to make a film about Jesus in the 1930s that had certain sacrilegious elements in it but the Danish Film Institute refused to fund the venture. Instead of banning it for blasphemy, the Institute invoked a unique precedent, revoking the subsidy on the grounds that the script violated the copyright of the authors of the New Testament!

In *Quo Vadis?* (1951) Jesus is a distant presence, and in *The Robe* (1953), he's nothing more than a disembodied voice from the cross. William Telford wrote in an essay on the subject, "The actor portraying Christ in any film is trapped in a maze of dramatic contradictions. He must be believably human yet also believably divine, gentle yet forceful, charismatic yet humble."[3] In Victorian times, Jesus was the archetypal blonde, blue-eyed, white-robed figure, ethereal yet somewhat bland, commanding yet somewhat passive, which is why any actor taking him on must be aware of the palimpsest.

Jesus occupied only a minor role in *Ben-Hur* in 1959. Sam Zimbalist, the producer, commented wryly to Graham Greene, one of the screen-writer *apropos* the script: "We would like you to pump up the final part. We find there is a sort of anti-climax after the Crucifixion."[4]

William Wyler, the film's director, was unfortunate because nothing, not even the crucifixion of Jesus, could top the chariot race. The bond between Ben-Hur and Messala was much more interesting than the one bond between Ben-Hur and Esther; therefore, the fracturing of that bond and Messala's execution in an amphitheatre under thundering horses' hooves outdid the martyrdom of a religious icon. The road to Damascus somehow doesn't seem as important to Wyler as the blood and guts of imperial Rome. Even Christ had to play second fiddle to this under Wyler's aegis. His film was always going to marginalize Christ, so per-haps it would have been expedient to eliminate him altogether. Jesus' inclusion in the project was always going to be tokenistic.

The scene where Jesus offers Ben-Hur water is effective because we never see Jesus' face. Wyler put all of the emphasis on people's reaction to Jesus: first, that of Ben-Hur himself and then the centurion who screams "No water for him!" Wyler didn't like the extra the studio pro-vided for these four words and had his assistant director send to Rome for a replacement—the man who was actually his original choice.

Waiting for him to arrive purportedly cost MGM $15,000. What Wyler wanted was a man with a cruel demeanor who also had a hint of sensitivity, which could be brought into play when he saw what we, the viewers, couldn't see: Jesus' face.

The crucifixion took four days to shoot and Wyler agonized over it. It may have been a postscript to the main story but if it fell flat it would tarnish everything that had gone before, including the spectacular chariot race. He felt frightened when he contemplated the great challenge that lay ahead of him, that of filming a scene so many artists had painted in the past. He wanted to portray the horrible bloodiness of it, but also the reverence. He was himself painting on a vast canvas, a celluloid one, and he didn't want to disappoint anyone who had been a witness to such a grand tradition.

He did his best, but not everyone was satisfied. The critic Dwight MacDonald, to name but one, likened the film to the experience of standing at a railway station as an interminable freight train lumbered by. Such a putdown would have crushed lesser men.

King of Kings was re-made in 1961 with Jeffrey Hunter as Jesus. This wasn't the worst Biblical movie ever made, but as Martin Scorsese commented, there was no way Hunter looked as if he had spent forty days in the desert. Nicholas Ray's direction was stately but the movie itself was too prettified for comfort, and Orson Welles' grandiose narration didn't help. Dilys Powell noticed "a kind of glazed seemliness" about Hunter's performance.[5] The film didn't seem to be so much about religion as Hunter's azure blue eyes, with which Ray was obviously fascinated. Did Hunter's eyes change the course of history? Hunter may have hypnotized Ray with them, but audiences weren't quite so swayed. Cynics dubbed the film *I Was a Teenage Jesus* because Hunter looked as if he came out of a beauty salon rather than a Bethlehem stable. One critic decried its "hackneyed pietism."[6]

In one scene, Jesus visits John the Baptist, played by the somewhat less beautiful Robert Ryan, in prison. Ryan asks him if he's truly the Christ. Hunter doesn't say yea or nay. Instead, the camera zooms in on his eyes and cross-cuts to Ryan's eyes afterward. In another director's hands this scene could have been profound but here it's a vaguely embarrassing affirmation of divinity. Once again, the eyes had it.

The film was an unmitigatedly glossy, Sunday School version of the Christ story. As Derek Elley pointed out in his book *The Epic Film*, it seems somehow right that Christ should still be in spotless white when brought before Herod and Pilate, "and that the blood from the crown of thorns should run down his face in perfect rivulets."[7] Elley notes that even the extras all wore spotless white headshawls in the bright sunshine. Ray's picture perfect Messiah is tailor-made for those who like their homilies dressed up in pink, or rather azure blue, ribbons.

Hunter is a Jesus who doesn't appear to feel, doesn't sweat and looks like he's on Prozac. Watching him is like watching a stained glass window instead of the unfolding of a destiny. Even when the death sentence is announced, he accepts it as a *fait accompli*. Edward O'Connor suggests that, far from demonstrating divinity in the film, Hunter actually seems to be "disclaiming" it.[8] Ray Kinnard describes the proceedings in general as "strangely uninvolving."[9] Clearly, Nicholas Ray was still in a DeMille time warp, but without the melodrama DeMille would have conjured up. In the end, the audience experiences no feeling at all, just the sense of a pin-up Christ rather than a nailed-to-the-cross one.

Hunter's Jesus was as perfect—and moribund—as a statue. He hadn't been bloodied, as it were. There was no heart ticking, no passion. He had a definite presence but didn't connect with people. You looked up at him, not across. His humanity was lost in Hunter's fabulously crafted features and shaved armpits.

Having been shown little of his humanity, one might have expected Jesus' divinity to be laid on with a trowel but this was played down too. Only two miracles are shown in the film, both of them done in silence and without showing Jesus. The only sermon Jesus gives is the Sermon on the Mount. We don't see the miracle of the loaves and fishes, or Jesus raising Lazarus from the dead. There's very little contact between Jesus and anyone, including those he heals. The film works on a suggestive level that's really quite old-fashioned. Only Hunter's "pop star" appearance is contemporary.

One of the lasting images of *King of Kings*, as the author Richard Walsh pointed out, is that of Hunter with his head bowed, waiting for Herod to decide his fate. He's not a salvific figure, Walsh opines, "but rather a victim of historical forces beyond his control." In fact, given the forest of crosses that climax Welles' introduction to the film, Ray's Jesus is "simply another Jewish victim of Roman oppression."[10] Far from being the man who single-handedly changed the course of history, he is, in Ray's hands—dare one say it—a rather ineffectual figure.

Ray also gives us a Y-shaped table at the Last Supper, the final curious touch in an inordinately curious film. Mary Magdalene looks as pure as the driven snow. Perhaps she should have been cast as the other Mary. Siobhan McKenna's red hair is also wrong. Are we to believe Jesus was actually Irish?

Bruce Babington refers to Ray's Jesus as "a rebel with a cause."[11] This is a neat phrase that aptly undercuts the film that made James Dean a teenage cult figure, *Rebel Without a Cause*. Ray directed this film too, and one suspects that if Dean had lived, Ray might have cast him as Jesus. Dean would have been just the right age, and would have carried the vulnerability much better than Hunter, if not the authoritative edge Hunter imparts.

Critical reaction to *King of Kings*, by and large, was negative. The Catholic Legion of Decency described it as being "theologically, historically and scripturally inaccurate."[12] Moira Walsh, writing in *America,* expressed the belief that "there is not the slightest possibility that anyone will derive from the film any meaningful insight into what Christ's life and sufferings signify for us."[13] *The New York Times* weighed in with this summation: "The spirit is hinted, but the projection is weak."[14]

Jesus was portrayed marginally in the 1962 film *Barabbas*, which explored the guilt of the freed thief of that movie. Barabbas, well played by Anthony Quinn, subsequently converts to Christianity. Jesus was forgettable in the film. "I am fire," Barabbas tells Judas at one point, "and he is water." One can't help agreeing. Director Richard Fleischer did use an interesting device during the opening sequence, filming it during an eclipse of the sun. The flares from the sun came out in the shape of a cross which caused Fleischer to emote, "I tell you, when she saw that, we said it was the hand of God. We've often been accused of doctoring the film but we never touched it. It's one of the greatest special effects of all time and it had nothing to do with computers or anything else."[15]

Perhaps the most moving Jesus of all was presented in 1966 in *The Gospel According to St. Matthew*, a low-budget black-and-white film directed by the gay, Marxist, atheist Pier Paolo Pasolini. Derek Elley succinctly summarized Pasolini's achievement when he said, "The attraction of Pasolini's film is its marvellous ambiguity. It promises deification, yet adamantly refuses to keep that promise."[16] The treatment was mutedly textured and meditative with a poignant attention to detail. The austere documentary style made few concessions to the kind of pietistic sloganeering that dogged more exploitative confections.

Pasolini was an unusual candidate to make this type of film as two of his earlier ones, *Accattone* in 1961 and *Mamma Roma* the following year, had both been cited for obscenity. He was brought to court then, and again in 1963 for his sacrilegious film *La Ricotta* and was sentenced to four months in prison for blasphemy. This ruling was overturned by the Appeals Court the following year but he was definitely coming to this project with his card marked. The long knives of the church were out even before he started shooting.

"I don't believe that Christ is the son of God," Pasolini declared, "but I believe that his humanity is so lofty and ideal as to exceed the common terms of the word."[17] This cautionary reverence didn't endear him to pastors of the liturgical flock.

The performers weren't professional but rather plucked from obscurity. Jesus was played by a young Spanish student named Enrique Irazoqui, who, for Pasolini, resembled the El Greco depiction of Jesus, though his voice had to be dubbed by a professional actor. Pasolini's own mother, Susanna, played Jesus' mother Mary, with friends and acquaintances rounding out the rest of the cast. A truck driver played Judas, a lawyer took on the role of Joseph, a writer played Simon and Matthew was played by a music critic. These people were chosen for their chiselled features and primitive gait. As stated in one book, there are "no well-manicured figures here, no soft focus lenses to erase minor skin flaws. Deep wrinkles are evident in nearly every leathery face."[18] The result was an absorbing authenticity that was light years away from Hollywood fabrication.

The film was shot in southern Italy because, as Pasolini observed, "Like Jerusalem, it is close to the Mediterranean and there are many humble people there." Herod's palace was a 12th century castle. The costumes were based on frescoes by Piero della Francesca. Jesus was dressed in subdued garb that didn't stand out too much from the rest of the cast, as was the way in former messianic movies.

The film had no screenplay, Pasolini being content to use only the words in the gospel itself. "I liked the Christ of Matthew," he said, "he was rigorous, demanding and absolute." This is the Christ who said, "I came not to send peace, but a sword," the Christ who will "burn up the chaff with unquenchable fire" and who dubs his contemporaries a generation of vipers."

Pasolini used a melange of musical scores as a backdrop, everything from Negro spirituals to Leadbelly's rhythm and blues to Bach and Mozart. Such eclecticism was indicative of the general tenor of the film. Overall it was a model of minimalism and gentle power, which of course was what Jesus was primarily about.

It may seem surprising to us that a Marxist would be interested in making a film about Christianity's pre-eminent avatar, but let's not forget Pasolini believed that the real Marxist must not be a good one. His function was to put orthodoxy and codified certainties into crisis. His duty was to break the rules. He admitted he was anti-clerical, but added that within him there was also a huge tradition of Christianity which was manifest in his devotion to Romanesque, gothic, and baroque churches and other forms of Christian architecture which had strongly influenced both his life and career and given him a philanthropic sense much greater than that of priests.

Apart from *The Gospel According to St. Matthew*, many of his works, particularly *Accattone* and *Teorema* are infused with religious themes like sin, guilt and expiation, but the atheist in him sees little hope of salvation, art alone offering the only tenuous form of apotheosis available. His vision of the world, he told a group of film students in the 1970s, was both epic and religious, and such a vision found fruition in misery, which was, in his view, always epic. *Teorema*, incidentally, was described as "mystical" by Canadian priest Marc Gervais, who saw it as a film about the need to reach the absolute by rejecting the bourgeois condition that alienates man. It even won a prize from the Office Catholique International du Cinema, despite the fact that many viewers slammed it as being a decadent mix of religion and sex. In it Terence Stamp played a priapic gentleman who could be construed as being either Christ or the devil.

The film was banned for obscenity, and the Pope described it as "inadmissible" because of its unhappy cohesion of religion and sex, while Marxists denounced it for taking a soft line on the bourgeoisie, unusual in this Pasolini's canon.

Mark's Gospel would have been closer to Pasolini political views but St Matthew's Gospel is more literary and better constructed, so it's safe to assume that Pasolini was more interested in art than polemic when he made the film. The stark Italian locations are also a refreshing antidote to the splendor of lush Hollywood barnstormers. On the negative side, by creating Jesus as a socialist figure rather than a primarily religious one, Pasolini, in a sense, divests him of his essence. Richard Walsh believed Pasolini filmed Jesus "less reverently" than his predecessors, noting that even though the director confined himself to just one gospel, his Messiah nonetheless spoke "less canonically."[19]

Pasolini said one of the reasons he made the film was that he felt Marxism had lost its way. He also believed it was possible for there to be a meaningful dialogue between Marxism and Christianity. Jesus himself, he emphasized, had many Marxist tendencies in his championing of the underdog, his predilection for social upheaval and his use of the sword as well as love.

Too much importance had been placed on "sins of the flesh" by Catholics, Pasolini held, and too little on social justice. Christ's main nemesis, he said, wasn't Mary Magdalene, the fallen woman, but the Pharisees with their whited sepulchres. The sixth and ninth Commandments, in other words, weren't as important as the seventh and eighth ones.

This may be an "à la carte" reading of St Matthew and a convenient mechanism whereby he could shoehorn his own ideology into the received wisdom of a 2000-year-old tradition, but if so, he did it with exceptional authenticity and persuasiveness. His Jesus isn't handsome, but rough-hewn. Jesus wasn't so much a man of letters as of the soil. He's a social crusader—a Pasolini, if you like.

Using a documentary approach to tell the story, backed up by the haunting scores of Mozart and Bach, Pasolini shoots Christ in close-up as if to distance him from his followers, a ploy that backfires from a cinematic point of view. The drama of his words is lessened and their impact impaired. Pasolini is better when inveighing against his pet hate of consumerism.

The great enemy of Christianity, he believed, wasn't communist materialism but rather bourgeois materialism. It's against this backdrop that he explores the fissure between the two traditions, using Jesus as the connective thread. Critics of the film felt he downplayed the conflict between the Jews and Romans, as well as that between Christ and the Pharisees, in favor of an abstractionist vision of demagogues and victims. While this theory holds some weight, we must remember he was making a film he hoped would outlast any particular epoch. At the end of the day all we can say for sure is that both Jesus and Pasolini loved the poor, even if one of them expressed that love in a hieratic fashion and the other in a sensual one.

From an artistic point of view, the film eschews traditional depictions of Jesus garnered from Renaissance paintings and elsewhere, stripping him down to his bare essentials as a man grounded in a particular place at a particular time. Unlearning the coordinates of eons of sacerdotal iconography, Pasolini crafted a work that would stand its ground as a relic of hagiography bereft of derivative clichés and plagiarized mannerisms. As such, it features what Shakespeare called "unaccommodated man," albeit in a precise socio-cultural context and captured in an improvisational way the kind of neo-realism beloved of independent film-makers. There were no corporate fingerprints in Pasolini's film; it was a work that galvanized the raw pain of the disenfranchised under the oracular tutelage of a pariah.

Dedicated to the memory of Pope John XXIII, the film won many artistic kudos. *Time* criticized it for its plethora of close-ups but praised it as being a "modest, unadorned movie that should satisfy the yearnings of anyone who has ever suffered through the pretentious piety of multi-million dollar orgies of Scripturama."

What Pasolini is is an awkward neo-realist who used the actors' inexperience to dramatic effect, i.e., to make their discomfiture before the camera a tool to create apostolic awe. If we carry the argument further, the inexperience of Irazoqui as Jesus can be deployed to convey his bashfulness.

Nobody in this film looks like they own a Porsche, or has a kidney-shaped swimming pool in their back garden. They're not reconstituted primitives but rather the real deal; a cast literally picked off the streets with all the facial flaws the rest of us unfamous souls try to live our lives with.

The film was recently included in a Vatican "Best of All Time" list so obviously Pasolini's Marxist agenda wasn't a problem, or perhaps the Vatican didn't pick up on it. Pauline Kael was its most denunciatory critic. She could hardly wait, she insisted for Pasolini's hero to become crucified! As a result of the strong Marxist reverberations from the film, Irazoqui had his passport confiscated after it was released and he was suspended from his university for a year.

On November 3, 1975 in a wry coda to its eclectic director's career and life, Pasolini was murdered on a backstreet in Rome. A young male prostitute confessed to the deed, but many felt, as they felt when John F. Kennedy was gunned down in Dallas a decade or so before, that he could have been a pawn for a wider conspiracy. There was a groundswell of discontent about Pasolini's work from a right-wing contingent almost from the moment he put his first image on screen. Maybe a bloody end to his life was inevitable. It could also have been a homophobic ritual.

For the man who'd made global headlines for creating the most austere Jesus yet, the event also had overtones of life imitating art in a vicarious form of mock-martyrdom, Pasolini himself, indeed, had even contemplated being crucified like Christ. As a young man he had written in one of his diaries that the experience of looking at Jesus on the cross had made him fantasize about imitating the sacrifice the Messiah had made for us. He saw himself hung on a cross with his loins scantily wrapped by a thin strip.

His martyrdom wound up by becoming a voluptuous image and, bit by bit, he was nailed up with an entirely nude body. With arms outstretched and hands and feet nailed, he was totally vulnerable and lost. There's a decidedly erotic edge to these images which makes it all the more amazing that *The Gospel According to St. Matthew* was so restrained. Reading about these images, one is surprised Pasolini didn't make a film more like Martin Scorsese's *The Last Temptation of Christ* a few decades later. Scorsese's images also evinced a pronounced masochistic sense.

While the world was still reeling from Pasolini's film, and not yet expecting Scorsese's one, George Stevens directed *The Greatest Story Ever Told*. As we saw, it was anything but that. Stevens was at the end of his career when he made it, and it showed. Much of the film looked confectionary. Max Von Sydow did his best as Jesus but his Swedish accent, which he didn't attempt to disguise, was off-putting. The general impact was corny and the direction was heavy-handed.

Richard Walsh wrote in *Reading the Gospels in the Dark*, the film "mythologizes the Jesus story along Emersonian rather than existentialist lines."[20] Pasolini is not interested in being revisionist, merely reverential. Michael Bliss makes a good point when he says that Jesus in Pasolini's film, and indeed in *Ben-Hur,* has "a halo of adoration" over his head. These films, as a result, only speak to people "already convinced of Jesus' divinity."[21]

Stevens opted for a mystical Jesus somewhat in the tradition of DeMille as evidenced by the film's hyperbolic title, but with a modernist perspective. There was a supreme irony in loading Ingmar Bergman's angst-ridden knight from *The Seventh Seal* with this responsibility. In the earlier film the divinity was silent. Now Von Sydow could reverse that silence in the most dramatic manner possible: by entering its soul.

Or could he? Maybe if the film was structured differently he might have had a chance, but it was weighed down by a raft of celebrity cameos—Charlton Heston, Carroll Baker, John Wayne, Sidney Poitier, Telly Savalas, Claude Rains, Dorothy Maguire and, perhaps most ridiculously of all, Pat Boone as an angel. They served more to distract from the action than enhance it. The overall effect, in the view of one author, is "totally crippling" to the film's credibility.[22] Also, putting Wayne in chainmail was tantamount to casting Cary Grant as Pontius Pilate.

The ludicrousness of casting the macho (and decidedly unsubtle) Wayne in a supposedly poignant role was alluded to by an anecdote that may or may not be apocryphal. Legend has it that Stevens was having trouble trying to drag a sense of wonder from Wayne, who played one of the soldiers at the cross during the crucifixion scene. His line was, "This truly was the son of God." Stevens wasn't happy with his cowboy drawl and asked him to inject more awe into it. Wayne paused for a second and then said, "Aw, this truly was the son of God."

There were other problems too: the duration of the movie for one thing. David Jasper, in his essay "On Systematizing the Unsystematic," rightly pointed out that the film was "far too long for the attention span of the commercial cinema audience."[23]

Critics like Stanley Kauffmann felt Stevens had sold out his integrity by putting a stellar cast into a work that ought to have been more muted.

Did Stevens feel that the "greatest" story also had to have the "greatest" cast? If so, his radar was on the blink. If Pasolini proved anything, it was that the street was a much more authentic place to find historical-looking faces than a film studio. The studio meant recognizability. Even the Nordic Von Sydow was a household name. Granted he wasn't a boy-next-door like Jeffrey Hunter, but people still knew him from other roles. One could hardly say the same for Enrique Irazoqui, who was hardly known to a dozen people in the United States, which meant he came without baggage. The audience could invest all their concentration into what he was doing instead of being distracted by his CV. To my knowledge, Irazoqui never made another film, but if an actor is to be associated with just one part, let it be this one.

Perhaps the most ludicrous aspect of the film is Judas' betrayal. He's played by a suitably guilt-ridden David McCallum, but when he describes Jesus as "the purest, kindest man I've ever known," one wonders why somebody who held such a view would be tempted by thirty pieces of silver. The precondition that he wants no harm to come to Jesus is surely naive in the circumstances.

Stevens put in the glitzy cast to help him recoup his enormous financial investment in the project, but they diminished the film's credibility dramatically. What was the point in having a "non-Hollywood" Christ if he was going to be surrounded with celebrities?

Rumors abounded that many of the cast offered to be in the film for free because they were eager to be a part of this much-hyped blockbuster. These offers would have been hard to refute, particularly with his spiralling budget. But where was the perfectionist of yore? Stevens would have been better off giving the cast members thirty pieces of silver and telling them to go home.

At any minute we expect Savalas to blurt out "Who loves ya, baby," like his Kojak persona. Von Sydow, on the contrary, is too haughty. It's as if Stevens was aware that he had too much of a Hollywood Who's Who on board and tried to upgrade matters in one fell swoop by putting an "intellectual" actor at the forefront. This might have sounded good in theory but it creates an imbalance that Stevens' schematic direction intensifies rather than mitigates.

The script was problematic as well. In one scene, Jesus asks James the Younger what his name is. "Little James," he replies. "What is your name?" James asks Jesus. "Jesus," says Jesus, to which James says, "Ah, that's a good name."

Sydow struggled with his dialogue, his halting delivery adding to the ponderous nature of the proceedings. The fact that Stevens storyboarded the film with setups drawn from the paintings of El Greco, Leonardo Da Vinci and others added to the studied aura. Sydow's dialogue is also too contemporary in tone. Wanting to be "relevant," the bane of many religious films, Stevens compromised the mystique of his main star. He ends up verbalizing bromides.

Stevens frames many of his shots in a self-conscious manner. This was also a problem with his earlier film *Shane*, where the actors seemed to be mere figures on a landscape. Exerting huge control over each scene, Stevens not only directed the film, he also produced it and co-wrote the screenplay. Such "God-like" control worked against its being allowed to breathe freely under the aegis of different voices.

The film is more faithful to the gospels than *King of Kings*, with less jarring cross-cutting and more of a sense of purpose, but it errs on the side of being too preachy. It also treads a middle-of-the-road path theologically. While there are cries to "Crucify him!," we can also hear voices saying "Release him." Stevens seems to be trying to avoid charges of anti-Semitism, something Mel Gibson also had problems with in his 2004 film *The Passion of the Christ*. The film was released in the same year that the Second Vatican Council declared that the Jews weren't responsible for Christ's death, so Stevens had to walk on eggshells to avoid a boycott. Stevens basically tried to Hollywoodize the Bible, with dire consequences. His crucifixion scene is over the top with its fancy flourishes. Couple this with the lush scenery—like John Ford filming Monument Valley, but without the atmospheric sense—and you've got rampant confusion. Similar Colorado backdrops were used to much better effect in *Shane*. In that movie, Stevens transposed a western into a mythic parable. Here, on the contrary, he was guilty of turning a Judaeo-Christian myth into the stuff of bad westerns. David Jasper put it in a nutshell when he said, "Alan Ladd in buckskin was a more acceptable saviour for the cinema than the rather unctuous figure of Max Von Sydow." Lloyd Baugh spoke for many when he wondered why Sidney Poitier, as Simon of Cyrene, wasn't given any dialogue or why the audience doesn't know what Shelley Winters suffers from before she screams "I am cured!," or why, in a film that swears by orthodoxy, does Judas end his life by throwing himself into a pit rather than hanging himself from a tree?[24]

The general tone of the film is somber. One is always aware that the director is pulling the strings, which gives the proceedings a sense of unalloyed contrivance. Stevens tries to force the audience to be awed, which is one sure way of making sure it *won't* be. Many of the scenes look like representations of paintings with all of the staidness that conjures up. The well-groomed Jeffrey Hunter wouldn't be out of place on this canvas, giving his Sermon on the Mount opposite the Grand Canyon. Baugh wrote of the "perfectly balanced composition" of the Last Supper scene, remarking that "When Stevens has Jesus extend his right hand over the bread and the chalice of wine in the liturgical gesture of epiclesis, he seems to be anachronistically presiding at a Catholic Eucharistic service instead of a Hebrew Passover meal."

Stevens' pretty cowboy scenery, coupled with his pumping music score and grandiose effects which hark back to an age of *The Miracle of Our Lady of Fatima*, make an unsatisfactory *melange*. He may have been sincere in his intentions but reverence often makes for bad art, as was the case here. The film was like Cecil B. DeMille meets John Ford in Norway, giving off all the profundity of a shampoo commercial.

Peter O'Toole played a much more fascinating Jesus figure with a particular edge in *The Ruling Class* in 1972. This riotous black comedy was originally a play but O'Toole felt it would work equally dynamically on the screen so he bought the rights to it. He commissioned Peter Barnes, the play's author, to write the screenplay and hired some of the most respected British character actors to fill the supporting roles. Arthur Lowe, Alastair Sim and Harry Andrews acted wonderfully, their collective stiff upper lips acting as the perfect antidote to his blithe derangement.

When O'Toole's father dies he becomes the 14th Earl of Gurney. Potential beneficiaries of the will queue up for a slice of the cake but he has his own ideas about what to do with the money. The insane O'Toole believes he's Jack the Ripper as well as Jesus and prances around in a white suit with his red hair hanging down around his shoulders. One critic compared his appearance to that of Barbara Stanwyck in *Double Indemnity*!

Convinced that he's God, O'Toole spends a lot of his time on a self-styled cross which he has positioned strategically at the top of a ladder in his study. He even says: "When I pray I find I'm talking to myself." He regales Lowe *et al* with his messianic gobbledygook as he fastens his Royal blue eyes on them, towering over them both in altitude and with the richness of his personality.

O'Toole is also a man of some mirth. Asked to reveal his Godhead, he starts to unzip his trousers. When a woman tries to kiss him on the grounds of his palace he says, "Don't. The last time I was kissed in a garden, it turned out rather awkward." When asked to perform a miracle, he ponders a moment before replying, "I can't raise Lazarus again—he's decomposed."

In addition to being a religious farce, the film was also a satire about the aristocracy. As Lowe succinctly puts it, "Privileged arseholes can *afford* to be bonkers." But O'Toole's insanity, of course, is leavened by bursts of incredible lucidity. It's here the film really shows its teeth as O'Toole hacks away at one sacred cow after another with delicious abandon. The film was way ahead of its time both in its abrasive script and vaudevillian dance numbers, but it ran for too long, 154 minutes originally, to be commercial. O'Toole finally agreed to shorten it by 6 minutes. The film was the official British entry at the Cannes Film Festival in 1972 and drew favorable attention but did less well in the United States Too few people know about it today but it remains a high water mark in O'Toole's career as well as being a work that paved the way for much of the Pythonesque lunacy that came in its wake—including *The Life of Brian.*

The basic question it poses is whether Jack Gurney is mad or is the world mad. In a discussion of whether he should be certified as insane, Lowe speaks for most of the audience when he opines, "They should all be locked up."

In his Jack the Ripper guise, O'Toole goes from the God of love to the devil of hate. After shooting a pheasant on his property, he remarks, "[I]t's a sign of normalcy in our culture to slaughter anything that moves." Like Hamlet, another eloquent nobleman who's lost his father, Gurney is but mad north by northwest.

The funniest scene in the film occurs when the man chosen to vet O'Toole for insanity turns out to be an old Eton classmate. Upon realizing this, the pair break into a rendition of "We'll Still Swing Together" in memory of their boating days, miming the motions of rowing as they sing. Monty Python's "Always Look on the Bright Side of Life" from *The Life of Brian* is more than a little derivative of this treasurable nonsense.

Significantly, it's only when O'Toole goes on a hunting expedition, and proclaims the merits of a barbarous, even medieval form of capital punishment, that he's accepted by his peers. Even his savage stabbing of Lady Clare comes to be regarded as "normal" by his doctor—who's twice as daft as he.

In the closing scenes of the film O'Toole becomes "Judas Jack Iscariot," making Lowe, a closet socialist, take the rap for the stabbing. "I stand outside myself," he tells us, "watching myself watching myself watching myself." His rehabilitation complete, O'Toole even brushes his teeth twice a day now. His sanity is conformity to the insanity of the status quo. He doesn't need to fly over the cuckoo's nest provided all the rest of the gentry are keeping the peasants down. All normal services are resumed for the horsey set once Jesus/Jack finally realizes that it's hate that makes the world go round. All you have to do is learn how to sing it properly.

Thus we have "Onward Christian Soldiers" trilled at his climactic, coruscating House of Lords speech where, surrounded by fossilized skeletons, he kisses the Bible and promises the wrath of an Old Testament God on those who threaten the establishment. All that remains now is for Jack the Ripper to kill the one person who could have meant something to him: his wife.

1973 provided two musical depictions of Jesus, both having had their debut on Broadway. *Godspell* was an updated version of Jesus' life which featured a slew of effervescent teenagers following Jesus around modern-day New York. The concept was original but many of the song lyrics were saccharine, to say the least.

Based on the Old English word for gospel, or "good news," *Godspell* is a cheery piece of street theater without any pretensions. If the film plays around with the Bible, it does so only in form, not content. There's no Martin Scorsese or Terry Jones here, just a bunch of street actors engaging in various slapstick routines against the backdrop of Scripture. Neither is there the frantic crosscutting of *Jesus Christ Superstar*. No miracles are performed, and the arrest of Jesus, which will become such a significant part of Franco Zeffirelli's *Jesus of Nazareth* in a few years' time, is sidelined. As was the case with *The Gospel According to St. Matthew*, the cast was comprised of unknowns. This gives the film more spontaneity, a quality it already has in spades.

It's simple and direct in tone, a "happening" experience with a strong sense of immediacy. The film is a flamboyant affair, carried along on a tide of infectious goodwill. Maybe it should have been subtitled

"Fairytale of New York." The spirited cast engage in a frothy love-fest, being baptised anew in a Central Park fountain before darting about the place to spread the word. There's nothing doctrinally new here, but the songs, most notably "Day By Day" are catchy and the light touch is refreshing. Cynics saw it as hippie mania firmly entrenched in the "flowers in your hair" era. While its message is age-old, it isn't shoved down our collective throats. One is invited to jump on this bandwagon only if one wishes, unlike the more aggressive dialectical stance of *Jesus Christ Superstar*, which is more deviant but also more pushy.

The God of *Godspell* is a clown figure, a frizzy-haired cross between Superman and a jubilant hippie. Jesus forgives Judas for betraying him by kissing him, an ironic reversal of the original kiss of betrayal. At the end, Judas carries the dead body of Jesus back into the city.

In the same year, Andrew Lloyd Webber and Tim Rice's rock opera *Jesus Christ Superstar* was brought to the screen amidst much fanfare. It was filmed by Norman Jewison in the Holy Land and featured a gay Pontius Pilate and black Judas. Many viewers felt the latter walked away with the movie. The same people might have argued that Satan was a more interesting character than God in Milton's 'Paradise Lost," which reminds one of Kirk Douglas' comment "Virtue isn't usually photogenic."[25]

Jesus Christ Superstar is more style than substance. The director moves around with the camera in a frenetic fashion as his motley crew of energized apostles soul-search, giving rise to what one writer called "audio-visual whiplash."[26] Lost somewhere in the middle of them all is Jesus, a decidedly subangelic and rather pedantic Messiah. The show belongs to Judas. To be fair, he doesn't have much opposition. Was this deliberate? Perhaps it should be pointed out that, heretofore, God has written all the books. We've never heard the devil's side of the story.

Judas moves to center stage in this movie just as he did in *King of Kings* and *The Greatest Story Ever Told* while Peter, by contrast, is shortchanged. Martin Scorsese will soon "re-invent" Christ in *Last Temptation*, the "enlightened" postmodernist era also being the one of the anti-hero. Jesus won't become sanctified but an attempt will be made to "understand" him. DeMille wouldn't have had anything to do with this kind of demythologization.

Jewison's Judas, to quote Richard Walsh, is "angry, fated. He, more than Jesus, is a victim."[27] Like the priests with whom he allies himself, Judas finds Jesus a threat to Jerusalem's precarious order. Finally, he betrays Jesus because he thinks this is Jesus' wish. Feeling used, Judas hangs himself, claiming God has murdered him. Walsh points out that Jewison "resurrects" Judas for the final song and dance scene as Jesus is crucified. Jewison won't even allow Jesus center stage in his final hours, focussing on the traitor rather than the betrayed. "Clearly," he notes, "Judas and Jesus have swapped places."[28]

"Stick to your fishing from now on," Jesus tells the apostles in a final gesture of frustration at his failure to gain self-respect. Because on the evidence of the film, being a follower of this fuzzy pariah seems like a recipe for disaster. It's a tempting offer.

The bus in which the cast arrive and leave bookend the narrative. Jewison also puts tanks in the desert to give it some semi-political topspin. Such details underline the artifice of a bold polemic that skates off in too many directions to have the lasting appeal it craves, the appeal its Jesus agonizes about losing in the next era. In Singapore, the Protestant church authorities insisted that a postscript be added to the film saying, "This is not a true or accurate portrayal of the life of Jesus Christ, Son of God. For that, please read the Bible."

The film has lots of jump-cuts and abstruse camera angles as the fragile Jesus looks for all the world like a disposable commodity. Maybe this is why even Mary Magdalene, by comparison, seems like a tower of strength as she entreats him not to worry. "He's just a man," both Judas and Mary Magdalene sing to drive the point home. In some ways he seems more in need of healing than somebody capable of healing others. "What's the fuss," he inquires like a rap artist, "Tell me what's a-happening." Everyone else seems more clued-in than the prime mover.

Jewison's Mary Magdalene is light years away from that of DeMille's— or indeed the evangelists. Far from being a *femme fatale*, she's more of a chastening, maternal figure. She could be viewed as the mother Jesus never had considering that his ministry began before he reached his teens. When she serenades Jesus with "I Don't Know How to Love Him," the future has indeed arrived for the Biblical movie. DeMille would have seen her as not too far removed from the serpent in the Garden of Eden, but here, just fifty years later from a 2000-year-old tradition, she's invited into the apostolic fold. Or rather, Magdalene has invited herself into it, all too well aware that even Jesus needs love. Already the markers are being laid for Martin Scorsese's "last" temptation.

The audience comes away from the film feeling that if God chose this Jesus to save the world, he mustn't have had much taste. Jesus doesn't act but rather reacts—principally to Judas, who would have made a much more dynamic savior.

Jesus also seems to have one eye on posterity, as when he says, "I must be mad, thinking I'll be remembered. My name will mean nothing ten minutes after I'm dead." This is an interesting piece of existential angst that foreshadows Martin Scorsese's *Last Temptation*, but in Jewison's fluffy milieu it comes across as just another example of a vacillating, publicity-hungry misfit.

Far from embracing his destiny, Jesus exhibits what the philosopher Martin Heidegger might call "a throwness into being." He appears to have no understanding of, or appreciation for his mission, being dependent on Judas to explain it for him, and to, him. "Why me?" is his attitude, even as he goes to his death.

Robert Powell did a bearable job of portraying the Messiah in the TV mini-series *Jesus of Nazareth* in 1977, but he was rather pacifist, and the film's treatment of Jesus in general didn't break any new ground. Director Franco Zeffirelli, a Catholic, drew heavily on Renaissance paintings for his visuals and he co-wrote the script with Anthony Burgess, also a Catholic, so it was no surprise that it was stringently Catholic–and catholic. Richard Walsh rightly remarked that the film anticipated the "swing towards conservatism" of the 1980s.[29]

Powell was originally supposed to play Judas but Zeffirelli was so impressed by his screen test that he offered Powell the lead role instead. Afterward Zeffirelli spoke of this decision as the Holy Spirit working through him. It's hard not to sniff a publicity stunt in the manner in which Zeffirelli described Powell as having "a kind of light not his own moving through him" at the audition. In our own time, we may be skeptical of Mel Gibson speaking in similar terms about events that took place during the shooting of *The Passion*.

Zeffirelli made the same mistake George Stevens did by recruiting his performers from Central Casting. Thus the film has people like Peter Ustinov, Rod Steiger, Anthony Quinn, Laurence Olivier, Anne Bancroft, Ernest Borgnine and a host of others decorating these ornate tapestries. Some of them even speak directly to the camera on occasion, which solidifies the didactic nature of the enterprise. Having said that, I agree with the view that the profusion of guest stars in this film never becomes the "liability" it was in *The Greatest Story Ever Told*.[30]

Jesus of Nazareth has become something of a perennial phenomenon on television at times like Easter and Christmas and has also made its way into schools for various religious purposes. So far, key rings or bumper stickers haven't been sold at the movie, but such a day may come. How sad that a work which concerns itself with removing consumerist concerns from our lives should itself become a victim of such merchandizing.

Even on a scriptural level the film has some significant shortcomings. Zeffirelli, for all his pretensions of comprehensiveness, leaves out scenes like the transfiguration, the storm on the lake, Jesus walking on water and his temptation in the desert. The reason he gave for the latter omission was that he saw it as "too interior" and risked "leading the spectator into a dangerous confusion." God only knows what he meant by such a patronizing cop-out. Surely this scene afforded the best audio-visual opportunity of the whole movie. Audiences were hardly likely to be "confused" by such a well-documented episode.

By playing things safe, Zeffirelli turned his film into a bland non-event. The middle of the road is a place where one is most likely to be knocked down. So it proved here. Lew Grade insisted there be a bar mitzvah in the film, despite the fact that this was anachronistic, which is yet another reason why we should be suspicious of it. The film is really nothing more than seven hours of undiluted piety. Lloyd Baugh noted that Jesus was "superficially characterized" and "domesticated," which ultimately meant that he had "little to do" with the Jesus we know from the gospels.[31] Zeffirelli promised us a contemporary Jesus but his conservative, please-everybody approach actually ends up as a big nothing. The film is a throwback to the DeMille/ Stevens era but there's little food for thought here, merely a long-winded retread of millennia-old orthodoxy. Zeffirelli also places huge emphasis on Jesus' arrest rather than his inner struggle, which makes the film a third-rate version of a story that, thankfully, wasn't made for the big screen.

On the credit side, Baugh praises Zeffirelli for giving us the first "Jewish-Palestinian" Jesus. This is particularly welcoming, he notes, after the "California-surfer-Jesus" of Nicholas Ray and the "Grand Canyon Old West" Jesus of George Stevens. Apart from this, though, the director has gone full tilt for a populist work and it snowballs on him.

Monty Python's *The Life of Brian* was released in 1979 to much consternation. A Biblical spoof that was originally entitled *Jesus Christ: Lust for Glory*, the film dealt with a humble amphitheater usher who's mistaken for Jesus. Directed by Terry Jones, the film polarized the population of Britain.

The film was originally to be bankrolled by EMI but they pulled out when the negative publicity began. George Harrison, a member of the Beatles, rescued it. The day after it premiered in Britain, cast member

Michael Palin took part in a TV debate with John Cleese, the Bishop of Southwark and various other guests about its merits.

"We were attacked by everyone, Lutherans, Catholics, even a rabbinical group," Palin declared afterward. Mary Whitehouse also entered the fray, as did Malcolm Muggeridge. The Bishop called it "tenth rate and miserable."[32] "He [the Bishop of Southwark] spent the whole show castigating us," said Palin, "as if we were the most loathsome dogs in London, eventually demanding that we be deported." After the show, however, Palin claims [the Bishop] gave him a broad smile and said "Jolly good." Palin said it was precisely this doublethink he was inveighing against in the film. "I'm wary of people imposing their morals on me," he bristled, "and I have little time for the hypocrisy of a lot of churchmen."[33]

The film tells the story of Brian of Nazareth, the son of a Roman centurion who's gone AWOL, and a mother who's reputed to be a virgin but won't talk much about the subject. Brian wants to destroy the Roman Empire and has little interest in religion. Preaching Christianity is imposed on him by his followers, who have preconceived ideas about him that eventually cost Brian his life. Brian's martyrdom is meaningful for his followers since they don't have to die but for him it's literally a waste of a life. Since life is absurd anyway, according to the film's sub-nihilistic compass, this fact merely compounds the agony.

Jones animates the credits at the beginning just to let us know he's in an anarchic mood. The soundtrack is similar to a James Bond film, Bond being a more tangible, iconic figure for Britain's youth culture at the time. There are also allusions to science fiction. Everything went into the mix.

To show his distaste for the Romans, Brian is forced to write abusive graffiti on the walls—making sure he gets his grammar right. He's also called upon to kidnap Pontius Pilate's wife, which isn't too difficult a task considering Pilate is gay. Brian is pursued by the Romans but escapes when he receives help from aliens aboard a spacecraft that has run into trouble.

After Brian is mistaken for a prophet, and then a Messiah, this gives Jones ample opportunity to satirize those who have vested interests in adoring him. They have, in a sense, made God in their image, in contravention to the Biblical concept of God making Man in His image. When Brian tries to exhort them to be individuals, they reply in perhaps the film's funniest moment, "We're all individuals." The people's need for a patriarchal figure has caused them to "invent" one, which is Jones' most devastating indictment of all.

"Blessed are the peacemakers," Brian exhorts the crowd at one point, but his words are misheard as "Blessed are the cheesemakers," after which Pythonesque frenzy and mayhem ensue.

After a while we realize that though the immediate subject matter is religious what the film really attacks is the bourgeoisie. It's primarily a political statement rather than a religious one. In an interview, Palin said its main target was "the extraordinary length to which authority must go to preserve its credibility."[34] To this extent, it could have been set anywhere, at any time. To be more specific, it's a critique of religious *films* such as *Ben-Hur, The Greatest Story Ever Told* and others rather than religion itself. Vincent Canby summed it up as a critique of the "sand and toga" genre.[35]

Eric Idle said, "I'm a very religious person; it's just that I don't believe in God." He was an adherent of Eric Hoffer's credo: "Faith in a holy cause is to a considerable extent a substitute for the lost faith in ourselves."

The film climaxed with a crucifixion scene in which a rent-a-crowd crooned "Always Look on the Bright Side of Life." The final depths of bad taste are thus plumbed. One of the echoing refrains of the film is the complaint that "the bloody Romans can't take a joke." Perhaps they couldn't, but there isn't much funny about crucifixion—unless you're Terry Jones.

The Life of Brian isn't so much an iconoclastic work as a satire on the stuffiness of organized religion. It trivializes the issues it deals with, not so much for the adolescent pleasure of that activity as to act as a forum for debate. It declares war on conformity, delighting in tearing down the sepulchres, but without being sure of what to replace them with. Crucifixion jingles are hardly the answer to life's eternal questions. "These are images of the Jesus of culture," Peter Malone points out in his book *Christs and Anti-Christs*, "not the Jesus of faith."

The fact that Brian is a fake messiah—the Three Wise Men rapidly withdraw their gifts when they become cognizant of this—gives Jones the opportunity to score points about the spurious manner in which the real Messiah has been worshipped through the ages. Brian enables the director to have fun with heresy, the undertaking of miracles and all the baggage associated with putting people on pedestals when they clearly don't deserve to be there.

Critics and audiences were divided as to whether the film was scabrously brilliant or childishly trite. What commentators were really airing in their various expostulations was a mindset they would have had before entering the cinema. Church-bashers loved it almost from the first frame, whereas the protectors of religious probity never allowed themselves to see the humor. Are some subjects too lofty to be satirized? That was the basic point at stake. If the answer was no, then it should have been evaluated on its own terms as a plea for pluralism trussed up in the guise of broad farce, or a silly satire infatuated with giving two fingers to an ancient institution.

In its first week of release, the film raked in a whopping $80,000, leaving one in little doubt that, whatever side of the fence people stood on, they were still interested in seeing it. Most of its patrons, it should be added, went to chortle rather than harrumph.

This wasn't the only "false" Christ committed to film history. In *Whistle Down the Wind* (1961) Alan Bates plays a murderer on the run who's mistaken for Christ by the three children who discover him in their barn. The film guns the unique storyline for all the sentiment and humor Bryan Forbes in his directorial debut can wring out of it. Forbes is careful not to conflate the quasi-religious undertones too much, drawing fine performances from the children, in particular Hayley Mills, whose mother actually wrote the novel upon which the film is based. The drama is cleverly built up by Forbes, which makes its eventual undercutting by one of the children—"He's not Jesus; he's just a feller"—all the more reverberative. In one scene, as Bates is being searched by a detective, he puts his arms out against the skyline 'in a Christ-like pose.'"[36]

In 1981 Mel Brooks also got into the heretical act with *History of the World—Part 1*, a film which parodies everything from the Stone Age to Hitler—and of course the Bible. One scene has Brooks himself as a waiter at the Last Supper inquiring "Are you all together or is it separate checks?" One almost expects Judas to bark at Jesus: "Enough of this water into wine business; you'll pay for your round like everyone else." According to Brooks, Moses originally had fifteen Commandments but dropped one of the tablets, leaving only ten.

If nothing else, Jones paved the way for the most revolutionary depiction of Jesus in screen history, Martin Scorsese's *The Last Temptation of Christ*.

Scorsese, a former altar boy who had once toyed with the idea of becoming a priest—a cleric of his ken told him he was "too much Good Friday and not enough Easter Sunday"—had first become intrigued by this project in 1972, but it would be fifteen years later before it finally reached the screen.

Barbara Hershey, whom Scorsese had directed in *Boxcar Bertha* that year, had given him the novel on the set. It was written by a man whose

name not many people knew and even less could pronounce: Nikos
Kazantzakis. It was years before Scorsese actually read the novel. When
he did, he was enthralled by its subversive splendor.

Scorsese visited Kazantzakis' widow in 1977 to try and persuade her
to release the film rights. Sidney Lumet had expressed an interest in it
as far back as 1971 but hadn't developed the project. In the end,
Mrs Kazantzakis gave Scorsese permission to make the novel into a film.
Scorsese then asked Paul Schrader, who'd worked with him almost as
often as Robert De Niro, to write a script for it.

Schrader obliged but they couldn't get it off the ground due to
Paramount's understandable vacillation about such a seething cauldron of ostensibly heretical material. As Peter Biskind pointed out,
Paramount decided to "pull the plug well into preproduction when it
realized the flak it would have to take from the religious right if it
proceeded."[37]

Hershey told Scorsese she felt she was "put on earth" to play the Mary
Magdalene role, to which Scorsese replied that he was put on earth to
direct it. But the film stayed in dry dock until 1988. Even at this point
Scorsese found himself as the object of derision in Hollywood. As he
remembers, "Big people in the business were turning around saying,
'Yeah, I know the pictures you make.' One guy introduced me to someone who was the head of some company. He says, 'This guy is going to
make *Last Temptation.*' The guy looked at me and laughed in my face.
'Yeah, right. Call me next week.' I mean, I'd come through all those
years to get that? It was like a kick in the heart."[38]

Schrader's script has Jesus saying to Mary Magdalene at one point,
"God sleeps between your legs." The dream sequence towards the end
also had Jesus making love to his mother. The general thrust of the movie
was to present a Christ riddled with indecision and struggling with carnal
desire. Dawn B. Sova remarked, "This Christ is wracked with doubt over
his destiny. He can't be certain if the voices he hears are those of God or
the devil."[39]

Scorsese first shows us his Jesus in a state of psychological torment.
As Richard Walsh points out, Scorsese shoots Jesus from a bird's eye
view, in marked contrast to the worm's eye view directors like Cecil B.
DeMille preferred.[40] Even in this detail we can see a seismic shift in religious appraisal. The camera isn't awed by the savior anymore but rather
curious about him. He isn't untouchable or invulnerable. Scorsese
catches him like a rabbit in the headlights. The Hunter has become the
Hunted.

In an early scene Jesus watches Mary Magdalene have serial sex. He makes crosses for the Romans and therefore feels God will consider him unworthy of his mission.

Scorsese's Christ is a reluctant savior. He revolts not only against Phariseeism and whited sepulchres but also himself. He feels he's weak-willed, and liable to succumb to such weakness in time. At one point he even curses a fig tree because it fails to bear fruit.

The "last" temptation Scorsese puts Jesus' way is the sexual one, and temptation must be vindicated on the grounds that it's probably the scenario most red-blooded males on the planet can quite easily identify with. We can't say the same about the devil's desert temptation, which doesn't have relevance to the lives most people lead, and therefore doesn't really allude to temptability at all in a being Christians are called upon to believe is half-man. It isn't easy temptations that test one's mettle but difficult ones. The greater the challenge the greater the victory in beating such a challenge.

Scorsese himself insisted the film was made with deep religious feeling. He said it was about suffering and the struggle to find God. He made it with conviction and love as an affirmation of faith, not a denial. The reason he wanted to emphasize Jesus' human side, he said, was because he felt people would identify with that more. Others disagreed. Two hundred members of the Fundamentalist Baptist Tabernacle in Los Angeles picketed outside Universal Studios shortly before the film's projected release date. The banners they held carried messages like "Universal Is Like Judas Iscariot" and "The Greatest Story Ever Distorted." Some of them even staged a mock crucifixion.

Scorsese has really built his whole film around the idea of Jesus in the Garden of Gethsemane asking God to "let this chalice pass from me." He felt this aspect of Jesus' life had been shortshrifted until now. If God had taken human form in Jesus, it had to follow that the human being who was called upon to die on a cross in enormous pain would balk at this notion at some point. Otherwise he couldn't really have been human at all. Such self-doubt didn't work towards the demolishing of Scripture but an endorsement of it.

Similar to this was Scorsese's attitude towards Mary Magdalene. How could Jesus not have been attracted to her? he asks. Temptation isn't the sin, our religion tells us, but rather succumbing to it. Jesus doesn't succumb to temptation any more than he did when the devil tried to tempt him in the desert but that shouldn't mean the temptation didn't occur. And yet sexual temptation is curiously absent from the gospels. That's why Kazantzakis' book was unprecedented in its import.

Whatever we may feel about Scorsese's inflammatory approach, in many ways it's more faithful to the Bible than DeMille's. This is a point well argued by Gerard Loughlin.[41] DeMille's *The King of Kings*, Loughlin points out, had Magdalene being deserted by Judas, her former lover, for "a band of beggars" i.e., Jesus and the apostles. This part of *The King of Kings*, Loughlin feels, is far more titillating than the "somewhat demure scene in *Last Temptation* that has Jesus waiting his turn in the brothel where Magdalene is offering her carnal services to all comers." Loughlin is also surprised that so many fundamentalist groups were revolted by Christ's "homely heterosexuality," considering such values are the bedrock of Christian domesticity. Christ longs for the "nuclear" family. What could be perverse about this?

Scorsese wanted to take things a step further. He asked Schrader to write a script about a common man possessed by God but fighting it. Scorsese's use of the word "possessed" is interesting. Usually we associate this with evil spirits rather than benign ones. Scorsese even told Schrader that God was a "demon" to Jesus in this sense. Clearly, such language is anathema to biblical scholars and could be expected to infuriate them, as it did.

Schrader told interviewer Kevin Jackson that his script tried to plow a middle course between the Arian heresy, which claimed Jesus was a man pretending to be a God, and the Docetian one, which contended that he was a God pretending to be a man.[42] This was a curious point to make considering most films featuring Jesus had already made that distinction in greater or lesser degrees. In any case, surely it was Kazantzakis who had the right to make it considering his was the original vision behind the project.

Paul Moore, the Episcopal Bishop of New York, explained to Scorsese that all of this was "Christologically" correct, and that his take on the "two natures of Jesus went back to the Council of Chalcedon in 451." Scorsese found it fascinating that the human nature of Jesus was "fighting Him all the way down the line, because it can't conceive of him being God."

Judas becomes politicized in the film, urging Jesus to revolt against the Romans. Jesus considers it, more because he would prefer to die on a battlefield than a cross, but then realizes his divine duty. Scorsese's Jesus wants Judas to betray him so that he can expedite his father's wishes for mankind despite his near-failure of resolve in the Garden of Gethsemane.

"Without you," Jesus tells Judas with some irony "there can be no redemption." It's a poisoned chalice. "Could you betray your master?"

Judas asks teasingly, to which Jesus replies in one of the film's best lines, "No, that's why God gave me the easier job—to be crucified." Later, in a classic role reversal, he even asks Judas to comfort him because he's afraid.

Jesus is tempted by a young woman in the film's extended final stages. Not too surprisingly, it's the devil in disguise. Women as Biblical temptresses go all the way from Eve to Salome and beyond, thus causing many feminists to see it as the ultimate misogynistic tract. This alluring Satan offers him sexual happiness, relief from pain, release from the cross and a harmonious family existence. She isn't quite as easy to resist as the diabolical apparition in the desert.

Scorsese defended himself against his detractors by insisting that the temptation of the film's title is more of a dream than Jesus succumbing to "bad" thoughts. Jesus doesn't sin, even in thought, but in the aftermath of the dream experiences the guilt anybody might feel in such a situation. In this way Scorsese gets around the awkward theology of a "lustful" messiah.

As for Mary Magdalene, Scorsese would have us believe she became a prostitute out of despair at the fact that Jesus couldn't love her in the way she wanted. Unlike Norman Jewison's Mary, she does indeed know how to love him, but Jesus' response isn't forthcoming.

This is all highly inflammatory material. Even his choice of Willem Dafoe to play Jesus was audacious since Dafoe had played mainly villains before. You couldn't say this about any previous screen Jesus. Scorsese was asking us as an audience to come to the film without preconceptions. We were to put out of our minds all those boring sand-and-sandal epics like *Ben-Hur* and *The Greatest Story Ever Told*. Religious history began here.

The film took its director down many roads, some of them conjecturally brilliant, others maybe just that tad too far of left field. But even when he misses the target it's intriguing. The idea of Jesus imagining that his godlike nature is a conceit implanted in his head by Satan is highly original and perfectly conveys the self-doubt Scorsese is looking for. At times like this, one remembers pride was the first sin of all.

Scorsese's Jesus is like something from Freud. He has fits of rage, he faints, he hallucinates. He also disavows his ministry. Can Scorsese get away with this? It's not canonically accurate, and neither does it read like the Jesus of history. By calling his work fiction he's warding off onslaughts from many different groups, but there are so many elements of the actual gospels in the film, we're tempted to accuse him of cherry-picking and then running for cover when he steps on theological toes. Only *á la carte* Catholics can have it both ways like this.

Richard Corliss called the film "a Billy Graham crusade for the lapsed Christian."[43] Corliss saw it primarily as a "buddy" movie, remarking that Scorsese's finest achievement in making it was to "strip the Biblical epic of its encrusted sanctimony and showbiz."[44] Further, "by jolting the viewer to reconsider Hollywood's calcified stereotypes of the New Testament, Scorsese wants to restore the immediacy of that time, the stern wonder of that land, the thrilling threat of meeting the messiah on the mean streets of Jerusalem."[45]

"I made it as a prayer," Scorsese insisted, "an act of worship. I wanted to be a priest. My whole life has been movies and religion. That's it. Nothing else."[46] Kazantzakis had captivated Scorsese with his depiction of Jesus as someone he could envisage himself breaking bread with.

Scorsese also liked the idea that Jesus "hung out" with tax collectors and prostitutes. The fact that Jesus engaged with people impressed him more than a prophet like John the Baptist, who fasted in isolation. Another idea that fascinated Scorsese was that of Jesus being "terrified" every time he performed a miracle because each one brought him closer to the prospect of his final fate on the cross, an event he dreaded as much as looked forward to as an expiation of humanity's sins.

Scorsese didn't believe his film would destroy people's faith but rather challenge and ultimately strengthen it. As he stated, he believed Jesus was "fully divine" but Catholicism placed an undue emphasis on such divinity. If Jesus walked into a room, Scorsese said, "you'd know he was God because he glowed in the dark." This being so, it would surely have been easy for Jesus to resist any kind of temptation, which diminished its impact. Equally, he could be expected to resist the temptation of sex and undergo his crucifixion because he was all too sure he was coming out the other end in no time. Schrader disputed the "carnal desire" emphasis, claiming it was normal family life his Jesus craved, with sex just part of the procreation process.

On the sexual end of things, at one point of the film Jesus is informed, "When you don't sleep with women your sperm goes up to your brain and makes you crazy." The next unasked question is "Is this what gives you your messianic sense?" Let's not forget that sexual deprivation also drove two of Scorsese's previous characters "crazy": Travis Bickle of *Taxi Driver* and Jake La Motta of *Raging Bull*. Betsy (Cybill Shepherd) denied Bickle in *Taxi Driver* and La Motta denied himself Vickie (Cathy Moriarty) in *Raging Bull*. Can we now add Mary Magdalene to that list? Schrader called the film "the final panel in the triptych" that contained the other two.

Scorsese is no longer a practicing Catholic. He wanted his movie to take people back to where they were alone with God without any churches. He wanted it to act as a conduit for people to get back to the real Jesus, to a person who wasn't just an ethereal symbol of omniscience but rather the being who gave ultimate meaning to every aspect of our existence here on earth.

He made an analogy to the character of Charlie in *Mean Streets*. Charlie goes to Mass and all the sacraments but outside the church his life is ruled by guns. How does one reconcile these antinomies? Is it impossible to do so?

The American Family Association contacted 170,000 pastors in the United States to stop the film's release. Mother Anjelica, the head of the External Word TV Network, claimed it was "the most Satanic movie ever made" and would destroy Christianity. In Britain it was condemned by Cardinal Basil Hume, who exhorted Catholics to avoid it. The U.S. Catholic Conference declared that its 40 million followers should studiously stay away.

Donald Wildmon, a Christian fundamentalist from the American Family Association, threatened a four-year boycott by his members of any cinema that had the gall to show it. His threat, alongside that of fellow-minded souls, caused General Cinema, one of America's largest chains, to shy away from it. Suddenly, we were back in the 1930s again with Mae West and her ilk.

Considering the masochistic nature of Scorsese's Jesus, and the strain of masochism that runs through Scorsese's entire *oeuvre*, many have concluded that *Last Temptation* is as much about Scorsese as it is about Jesus. There's no doubt that he used the film to get some of his obsessions off his chest, and maybe some Catholic sexual guilt too. He also devotes double the time to the temptation itself as Kazantzakis did, a telling indication of why he was first excited by the project.

I'm inclined to agree with Michael Bliss, who wrote "The Christ in films such as *The Greatest Story Ever Told* and *Ben-Hur* passes through each film with a halo of adoration swirling above his head. These films speak only to people already convinced of Jesus' divinity so they accomplish nothing in the way of widening his appeal."[47] Scorsese, on the contrary, makes him earn it. It's precisely Jesus' uncertainty, Bliss argues, that makes the crucifixion story so glorious, "since it shows us a man dying for a cause whose validity is not—indeed, cannot be—firmly established. Jesus' triumph derives from his sacrificing himself solely on the strength of his faith."[48]

On the night before the screening, vandals ransacked the L.A. cinema at which it was going to be shown. The following day a group of directors held a press conference to support Scorsese. Sydney Pollack concluded, "Christianity survived for 2000 years. It will survive Martin Scorsese's movie."[49]

The film opened to packed houses amidst tight security in nine U.S. and Canadian cities. Most of the people who bought tickets did so because they were interested in seeing it; others did so to make a statement against the protestors. At one showing a man stood up in the middle of the film and shouted out, "Blasphemy!" He was told to shut up. There were a few incidents of vandalism and violence. A suspicious package was sent to Scorsese's daughter's home but it turned out to be just a rock and a letter of protest. An Arkansas cinema was set on fire and in Salt Lake City a print of the film was stolen. Some protestors lobbied the government to halt the progress of the pernicious beast unleashed by the former seminarian. One congressman, Robert Hubbard from Kentucky, went so far as to say, "There's one difference between Judas Iscariot and Martin Scorsese. Scorsese will earn more than thirty pieces of silver for betraying Jesus Christ."[50]

Worldwide the film opened to violent demonstrations. Molotov cocktails were thrown in some countries, while in others tear gas was sprayed at cinemas. The film was banned in both Israel and Greece. In Ireland it was given an Over-18s certificate, with the proviso that nobody be admitted after it had begun so as not to miss the opening statement that it was based on a work of fiction and not the gospels. Such a caveat didn't defuse the anger. Audiences globally were frisked for knives, in case they'd slash the screen and spray paint. Bill Bright, the leader of the fundamentalist group Campus Crusade for Christ, even expressed an ambition of buying up all available prints of the movie, which would have cost him in the region of $10 million to destroy them all.

The critic Bruce Bawer, writing in *American Spectator*, had a different kind of problem with it. When Jesus was with Mary Magdalene, he wrote, "The two of them look and behave like one of those ageing flower-child couples who live in Topanga Canyon, drive around in pickup trucks and analyse each other in pop-psych fashion." The film was over-acted throughout, he felt, which meant that Dafoe and Hershey in particular "seem incapable of saying hello without putting on an intense Actors Studio expression." It's true that the naturalism of the piece conflicts with its mystical aspirations but we may allow Scorsese a certain amount of license considering the audacity of his ambition. Alice Ellis, in the *Daily Telegraph*, was even more scathing, telling us that if Christ were reincarnated as a film critic, "I don't see much hope for Martin Scorsese." When the film was shown in Ireland at the Cork Film Festival, a vocal group of protestors, one carrying two cans of paint, demonstrated and prayed outside the Opera House, thereby delaying the performance. One protestor carried a placard saying "Jesus was Nailed, Not Screwed."

Not every Catholic disapproved of it. The progressive Jesuit Andrew Greeley said its critics were guilty of the aforementioned Docetism, which stated that Jesus wasn't really human. "Those who would exclude the poignancy and joy of erotic desire from his life," he stated, "deny him his full humanity."[51] Greeley added significantly, "Although Mr Scorsese's Jesus is not the Jesus of the Scriptures, the film makes us think seriously about just what God represents for us."

Robin Riley wrote, "Scorsese's fully human Jesus, a demystified and highly subjectivized Christ, radically altered the traditional function of the sacrificial victim as well as the formal relations between good and evil."[52] In other words he opened all the floodgates, launching a full frontal assault on the father–son dichotomy that stigmatized Christian thinking in his view.

What Scorsese said about the church isn't as interesting as what the church said about Scorsese. He brought everybody out of the woodwork, his film exposing as much tunnel vision as righteous indignation. A black minister wrote to him after seeing the film, saying that he loved it and was going to use it as a study guide in discussion groups. He felt it challenged traditional images of Jesus which were so comfortable they had practically no relevance to the depravity of many people's lives. Such people wanted their Jesus in a place far away from those lives, unconnected to them, a distant ideal. Scorsese took him down from that distant place and as such his film was valuable. "The great hook of the film," Schrader said, "is the idea of the reluctant God, the person whom God is imposing himself on. . . . It's a tortured human struggle about a common man possessed by God and fighting it . . . God is a demon in that way."[53] Marlon Brando, it's said, brought doubt into the locker-room. With *Last Temptation*, Scorsese brought it into the Garden of Gethsemane.

The following year Denys Arcand also made a brave effort to render the Messiah relevant to modern society with *Jesus of Montreal*. People have often asked what would happen if Jesus came back to present day society. Would he be crucified again? Would he be listened to, recognized for what he was? In this offbeat movie an actor recreates Jesus in a passion play as Arcand draws parallels between the actor and his God. Perhaps the point is baldly made, making one feel that it might have sounded better as a Sunday night idea rather than a Monday morning working project, but it took a brave man to be so audacious as to update the Gospel story. The film is flawed, but maybe the surprise isn't that it was done imperfectly, but that it was done at all.

As the film begins, a priest who's been putting on the play for years with increasing levels of boredom hires Daniel, an actor to revive it. Fr Le Clerc, a man with many problems of his own, wants the play revitalized, but he gets more than he bargained for with Daniel, who ends up rewriting it totally until it starts to merge osmotically with the circumstances of his own life.

Daniel, played by Lothaire Bluteau, gathers his cast from a bunch of struggling actors from the lower strata of the profession. He blends into their lives, inspiring them to get the best out of themselves. It's a case of "take up your script and follow me." He isn't ostentatious about his mission but his words have a quiet profundity. As Bryan Stone noticed, he greets one cast member with the very Biblical invocation, "I've come for you."[54]

The new play, re-working the precepts of Jesus, contains lines like "Harlots will go first into God's kingdom," "Never say I am the Christ; I am the son of man," and "You must find your own path to salvation. No one can help you." It even manages to quote Shakespeare's most famous soliloquy from *Hamlet* to fulfill an ambition of one of the actors. Daniel places Jesus' divinity and resurrection in question. He makes Jesus the illegitimate son of a Roman soldier, which outrages Le Clerc. Le Clerc tries to stop the play in its tracks but it's too late. It becomes a hit. Fr Le Clerc is the last man who should cast stones. In an earlier scene Daniel finds him sleeping with one of his cast members. "I am not a good priest," he confesses to Daniel afterward, revealing that he dearly wanted to leave the priesthood but hung on because of the creature comforts. Rome, he says, would offer him pittance if he renounced his vocation.

Daniel begins to act like Jesus after playing him on stage. He then has to deal with Phariseeism in the form of the church that persecutes him.

One of Daniel's cast members, the beautiful Mirielle, bears more than a passing resemblance to Mary Magdalene. She has "prostituted" her talent by appearing in tacky advertisements for TV, but Daniel "redeems" her by giving her a more fulfilling role. In a seminal scene, Mirielle auditions for a beer ad. She's told to lip-synch a song but would prefer to sing it. The director of the ad tells her not to worry about her

voice; that her main talent is in her body. She's asked to take off her
sweater for this reason but refuses because she has no bra on. When the
director persists, wishing her to do the song topless, Daniel blows a fuse
and wrecks the TV studio, breaking thousands of pounds worth of equipment. Arcand allegorizes the incident of Jesus throwing the moneylenders out of the temple here. It's hardly a subtle metaphor but it blends
into the warp and weft of the narrative. After being arrested for wrecking
the studio, Daniel refuses to employ a lawyer because, like Jesus with
the Romans, he doesn't recognize the court.

Another scene has a lawyer in a skyscraper—no prizes for spotting the
Satanic allusion here—endeavoring to persuade Daniel to sell out his
artistic integrity for financial gain. "The city is yours if you want it," he
enthuses tantalizingly, gazing out over the concrete jungle that's also a
desert. Jesus is "in" these days, he tells Daniel. The lawyer suggests that
Daniel write a book, adding that it would be helpful if he had a drink or
drug problem. Perhaps he could even put his face on a salad dressing,
like Paul Newman. He knows there are big bucks to be made from the
play if Daniel plays his cards right. But this Devil is eminently easy to
resist.

A lot of the dialogue is loaded. When a policeman arrests Daniel, he
says he'd like to have seen the ending of the play. Daniel replies, "You'll
be back." One is reminded of Jesus saying to the good thief, "This day
thou shalt be with me in Paradise."

After Daniel is arrested, Fr Le Clerc tries to get the cast to perform the
old version of the play, a suggestion they respond to by mimicry. They
do a mockery of it for him in a variety of styles: vulgar street theater,
melodrama, "comedie francaise," even a Method version. Daniel arrives
while they're in mid-act and mimes hara-kiri, ironically presaging his
own death as well as a humorous reaction to their over-acting.

The priest is humanized in the scene where he tells Daniel he once
tried to fight authority himself but it didn't work. His ministry is compromised now, but it's all he has. He also knows he performs a service.
He gives illusions to people who "can't afford psychologists." Religion
is the Great Lie, but a necessary one. Daniel counters by arguing that
there must be more to life than "waiting to die," a significant phrase in
the circumstances as his own short life is nearing its end. Fr Le Clerc is
intelligent enough to realize Daniel's play has much more quality than
his own but he also realizes that his survival rests on a return to the melodramatic version of the play. Otherwise he'll end up "a chaplain in an
old folks home in Winnipeg," almost as chilling a fate as the pittance he

would receive from Rome if he took off his dog-collar. His church is full of worshippers who don't want too much reality. Maybe they're like the audience targeted by the beer-ad people, with the collective IQ of a gnat. But they're all he's got, and he's all they've got. They're each other's mutual comfort zone.

Constance, the cast member he's been sleeping with, would like him to leave the priesthood and go away with her. "I'm too old," he tells her. "You're not too old to make love," she replies. Fr Le Clerc pulls the plug on the play but Daniel decides to put on one last performance. Before he goes on stage, Daniel and his cast have their own "last" supper of bread in the form of pizza and wine.

Police show up toward the end of the show to close it down. A *melee* ensues, during which Daniel, who's on the cross, is knocked down. He hits his head on the wood and seems to have a concussion. Constance and Mirielle accompany him to a Catholic hospital where he gets shabby treatment. He's nobody; just another actor without a medical card—dispensable. At a second hospital, a Jewish one, more attention is given.

Daniel goes to a subway—a metaphor for the underworld. Here he starts spouting apocalyptic messages like one of those Old Testament deities. He collapses and is rushed to hospital again, where he dies. His organs are donated: one person receives his eyes and another his heart. In death he's allowed two people to see and feel respectively. The words of the surgeon are pointed, "He's blood type A. That's a godsend!" Mirielle and Constance, who represent Martha/Mary, sign his organ transplant forms. The operating table on which he lies is cross-shaped. The surgeon puts red disinfectant on his chest in an obvious "sacred heart" motif.

Richard Cardinal, the lawyer, continues the theater company after Daniel dies, but his motive is profit. In both his name and gesture, Arcand seems to be casting Cardinal as the spokesperson for the institutionalized church that will continue after his demise, with all its attendant compromises. Richard Cardinal's name is possibly a pun on Cardinal Richelieu.

Arcand isn't a believer but in his depiction of the actors rehearsing their play he gives us a poignant evocation of the seminal elements of Scripture. He presents us with a play-within-a-play, the subtext being the fact that we, like him and his bedraggled cast, are all members of both merely by being alive. If the film has a Satan, a Mary Magdalene and a Martha, it's also got a Pontius Pilate—Fr Le Clerc—who washes his hands of the production and stands inside a closed window near the end as the rain pelts down.

It's also got a Judas. As the film begins, a young actor playing a murderer in a different play ends up by killing himself. After the show is over we learn that he's both a friend and admirer of Daniel. An advertising executive who attends the show says to her friend, "I want his head," meaning on a poster, but the allusion to John the Baptist is obvious. In the words of one commentator, "in allowing his face to be prostituted, he metaphorically hangs himself spiritually."[55]

The advertising executive secures this, as we see in the scene where Daniel starts screaming the apocalyptic messages from the Bible. At one point he sees the young actor in a life-size poster on the wall. He vomits into a trashcan as a result. In contrast to Mirielle, this man has been unable to resist the blandishments of the celebrity culture. Put simply, he's taken the thirty pieces of silver, metaphorically "betraying" his friend Daniel by reneging on his artistic integrity. Just as Daniel has morphed into the character of Jesus by playing him on stage, so has the actor who killed himself committed artistic suicide.

The idea of art as religion and artistic sell-out as prostitution runs through the film. It's even apparent in the words of the idiotic beer ad Mirielle auditions for "The young crowd's here, we worship beer. Nothing's sacred to you, but a good glass of brew."

The film has worn well since it was made and has found favor with students of the Messiah in movies. Peter Fraser spoke for many when he said it "recontextualizes the gospel and renders Christ in a somewhat idiosyncratic manner, yet still carries the viewer towards a climactic embrace with incarnate divinity." Arcand's Christ, he concludes, "has the integrity of a character without guile."[56]

Mel Gibson gave us a more traditional Jesus in *The Passion* in 2004, an ultra-violent treatment of the Messiah's last twelve hours on earth which laid on the gore in rather gratuitous fashion. We're all aware crucifixion is excruciatingly painful when administered by nails rather than ropes. This wasn't news. Gibson also made a meal of the scourging at the pillar. Was there any need for this megabucks movie to be made? Hardly. The characters are one-dimensional, and even though Jim Caviezel is adequate as Jesus, we don't see any new layers to him. The film was controversial for stirring up discontent in the Anti-Defamation League for alleged anti-Semitism, largely based on a line that was supposed to have been cut from the script, the mob's cry of "His blood be upon us and on our children." In fact the line is still in the film, contrary to popular belief. Gibson kept it in Aramaic and didn't subtitle it, a mischievous gesture.

Gibson is a traditional Catholic who recently built a church in L.A. which celebrates the Tridentine Mass so this was never going to be *The Last Temptation of Christ*: *Mark 2*. Caviezel is also a devout Catholic who's reported to say the Rosary daily and shy away from love scenes with sexy ladies. Gibson bankrolled the project himself, at a cost of over $25 million, his ambition being to convey the graphic nature of the suffering Christ endured. He found it difficult to get studios interested in it at first but the controversy generated by the ADL gave it a huge amount of publicity.

Gibson told Caviezel that before making the film he "began meditating on the passion and death of Jesus and in doing so the wounds healed his wounds."[57] He also said that a real-life miracle took place on the set when a six-year-old girl, the daughter of a member of the crew who'd been suffering from regular epileptic seizures, was healed of them once filming began.

The Holy Ghost was working through him on this movie, he told an evangelical group, he was just the messenger boy. Some of his critics accused him of trumping up such incidents, real or imagined, for publicity. Similar charges were levelled at films like *The Exorcist* from an inverse point of view, i.e., when on-set *accidents* took place.

A man who disapproves of the "reforms" of the Second Vatican Council, Gibson alienated America's left with many of his theological pronouncements in the past, and *The Passion* continued that trend. Gibson was also hit by reports that his father, an alleged Nazi sympathizer, said that Hitler's decimation of the Jews during World War II was exaggerated. Gibson's father said "It takes one litre of petrol and twenty minutes to get rid of a dead body. Ask any undertaker, or the guy who operates a crematorium. Now six million?"[58] He also insisted that there were more Jews in Europe after the war than before. Calling himself the champion of true Catholicism, Gibson's father cherished the Latin Mass and was opposed to ecumenism as well as birth control and alcohol. He also banned television in the family home while Mel was growing up.

In Gibson's movie it's the Jewish high priest Caiaphas who's primarily responsible for whipping up the ire of the mob rather than the relatively cowed Pontius Pilate, which spearheaded all the anti-Semitic charges. Pilate actually tries to save Jesus, saying to Caiaphas, "Isn't he the prophet you welcomed into the city? Can anyone explain this madness to me?"

The fact that Caiaphas could over-rule Pilate doesn't seem realistic because politically speaking he was subservient to him. "If I don't condemn [Jesus]," Pilate says to his wife afterward, "Caiaphas will start a rebellion." Again this isn't borne out by the facts as Caiaphas didn't have the clout to do this. Neither would the bullish Pilate of history have kow-towed to the relatively ineffectual Caiaphas. And there's no scriptural evidence of Pilate's wife comforting Jesus' mother and Mary Magdalene while he was being whipped, as takes place in the film.

Gibson takes a "pick 'n' mix" approach to the four gospels for his script. Every Jesus film alienates some people but this one more than most, possibly because it tries to be so user-friendly. Gibson denies that he singled out any one group for deicide. "We're all culpable," he said, "I don't want to lynch any Jews. I love them. I pray for them."[59] Billy Graham is alleged to have wept when he saw the film, and to have described it afterward as "a lifetime of sermons in one movie."[60]

After Scorsese, this is a step back toward the straight-laced interpreta-tion of Zeffirelli, with a touch of Pasolini evident in the Aramaic and Latin dialogue. Maybe DeMille is even in here, because we're expected to be moved to tears after the kind of violence you might expect to see in a Tarantino movie. Is this not trying to have your cake and eat it?

The main weakness of the film is that the support for Jesus seems thin on the ground during his trial and sentencing, leaving one to assume that both Caiaphas and Pilate over-estimated the threat he posed. That posterity would prove them right is irrelevant, unless they too were pre-scient like the Messiah they condemned. Gibson is more conservative elsewhere, shying away from any experimental stance as he soups up the violence. It's hard not to be cynical about this. Everyone in Hollywood knows violence sells, and nobody more than this man, who's been down a similar road with *Braveheart* as well as the *Mad Max* and *Lethal Weapon* movies. In one scene from *Braveheart* he lies stretched out on a rack with his arms spread out as if he's on a cross.

The film opens with a riveting evocation of the agony in the garden. Caviezel's Jesus is resoundingly real here as he undergoes his dark night of the soul. A foggy backdrop underpins the atmospheric mood. There-after we get the Judas kiss, the denial of Peter and so on: all of the expectable staples of most biblical films of yesteryear. Which is why one can't help thinking, if Gibson has had this project in gestation for almost a decade, as he claims, surely he should have something more original to offer us. His dialogue is succinct but it doesn't shed any new light on the story of Christ, delivered as it is in a manner anyone with even a passing knowledge of the Bible would find instantly recognizable. This isn't to suggest one should play around with Scripture for the sake of it, but so many Christological films have been made already, one feels anyone negotiating a new one, particularly one that came with the amount of hype this did, should give us an innovative emphasis, or at least some directorial versatility.

The Passion is a powerful film both visually and aurally but here again one feels something of a disjunction. The choral music uplifts the spirit but the relentless images of Jesus being tortured beyond the degree of anything we've ever seen before works against the emotional involvement Gibson works so hard to muster up. He appears to have adopted a strategy of "shock and awe," to use George Bush's expression, but unfortunately the two components are mutually exclusive. Just as we're starting to feel empathetic toward the divine suffering, another graphically ghoulish blow rains down, breaking the spell.

Overall, the film leaves one with a sense of annoyance. Its production values are exemplary, and none of the cast are less than adequate, but the powerhouse special effects, with the possible exception of the post-crucifixion ones, are unashamedly sensationalistic. Caviezel carries the film as well as the cross. He has little to say, and no real range of emotions, so he has to try twice as hard as anyone else. From the opening scene, with its horror movie full moon and tempting serpent, his torment is heart-rending. Sadly, the film as drama declines from this point.

Gibson said he was inspired by the writings of 19th century eccentric visionary Anne Catherine Emmerich but there's nothing eccentric here. As in DeMille, we go from sublime to ridiculous repeatedly. The baying Jewish mob and grinning, yobbish Roman soldiers remind one of other, slightly better Gibson movies which also had these bold brushstrokes and lack of subtlety. We're never in any doubt where his sympathies lie because he bludgeons us in the face with them.

One of the few realistic characters in the film, intriguingly, is Pontius Pilate. He has a sense of fair play. Yes, he does metaphorically wash his hands of Jesus in the end, but not before he's made every effort to have him released. In a film that trades derivatively on received wisdom, one is quite amazed at this three-dimensional representation. Satan is played by a woman but you wouldn't know this until you see the name on the credits. She has no eyebrows but is still attractive. Her seductive tone, as she tells Jesus the burden of redemption shouldn't rest with one person alone, is well caught. This is a cowled, wraith-like figure. A maggot crawls up her nose at one point. Gibson handles this detail much more delicately than others, which seem to owe more to John Carpenter or Wes Craven than Biblical lore.

Jesus is struck approximately a hundred times in the film. Mark Green, director of the London Institute of Contemporary Christianity, said that his sympathy for Jesus was reduced because of this, not increased. His logic was that it couldn't have been this bad.[61] Dominic Wells came down heavily on Gibson's heady mix of imagery, "Mere bloody scourging is not enough; there must also be flesh ripped off to expose the ribcage. Nailing Christ's hands to the cross is not enough. His shoulder must also be dislocated. Christ dying is not enough; God must also drop a celestial tear which explodes into an earthquake that rends the veil of the temple asunder. Even the presence of Christ is not enough; there must also be a Satan wandering about with insects crawling up his nose."[62]

Rabbi Dr Jonathan Romain felt that a film that emphasized the teachings of Jesus rather than his death might have been more advisable. The film, he contended, "sends the religious clock spinning backwards and undermines all the current efforts towards religious harmony."[63]

Gibson wallows in filming large chunks of Christ's flesh being torn from his body by soldiers who take an inordinate delight in their handiwork. Many people watched such scenes with their hands in front of their faces. In Wichita, a 57-year-old woman died of a heart attack during the final scene. When the soldiers are finished with the "conventional" scourging, they then whip Jesus with whips that have iron-tipped hooks on them, clawing into him from both sides.

By the time we reach the crucifixion itself, the soldiers continue to display a sadism that seems both unseemly and implausible under the circumstances. Why would they be as threatened by Jesus as, say, Pontius Pilate? At times like this, one feels Gibson is laying a *Braveheart*-with-chain-mail on us. Some of the melodramatic touches work, like the celestial tear that hits the ground as Jesus dies. Again it's not the most original special effect in the history of film, but in comparison to some of the more offensive directorial flourishes it holds up well. Gibson plays around with history if not theology. First off, the characterization of Pilate as a kindly man doing his utmost to secure the release of Jesus is antithetical to the actual despot. Secondly, anyone claiming to be a Messiah wasn't automatically sentenced to death.

The *L.A. Times* made a good point when it said that even worse than the violence is the film's cardboard view of Jesus, "reducing his entire life and world-transforming teachings to the notion that he was exclusively someone who was willing to absorb unspeakable punishment for our sins."

There are flickers of Jesus' humanity, as in the flashback vignette of him laughing with his mother after he's made a table she thinks is too high. When have we ever seen Jesus laughing in a film before? Perhaps this is the one quality the Bible lacks, humor. Sadly, moments later we're back to violence again. When Jesus falls under the cross one imagines he would be knocked unconscious, or even dead, but instead of this he looks at Mary, who has run over to him, and says, "See, mother, I make all things new." It's hard to know whether to laugh or cry at moments like this. One would have to be well and truly hooked by the film's mystical moments to accept them. How could Jesus even talk, never mind transmit a rose-hued optimism?

Gibson's notion of suffering is almost medieval in tone. The fact that he's done this sort of thing so many times before, e.g. in *The Patriot* and *Payback* as well as *Lethal Weapon* and *Braveheart*, de-contextualizes it. The protagonists become Gibsonesque rather than biblical.

Also overly sensationalistic is the raven that plucks at the eye of the "bad" thief on the cross after he challenges Jesus. This is much too obvious a manner of letting us know where he's headed after he dies—a touch of Cecil B. DeMille, one might say. It's very definitely the Old Testament God of wrath rather than that of love, though this isn't too surprising considering the foregoing. One critic estimated that, of the film's 126 minutes running time, a whopping ninety of these are devoted to violence. Clearly, Gibson is more interested in agony than ecstasy.

By the end, after the tokenistic resurrection vignette, one feels all Gibson has to preach to us is that (a) whipping can be agonizing, and (b) crucifixion by nails is even worse. Was this why all those who viewed the film before it went on public release had to sign a confidentiality agreement blocking them from writing about what they saw until the embargo date had expired? So that they wouldn't spoil the "surprise" (i.e., Jesus dies on the cross) ending?

The fact that Caviezel dislocated a shoulder, suffered various skin infections, headaches and even hypothermia is an indication of the uncompromising nature of the violence, particularly in an age where there are so many ways of protecting actors from such ailments. He went through most of the shoot looking like a boxer who'd gone fifteen rounds with Mike Tyson, one of his eyes closed and swollen and the other gone back in his head.

Gibson made him spend up to eight hours in make-up every day "to have the look of a man who has been scourged and beaten until the flesh hangs in shreds from his body."[64] He also had Caviezel strapped to the cross in freezing weather on and off for a night without clothes. The cross he carried weighed 150 pounds. It felt more like 600 as the days wore on, he revealed. Then they stuck him up on it in a temperature of 25 degrees with thirty knot winds.

Caviezel claimed he was hit by lightning just before the Sermon on the Mount scene. He knew it was going to happen, he said. People started screaming, telling him he had fire on both sides of his head and a light around him. They started shrieking the way the people did when the jet plane ran into the World Trade Center on 9/11. It was a sickening feeling. He thought he looked like Don King's hairstylist. He's put everything into the mix here. The last image is particularly inappropriate, trivializing the event, whatever it was that happened.

Caviezel rose to Gibson's defense on the anti-Jew charge. It would have been a lie to his faith as well as a mortal sin to make a film that had that element in it. He claimed he was the most Semitic-looking Jesus in history. Mel didn't want a blonde, blue-eyed Aryan Christ.

Asked what he thought the overall impact of *The Passion* would be, apropos the divisiveness that seemed to be turning it into a cause, he replied that in the film there were three different types of people—indifferent, sympathetic, and those who didn't care about God. That's the way it was in the world too he believed.

The Italian sex siren Monica Bellucci was cast as Mary Magdalene. She spends most of her scenes with the other Mary, Jesus' mother, as they helplessly watch him being flogged and tortured. They're both under-used, and fail to convey the extent of the horror they should. You feel their entire performances could have been shot in a few days. All they're called upon to do is huddle together and look pained.

The cast do their best against almost impossible odds, speaking Aramaic as if it's their natural language and in general looking as committed as they can while not called upon to do very much except administer suffering or witness it. Indeed, as the critic Deborah Orr remarked in the *Evening Herald,* "I could detect no spiritual context in this horrific film at all. In fact the implication seemed to be that it was the extremity of the violence used against Christ which alone made him special."[65] Ms Orr went on to note the irony of this, considering the fact that the world's obsession with violence was many people's main stumbling block against a steady belief in any religious system. Gibson's dubious achievement, she wrote, lay in "marrying the aesthetics of medieval obsession with the unflinching shock values of popular culture."[66] Those who were accustomed to soaking up such medieval violence with their daily bread now got on a soapbox against violence, she said, while thin-skinned evangelists, on the other hand, suddenly developed stomachs of steel. Everyone, it appeared, had turned into their opposite because of the baggage they brought to the film.

Other writers bemoaned the fact that Gibson hadn't chosen a more palpable atrocity like, say, the Holocaust to shock audiences rather than a tragedy that was shrouded in conjecture. Orr claimed he failed to bear in mind the context in which the gospels were written during the Roman Empire, which could have accounted for the reluctance to blame those same Romans for Christ's crucifixion nor the context in which the film was being viewed during the Arab-Israeli conflict and against a backdrop of rising anti-Semitism.

"Who killed Jesus?" Gibson asked rhetorically, "I believe we all did."[67] The film was meant to be an apologia, for all his sins and for everyone else who ever committed a sin. It was the vehicle by which Gibson would publicly apologize to his creator for misdemeanors of yore. "I reached the pinnacle of secular utopia," he revealed in an interview coinciding with its release, "I dipped my proboscis into the font and found it wanting." Having secured the help of Alcoholics Anonymous in 1991 for his excessive drinking, maybe the concept was born right there.

Bellucci defended the film on the anti-Semitic charge, reminding people that Maia Morgenstern, who played Mary, was herself Jewish. It's also a fact that the Romans are just as bloodthirsty, if not more so, than the Jews. Which brings us to the nub of the issue: why so much blood? Apologists for Gibson defended him by saying that most previous films about Jesus "protected" viewers from the horrors of what he suffered. Perhaps, but having made this point, did he need to hammer it home—no pun intended—again and again?

The second main problem with the film is its lack of imagination. The sets are moodily arresting, at least in the subdued scenes, few and all as they are, but the script's predictability rankles. Was this why Gibson originally planned to exhibit it without subtitles? Would such a cut have neatly sidestepped the vexed charge of such a lack of imagination? It's difficult to avoid such a conclusion. Why else would somebody shoot a movie in a foreign language and fail to provide subtitles? This would have been an unprecedented phenomenon in film history.

Gibson's answer might have been that the old Mass was in Latin too, and most people didn't know what the words meant, but still responded emotively, at least in theory. This is a tenable position but in a post-Vatican II era it would have been unlikely to net the film the $300 million-plus it earned as cineastes of the 21st century, even fundamentalist cineastes, aren't noted for attending films whose scripts fly over their heads. Having said that, Gibson leaves us in little doubt that his priority with *The Passion* was the visuals, which have been constructed like paintings, thereby following in a tradition set by everyone from DeMille onward. Former directors usually went for Da Vinci or Rembrandt; Gibson's preference is for Caravaggio.

It's a pity he didn't build on his undeniable strengths as a film-maker to give us the Christ we deserved here. He hints at profundity in the flashback sequences which are, unfortunately, mere blips on the overall tapestry. If he'd made a film about the entire life of Christ rather than just his last hours, one feels there would have been better opportunities to develop the richness of character he only hints at sporadically. The film also became a product with memorabilia like nail pendants being sold in conjunction with its release. Over a million "witness cards" as well as various items of "Passion jewelery" are also reputed to have been sold.

Tie-in deals like this are fair game for, say, *Star Wars*, but with a venture like this they trivialize, nay vulgarize the vision. Could Gibson not have clamped down on such spin-off escapades? Somebody who worked on *Braveheart* with him in 1995 in Ireland claimed he stopped some locals from making a meager profit on *Braveheart* T-shirts. Would that he employed similar restraints here before people lose sight of what the film is about. Is there not a point to be made about throwing the moneylenders out of the temple, or is he content to render to Caesar what is Caesar's?

The general consensus among people was that at a time when religion was on the ropes throughout the world, the film could re-invigorate it, at least in theory. What happened was that it had a thoroughly polarizing effect. Fundamentalists loved it, but for all the wrong reasons. Liberals hated it, also for most of the wrong reasons. Most people had their minds made up about it before they entered the cinema. The issues it raised—or rather failed to raise—became an ideological tug-of-war between factions with vested interests.

"It is as it was," the Pope is alleged to have said, rather biblically.[68] One is reminded of Jesus' "I am who I am." But was it? Could Jesus' life, and death, have been this devoid of complexity? When one analyzes the film, and every critic with even the most minute interest in religion apparently did, one was forced to conclude that everything after the opening scene was something of an anti-climax.

The fact that so many religious groups were heartened by the fact that a traditional Catholic like Gibson was getting such a profile meant that his Tarantino-like escapades were going to be given a fool's or saint's pardon. One critic suggested that if the same viewers saw such raw exploitation of suffering in a movie that wasn't about Jesus they would have been aghast. The scourging at the pillar went on so long, and in such grueling fashion, that even the most sympathetic Christian felt drained for the crucifixion. Most objective viewers underwent burn-out long before the walk to Golgotha. They had no tears left to shed by the time Jesus said, "It is consummated," Gibson having bludgeoned his way through the stations of the cross in such a grotesque fashion that some people went so far as to dub it a horror movie. Children were even warned to stay away. The expression "Suffer the little children to come unto me," had ironic ramifications as applied to this orgiastic bloodbath.

In the Garden of Gethsemane Jesus replaces the ear of the Roman soldier in the film's only gesture toward an anti-violence agenda. Thereafter it's more akin to the "earectomy" antics Tarantino employed in *Reservoir Dogs*. One writer dubbed it *Good Friday* meets *Friday the 13th*. Would *Reservoir God* be more apt?

Bellucci described it as a violent film against violence. Gibson claimed the violence was necessary to raise peoples consciousness but said he gave audiences escapes from it. He was presumably referring to the flashback sequences here.

Caviezel believed there was something providential in him getting the role. He was thirty-three when he played it, the same age as Jesus himself at the time of his crucifixion. Also, his initials were J.C., like Jesus. He felt such details were significant—as indeed were the initials of Maia Morgenstern, M.M. After the film wrapped, Caviezel visited the Pope and engaged in banter with him. "I've always believed Jesus was Italian," he said to the Pontiff, "because he lived with his mother until he was thirty, hung out with the same twelve guys all his life, and his mother believed he was God." He was wondering how this joke might be received but the Pope actually laughed. "As for me," the Pope is alleged to have replied, "I always thought he was Polish."

Though the cross Caviezel carried was "only" 150 pounds, or about half the weight of the one Jesus would have carried, it gave him severe shoulder pains to add to the splitting headaches he got from the crown of thorns digging into his head. Is this authenticity? One is reminded of the movie *Marathon Man*, where Dustin Hoffman stayed up all night one night, like his character in the film, so he'd look tired the next morning. When his co-star Laurence Olivier, who wasn't a fan of the Method school, heard what he'd done, he guffawed. "Why not try acting, my dear boy." (Nigel Rees relates this anecdote in his book *Cassell's Humorous Quotations*, Cassell & Co., 2001, p. 18)

The point is that there's such a thing as emotional truth. Carrying a cross of that weight on one's shoulders might very well have the effect of making an actor unable to call up the necessary expressiveness in his face when it's called for. Which is another way of saying that Caviezel was much more impressive in the Garden of Olives—where he could afford the relative "luxury" of concentrating on his performance—than on the tortuous climb to Calvary.

What the film really proved was that the church was so much on the back foot, as the result of global agnosticism as well as the epidemic of clerical child abuse scandals, that it was willing to hold a mega-violent and not very original film close to its bosom and tout it as high mysticism. A couple of decades previously, one feels it would have been denounced by the Vatican as inane fodder dedicated toward little but beefing up Gibson's bank account. Neither did anyone expect him to dedicate the profits to charity. What was that about rich men and the eyes of needles?

Eilis O'Hanlon wrote, "It's Hollywood that's glorified by the film, not the church. For the church, therefore, to try and hitch a return ride to significance on the back of it only risked exposing their own inability to rise to the challenge of transcendence. Hollywood simply took a story that the church was failing to sell and turned it into box office heaven."[69] O'Hanlon added that there was a website offering film viewers a "replica nail" as a symbol of Christ's love, "though such love was only available to anyone with a credit card."[70]

After the film opened in the United States on Ash Wednesday it was shown in 2800 cinemas simultaneously, comprising over 4000 screens. It raked in $8 million in ticket sales that day, a figure that had risen to $30 million by the weekend. Having been all but ignored by the major studios when Gibson first introduced it, it later became a cover story on *Newsweek* magazine.

People were suddenly talking about religion again, and not just in the context of the movie. This was a revelation in an age in which, as one author pointed out, only 42 percent of Americans attended church weekly as opposed to 70 percent visiting malls.[71]

Reaction to the film varied widely. Jews feared it would incite a backlash against them and asked for police protection in certain areas of New York. Evangelicals, on the contrary, felt it was such a powerful tool for accentuating conversion to Christianity that they bought out certain cinemas, encouraging their members to bring along "unchurched" friends with this in mind. Jon Meachan called it "the most watched Passion play in history."[72] Nick James remarked, "If Mel Gibson is to be congratulated for one thing that everyone might agree on, it's that no film in recent memory has generated such high quality commentary."[73]

There were some uncanny events surrounding the film after its release. In Houston, a 21-year-old man who had murdered his pregnant girlfriend and made it look like suicide was so moved by it that he confessed to the murder. The police had assumed that the death of Ashley Wilson two months previously had been suicide as she was found hanged in her apartment with a letter nearby explaining that she was depressed as a result of an unwanted pregnancy. Dan Leach put that theory to rest when he walked into a police station and admitted he'd strangled her after persuading her to write a letter describing her unhappiness. He used a cord from her high school graduation gown to hang her, having got the idea from a TV program. Overcome by guilt after seeing *The Passion*, he turned himself in to the police. "The film moved him so spiritually," Detective Mike Kubricht concluded, "He wanted redemption."[74]

Parishioners from the First Baptist Church in Woodstock, Atlanta, bought out all the seats at 53 screenings in their local cinema for $63,000 so anyone who wished to see the film could do so for nothing. Rodney Sampson, an Atlanta businessman, paid $20,000 to take all twelve screens at his local cinema to spread the word. He described it as a masterpiece that would have an infinite shelf life.

The film critic from the *New York Times* disparaged its gratuitous use of violence, which caused an enraged Gibson to comment, "I want to kill him. I want his intestines on a stick. I want to kill his dog."[75] Not a very Christ-like response, one would have thought, from the man who has his Messiah exclaiming as the Romans drive nails into his hands and feet, "Father forgive them for they know not what they do."

─── 3 ───

Members of the Cloth

"Dial O for O'Malley if you're ever in trouble," Bing Crosby's Fr O'Malley tells Sr Benedict, played by Ingrid Bergman, the Mother Superior of an American school in *The Bells of St. Mary's*, the charming sequel to *Going My Way*. Made in 1945, it was an even bigger hit than its predecessor and garnered Bergman her third Oscar nomination. Crosby was also nominated.

Circumstances would change dramatically for Bergman after she conceived a child outside marriage by Roberto Rossellini. The woman who played Sr Benedict, and before that Joan of Arc, would become a pariah of American society. David Shipman wrote "Fortunately for Hollywood she was Swedish and her misdemeanour had occurred in Italy. With the films that Europe was now exporting, the Bergman affair only went to confirm the decadence of the old world."[1]

The film's main storyline is the friendly rivalry that develops between Crosby and Bergman and their differing opinions about how the school children should be taught. Meanwhile, the pair is trying to get a rich tightwad to part with his money so that their school can be upgraded. The story of the rivalry was humorous and, against the odds, it repeated the allegedly unrepeatable feat of outdoing its predecessor.

At the film's opening, St Mary's School is in dire need of repair. It was under the strict rule of Sr Benedict, which Fr O'Malley does his best to loosen. Both Benedict and O'Malley have a common aim in saving the school from closure but there's always a bit of needle between them.

When Bergman contracts tuberculosis it necessitates her being moved to another parish. Since Crosby gives her the news of her impending departure without telling her the reason, she feels it's personal. Allaying her fears on that score makes her happy in the final reel. On paper the plotline looked pretty straightforward, and it was. But the film struck a chord with audiences, who turned out to see it in droves, in large part due to Bergman's multiple charms. Director Leo McCarey said: "When she walks on screen and says, 'Hello,' people say, 'Who wrote that wonderful line of dialogue?"[2]

Her depiction of Sr Benedict, according to her biographer Donald Spoto, was in marked contrast to previous celluloid nuns, who were either "dipped in honey," "darling caricatures of mature women," or "silly examples of girls caught in a protracted pre-adolescence."[3] Bergman, on the contrary, was a "clear-headed beauty shining with tranquillity in her wisdom and a spirit of genuine self-sacrifice."[4] After the film she became a role model of sorts. People came up to her on the street saying they wanted their daughters to be like Sr Benedict. At this point Bergman's adulterous love life off-screen wasn't common knowledge. Neither, for that matter, was Bing Crosby's cruelty to his children.

Two years later Deborah Kerr donned the habit for *Black Narcissus*, a film about a group of British nuns stationed in Calcutta trying to establish a mission in a remote Himalayan outpost by turning a palace perched on the edge of a cliff into a hospital and school. The nuns have to struggle against the wild winds and also the psychological weather of their respective hearts and in the end it's all too much. After one of them goes insane and dies they return to Calcutta. It's a challenging and bittersweet film with a deep understanding of the conflicting forces that drive people–or fail to drive people.

An early decision was made not to have the nuns wear make-up. Jack Cardiff, the movie photographer, wrote in his autobiography: "How many times have we seen Joan of Arc or Mary Magdalene with lurid eyeshadow, artificial eyelashes, plucked eyebrows and bright red lipstick?"[5]

Maybe the most well-known movie novice of all is Audrey Hepburn's Gabrielle Van Der Mal in 1959's *The Nun's Story*. The daughter of a surgeon, Gabrielle longs to become a nursing nun in the Belgian Congo and so leaves her devoted family to join a convent. After a rigorous novitiate, which includes a time in an asylum where she's almost killed by a homicidal patient played by Colleen Dewhurst, she takes her vows and is sent to the Congo as she wished. Here her faith is tested by an agnostic doctor (Peter Finch) and at the outbreak of war she returns home. After her father is killed by the Nazis she undergoes a crisis of faith and renounces her vows.

The film was based on a novel by Kathryn Hulme, which derived from the memoirs of Marie-Louise Habets, a soul-searching nun-turned missionary who spent twelve years in the Belgian Congo, now Zaire. Habets left the Order she belonged to after seventeen years to work with the Belgian Resistance against the Nazis. Gary Cooper sent the novel to the acclaimed director Fred Zinnemann, imagining he might find it interesting.

Zinnemann was highly impressed by the book. "It was a whole new world to me," he enthused in his autobiography. "I had always thought of nuns and the whole institution as being medieval, a remnant from the Middle Ages that was dying and had no vitality left. I also thought of it as a refuge for people who didn't have strength enough to stay in the world." Hulme made him aware of the fact that, after a thousand years, it was as strong and alive as though it were contemporary. Suddenly he realized "There were tens of thousands of people who live this way under our noses, unbeknown to us. This made the film a voyage of discovery for me, not primarily geographic. You could open the door of a convent and be in a new world."[6] If, that is, the convent in question permitted him to enter its door.

The bishop of Bruges refused Zinnemann permission to shoot the film inside Habets' original convent in Ghent, feeling she hadn't depicted it authentically in her book, focusing as she did on the humility, if not humiliation, the novices were asked to adhere to. They were even ordered to fail their examinations in order to better appreciate disappointment. Zinnemann found the French much more forthcoming when it came to providing a convent. First of all the French had no axe to grind about the book. Secondly there had always been a rivalry between the two countries. They were also glad of the money Zinnemann was offering them for the privilege of shooting there. The fact that Hepburn had a lily-white off-screen reputation helped too.

After securing a convent at which to shoot, Zinnemann approached the Catholic Church to have the script vetted. A Dominican priest examined it to determine if it would meet with liturgical approval. He took exception to the line, "The life of a nun is against nature," insisting that the word "against" be replaced with "above." "More than two hours were spent in discussion of that one word," Zinnemann revealed "We went back and forth until a Jesuit friend said, 'Why can't you say, in many ways it's a life against nature?'" And so the Jesuitical addition of 'in many ways,' was added to the screenplay.

At the outset Zinnemann had a problem getting the studios to bankroll the project. The general reaction was, "Who wants to see a documentary about how to become a nun?"[7] But when Hepburn came on board, Zinnemann wrote, "The studios suddenly became intensely interested."[8] She was a "name" name, as they said, so they knew she could "open" such a movie. However it fared after Hepburn agreed to be in the film was up to how relevant Zinnemann could make Habets' plight to an audience composed primarily of people who hadn't stepped inside a convent since their schooldays. Hepburn was an ideal choice for the part. Apart from her undoubted acting ability, her private life was remarkably free of any whiff of scandal, unusual at that time for a star. To prepare herself for the role she met both the nun she would be playing and the author who wrote her story.

Habets and Hulme had been friends for years before Hepburn, the third 'H' in this triumvirate, met both. Hulme was initially reticent with Habets because she felt Habets' book was so confessional. Reading it was like eavesdropping on an intimate chat. But Hulme was soon relaxed by the casual bonhomie of the jolly ex-nun.

The church was also worried that Zinnemann might exploit the physical attraction of Finch's character to Hepburn. They wanted him to emphasize that the main reason Habets couldn't finally stay in the convent was because of her headstrong nature, which was at odds with the vow of obedience she was required to take. This was much more difficult for her than the other two vows, poverty and chastity. Though there's no physical contact between Finch and Hepburn, an unspoken sexual chemistry simmers below the surface. "Don't think for an instant that your habit will protect you from him," another nun warns her in the film's early stages, testifying to his wandering eye for women. Nothing becomes of Finch and Hepburn's sexual chemistry, but the seed is planted in the audience's mind, which gives their scenes together an added *frisson*.

Once in the order, Gabrielle becomes Sister Luke and has to curb her naturally independent spirit, something she finds very difficult. In one scene where she's asked to lie prostrate on the floor by the Mother Superior, she peeks out at the other nuns: a small but significant detail that hints at a later inability to totally immerse herself in the discipline demanded. The scene where Hepburn takes her final vows is forceful in its simplicity. "You're only an instrument," the bishop informs all the postulants, "you are nothing in yourself." Even now we seem to sense that her vibrant spirit—the self she's called upon to renounce unequivocally—won't be given up easily, no matter how much she struggles to conform to the harsh regime.

Habets starts working with Finch in Africa and he's struck by her unconventionality. "I've seen nuns come and go," he tells her ominously, "and you're not like them. You have not got a vocation."

She loves working in the Congo but after she gets tuberculosis she's sent back to Belgium. When the war breaks out, it destroys any hope she might have had of returning to the Congo. While in the hospital in Belgium she helps a member of the underground, thus disobeying a directive of the Order. Then her father dies at the hands of the Nazis— the final blow. From now on it's only a matter of time before she changes her course of life.

Zinnemann directed the film all with his customary dedication. His punctiliousness extended into all sorts of areas, right down to demanding that the actresses playing supporting roles as nuns stay out of the sun the night before shooting to make sure their skin looked suitably white. He said he saw Habets as having not so much a crisis of faith as one of "worthiness." She didn't leave the Order because she stopped believing in God but because she stopped believing in herself—or rather that part of herself that wanted to fly higher than was good for her personality. She was an unusual mixture of fragility and forthrightness, which created the confusion. The critic Stephen Whitty claimed he couldn't make up his mind if she was "holy or wholly neurotic," something of an over-reaction in the circumstances.

When I interviewed Hepburn two years before she died I mentioned this comment to her and she said she found it totally unreasonable and a misreading of the film. "Marie-Louise was simply an independent woman who couldn't conform to the rules of the Order," she said. "That's the beginning and the end of it. Right from the first day in the convent she finds it difficult to stop working when a bell rings. Such restrictions to natural behavior are anathema to her. You get the feeling she'll leave long before she does, but that doesn't make it any the less dramatic."

"Did you enjoy working with Zinnemann?" I asked her. "It was an utter pleasure," she said. He was a disciplinarian, but not in a life-denying way. He set up the meeting between myself and Marie-Louise, and of course Kathryn. I would have been much more nervous in the part if I hadn't met them before shooting began. I was never as daunted by a project before it started but never as fulfilled when it was over.

I found the use of the term "fulfilled" unusual in the context, considering her character left the Order. "I mean it in the sense that sometimes a negative is a positive," she said. "Marie-Louise wasn't quite sure where she was going as the film ends but she still knows she has to go. This is her new self. She's growing into the person she has to be but of course there's a huge yearning there too. You can't just walk away from seventeen years without a tear in your eye. But we didn't want to over-do the sentimentality. Fred played it down and time has proved him right. I don't know how many people have come up to me over the years and said they thought the ending was moving simple because it didn't try to be."

The film finishes with Habets walking quietly away from the convent. Zinnemann chose to film this scene without music, contrary to the way many Warner Brothers films ended. He didn't want an upbeat tempo or a dying fall, preferring to let the facts speak for themselves. "Festive" music would have sounded like a congratulation of Sr Luke, whereas "heavy" music would have depressed the audience. There was neither victory nor defeat in Habets "kicking the habit"; it was just a fact of life. He wasn't making a statement either against God or convent life, merely one about an idealistic woman who needed a different kind of environ-ment in which to be fulfilled.

"I was humbled by the part," Hepburn told me. "Wearing a habit makes you feel different about yourself. It's like a prop. It made it easier for me to immerse myself in the heart and soul of Gabrielle. Sometimes you nearly feel you're cheating. It was so easy and so obvious. On the other hand I didn't have a lot to work with. Nearly all your face is cov-ered so you can't show much expression. You have to make a little count, to exaggerate it. Marie-Louise was a wonderful help to me on this even though she wasn't an actress. She also showed me how to use surgi-cal instruments for the hospital scenes, and even how to genuflect. I would have overlooked the importance of things like that if it weren't for her. Maybe I should have given her a portion of my fee!" When I asked her how much she became involved in the character, she said, "Probably more than ever before. This was a role I dearly wanted to get my teeth into. You're probably aware I suffered at the hands of the Nazis as a child. Fred also arranged for me to go into a real convent to prepare for the part. When I was there I practically starved myself."

I remarked that, looking at her, that wouldn't be too far to go—Orson Welles once referred to her as the Patron Saint of Anorexics. "I eat as much as anyone," she said, "I just don't show it. Women hate me for that. But in the convent I made a conscious effort to cut down." She also denied herself the pleasure of looking at herself in mirrors because the

Order forbade it. "You can imagine how difficult that is for an actress," she remarked.

I pointed out that she didn't look like someone who was egoistic. "Don't be fooled," she told me. "For the end of the film when I take off the veil, Fred wanted me to dye my hair grey but I refused point-blank. It was stupid of me. How can a woman's hair stay the same color after all those years? It's the one blemish on a very authentic film and I have to put my hand on my heart and say it was all my fault. I knew he disapproved but I wouldn't give in. I'll always regret that." Hepburn made up for her regret in other ways. One day when a make-up man turned on a phonograph during a break in shooting, she asked him to turn it off as "Sr. Luke wouldn't be allowed to listen to it."[9]

Some of the cast thought she took her ascetic aspirations a bit too far. Another time when she and the other crew members were thirsty, she gave everybody water but took none herself. Was she being a Goody Two Shoes? "It's that princess bit again," said one of them, "be a shining example to the populace."[10] She begged to disagree. "I'm afraid that my strenuous advance preparation," she confessed, "is part of my obsessive worry that I won't be ready."[11] The irony was that she wasn't even Catholic. Asked if she would convert after the film was made, she respectfully declined, preferring to stick with her Protestantism.

The shoot wasn't without its humorous aspects. Between scenes, some of the nuns could be seen smoking cigarettes and putting on their make-up. "The blacks who came to watch the shooting couldn't believe their eyes," Zinnemann wrote in his autobiography. "Then someone said, 'These are American nuns,' and the blacks said, "Ah yes, now we understand.""[12] Hepburn had an obvious motivation in taking on the role, as she explained to me. "Marie-Lou's war-time experiences were in some ways like my own. She rescued British pilots from the Nazis. I couldn't claim that kind of heroism, or involvement, but I like to think I would have done what she did if I had the opportunity. In a strange way, what she did before donning the habit made me empathize more with her than her work in the convent or even her medical contribution."

I asked her if she had any worries about whether she'd be "up" to the part? "More than you'll ever know. There are so many things we take for granted when we look at a nun or a secretary or anybody in any walk of life. You think you can step into their shoes and become them. It doesn't work out like that. I'm not a Method actress but it's not often you can talk to the person you're playing and I wanted to make the most of that." "In what ways did Habets help you most?" I asked her. "Every way. I asked her about all the little details people mightn't notice—how she folded her hands, how she performed all the church rituals, what expressions to put on without trying to appear too pious. And as I said, the medical procedures. It was really like playing three women in one for me. She was chuffed when I told her that. It was an experience for her too. Maybe that's why she put so much into it. She was extremely gener-ous with her time. If I wasn't good in the part she would have blamed herself. But when it was successful she praised me. I felt she should have got the plaudits. I was just the middle woman in it all. I tidied up the loose ends, if I can put it that way."

"Did you ever consider being a nun yourself?" I asked. "No. There's too much of Sr. Luke's independence in me. I'm more Holly Golightly material. I couldn't have gone through life without men, or having chil-dren." I balked at asking her how she felt about William Holden. She'd had an affair with him on the set of *Sabrina Fair* which almost broke up both of their marriages at the time. He would have left his wife for her but he'd had a vasectomy and she dearly wanted more children. Billy Wilder, the director of that movie, afterward said that it was easy to fall in love with Audrey. He did so himself, but he never had affairs with any of the actresses in his films. He felt it would have been even more of a disloyalty to his wife than the films. The funny thing was he could have got away with it with Audrey Hepburn because his own wife was called Audrey too. If he called out her name in his sleep, nothing would have been suspected!

Habets' story, according to Charles Higham, wasn't liked in many church circles "chiefy because there was general disapproval of a nun who had broken her vows."[13] Many church people felt she exaggerated the harshness of convent life. There was also controversy surrounding her description of "kissing her superior's feet, undergoing flagellation, and being ordered to fail her examinations to teach her humility."[14] Hep-burn feared it might all prove too downbeat to succeed commercially but she couldn't have been more wrong. The reviews for it were ecstatic. The public also voted with their feet, standing in lines that streamed around corners wherever it was shown. The film made a fortune for the studio.

According to respected critic Albert Johnson, the film was "the best study of the religious life ever made in the American cinema." It was also a very moving analysis of a free-spirited young woman's efforts to reconcile her worldly desires with the regimentation of the order to which she belonged. The official Vatican radio station warmly praised it too. Zinnemann summed it up when he said, "Although it's the story of a woman who loses the way to her vocation, the strongest memory I retain is the total faith of so many nuns we met and the marvellous serenity with which they went about their duties and devotions."[15]

The film was nominated for eight Oscars but won none. *Ben-Hur* swept the board that year, Hollywood usually preferring to cast all its laurels, or at least most of them, in the one direction. Epics always did best at this annual circus anyway. Hepburn lost to Simone Signoret, who played a quite different type of fallen angel in *Room at the Top*. At the end of the film Signoret more or less kills herself at the wheel of her car in a drunken stupor when Laurence Harvey dumps her for the bosses' daughter. The Vatican was hardly impressed.

Though Sr Luke left her order and Hepburn got out of her habit as soon as shooting stopped, she returned to Africa three decades later to work with UNICEF as a good will ambassador. The experience on *The Nun's Story* was probably the catalyst for this. As she said herself, "After looking inside an insane asylum, visiting a leper colony, talking to missionary workers and watching operations, I felt very enriched. I developed a new kind of inner peacefulness. A calmness. Things that once seemed so important weren't important any longer."[16]

In 1957, Deborah Kerr played an Irish nun stranded with a rugged Marine played by Robert Mitchum on a South Pacific island in *Heaven Knows, Mr Allison*. In between fighting off Japanese soldiers and wading through swamps, which gave her nightmares after the movie was over, she engaged in much witty interplay with Mitchum, whom she found to be much gentler and more affable than press reports had led her to expect. She enjoyed the experience so much she worked with him again in *The Sundowners*. Less appetizing to her was the heavy nun's habit which had to be worn from dawn to dusk in the sweltering tropical temperature. "Talk about mad dogs and Englishmen going out in the midday sun," she quipped afterward.[17] John Huston directed it.

The film was widely compared to the Humphrey Bogart caper, *The African Queen* and *The Bells of St. Mary's* in the manner in which it chronicled the budding relationship of two people initially at odds with one another. It doesn't quite reach romance, but the pair manages to put their differences aside to join forces against the Japanese, hiding out during the days and foraging for food at night.

From the outset, considering the nature of the relationship between Kerr and Mitchum, there were going to be problems from the Legion of Decency. William Wyler, who was originally slated to direct the film, found a way to circumvent this. He suggested that there could be a surprise ending in which Kerr was revealed not to be a nun at all but rather someone who wore the habit "to keep her safe from Japanese invaders."[18] Huston felt this was a cop-out so he dispensed with it.

Off-screen Kerr and Mitchum fabricated a romance the day a Legion of Decency priest visited the set to verify that Kerr was depicting her nun character with due respect. Unduly fussy in his demands, Mitchum eventually became irked by the man and thought of a way to shock him. After Huston shouted "Action," Mitchum started to fondle Kerr's breasts lasciviously. Kerr grabbed his rear end, after which they both began kissing passionately. The priest was apoplectic and asked Huston for an explanation for this unseemly conduct. Unperturbed, Huston gave him a frosty glare and said, "Damn it, Father, you've just ruined a perfectly good take with your talking!"[19]

Kerr's accent is a tad too stage-Irish for comfort, and matters get somewhat far-fetched when Mitchum proposes marriage to her one night after drinking too much saki. "If you had to be a nun," he challenges, "why couldn't you be old and ugly?" He compares the pair of them to Adam and Eve, stranded as they are on the island without much hope of being discovered in the foreseeable future. She lets him know that she's already married to God. God, according to one viewer of the film, is "almost like a third character in the movie."[20] Mitchum fails to get her to renege on her vows but after the Allies land you get the feeling that Bob will forget his attachment to this unlikely damsel as soon as he sees the next uninhabited female.

Lilli Palmer played the Mother Superior of an Italian convent in *Conspiracy of Hearts* in 1959. This moving film dealt with the efforts of a group of nuns to free orphaned Jewish children from concentration camps and transport them to foster homes toward the end of World War II. It was interesting for the manner in which it depicted the growing rift between the Italian and German soldiers. The Italians turn against the ruthless Colonel Horsten (Albert Lieven) in the climactic scene where they're ordered to kill three of the nuns but turn their guns on Horsten instead. In a subplot, the Italian Major Spoletti (Ronald Lewis) has a crush on a novice in the convent played by Sylvia Syms.

The film is also interesting for its appreciation of Jewish culture, the nuns having to "educate" themselves as to the significance of Yom Kippur in an early scene where the children berate themselves for having broken the Jewish fast. A rabbi is later smuggled into the convent, which reminds one at times of *The Diary of Anne Frank* with its secret panel for a service. However, when the Nazis step up their campaign against partisan Italian activity, which has also caused the dynamiting of some German supply trains, the rabbi is shot, as is a pig farmer helping to transport the children to and from the convent.

The film was made mainly at Pinewood Studios and director Ralph Thomas makes no attempt to persuade his cast to develop anything approaching Italian accents. Some of the children remind one of refugees from *Oliver Twist* and Sylvia Syms sounds like, well, Sylvia Syms. But the acting is impressive, particularly that of Palmer, whose willingness to martyr herself for the cause never becomes saccharine. Even under sentence of death she manages to banter effectively with Horsten.

Neither is Horsten a one-dimensional figure. Though ruthless, he makes it clear it gives him no pleasure to execute nuns, or indeed children. When Spoletti suggests that Horsten may be acting unreasonably in his pursuit of those responsible for the transportation of the children, he replies, "If an army were totally reasonable, it wouldn't fight at all." Earlier, he describes one of his subordinates who is indeed a bloodthirsty stereotype of the "Evil Nazi" as "an invaluable man—completely obedient, completely stupid. With a regiment like him, I could conquer the world." Spoletti replies laconically, "Haven't you such an arrangement already, Colonel?"

Most moving of all in this interesting cameo of the war is a scene where the children—one of whom asks to be "protected" from God, feeling that God has been the cause of all her problems—are asked to make a list of loved ones they've lost. A little girl with a face that exudes pain says, "My father, my mother, my sisters, my aunt." When Syms asks for their names, she says "I can't remember" as she breaks down in tears. Details like this rather than the documentary footage of Nazi cruelty at the beginning of the film are what really bring home the full horrors of the Holocaust.

In 1965 Julie Andrews played a postulant struggling with inner turmoil in a World War II Rodgers & Hammerstein adaptation, *The Sound of Music*. The most commercially successful musical of all time on the strength of its slick production values, it had Andrews being entreated to "Climb Every Mountain" by her Mother Superior, i.e., experience life outside the cloisters before she makes her final decision. Andrews goes on to become a singing nanny to the Trapp family and helps them escape from the Nazis while falling in love with the widowed father of the house, played by Christopher Plummer.

In Germany, much of the material dealing with the escape from the Nazis was edited out; the war wounds still too raw even after twenty

years. Pauline Kael, who sensibly complained that the film turned viewers into emotional and aesthetic imbeciles, wondered why there wasn't
even one little Von Trapp "who didn't want to sing his head off, or who
screamed that we wouldn't act out little glockenspiel routines for Papa's
party guests, or who threw up if he had to get on a stage." These weren't
issues which concerned any of the people involved in the film, who'd
laughed their way to the bank. The film is now almost a mandatory
Christmas TV offering along with *Miracle on 34th Street, It's A Wonderful Life* and *Willy Wonka and the Chocolate Factory.*

Plummer afterwards referred to the film as *The Sound of Mucus* for
the manner in which it exploited anti-Nazi feelings as well as sugar-
coating domesticity to make it palatable to the masses (it was dubbed
The Sound of Money in movie circles). He described the experience of
working with Andrews as being akin to "being hit over the head every
day with a Hallmark card."[21] Another cast member commented on her
combination of good manners and steely determination. "She may be a
nun," he said, "but she's a nun with a switchblade."[22] She had that
wonderful British strength, Moss Hart believed, that made one wonder
why they lost India.

The film is an evergreen nonetheless and went on to win many Oscars.
If we're to be unkind we could say the Austrian Alps give the best
performance of all. For Andrews it was an opportunity to build on the
success of the previous year's *Mary Poppins.* Her image became synony-
mous with these formative films. This became something of a poisoned
chalice for her in that they prevented her breaking out of the pigeonholes
in which they entombed her for decades. Her cross-dressing antics in
Victor/Victoria in 1992 looked like somebody protesting too much, as
did her previous baring of a breast in *S.O.B.*

Andrews was aware of the problems of playing a Goody Two Shoes
character. Upon first receiving the script she said, "I thought it might be
awfully saccharine. After all, what can you do with nuns, seven children
and Austria?" Director Robert Wise—wisely—decided to dispense with
certain sugar-coated images associated with Austria to snuff out this danger. In his film, he announced, there would be "no filigree, no carved
wood, no Swiss chalets"[23] His damage limitation exercise worked.

The following year we had another clerical chanteuse in *The Singing
Nun* where Debbie Reynolds has a surprise chart hit with "Dominique"
and goes on to split her time between religious duties and practicing her
octave. This was based on the true story of a Belgian nun who formed an
attachment with an orphaned child and wrote a song for him. A kindly

priest approached a record producer with it and it ended up becoming an international hit, with the nun even being invited onto the Ed Sullivan Show.

In 1969, Mary Tyler Moore played a nun opposite Elvis Presley in the last film he made before his return to live stage performances. Aptly named *Change of Habit* the title could have referred to both of their predicaments. It had Moore and her fellow nuns taking off their habits to go undercover as nurses at a hospital run by Elvis who plays a doctor as part of an experiment by the local Catholic Church to allow them learn about life outside the convent before taking the veil. In the final scene she watches Elvis sing "Let Us Pray" in a church and as the camera pans from his face to a statue of Christ she's faced with a dilemma: Elvis or God. She chooses God.

Surprisingly enough, one of Elvis' co-stars in an earlier movie—Dolores Hart, who appeared with him in *King Creole*—went on to become a nun in real life.

Elvis must have felt she made a wise choice considering the way his own film career went down the drain since that promising early movie. A man who once had ambitions to be a Dean or a Brando, such ambitions became scuttled by thirty-one candy floss disasters which made him very rich and very frustrated. By *Change of Habit* the audiences were finally starting to trail off. It seems to have been this fact alone which galvanized him back toward live performing, where his genius had always lain. So perhaps we should be grateful to this dreadful swansong movie for such a minor blessing.

The Nun, an unusual French film, was released in 1971. It dealt with a poverty-stricken young woman forced into a convent against her will and then plagued by the other sisters before being betrayed by a clergyman who befriends her. *Nasty Habits* (1977) was a thinly-disguised satire on Watergate, using a Philadelphia convent as the allegorical fulcrum. Glenda Jackson played a sneaky Mother Superior, with Sandy Dennis as the John Dean character. The nuns did everything from having affairs with priests to playing football in this lame one-joke comedy. In *Agnes of God* (1985) Meg Tilly plays a nun who's been abused as a child and as a result has grown up with a distorted self-image which manifests itself in deranged behavior similar to that of an extreme anorexic. When Tilly has a baby and it's subsequently found strangled and thrown into a garbage can, Jane Fonda is called in as a psychiatrist to try and solve the mystery. Director Norman Jewison is more commanding here than he was in the frothy *Jesus Christ Superstar* and wrings fine performances from both Tilly and Fonda, as well as Anne Bancroft who played the Mother Superior.

Tilly is a case of arrested intellectual development, her mind stuck in the dismal past that's unhinged her. She's in denial about both the birth of her child and and its murder, as well as some stigmatic wounds in her palms. Her attitude to suffering is almost medieval. She believes she has to purge herself of an inner evil to enter heaven. Fonda and Bancroft become embroiled in a confrontation about the adverse effects of religion on certain sensibilities. Bancroft almost goes as far as to suggest a virgin birth, which causes Fonda to fume.

At the court hearing that occupies the latter part of the film, Tilly claims she was impregnated by an angel. Jewison fails to satisfy our curiosity as to exactly what happened. The film asks many more questions than it answers and the viewer feels short-changed as a result, the science-versus-religion debate remaining firmly grounded as the final credits roll.

Two male nun impersonators were provided by Robbie Coltrane and Eric Idle in *Nuns on the Run* in 1990. It was a rather trite confection, made vaguely bearable by frequent cash-ins on Pythonesque lunacy. The following year Whoopi Goldberg appeared as a brassy lounge singer whose life is changed irrevocably the night she sees her hoodlum boyfriend (Harvey Keitel) shoot a snitch in *Sister Act*. Spooked, she makes a run for it and Keitel's henchman give chase. She ends up in a police station and is put in the Witness Protection program. What safer place to hide someone than a convent? But lounge singers don't usually make good nuns, even for temporary stints, and so it proves here. "What am I going to do there?" she asks the police detective. "Pray," he answers.

Her initial meeting with the Mother Superior, a suitably prim Maggie Smith, provides some easy laughs. "I've always admired you people," she tells Smith, "You're married to the big JC. You're his old lady." Goldberg is reluctant to conform to convent rituals, which sees Smith's patience give way. "People wish to kill you," she reminds Whoopi, adding tartly, "Anyone who's met you, I imagine." Smith tells Goldberg she'll have to take three vows if she's to stay in the convent: poverty ("Uh-huh"), obedience ("Uh-huh") and chastity ("I'm outa here"). Soon afterward, when called upon to recite the grace before meals, Goldberg draws upon her biblical and political sources to create a unique prayer: "Bless us O Lord for the gifts which we are about to receive, and yea though I walk through the valley of the shadow of no food, I shall fear no hunger. We want you to give us this day our daily bread, and to the republic for which it stands. By the power vested in me I pronounce us ready to eat. Amen."

Goldberg brings some serious soul rhythms to the nun's choir and before you can say "Dig those Motown blues" the congregation is coming back in droves. Even the Pope gets interested, which panics Smith. Smith wants the nuns to perform a traditional ceremony for His Holiness but is outvoted by her own Order, which results in her handing in her resignation. Before this comes to pass a bent cop leaks Whoopi's whereabouts to Keitel's men and they head for her. Goldberg is warned by a detective that she has to leave the convent. "I can't," she pleads, "I'm playing for the Pope." "If you stay here you'll be playing for St. Peter," he replies.

Goldberg gets nabbed by Keitel's henchmen and brought to Reno to be executed. Somehow, they can't pull the trigger. They go to Keitel and tell him the habit is upsetting them. Maybe she's a real nun, they surmise. "I know her," Keitel drones, "in the biblical sense. She ain't no nun." When they go back to her she escapes from their clutches, having hit them both in a very sensitive area of their respective anatomies, which must convince them that Keitel is right about her status. By this time Smith and her array of nuns have also come to Reno to rescue her. They arrive at a casino. "Try to blend in," Smith exhorts, as a gang of what look like penguins descend on the high rollers. All we're missing is the Pope trying his hand at blackjack.

Critics disliked the film but the public loved it and it went on to make megabucks, like Goldberg's sleeper of the previous year, *Ghost*, also built around a tenuous religious theme. Hollywood is never shy to milk a cash cow so two years later it made *Sister Act 2: Back in the Habit*. Only this time there was no criminal plot so all we got was Whoopi being called back to the convent to remobilize the choir, and stop surly administrator James Coburn from closing down a nearby school. We might as well have been back in St Mary's with Bing Crosby and Ingrid Bergman. Goldberg's adrenalin made it bearable but the concept was tired and threadbare. Its treatment of inner city poverty was also naive and condescending.

Nunsense was released in 1993. The title says it all. It's the story of a group of nuns who suffer food poisoning while their colleagues perform a musical to pay for their medical care. Two years later Susan Sarandon won an Oscar for playing Sr Helen Prejean in *Dead Man Walking*, which was based on Sr Prejean's book, with a screenplay by Tim Robbins. Sarandon plays the spiritual advisor to double murderer Patrick Sonnier

(Sean Penn), who appears to have no remorse for what he did. As the film goes on, however, her influence over him humanizes him more and more. The story is played out with great feeling without being sentimental and draws compelling performances from the two main leads. Neither is it a smug denunciation of capital punishment, taking time out to see both sides of the coin as the beleaguered Sarandon also has to deal with the raw emotions of loved ones left devastated by the deaths.

Sonnier's name is changed to Matthew Poncelet in the film. Robbins, as Penn's biographer Nick Johnstone says, "never lets us forget that he's a sick individual who participated in a horrific and senseless crime." But he's still written a script of great poignancy.[24]

Sarandon plays Sr Prejean as a full-blooded woman rather than a plaster saint. One of her faults is arrogance, which she accepts. Her relationship with Sonnier isn't sanitized. They laugh as well as cry together. He even makes a pass at her which she, of course, rejects, but with humor. This couldn't have happened in, say, *The Nun's Story*, particularly if the man in question was a murderer. Another scene has Penn actually comparing his execution to that of Jesus, a conceit swiftly guillotined by Sarandon, who reminds him that Jesus changed the world with love, while he, on the contrary, slaughtered two innocent people. The main objective of the film, Sarandon believed, wasn't to make a statement about capital punishment but rather to tell a love story. "How do you unconditionally love someone who isn't your child?" she asked. Sr Prejean, she said, was struggling with the attempt to love "this really despicable person, this Nazi racist. That's the task she set for herself, despite the terrible crime he's committed."[25]

Prejean is contrasted sharply with the prison chaplain, a severe man who has little of her humanity. Prejean doesn't wear a habit, which makes her better able to connect with Penn on a secular level. She's frustrated about the fact that she's not better at getting through to him, and bangs her fists against the wall at one point to convey that. The chaplain isn't interested in Penn's reformation, or indeed in Sarandon attempting to bring it about. Her job, in his eyes, is to make sure Penn receives the sacraments. Anything more deeply felt is, to his way of thinking, irrelevant. "You can save this boy by getting him to receive the sacraments of the church before he dies," he tells her, "this is your job. Nothing more. Nothing less." As Bryan Stone states, "The chaplain has reduced forgiveness to a mechanical transaction that takes place outside both the giver and receiver."[26]

Her best quality is her ability to take Penn as he is. It's this he appreciates and this which, in the long term, makes him confront the horror of what he's done. She's non-judgmental with him throughout, offering him love instead of censure, but not in a wispy, otherworldly way. She's down-to-earth, which lends added force to her whispered "I love you" to him as he's about to die. The last sight he sees is "the face of love." Afterward Sr Prejean prays with the aptly named Delacroix, meaning "of the cross".

The title of the film is ambiguous. As well as being the traditional reference to a condemned man on death row, here it has added reverberations of resurrection. Before Sr Prejean became involved in campaigning against capital punishment, she worked in a New Orleans housing project with poor black residents. "Not death row exactly," she joked, "but close." Even then she was concerned about the prevalence of capital punishment in the deep South, particularly for black people who killed white ones.

One day in 1982 she was asked to be a "penpal" to a death row inmate in the state of Louisiana. Without thinking she said yes. And thus began a ten-year correspondence that led her into death row herself, and into advocacy groups for homicide victims' families. It was, she said afterward, the most important decision she ever made in her life, a journey from a protected middle class environment to the seventh circle of hell.

Sonnier killed two teenagers, David LeBlanc and Loretta Bourque, in cold blood, shooting them both after raping Loretta. Sonnier's brother Eddie was also involved. After the murders Sonnier confessed to everything but later tried to pin the murders on his brother. The jury didn't buy the change in his testimony and he was sentenced to death. After the sentence was handed down he tried to commit suicide in prison by slitting his wrists.

When Sr Prejean first wrote to him he found it hard to believe that somebody would be trying to communicate with him who didn't have a vested interest. The fact that she was a nun made it even more incomprehensible. Nuns, he said, were the people who whacked him at school with rulers if he failed to remember the catechism injunction that God was love. Sr Prejean started to visit him after a time, becoming his spiritual advisor. Initially guarded, he eventually opened up to her about why he did what he did. She was the catalyst for a torrent of emotions he had buried. He, on the other hand, politicized her. She met him as a nun and left him a social activist.

Such activism was initially focused on issues like poverty but after her experiences in death row it became re-directed into a campaign against the bloodlust that demands the ultimate penalty for crime. Shortly after meeting him Sr Prejean said, "If you die, I want to be with you at your execution. I can't bear the thought that you would die without seeing at least one loving face. I will be the face of Christ for you."[27] Sonnier told her he didn't want to put her through that, that it could scar her for life. She knew she would be terrified of the ordeal but stood by her promise. "God will give me the grace," she said.[28]

Sonnier told her he didn't want any prayers at his execution, at which point she asked him if he thought God had forgiven him for what he did or if he felt condemned to an eternity of pain. "At first I felt even God hated me," he said, but then he went to confession and felt he'd be forgiven. He stressed that the killings weren't planned, and were motivated by fear and excessive drinking. He'd kidnapped the teenagers first and thought they would squeal on him, which would have resulted in him being sent back to prison. Afterward, he said he was filled with remorse and self-loathing.

Sr Prejean believed, as the writer Albert Camus did, that "Every murderer, when he kills, feels innocent, and excused by his particular circumstances."[29] A graphic illustration of this theory is evident in Camus' novel *The Outsider*, where the main character, Meursault, is condemned to death for what appears to be almost a nonchalant shooting of an Arab on a beach for little or no reason. It was as a result of this belief, along with many others, that she opposed the death penalty so vehemently.

She also argued against the deterrent value of capital punishment, citing the state of Texas as one state that executed more prisoners than any other U.S. state and yet also had one of the highest murder rates. She said it cost more to kill a prisoner than keep him alive because of the huge cost of capital crime cases and of incarceration. She also cited the grotesque phenomenon of states that in the past authorized the execution of the mentally handicapped, giving one example of a Florida inmate named Gary Alvord who was adjudged to have been insane while on death row and afterward moved to a mental hospital where psychologists "restored" him to sanity before he was re-admitted to death row and executed.

In addition to befriending Sonnier, Prejean bonded with Lloyd LeBlanc, the father of one of Sonnier's victims. This was perhaps a bigger challenge than getting through to Sonnier himself. The friendship wouldn't have been possible if LeBlanc hadn't forgiven Sonnier. Even then it was difficult for him to meet Sr Prejean, and more difficult again for his wife Eula, who used to leave the house at first when she called, unable to countenance the fact that somebody would wish to comfort her son's killer. At first Prejean stayed away from Lloyd LeBlanc, all too aware of her conflicted position. By visiting him she felt she'd re-open a raw wound. This wasn't the way he looked at it. "I need you too," he said to her once. Trying to straddle twin loyalties was her main challenge.

LeBlanc told her Sonnier was a ghastly individual, a man who hung around bars with scum and was a serial rapist of young girls as well as an abductor of teenage kids. This, she replied, wasn't the man she knew. All she saw when she went into death row was a man in a denim shirt who was always delighted to see her and who thanked her profusely for her interest in him. Reflecting on the question of doing unspeakably evil things, she thought back to a time as a child when she made fun of a fat girl at a slumber party, or when she joined in the beating of an opossum another time and had nightmares about it afterward. Did Sonnier have nightmares about the things he did, she wondered. But she never judged him. What was done was done; all she could do was try to mitigate the aftermath. The mistake she made, she realized, was in not getting to know the LeBlancs at an earlier stage because to them her continued empathy with Sonnier appeared as if she didn't really care what they were going through.

Her appointment as Sonnier's spiritual advisor also drew dissent from sexists, who felt that only a priest could deliver the kind of solace she purported to give to the condemned man. She was accused of being naive, and blind to the fact that Sonnier may have lost his soul because he had chosen not to receive the Last Rites just prior to his death. He told her he had already confessed his sins and received holy communion and didn't see the point of doing it again. Movies, Sr Prejean says, always show a "man" of the cloth raising his hand in blessing to the man on the scaffold: maybe, she thought, they were insecure about the prospect of women displacing them. Nonetheless, she fought her corner and continued her work long after Sonnier's death.

Sonnier was impressed by the fact that Sr Prejean talked "natural" and "didn't quote the Bible all the time."[30] She wasn't a nunny nun, in other words, relating to him on a human level rather than pushing any agenda down his throat. She was sympathetic to the fact that, though what he did was horrific, she felt he wouldn't have been sentenced to death if (a) he wasn't poor, (b) his case had been defended more professionally, and (c) his victims were black rather than white. Such details often meant the difference between a life sentence and the death penalty.

Dead Man Walking is essentially about forgiveness and repentance, the purgation both victim and aggressor must go through in their dark journey toward peace. In an ideal world maybe the state would forgive too, but this isn't an ideal world. Sonnier had to suffer the final indignity in the death chamber as Sr Prejean watched on helplessly. Or maybe she wasn't totally helpless, for she'd saved Sonnier in another way by persuading him to look inside himself for the answers to his dire predicament. She gave him the gift of thoughtful introspection. In addition to being interested in the spiritual dimension of his predicament, she was aware that in many ways he was a symbol of a society that had lost its way. In addition to being a protagonist he was also a victim of social injustice, of a world where those born on the wrong side of the tracks had little chance to make it. As he says in one scene, "There's no one with money on death row."

Sr Prejean has widely documented the callousness of death by electric shock and the fact that it isn't, as many claim, painless or always instantaneous. She repudiates those who quote scripture, particularly passages like "Vengeance is mine, saith the Lord" to bolster their argument for its continuance. She's always found it difficult to appreciate the fact that otherwise compassionate human beings seem to draw a blanket over logic when advocating capital punishment. She can't imagine the Lord throwing a temper tantrum to exact this kind of retribution.

Pat Sonnier, in her view, was "tortured" by the 1900 volts that ended his life, using the Amnesty International definition of torture as "an extreme mental and physical assault on a person who has been rendered defenseless." She can't believe in a God who believes in an eye for an eye or a tooth for a tooth, nor a God who invests human representatives with such power, i.e., those who sign the death documents. The paths of history, she says, are stained with the blood of those who've fallen victim to "God's avengers." If she were to be murdered, she insists, she wouldn't want her murderer executed or her death avenged.

Not only does Prejean not believe that God has fits of rage and goes about searching for retaliation for horrendous crimes. She can't believe that it's permissible to kill people even if you prepare them with good spiritual counsel to meet their maker. No matter how the procedure is dressed up, it still continues the cycle of violence and is thus fundamentally wrong. If we're to have a society which protects its citizens from torture and murder, she argues, then such stratagems must be off-limits to everyone, including the state, particularly when some executions have been shown to be of innocent men when posthumous evidence came to light, or when executors failed to kill the "dead man walking" within the time allotted, either due to an electrical fault or some item on his or her person catching fire and thus causing unspeakable and lengthy pain.

In the case of Sonnier she was upfront with him about everything that would happen to him on the day of his execution: the manner in which his head would be shaved, his trouser leg cut at the knee, a diaper put over his underpants, the straps that would fasten him to the chair—including his jaw—and the mask that would be placed over his face. She became emotionally involved in his plight. Too much so, some would argue.

Why do we kill people who kill people to show that killing people is wrong? Thus goes the bumper sticker. Another one echoes the words of Gandhi: "An eye for an eye leaves the whole world blind." Statisticians argue about the deterrent value of capital punishment but Sr Prejean was more intent on the terrible human fall-out of terrible crimes. She isn't woolly in her thinking, or walking on clouds dispensing vapid consolation. She's the living breath of religion in practice, at the coalface of grief and desolation.

In 2002 Peter Mullan's *The Magdalene Sisters* also set clerical heads thinking when it was first shown at the Venice Film Festival. Telling the story of three young girls psychologically bruised by the nuns entrusted to care for them in the infamous Magdalene homes, which were really little more than laundry sweatshops with quasi-religious overtones, it was like a napalm bomb dropped on an institution already reeling from a brace of pedophilia scandals. The laundry mat here is run like a concentration camp. Dickensian conditions prevail as Gestapo-like nuns terrorize the girls with beatings, insults and sadism. One of the girls has been raped, but blamed for it herself. Another girl becomes pregnant outside marriage but is forced to put her child up for adoption almost as soon as it's born. A third is adjudged to have flirted with some boys and is severely punished for this horrendous breach of discipline. A fourth suffers from psychiatric problems.

Mullan makes this a savage indictment of an era. It would have been more effective if he leavened the dosage, or gave some of the nuns human traits. A Manichean sense of loathing for all things sexual permeates the film. The acting is creditable but there's also an element of farce present, which diminishes its power. In the old days the church used sex as a weapon to beat the laity; now the roles seem to be reversed with this film and others like *Song for a Raggy Boy* (2003).

The Magdalene Sisters won the festival's main prize but received the wrath of the Vatican. Cardinal Ersilio Tonini condemned it for being untruthful and libellous, two charges Mullan strenuously refuted, accusing Tonini of "still living in the Middle Ages."[31]

Mullan denies that his film is an attack on religion. "It implicitly admires faith," he says, "while making an attempt to look an the gulf between the truly faithful and those who merely happen to be in control of the faithful."[32]

There were some very moving scenes and while nobody denied the pain inflicted on the residents of the laundries, Mullan overplayed his hand in two ridiculous scenes, one involving an itchy priest and the other an erotically charged nun. These reduced the film's credibility and made it into a gratuitous polemic. Less would have been much, much more.

The depiction of Hollywood priests has been more varied and challenging than that of nuns. In Hollywood's Golden Age they tended to be personified by the kind of character Spencer Tracy played in *Boy's Town* in 1938. Here, as Fr Flanagan, he built a community for juvenile delinquents and helped reform teenage firebrand Mickey Rooney. The film was immensely popular despite some charges of schmaltz. It had so much influence, the Boy's Town charity it spawned became one of the wealthiest in the world, living off its interest.

Bing Crosby played a similar type of priest in 1944's *Going My Way*, another Oscar-nominated film dealing with a member of the cloth helping to reform rowdy children, the main difference here being that Crosby, unlike Tracy, was also able to sing. It resulted in an equally successful sequel the following year, the aforementioned *The Bells of St. Mary's*.

Crosby could have done the film in his sleep. Cynics would contend he actually did. But this laidback form of clerical affability touched a chord, as did Barry Fitzgerald riding shotgun with a tad more vivacity. As a package it was just what the public wanted, though James Agee, writing in *Nation*, found it all exploitative and twee. "It would have a little more stature as a 'religious' film," he wrote, "if it dared suggest that evil is anything worse than a bad head cold."

Father O'Malley is sent to rehabilitate a New York parish and replace Fitzgerald without making him aware this is the reason for his being there. Crosby's ways irritate Fitzgerald but he comes to a grudging appreciation of, and eventual friendship with, Crosby. Crosby also reforms the local youths. An Ohio priest called Paul Glenn surprisingly called the film both "un-Catholic" and "anti-Catholic."[33] He was disappointed neither Crosby nor Fitzgerald were at any point shown saying Mass or their prayers. Their ministry, to his way of thinking, was purely—or rather impurely—secular. Neither was he overly impressed with a scene in which the two priests have a nightcap before retiring to their chambers. For Glenn this would cause viewers to conclude that "To be Catholic is to be Irish and to be Irish is to be a whiskey drinker."[34] Ironically, Pope Pius XII actually enjoyed this scene according to the film's director Mervyn LeRoy.[35]

The film won Best Film of the Year, an incredible achievement considering it was up against opposition like *Double Indemnity*, possibly the greatest *film noir* ever made. People were obviously voting with their hearts—or rather handkerchiefs. It was, however, unpopular in some countries. Crosby recalled, "When it was first released it couldn't play any Latin American countries for several years because the priest wore a sweatshirt and a baseball cap. To them, that was absolutely sacrilegious."[36]

Crosby, as film author Frank Walsh noted, represented an era where a priest almost had mythical powers to transform potential ne'er-do-wells into model citizens merely by his presence. As soon as he showed up at the local parish house, everyone became miraculously reformed all the way from misers to juvenile delinquents to couples intent on lascivious acts with one another. Seeing as Crosby was "Mr Clean" during these years, and an avid churchgoer, it's somewhat disconcerting to hear stories of his extramarital dalliances, his fearful tempers with his children and a general Jekyll & Hyde existence. One thing he never missed, according to his friend Joyce Whiteman, was Mass. She believed he would have crawled to church in a drunken stupor if the occasion called for it. She felt this was a beautiful trait. To which one might add: Would he not have been better off to stay home and sober up some of these times? Or be more paternal to his children instead of wearing holes in the knees of his trousers?

Crosby ruled his house with an iron fist, tolerating no resistance. He beat his children, particularly his son Gary who refused to toe the line, repeatedly with a belt that was dotted with metal studs. He was also an absent father, which meant the children grew up primarily with just their mother, Dixie, as a parent. She in turn became an alcoholic and died young. Crosby quickly re-married.

On a film set wearing a collar he had control over his life, and happy provisions for the one to come. When problems arose not even Father Crosby could handle them. He couldn't deal with Dixie's drinking, or indeed Gary's, retreating to the comfortable cocoon of a movie set, or church, to assure himself that God was in his heaven and all was right with the world. It was a question of, Lights, Camera . . . Faith.

Pat O'Brien was another beloved priestly character from this time. In his autobiography he joked, "I've played so many priests in pictures and television that at every meal our entire family discusses everything in Latin."[37] In 1938 he appeared in his most famous role opposite James Cagney in *Angels with Dirty Faces*.

Cagney plays Rocky, a rough diamond from New York's Lower East Side, while O'Brien is Jerry, his childhood friend. Rocky takes the path of crime while Jerry goes on to become a priest with a particular interest in reforming children like Rocky and steering them away from their wild ways. When Rocky returns to his home town the priest knows this spells trouble for the boys in his care. It isn't long before Rocky has become their hero. When Rocky is caught and sentenced to death for his crimes he receives the news almost with nonchalance, refusing to see a priest. In the climax of the film, Rocky is on death row awaiting execution. He wants to die as he has lived, with guns blazing, rather than go out on a whimper, but Father Flanagan (O'Brien) visits him in his cell with a unique request. He asks him to fake fear as he walks to his execution so that the children in his care won't see him as a role model.

To do this, Father Flanagan tells him, would be "a different kind of courage, the kind that only you and I and God know about." He asks Rocky to "let the children down." He wants them to "despise" Rocky's memory. For Rocky this is a thunderbolt. He's about to lose his life and now his old friend Jerry—whose life he once saved—is asking him to lose his dignity as well. Will he do it for him? Or for the children?

As he starts along his final walk of shame this doesn't look likely but then he breaks down. "I don't want to die!" he screams, "Don't do this to me!" Is the fear real or is he doing it as a favor for his old friend? We never know. Cagney himself, when asked the question in many interviews about the film afterward, said he wasn't sure himself. He claimed he played the scene with "deliberate ambiguity," which forced the audience themselves to decide what happened. The next day's newspapers had the headline "Rocky Dies Yellow."

The ending pleased those who felt that other movies of this decade glorified criminals. It was a bending of the knee not only to Father Flanagan but to a generation of viewers the Catholic Church felt was weaned on violence with their mother's milk. Rocky caved in at the end and thus his followers, the "Dead End" kids, were forced to look for other idols. Like Father Flanagan? In the moral compass of the movie this is a reasonable assumption, but hardly in real life. The ending is soppy Hollywood fairytale and a betrayal of the character the film puts before us.

Yellow streaks don't come from nowhere and this one wasn't tele-graphed by anything before. As for the "favor to an old friend" possi-bility, this too is unlikely.

To round things out, Rocky's saving Jerry's life in youth is balanced by Jerry saving Rocky's soul in adulthood. In this way the film serves two dialectical masters, giving us ninety minutes of a shoot-'em-up before finally imploding on its own convenient duplicity. "Did he die like a yellow rat?" the Dead End Kids ask Father Flanagan in the finale, and he tells them he did. The film ends with a prayer for a lost soul redeemed at and by his death.

The following year Cagney made another gangster movie, *The Roaring Twenties*. He died in the end here as well, fiery criminals of this era never allowed any other fate, but there was no Father Flanagan on hand this time to administer the Last Rites. Significantly, though, the location of his death is outside a church. The symbolism isn't exactly subtle.

Gregory Peck played a liberal Scottish priest in *Keys of the Kingdom* in 1944. The film was based on A.J. Cronin's 1941 novel focusing on the efforts of Father Chisholm, played by Peck, to open people's eyes to the wider message of the gospels. Darryl F. Zanuck, the director, chose Peck because he wanted Chisholm to be conveyed as a strong man rather than the "anaemic clergymen seen too often."[38]

Peck was impressed with his character, a man who wanted to serve the poor and needy rather than climbing the "clerical ladder to success."[39] He became so immersed in his role he had his entire dialogue memorized before even turning up on the set the first day.

He used an actual priest to inspire him. A Catholic missionary in China, Fr Albert O'Hara, was the technical advisor on the film. In one particular scene Peck wasn't sure how to preach to a gathering of Chi-nese people until the priest showed him that it was by evincing "grave courtesy and respect for each person as an individual."[40] The priest, who spoke fluent Chinese, taught Peck "the necessary humility" he needed to get into the part.[41]

A.J. Cronin was also delighted with Peck's interpretation of the part. He met Peck for lunch one day and blurted out, "I just can't understand how any actor could so well catch the clumsiness and beauty of Father Chisholm's character."[42] Peck did what he always did in his movies, convey a deep sense of principle. This got him a lot of fan mail, much of it from women who wanted to sleep with him, which was ironic given the circumstances. "Tell 'em I'm all booked up," he advised his secre-tary when she was fishing her way through the fan mail.[43]

One critic who didn't enjoy Peck's performance was Pauline Kael, a woman who never minced words. "His saintliness comes across as lack of imagination," she wrote, "utter sterility.[44] Which begs the question, how did Bing Crosby get away with clerical performances that had such blandness by comparison? Crosby won an Oscar the previous year for playing Fr O'Malley in *Going My Way,* quipping at the ceremony, "I didn't even have to wear a necktie." Peck was nominated for *Keys of the Kingdom* but lost out to Ray Milland's blistering depiction of an alcoholic in *The Lost Weekend.*

Cronin gives Fr Chisholm some choice comments in his book. At one point he states that atheists may not all go to hell, a rather daring assertion for the time. Elsewhere he notes that though Christ was a perfect man "Confucius had a better sense of humor."

At the beginning of the film Chisholm considers marriage as a lifestyle instead of the church but when the woman he loves commits suicide after becoming pregnant by another man he commits himself totally to his vocation. In a Spanish seminary where he trains to be a priest he finds himself at odds with his narrow-minded colleagues. One day in frustration he goes on a long walk to clear his head and ends up spending the night in a prostitute's cottage—though not, one hastens to add, in her bed. In a Biblical gesture this Magdalene clone bathes his feet instead.

After his ordination he exposes a fake miracle that has duped his pastor. Thereafter he travels to China where he finds himself more fulfilled, despite some friction with a domineering nun, Mother Veronica. A local pestilence follows which results in the death of an old atheistic friend of his. As he dies he tells Chisholm he still doesn't believe in God. "God believes in you," Chisholm replies.

Subsequent scenes have Chisholm in conflict with the local mandarin, a warlord he puts out of business, and also his bishop, who initially disapproves of him but comes to a final awareness of his rich spirit. The film was produced by David O. Selznick, Selznick was often at odds with a Father John Devlin, who was delegated by church authorities to vet it. Fr Devlin had many problems with the script, which included lines like, "We're all going to heaven by different gates." He felt this was unacceptable because it intimated that all religions were, in a sense, equal. At another point Chisholm declared, "Religious belief is such an accident of birth, God can't have set an exclusive value on it." Father Devlin also had problems with Chisholm's tacit acceptance of his atheistic friend, and his inability to "convert" him. Finally, he didn't want the aforementioned pastor embarrassed by the fake miracle so demanded that this character be written out.

The line about everyone going to heaven by different gates was changed to a watered-down "Each of us travels his own road to the Kingdom of heaven. Though I know another's to be wrong, I still have no right to interfere with his choice." Chisholm's failure to convert his atheist friend was also dealt with in a heavy-handed manner; the atheist's dying words changed to "I never loved you as much as I do now because you haven't tried to bully me into heaven." God only knew how Cronin would have felt, having his book mangled like this.

John Ford based his 1947 film *The Fugitive* on Graham Greene's novel *The Power and the Glory*. The priest here has feet of clay, which isn't too surprising from Greene, but he transcends himself in the final reel by giving his life up for the people he serves. Henry Fonda was effective in the main role of the beleaguered priest who's finally betrayed by a former friend. The film was set in Mexico under a government that outlawed worship.

Three years later France produced what Hollywood couldn't, a downbeat clerical drama that resonated with minimalistic power.

Robert Bresson's *Diary of a Country Priest* (1950) is a thoroughly moving story of a young priest in an isolated parish in France. It was based on the classic novel by Georges Bernanos, whose favorite theme was man's struggle between good and evil. His depiction of this struggle in simple unadorned language is evident even from the first sentence of the book: "Mine is a parish like all the rest."[45] The young priest is suffering from stomach cancer. Claude Laylu plays him touchingly and with candor. The manner in which he tries to inspire his parishioners, even as he struggles with his own imminent demise, is starkly captured by the striking directorial powers of a man at the height of his powers. It's a strangely enchanting parable of loss, its slow pace allowing the viewer 'to step into the film and walk through its images in a rather sentimental way."[46] The pace may be plodding and meditative but the overall impact is truly cathartic.

The priest, who's never named, negotiates his physical and psychological hell with a certain amount of stoicism, the "big" moments in his life not coming from "marvellous and extraordinary" feats but rather humdrum acts like peeling potatoes.[47] "In Bresson," Raymond Durgnat contended, "the monotone and the deadpan represent, not a mask but a revelation of the essential man."[48] This "essential man" is totally out of his depth in the parish, unable or unwilling to communicate. A woman pours her heart out to him about her dead son in one scene but in general he's mocked and/or ignored. An old priest tells him "A true priest is never loved," which is Job's consolation. Bresson doesn't make any play for our empathy here; he just throws a bleak scenario at us to make of it what we will. The result is his most engaging film of all.

It's unsentimental and uncompromising, but curiously uplifting, even in the raw pain of the awkward priest whose diary we take into our hearts as though it were our own. Paul Schrader believes the priest's alienation originates neither in the environment nor himself, but in an overpowering, transcendental passion—a beautiful insight into a beautiful, heartbreaking film.

Bresson even gives his priest some Christ-like qualities, as in details like the fact that he can only eat bread dipped in wine. The overall form of the film, to quote Joseph Cuneen, "depends on the duplication of sound and image, emphasising the interiority of all the action."[49]

Nineteen fifty-three saw a moral-dilemma introduced into a religious movie with Montgomery Clift playing a tortured priest, Fr Logan, in Alfred Hitchcock's brooding *I Confess*. The plot involved a German refugee who lives in Quebec robbing and killing a local lawyer having used a priest's cassock as a disguise. He hides the cassock and then confesses everything to Clift in the full knowledge that the seal of the confession box will preclude the priest from divulging what he's heard to the inspector investigating the case (Karl Malden).

Malden becomes suspicious of Clift as the film goes on, in large part because of Clift's edgy reluctance to speak to him about the evening of the murder, which he spent with old flame Anne Baxter, now married to Roger Dann. Baxter and Clift had been engaged to be married some years before but Clift left her to fight in World War II. She then married Dann, a man she didn't love. Clift entered the seminary but she still loved him. It's not made clear whether Clift became a priest out of bitterness that she hadn't waited for him to return from the war or for some other reason.

One day when Baxter and Clift are together they meet the man who will subsequently be murdered. The man says he'll tell her husband she's seeing Clift unless she helps him deal with his tax problems. After Malden hears all this he now knows that Clift had a motive for the murder. Tied to the bloody cassock, which the refugee has planted among Clift's effects, this leads to an almost watertight case against the beleaguered priest. At this point one expects Clift to tell Malden he knows who the real killer is without mentioning his name, thus adhering to his conscientious dictates but instead of that he continues to be distant and non-committal.

When he takes the stand, his demeanor is somewhat similar to the character of the traumatized Jew he played in *Judgment at Nuremburg*, which reminds one of Marlon Brando's reflection that Clift had an anal quality to his acting. There's a lot of Method huffing and puffing which at times almost appears masochistic, as if he seems hell-bent on spending his life in jail.

Clift is guarded in his comments because of the compromised situation in which he finds himself, despite the fact that the real murderer has done everything in his power to incriminate him, including lying about the fact that he saw him acting suspiciously on the night in question. The jury, amazingly, find Clift not guilty, but outside the court he's jeered by a horde of people who demand that he remove his clerical collar. At this point the murderer's wife, plagued by guilt, screams out the truth and her husband shoots her. The murderer is subsequently shot and begs for forgiveness from Clift as he dies in his arms. The man's dying words to Clift "I am as alone as you are" underscore the pretentiousness of the foregoing.

It was largely a dour, foreboding affair, not helped by Clift's nerviness, which was suitable for the character's plight, but unmitigated and therefore making for heavy going in a film already overburdened by depressing events. Hitchcock had been brought up in a Catholic house and educated by Jesuits so he was well aware of the intricacies of confidentiality demanded by a member of the cloth, but it was a very slender thread upon which to base a whole plot.

Idea-driven films are always much more difficult to sell to the public than plot-driven ones and so it was with this. The fact that Hitchcock was a Catholic made him empathize with Clift's absurd predicament but the public were harder to win round with all the talk about confessional secrecy. Richard Blake sympathized with his problem: "To a non-Catholic, Hitchcock believed, the seal might be conceived of as a form of professional confidentiality similar to the notion of privileged information in a lawyer-client or physician-patient relationship. Not realizing the differences, most of the audience would find it absurd that the priest could not use his knowledge, however privileged, to extricate himself from suspicion for a crime he did not commit, especially after the seal had been cynically used by a penitent to escape a murder charge."[50]

John Russell Taylor said the same thing in a different way, "Hitchcock blamed himself for allowing his "specialized knowledge as a Catholic to get the better of his judgment as a film-maker."[51]

The film got off to a bad start when screenwriter George Tabori bailed out after Hitchcock told him it was going to end with Fr Logan being spared the electric chair. The local diocese demanded this change. It was the first of the film's many compromises made to bring it in on time. Clift also felt he should die. If he didn't, he said, the momentum created by the false allegations would cause the film to piffle out at the end—as indeed it did.

Hitchcock was unwise to roll over like this. If an audience sniffs fear, or lack of commitment, a film can die. *I Confess* is a classic example of the lack of moral courage on a director's part leading to a non-event. It might not have taken off anyway but better to fail gloriously than tamely.

Clift was theoretically a good choice for the part. He was fascinated by the subject of martyrdom and indeed was shortlisted by George Stevens to play Jesus in *The Greatest Story Ever Told*. One of the books he always wanted to read was Nikos Kazantzakis' *The Last Temptation of Christ* which would be filmed some decades later by Martin Scorsese. "I'm surprised no priest ever got to him and converted him," an acquaintance said, impressed by his ascetic demeanor. Michael Berson argues that he was "constipated with anguish" and that Hitchcock was always better when he used "guilt and expatiation as covert themes" rather than overt ones.[52]

Hitchcock gave Clift a lot of latitude during shooting, making it obvious he didn't want any discussions about motivation or interpretation, though one day he asked him if a penitent came into him in confession—presuming Clift was really a priest—and informed him he'd put poison in the altar wine he was going to drink later that day at Mass, would he drink it? Not doing so would be to use information gleaned from the confessional, which was prohibited. Hitchcock was being puckish here but Clift merely shrugged his shoulders as if it was irrelevant to the film.

In this small anecdote resides the failure of *I Confess*. Hitchcock was fascinated by the concept behind the film whereas for Clift it was just another excuse to act out his nascent neuroses. This was fine insofar as it went but dragged over the length of the movie resulted in the film being turgid. It became a one-note performance. The film was fraught with other tensions between Clift, who wanted to get into the inner torment of the priest, and Hitchcock, whose storyboarding techniques virtually meant his films were shot in his head before he ever got to a film set. He had famously, or infamously, once said that actors should be treated like cattle, a remark that infuriated Clift. This cow would resolutely refuse to chew the celluloid cud. Clift took the part so seriously, as his publicist friend John Springer revealed to one of his biographers, that he actually spent a week in a monastery in preparation for the role.[53]

Clift took very little direction from Hitchcock, generally deferring to his acting coach Mira Rostova when he was in doubt about a scene. This could have led to an all-out war between them but Hitchcock was all too well aware it was a battle he was unlikely to win so he left Clift to his own devices and tried to keep his eye on the unity of the film in general. We may blame Clift in part for the fact that he failed in this latter ambition—uncharacteristically for him. Hitchcock admitted he felt uncomfortable around Clift. He was, he accused, "very neurotic, and a Method actor."[54] One imagines the second part of that sentence to be the more insulting, coming from this man.

Hitchcock was fascinated by Clift's homosexuality, though, and his excessive drinking—so long as they didn't interfere with the shoot. In addition to being a stern disciplinarian, Hitchcock had a mischievous side to him. He enjoyed the wild antics of stars and also probably suppressed a lot of his own wildness, or channeled it through his work.

Hitchcock was particularly disconcerted because he'd looked forward to working with Clift, and the "seal of the confessional" was the ideal "McGuffin" in which to do so. Every Hitchcock film had a "McGuffin", i.e., a catalyst to spur the plot onward. The fact that he labored the point made this perhaps the most un-Hitchcockian film he ever made, which probably explained why it failed.

Neither director nor actor was comfortable, and it showed. Catholics found it feeble while for non-Catholics it was unreasonable. It was over-laden with a sense of portent and discernibly lacking in pace. This was due in no small part to Hitchcock's confused mindset. As one biographer put it, though his films often deal with questions relating to God, "their characters aren't gripped by an anxiety that is properly speaking religious."[55]

The casting of Anne Baxter was also disingenuous. For the Quebec setting Hitchcock had wanted an unknown actress with a European accent. He found one such in the Swedish actress Anita Bjork, who'd received good reviews for her performance in *Miss Julie*, based on August Strindberg's play. She arrived in America, however, just two weeks before shooting of the movie was due to begin, with her lover and their baby. She was married to another man whom she intended to divorce.

This might have been acceptable in her native Sweden, but not in America where the League of Decency held such sway. Her predicament was reported in the press as a scandal and Warner Brothers put pressure on Hitchcock to pay her off and send her home. Jack Warner said that the only way he would have her in the film was if she obtained a quickie divorce and married the child's father but she was stern in her objection to this ploy.

Baxter came on board at very short notice. Hitchcock only accepted her grudgingly as a last resort and the atmosphere between them was as chilly as the Quebec air. It was an ominous sign that the film was destined to die at the box office. Hitchcock realized it lacked both humor and subtlety. He was also unhappy with Baxter's final reconciliation with her husband, which was always going to be unlikely. Third, he wanted Clift to be hanged at the end to drive his message home further but he realized this would be a very unpopular conclusion as far as the studio was concerned, not to mention the Catholic authorities.

Father John Devlin, a priest who vetted the film to make sure it acceded to Production Code tenets, was unhappy with one of the early scenes where Clift goes to the location of the murder. Even doing this, he felt, was an abrogation of the privacy of the confessional. In the courtroom scene he told Hitchcock that "under no circumstances" was Clift to look in the direction of the murderer as this would also be to breach it.[56] On a more serious note, Father Devlin was worried that, because the murderer had confessed his crime to Clift, audiences might deduce from this that he'd been absolved of his sins. He made it clear to Hitchcock that a requisite degree of remorse was necessary for this to be expedited.

A further bone of contention between the priest and Hitchcock was that in the play upon which the film was based, the Anne Baxter character had had a child by Clift. When Hitchcock first approached the Canadian church authorities for approval for his film he found the priests he dealt with more than accommodating. No eyebrows were raised over the illegitimate child.

As time went on the Canadian Censorhip Board objected. It was unacceptable that the married Baxter would have a child by Clift even though he didn't know she was married when he slept with her and hadn't yet become a priest. So this had to go, much to Hitchcock's chagrin. Clift's execution went too. This would probably have been too similar to *A Place in the Sun*. From this point of view, it was best for Clift's career that the film ended less sensationally.

The Canadian Censorship Board also removed a crucial three minutes of footage between Baxter and Clift which makes it clear they slept together. Hitchcock was infuriated, giving in only reservedly. "There will be one version for the province of Quebec," he insisted, "and one version for the rest of the world."[57] Everything seemed to be conspiring against him. He hadn't even got his way with his choice of a screenwriter. He'd really wanted Catholic convert Graham Greene to do it but Greene politely refused on the grounds that he didn't write pictures for hire. "It is a resolution I made some years ago," he explained, "and I don't want to break it, even for Hitchcock."[58]

There were some saving graces. Whatever else we may say about Clift, he certainly conveyed intensity. He also looked the part. He'd spent a week in a Quebec monastery prior to shooting, as I said, to prepare himself for the role. Karl Malden paid him an unusual compliment when he said he had "the face of a saint, but when you looked into the eyes you saw a tortured soul trying to make its way out of utter bewilderment."[59] For Hitchcock, though, it was a dream gone sour. After a barrage of straightforward thrillers he had been looking forward to making his "Catholic" movie. Not many people realized how much Catholicism meant to him. He'd been an altar boy in youth. He had many friends who were priests too and was a frequent donor to Catholic charities. In 1962 he contributed $20,000 toward the construction of a chapel at his *alma mater*.

The film premiered in New York during Holy Week in March 1953, which caused him to chirp, "A nice Lenten date!"[60] Perhaps it was, but it looked like audiences were content to observe the day at home rather than go and see a film about an emotionally distraught priest going through his dark night of the soul. They were unimpressed by Clift's "introspective pouting and oh-so-sincere inner conflicts."[61] As Hitchcock had half-expected, the film died a quick death. Nonetheless, he took it all on the chin and went back to what he knew best with his next venture, *Dial M for Murder*.

There were no theological conundrums in this whodunit, and the villainous nature of the main character, played by Ray Milland, also seemed more watchable than Clift's earnest *angst*. Grace Kelly also helped as the victimized wife. It takes a good director to know his limitations and Hitchcock did. Even psychodramas need oomph. The skill of actors like Clift belonged in different types of roles, and with directors who would nurture their nuances. This wasn't Hitchcock's way. For all concerned it was a learning curve.

The following year, Karl Malden excelled himself as a socially crusading priest opposite Marlon Brando's vacillating longshoreman in the riveting *On the Waterfront*. Brando is affiliated with the mobsters, getting "kickbacks" on the Hoboken docks, but doesn't know the full extent of the corruption. When the brother of his girlfriend is killed, however—partly due to Brando's actions—Malden sees an opportunity to galvanize the slowly awakening conscience of the impressionable Brando to break up the gang. Malden, along with Brando, picked up an Oscar for his performance, dynamically taking religion onto the streets to upend the stranglehold Brando's henchmen held on the local workforce.

Malden based his performance on the life of a Father Corridan, who was a special advisor on the set of the film. This was a man who took on the vested interests not only in secular institutions in his reforming work but even the church itself, which received monies from benefactors with links to waterfront criminals. Budd Schulberg, who wrote the movie's screenplay, said in Fr Corridan's obituary in 1984 that, more than anyone else he knew, he represented the true essence of Christianity.

When Schulberg first met Fr Corridan he described him as "a tall, gangling, energetic, ruddy-faced Irishman whose speech was a fascinating blend of Hell's Kitchen jargon, baseball slang, the facts and figures of a master of economics and the undeniable humanity of Christ."[62] Malden captured his passion right from the moment he gives his first waterfront "sermon" aboard a ship after a stevedore is murdered. "Everyone who keeps silent," he urges, "is just as guilty as the Roman soldiers who pierced the flesh of our Lord." He appeals to the niggling conscience of Brando, the film's unlikely Christ-figure in a *denouement* that came to be called "a crucifixion without nails." Fr Corridan himself believed that Christ was present among all workers all the time—even at union meetings.

Though Fr Corridan extolled the merits of whistle-blowing in the movie, the manner in which Malden persuaded Brando to do so wasn't without an ironic undertone, for Kazan had "named names" during the McCarthy House on Un-American Activities Committee (HUAC) investigations and many people saw his extrapolation of Schulberg's screenplay as being engineered toward a rationalization of this. To use the parlance of the film itself, he "sang like a canary" to Joe McCarthy. As a result, Kazan lived under a cloud for the rest of his career, right up until the moment he was awarded a Life Achievement Award in 2003, its presentation compromised by dissension among the ranks of those who felt friends and acquaintances had been betrayed by his spineless revelations half a century before.

Kazan first testified to the HUAC in January 1952 but refused to name anyone with Communist sympathies. Three months later, however, when called upon to testify again, he did. His attitude wasn't apologetic but forthright, even belligerent. Perhaps he felt attack was the best means of defense, but he took the high moral ground in denouncing the "red threat." Part of his anger, he said, was as a result of being "booted out of the Party" sixteen years earlier, which of course made a mockery of his testimony because it suggested that he didn't lose his affinity with the left willingly, but by default. He played the martyr like one of his own Method heroes and continued his career uninterrupted for the next twenty years. Meanwhile, men with infinitely more integrity fell like fleas around him, scrambling for the odd screenplay usually done anonymously to keep the wolf from the door.

Nineteen fifty four was also the year in which Alec Guinness played G.K. Chesterton's famous clerical sleuth in *Fr Brown* with inventive relish. This much-loved movie had Guinness on the trail of a valuable church cross that had been stolen.

Robert Mitchum appeared in *The Night of the Hunter* in 1955. Mitchum plays a fake preacher who marries widows so he can rob and kill. His latest victim is Shelley Winters, whose children hold the secret to where a stash of money is buried. He's heard about this from a man he was in prison with. Mitchum, who has the words "Love" and "Hate" tattooed across his knuckles, gave one of the most riveting performances of his career in this bleak parable directed by Charles Laughton. The story goes that when Laughton approached him to play the role, he said, "The character in this film is an evil shit," to which Mitchum chirped in reply, "Present!"[63]

The film is directed in bold strokes, the black/white dichotomy forgivable because we're in the children's mindset. At times Mitchum seems to be laughing at his own revolting qualities but there's no gainsaying the shiver he sends down one's back when he plays it for real, thumping his black Bible with chilling portentousness. The film is a mixture of *noir, grand guignol* and farce which is probably why it bombed at the box office. Audiences expected more streamlined packages in 1955, an age before "indie" film-making put everything up for grabs. In this dark celluloid nightmare, childhood innocence is whisked away into the forest of a dark, amoral mind, and it was just too much for the public.

Laughton worried about Mitchum and about the fact that the film might be "bad for his future." Maybe, he thought, he should "break the evil" with some amusing diversions.[64] But this would have been an abominable compromise. At least the critics appreciated it, but Laughton never directed again, disappointed at its commercial failure. People didn't want to see Mitchum being this ghoulish, or Laughton being revisionist. It was regarded as too brooding and self-conscious by far. Lillian Gish had a small role as a woman who provides sanctuary to the children in an orphanage but her quasi-angelic aura only skewed the imbalance further. A film ahead of its time, posterity has been kind to it.

Danny Peary described it as "part gothic horror film, part religious parable, part children's nightmare, part fairytale."[65] Laughton, he said, paid homage to the novel on which it was based, written by Davis Grubb, which harked back to the "Dark Ages, to biblical times, to mythical times." Laughton himself described it as "a nightmarish sort of Mother Goose."[66]

Ireland lagged behind other countries with regard to what was deemed admissible cinematic fodder at this time with a patronizing attitude being adopted by many members of the clergy toward their less well-educated brethren. Some priests tried to change this. As Louise Fuller wrote in *Irish Catholicism Since 1950: The Undoing of a Culture*, "A number of 1950s clerics began to voice fears that Irish Catholicism was underdeveloped intellectually, precisely because it was too closed off and over-protected from what were seen to be corrupting influences." She mentions one man in particular, Fr Peter Connolly, who was Professor of English at St Patrick's College in Maynooth, and a member of the jury at the Cork Film Festival. He wanted to drag Ireland kicking and screaming into the twentieth century.

Fuller put it like this: "In order that a mature Catholic elite might develop, it was necessary, Connolly felt, that Irish Catholics be exposed to ideas that were different, and maybe sometimes even shocking to their sensibilities." A feature of Irish Catholicism at this time, she notes, was that "clergy were placed on a very high pedestal and seen as almost superhuman."

Against this background, she refers to a 1956 film called *Le Defroque* which depicted "the fall and resurrection of a priest." Connolly felt that this might contain drama and conflict "too strong for the moral or artistic palate of the average cinemagoer." He allowed that it made for good drama, but was concerned that "human sin and weakness . . . might not measure up to the Pope's ideal film" since if priests were on a pedestal, the Pope was almost sacred. Connolly surmised that the reason the French film didn't make it to Ireland was probably because of cinema managers' fears that it would make them pariahs. He showed his utter condescension toward people from rural areas when he surmised that they were probably "unequipped to face a priest as a tragic hero." "Educated audiences and seminarians," on the contrary, were recommended to view it.

He also had reservations about the 1955 film *The Left Hand of God* being shown in Ireland. This had Humphrey Bogart as an aviator in post-World War II China posing as a priest to evade the clutches of a nefarious warlord. Another film released at this time, *The Prisoner*, featured Alec Guinness as a Cardinal behind the Iron Curtain being brutally interrogated and brainwashed by Jack Hawkins. It was banned in Ireland but went on to win the Catholic International Cinema Office's Grand Prix Award. Was it for this the wild geese spread their wing on every tide?

Such circumstances underline the massive gap of tolerance that existed between Ireland and Europe at this time. It wouldn't be until the Second Vatican Council at the end of the 1960s that the laity were allowed to have minds of their own. It was then they came to be seen as an endemic part of the church rather than primitive people being told what to approve of. The Irish film censor James Montgomery summed up the sea-change in attitude. He saw himself between the devil and the Holy See, struggling against the possible "Californication" of Ireland.

Bogart's biographer Jeffrey Meyers had different kinds of problems with *The Left Hand of God*, rubbishing it totally. "Offering religiosity instead of religion," he fumed, "the movie neither emphasises the ironic aspects of Bogart's impersonation nor exploits the dramatic potential of Gene Tierney's forbidden love for a 'priest'. The audience could get more authentic atmosphere by sending out for Chinese food."[67]

Meyers has a point. Even the scenery looked fake. Tierney was also in the middle of a nervous breakdown during the shoot, and Bogart himself in the first stages of terminal cancer, though he wasn't to know that yet. He coughed incessantly between takes but still found time to be patient with the unhinged Tierney. As the pretend-priest with a gun under his cassock, he was always going to struggle with the duality of the role. The fairytale end, where he defeats the villains and wrests control of the village from the warlord played by a bald Lee J. Cobb was also contrived. And the dialogue, which should have been a lot better considering it was written by Nobel Prize-winner William Faulkner, was cringe-inducing. He tells a peasant whose wife has just died in childbirth, "She's now with someone who loves her as much as you do." Bromides like this give terms like "Job's consolation" a new dimension.

Bing Crosby played a church pastor in *Say One For Me* in 1959 but by now his clerical mystique seemed to have waned and the film was panned as being treacly and inconsequential. In the few short years since *The Bells of St. Mary's* the public's taste seemed to have changed, Crosby having been widely praised for playing an alcoholic with great poignancy in *The Country Girl* five years earlier. He was puzzled by this. He didn't seem capable of appreciating that what the public was reacting to was that rare Crosby gift of good acting, not the actions of a bland padre preaching to the converted in a hermetically sealed environment of easy virtue and contrived reform.

In 1961 John Mills played a priest in the taut but rather dour *The Singer Not the Song*. He tries to reform a sleek Mexican bandit played brilliantly by Dirk Bogarde but the film itself suffers from turgidity. The final scene, however, is interesting. As Bogarde lays dying, Mills asks him to clench his hand if he's praying. Bogarde isn't, but clenches it all the same, because of his respect for Mills. It's a poignant touch in an otherwise languid affair—though we could have been spared Bogarde's final and very pretentious namecheck of the film's title.

The *Hoodlum Priest*, in the same year, brought us back to the socially committed padre, with Don Murray, who also co-wrote and produced the movie, trying to steer potential criminals back onto the straight and narrow. He involves himself particularly with the edgy, dysfunctional Keir Dullea but his efforts are in vain and Dullea is executed in the end.

Two years later in Otto Preminger's blockbuster *The Cardinal*, Tom Tryon goes from humble priest to the titular rank in a film that was overblown and melodramatic, though it did raise some interesting concepts. In a seminal scene, Tryon refuses to allow a doctor to perform a craniotomy on his sister, who's having problems delivering her child. The operation would result in the child's death but save the mother. His loyalties are divided. Obviously he wants his sister to survive and without the craniotomy she still might. With the craniotomy the baby will definitely die, which to him is murder. It was a grey moral area which caused many tongues to wag at the time. The Nazi backdrop to the film, and a dalliance with Romy Schneider, was more capably handled. The Legion of Decency, as might have been expected, became inflamed about the craniotomy scene, complaining that it made Tryon seem like a cold fish, adhering rigidly to pro-life concerns despite the heart-rending circumstances. The Legion also had problems with Tryon's relationship with a young girl while on leave of absence, and the general implication of the film that he became a priest more from parental pressure than a genuine vocation.

Preminger spent most of his time roaring at Tryon for what he deemed to be a substandard performance. Tryon was devastated and perhaps as a result never really got his career back on track. In fact few people know much about what he did apart from this role. Even here he was plagued with insecurities during the shoot. Minaret director Preminger terrorized and terrified him, scraping away what little confidence he had. The story goes that one day a crew member told Preminger he was making Tryon nervous with all his roaring. Preminger reacted by going over to Tryon and screaming "Relax!" into his ear.

Carol Reed made *The Agony and the Ecstasy* in 1965. The film was a drawn-out psychological tussle between Pope Julius II, played by Rex Harrison, and Michelangelo (Charlton Heston). Almost from the moment it began there was friction between the two on the set. It should have been a better film as they sparked off one another in the script as well but it was really just one long yawn. Pope Julius, known as the Warrior Pope, was as much at home on the battlefield as in the papal residence, which also could have made for interesting subject matter, but the film chose instead to focus primarily on the commission he gave to Michelangelo to paint frescoes on the ceiling of the Sistine Chapel.

"Now there's a part," Harrison was quoted as saying when he first read it, "a Renaissance bull of a man, an unpopelike pope, fighting duels and siring illegitimate children."[68] None of this saltiness, sadly, comes across in the film, which spends most of its time obsessing on the manner in which the two men, equally headstrong in their way, barrack one another. A subplot dealing with Harrison's fight to preserve his power over the Papal States goes for nothing, not even when Heston arouses him from his deathbed to drive French and German invaders from Italy toward the end of the film.

An impatient Harrison keeps enquiring of Heston, "When will you make an end?" but as Harrison's biographer Roy Moseley pointed out, this comment could equally have been addressed to Reid about the movie. Bosley Crowther rightly emphasized the fact that its leaden-footed pace mirrored Michelangelo's inability to make decisions about his work. The painter is too punctilious for the Pope, who mutters at one point "I planned a ceiling; he plans a miracle." He goads him to speed up, threatening to employ a rival if he doesn't, but still he dawdles interminably. The film isn't helped by lines like Harrison's "Do you dare to dicker with your pontiff?" which sounds like some naughty *double entendre* from a *Carry On* script. The scale is big and the stage set for a solemn exercise in duelling egos but it never reaches lift-off. Harrison's frustration and Heston's stubbornness fail to flicker off each other in the way intended, with the result that one seems more aware of two rather petulant misanthropes than anything else.

"Heston very politely and very nicely made me feel that it was extremely kind of me to be supporting him," Harrison taunted.[69] He added, "Unfortunately, he thinks the whole world is his supporting cast." The pair of them tried to upstage one another, believing the film belonged to each of them respectively instead of being a collaborative effort. This weakened the fragile structure upon which the central dynamic revolved. In a diary published years after the film was completed Heston wrote, "Harrison has the temperament of a thoroughbred racehorse . . . highly strung, with a tendency to snort and rear and kick at the starting gate." He magnanimously conceded that he was a fine actor nonetheless and therefore worth all the "megrims."[70] The irony was that Harrison could probably have written the very same words about Heston if he himself had kept a diary. To coin a phrase, it was really all more agony than ecstasy, both on and off the screen. The frescoes may have been ornate but the film itself was a fiasco.

Asked if he felt he was too tall to play Michelangelo—the painter was six inches smaller than him in real life—Heston replied that on the contrary, he felt too *small*. It was a gracious comment but unfortunately such humility didn't translate itself onto the screen. Philip Dunne, who wrote the screenplay, felt Heston was miscast in the role. "Michelangelo was a small, gnarled, ugly man," he said, "Chuck is a tall and blonde Greek god."[71] He wanted Marlon Brando for the part. Darryl F. Zanuck, the producer, told him Heston was "the only American actor who can wear a toga."[72] Dunne suggested Spencer Tracy rather than Harrison as the Pope but was again shot down by Zanuck, who felt that "aristocratic figures like kings and Popes should be played by English actors."[73] The film foundered in its deference to such lazy pigeonholing.

David Lean made *Ryan's Daughter* in Ireland in 1968. This was a remake of Gustave Flaubert's *Madame Bovary*, featuring Trevor Howard as Father Collins, the film's moral barometer. A flabby epic laughed out of many cinemas thanks to some very amateurish love scenes between the eponymous Sarah Miles and her prematurely ejaculating husband (an unlikely Robert Mitchum as an Irish schoolteacher) it became even more risible when she went frolicking in the woods with her secret lover

Christopher Jones, a moody James Dean lookalike, playing a shell-shocked soldier.

Lean originally wanted Alec Guinness for the part but he turned it down so he went to his old ally Howard, whose last two roles were as marriage wreckers (*Brief Encounter* and *Passionate Friends*). "Whose wife do you want me to fuck this time," asked Howard, deliciously.[74]

Maybe if something like this *had* occurred, the film might have had more fizz. As it was, Howard felt marginalized both by the material and Lean's punctilious directing methods. The film took a year out of his life, an amazing amount of time considering he was only on screen for relatively short periods, and left him with a sour taste in his mouth. The shooting was plagued by rain and storms, and a director who refused to settle for anything less than what his storyboarding technique dictated.

At one point Howard left Ireland to check out the cricket games at Lord's—he actually had provision for this privilege in all of his movie contracts—and when he returned to the set three weeks later realized he'd hardly been missed. The snail-like pace, combined with the straight-laced character he was required to play, made it all something of an ordeal for him, but he did imbue the part with his customary square-jawed credibility.

A political subplot was threaded into the action but this was perhaps unwise. As a spectacle it was a luscious affair and Mitchum was uncannily impressive as the decent, unworldly clod, but it was too lengthy to support the wafer-thin plotline and imploded as a result. As Howard himself remarked wryly, "Three hours is a bit long for a trifling little love story."[75] Alexander Walker added equally phlegmatically, "Instead of looking like the money it cost to make, the film feels like the time it took to shoot."[76]

Today it's regarded as a quaint pastoral with Howard coming across as a well-intentioned, unimaginative padre who was quintessentially of his time but hardly fleshed out as a character. He's really there as the token spokesman for the official church line on infidelity in an Ireland not long into the 20th century. Though he does befriend Rosy (Miles) beyond the call of duty when she's hung out to dry for suspected snitching on the gunrunners, he's very much a clichéd figure on an over-elaborate landscape. All the same, his performance was Lean's favorite, probably because a fundamental core of decency shone through the crusty exterior.

Pauline Kael, not too surprisingly, also denigrated the film, describing it as "gush made respectable by millions of dollars tastefully wasted."[77] In Britain, however, Dilys Powell contended that Howard dominated the film, claiming that it was his compassionate nature that stood out over the general sourness of the other rural characters. This was a strange view indeed for Howard was dwarfed by everything around him, the scenery, the other cast members, Lean himself and the "rural characters" weren't so much sour as wild, dog-rough and xenophobic. Howard's most memorable experience on the set, in fact, was falling off a donkey one day when he wasn't shooting, and ending up in the hospital for his troubles. Somebody must have been trying to tell him something.

Gene Hackman played a distinctly unpriestly priest in *The Poseidon Adventure* in 1972. This is one of Hollywood's better "disaster" movies, largely due to his desperate efforts to make most of the other cast members behave hysterically. Early on we see the collar but there are few religious sentiments here, or admonitions to pray, when the luxury cruise ship on which he's travelling gets upended by a tidal wave. He becomes the self-appointed leader of the survivors, roaring at them more like a navvy than a curate. If this is Christ—he gives his life to save the others in the end—it's a Christ of the streets. He's resourceful but impatient, kind but gruff. Whenever be sees anybody going the "wrong" way—terms like "right" and "wrong" are open to conjecture in the uncertainty of their situation—he blows a fuse. Some of the passengers seem to almost have a death wish. They certainly have a sheep mentality.

Hackman gives them true grit rather than homilies, pushing them beyond their limits. Some of them die and he takes the heat for this. Ernest Borgnine is his main adversary. In some ways the film is about this man's softening. When Borgnine loses his wife he blames Hackman personally. "I just started to believe in you, Preacher," he wails, "but you took the only thing I loved in this world." Hackman has nearly led them all to safety when the final disaster strikes. Steam is escaping from a valve and he has to turn it off. The only problem is it isn't within reach. If he jumps onto it there's no way back. But he still jumps. Dangling from it, he turns the wheel until the flow stops. "What more do you want of us?" he screams at God, "How much more blood? How many more lives?" And then, "You want another one? Take mine."

He hangs like Jesus on the cross, telling the others they can make it even if he doesn't. Then this latter-day savior dives to his death in a flaming pool of water. Not long afterward the rest of them are rescued. "The beautiful son of a bitch was right," Borgnine exclaims. Too little praise, delivered too late.

Jack Gold directed *Catholics* for TV in 1973. It was based on Brian Moore's novel dealing with the refusal of an embittered abbot to modernize the Mass after being ordered to by his superiors. Using a screenplay also written by Moore, *Catholics* captures the collision of two cultures in microcosm as per its two main characters. It's set in the future, an era where not only has the Latin Mass been done away with but confession is also outlawed. Liberalism rules—except on a small island off Cork where an old abbot (Trevor Howard) prefers to stay with the old verities. He attracts a large following of like-minded souls so Rome sends a priest, Fr Kinsella (Martin Sheen) to quash it. There follows an ideological tussle between the two men, the irony being that Howard himself is undergoing a crisis of faith.

The final scene of Howard's quiet desperation is the stuff of great acting, and it didn't go unacknowledged. The director Peter Brooke wanted to know what monastery Howard had entered to prepare for the part. The answer Howard gave was simple: "None. I'm an actor." Asked if he had done any preparation at all for the role he replied brazenly, "Of course not."[78] Greene himself actually wept as he watched it and had to take a pill to sleep afterward. He wrote to Howard to tell him it was "one of the two finest performances I have ever seen on the screen or the stage."[79] He didn't mention what the other one was.

An even more effective priest than this was created by Robert De Niro in Ulu Grosbard's 1981 movie *True Confessions*, based on John Gregory Dunne's explosive novel. De Niro played Monsignor Des Spellacy, an ambitious clergyman whose vocation has "long been lost in his rise up the ecclesiastical ladder."[80] He's also vaguely involved in a killing being investigated by his brother Tom (Robert Duvall), an LAPD detective. De Niro has been getting money to build diocesan schools from corrupt property developer Jack Amsterdam (Charles Durning). Duvall makes it his business to bring Durning down but in the process he also seals the fate of his own brother. To quote Keith McKay, it's a film about the conflict between "Holy Orders and law and order."[81]

The film very effectively combines the brutality of street life with some tender scenes involving both brothers visiting their Irish mother, who's going senile, against the backdrop of a haunting "Carrigfergus" score. The central scene has de Niro hearing Durning's confession and giving him absolution while on the other side of the confession box sits Duvall, who's heard it all. Earlier on, the beleaguered Monsignor Fargo (Burgess Meredith) tells De Niro, "You have a mind like an abacus. You do everything, in fact, but feel." All the years of glad-handing politicians and bagmen have transformed him into a mover and shaker, the sacraments coming a poor second. Golf seems to be the center of his life. But his compromised past is catching up with Des. He knows too many of the wrong people. His downfall is his former familiarity with a murdered prostitute. It's this that finally nails him.

After Durning is exposed, De Niro's "career" is over and he becomes exiled to a remote parish in the California desert. Duvall visits him years later and asks for his forgiveness. De Niro feels he's been purified by suffering. "I'm going to die, Tom," he says, and proceeds to show him where he wants to be buried. It's a beautifully elegiac finale.

De Niro's preparation for the role bore all the hallmarks of his usual perfectionism. Patrick Agan wasn't exaggerating when he said he "practically joined a seminary" for the role.[82] Months before he began filming he studied and practiced the liturgy of the Mass, doing so in Latin because the film was set in the 1940s. He also studied church dogma, and insisted on rehearsing in the clerical garments he would wear in the film. Grosbard said of him, "By the time he was ready to start the movie, he talked like a priest, he *was* a priest."[83] Father Henry Fehren, who acted as his tutor, added, "He wanted to master not only the fundamental routines of an ordained priest, but to feel within himself the tradition of what the church was in 1948. He may be the most authentic priest ever seen on the screen. How holy we would be if we worked as conscientiously [as de Niro did] at becoming saints as he did for his role."[84]

The Catholic hierarchy also praised his performance, agreeing that he was the most convincing cleric seen on screen in years. Andy Dougan believes part of that credibility could have been the result of the fact that De Niro was still slightly overweight from *Raging Bull*, in which he'd put on an astounding seventy pounds, and was thus better able to convey the persona of a "fatcat" priest.[85] De Niro's biographer John Baxter quotes Rex Reed commenting on him "whispering piously through his stoic double chins."[86] Baxter thinks this is a "bitchy" comment but it's actually a flattering one because this is precisely the effect De Niro was seeking to conjure up.

What made it all the more impressive was the manner in which his character was struggling with duplicity. In between performing the sacraments he spends a lot of time "networking" with Durning, behaving more like an accountant than anything else. As one of the characters puts it "He looks like a leprechaun and thinks like an Arab." At one point he even arranges an audience for Durning with the Pope.

The cast is first-rate. De Niro and Duvall, who'd appeared together before in *Godfather 2*, tied for the Best Actor award at the Venice Film Festival but in America the film died at the box office. It was too dark and reflective to sell, like much of De Niro's early work. Richard Corliss wrote in *Time*, "Characters who should percolate and rage simply simmer . . . De Niro's big scene has him hanging up vestments."[87] This is harsh, but Grosbard himself admitted that plot wasn't the film's priority, "Oh you find out who dunnit. But it doesn't really matter."[88]

Dunne was also a party to this approach. One of his stipulations was that a scene in the film—it could be any one—should have no dialogue at all. This was achieved over two minutes and two seconds when Grosbard follows De Niro from his car to his bedroom after a game of golf. For the movie connoisseur it was a perfectly realized sequence, though perhaps more suited to an art-house audience than a mainstream one.

The following year Christopher Reeve now, alas, gone from us, played a priest in the ill-advised venture *Monsignor*. This concerned a cleric who not only befriends mobsters but also has an affair with a nun (Genevieve Bujold) while operating as the Vatican's business manager. The film was both an artistic and commercial disaster, so much so that it was three years before its director, Frank Perry, was given another job. *Newsweek* magazine rubbished it as an unabashed turkey. Reeve, a lapsed Episcopalian, said in his defense, "I played a corrupt character, not a real one. They tried to homogenize him." One critic claimed the film was so unintentionally laughable that when the nun asks him what his secret is, you expect him not so much to say "I'm a priest" as "I can fly." (Reeve, of course, also played "Superman" before the tragic riding accident that paralyzed him.)

Some of the dialogue is cringe-inducing. In one scene Bujold gushes to Reeve before seducing him: "God gave me a strange gift. He made me attract love affairs that quickly become disasters. That's why I decided to become a nun. But here I am, ready for another disaster. I'll have some champagne." Rarely has the principle of "I might as well be hanged for a sheep as a lamb" been more hilariously enunciated. *Time* magazine justifiably felt the Legion of Decency should have intervened to end everyone's pain. But then this wasn't so much indecent as palpably juvenile, so perhaps that's why it was given free rein. Bad anti-clericalism is, if anything, a boon to the church.

A more interesting movie by far was the 1984 drama *Mass Appeal* in which Jack Lemmon, a decent if populist priest, has his life shattered by a cocky young seminarian whose revolutionary ideas about what it means to be a cleric rock Lemmon's complacent habits to the core and force him to confront hard questions about the authenticity of his vocation. The formula was old hat. The young seminarian (Zeljko Ivanek) comes to his parish full of idealism and it's Lemmon's job to put him through his ecclesiastical paces in preparation for donning the collar. Pretty soon the pupil is lecturing the teacher. He tells Lemmon that his ministry is hollow and superficial and that he also sucks up to the congregation too much. Ivanek's own vocation is one of challenge so when he gives a homily he berates the congregation. "Jesus is not impressed with your mink hats, cashmere coats and blue hair," he tells them, to their pronounced disdain. "The purpose of the church," he declares in another homily, "is to make itself obsolete." This isn't the kind of thing his smug array of worshippers is accustomed to hearing on Sunday mornings before they drive home to their duplexes for the weekly pot roast.

Ivanek's belligerence with his flock, and his prickly Catholicism, earns the displeasure of a senior priest played with just the right degree of menace by Charles Durning. He tells Lemmon to get rid of Ivanek even if he has to lay a gay charge on him to do so. (Ivanek has expressed a certain leaning in this direction).

Lemmon is now in a quandary. Does he put his neck on the block for this callow youth who has experienced little or nothing of life or should he have him removed so he can get back to his cozy ways of preaching to the converted? In the end he chooses the brave path, telling Durning what he thinks of him and, by extension, what he thinks of himself. The film is really about Lemmon's life rather than any revolutionary ideas Ivanek may or may not have about one's noumenal relationship to God. He's reformed by the young man who makes him realize he's been living a lie for most of his life, The message is fine but the delivery is rather wishy-washy. Ivanek's earnestness is irksome and there are times one feels Durning is right: i.e., that the lad should be kicked out of the parish, not because he's a radical, but for his ill-disguised narcissism and squeaky clean self-righteousness. "What you believe," he tells Lemmon in one of his smug exhortations, "has got to be more important than what your congregation means to you."

There are too many boringly earnest lines like this and the film implodes as a result. Lemmon does his best in a role that calls on him to be stuck between a rock and a hard place but just this once his twitchy mid-life crisis *shtick* doesn't work. Michael Freedland summed his performance up, calling it "Barry Fitzgerald . . . without much of the fun."[89]

Kenneth Turan in *California* magazine felt Lemmon's character's main problem in the film appeared to be "over-exposure to Jack Lemmon movies" and that he seemed to believe that being "a facile entertainer is all a clergyman can manage these days."[90] David Edelstein came down even harder on Lemmon in *The Village Voice*, accusing him of playing the same character in every movie, "the jokester whose flip persona is a mask for cowardice and the inability to love." From his first weary look at the deacon, Edelstein contended, "he knows he's done for—it's like he recognized his executioner from a prophetic dream."[91]

Linus Roache played a gay Liverpudlian curate in *Priest* (1995); a film in which he discovers that his supervisor (Tom Wilkinson) is having an affair with their housekeeper. In a nod to *I Confess*, an early scene here has a man confessing to an incestuous relationship with his daughter, safe in the knowledge that the confessional seal will prevent his confessor from "outing" him. The priest prays to God for a way to solve his dilemma but fate intervenes because the man's wife catches him in the act shortly afterward. When Roache is finally exposed as a practicing homosexual he finds an unlikely ally in Wilkinson. There were so many hot issues in *Priest*, the floodgates were open now for films like *The Magdalene Sisters* to further tilt at clerical windmills, a phenomenon obviously related to the slew of scandals breaking out in the church at this time. Suddenly, the worlds of Spencer Tracy, Bing Crosby and Pat O'Brien seemed from a far-distant era.

In the aftermath of such rose-tinted portrayals, we also had the phenomenon of priests in horror movies like *The Exorcist* and its sequel *The Heretic*, where Max Von Sydow and Richard Burton did the respective honors, playing characters almost as tormented as the children they were employed to exorcise. Gabriel Byrne did a similar turn in *Stigmata*, as well as playing Satan opposite Arnold Schwarzenegger in *End of Days*. *The Exorcist* spawned a number of other sequels, each more exploitative than the last, but this didn't seem to bother the distributors, who regarded it all as something of a license to print money.

Robert De Niro played a mercenary-turned-Jesuit in *The Mission* in 1987. While he gave a committed performance especially where he climbs up a sheer cliff-face in his bare feet there wasn't much opportunity to engage in the kind of intimate, highly-personalized tics that could have lifted the film onto another level. As a study of events that took place in Paraguay in the mid-1700s it's a worthy exercise but his role is really only a cameo. He donned a soutane again in *Sleepers*, the 1996 adaptation of Lorenzo Carcaterra's best-selling novel about four ex-inmates of a boy's correctional institution who, as adults, take revenge on the vicious guard who brutalized them as children. They're tried for his murder but De Niro, who sees a kind of justice in their revenge, perjures himself on the stand to help get them acquitted. The film raised the old question of whether the end justifies the means and was roundly castigated by the church for this, as well as appearing to endorse vigilantism. What raised even more hackles was the fact that it was allegedly based on real-life incidents.

De Niro played a criminal on the run who dresses up as a priest in the earlier *We're No Angels*, a Neil Jordan re-make that was embarrassingly amateurish. It was a one-note performance from the Method guru, confirming many in their belief that some great actors (Brando was another example) aren't ideal candidates for comedy. All he could do was pull silly faces in a hamfisted attempt at whimsy.

Brando was actually slated to play a priest in the 1995 production *Divine Rapture* which was to be shot in Ireland. He was starring opposite his good friend Johnny Depp, who'd appeared with him not long before in *Don Juan De Marco*. Depp was given the part of a journalist investigating religious miracles. Debra Winger was cast as a fisherman's wife who dies and is brought back to life. Two Cork priests refused Thom Eberhardt, the director, permission to use their churches for certain scenes, informing him bluntly, "Churches are not film sets."[92] Not too much had changed since *The Nun's Story*. He also felt Brando's character was "an insult to Catholicism."[93] A bishop rallied in behind the two priests in question, unimpressed with the kind of film that was being made. It had blackly comic aspects, one scene having fish raining from the sky.

Brando was highly enthusiastic about filming in Ireland. He felt totally at home in the country, so much so that he even contemplated taking out Irish citizenship. But he came with a large price tag—his living quarters alone were £4,000 a week and this, combined with the difficulties in getting places to shoot, and the direly unpredictable Irish weather, caused severe financial problems.

The overall budget of $16 million wasn't exorbitant but after only twenty minutes had been shot the production was shut down. Brando had been paid $1 million upfront but many of the other cast members ended up with nothing. The French backers pulled out and everybody was told to go home. Johnny Depp's summing up of the experience was succinct: "It was like being in the middle of good sex, and then having the lights turned on and fifteen people with guns come in and say, 'Stop or die.'"[94] The film subsequently came to be dubbed *Divine Rupture*.

A Love Divided (1997) investigated the massive degree of religious bigotry that existed in Ireland in the 1950s. The plot, featuring a Protestant woman who refused to have her children educated in the local Catholic school in Co. Wexford, was based on a real-life incident. At her child's baptism she had signed a pledge saying she'd do so but changed her mind after being intimidated by the parish priest. She was also annoyed that he seemed to have her husband—and indeed the rest of the community—in his pocket. When her decision met with the wrath of the clergy and her submissive husband sided with the priests she ran off with the children. She opened a can of worms in the village, giving rise to much violence against the Protestant community. After fleeing the nest she was branded a kidnapper by most of the villagers. She hid out in the Orkney Islands, her case brewing up a national, and then an international storm. The Protestants in Fethard-on-Sea, the village in question, were boycotted at the priest's behest and the Papal Nuncio was eventually called in to quell the unrest.

Her predicament became a test case for the church and crystallized just how powerful the Catholic Church was. It took a plea from the president of Ireland to the Pope to finally restore order.

Tony Doyle is brilliant as the priest, as is John Kavanagh as a particularly oleaginous bishop. Orla Brady is the plucky woman who risks all for her principles and Liam Cunningham her husband. Ms Brady is more motivated by feminist than religious concerns, anxious to make a man out of her husband by her dramatic actions, rocking the boat on what appeared to be an idyllic marriage in an equally idyllic community. But as he remarks in the film's closing stages, the tension was always there; she merely brought it to the surface.

In a way the film is really about how Cunningham matures. There's a bit of good cop-bad cop in the treatment of Protestants versus Catholics. The former are almost all gentle and the latter nearly all bigoted but this is still a searing treatment of a much-neglected issue.

The Third Miracle (1999) was a quietly effective study of a priest undergoing a crisis of faith, falling in love with the daughter of a possible saint and trying to square his vocation with his alleged practice of "miracle-killing." Frank Shore, played by Ed Harris, investigates the authenticity of miracles. When he was a boy his father, a police officer, was seriously wounded and he made a vow to God that if he recovered he would become a priest. Both events took place but a few months later his father died. Shore felt cheated. He also felt cheated when, shortly before the film begins, he was called upon to investigate the cause of a priest who was reputed to have effected cures. Shore discovered this cause to be unsafe when he learned the priest in question committed suicide. As the film begins Shore is called upon to investigate another cause, that of an "ordinary" woman named Helen O'Regan. He's reluctant to take the case, so soured by his last assignment that he's taken an unscheduled sabbatical.

The church where Helen worked has a statue that bleeds in her blood type and Shore is sufficiently intrigued by this to take up the case. He initially suspects the bleeding could have a chemical source, but as the film goes on, his belief in her authenticity increases. This causes problems for him as he's begun to fall for her daughter Roxanne (Anne Heche). When he tells Roxanne he has to call off their relationship because of his compromised position Roxanne taunts him by saying "I have a friend who wants to be a Catholic. She says you can do anything you like if you go to confession afterward and say three Hail Marys." She finishes by saying, "God won."

The blood from the statue is believed to have cured a young girl called Maria who was dying from lupus. During the course of the film Maria undergoes another miraculous cure when she recovers from a coma for no explicable reason. The third miracle of the title either refers to an instance during Helen's childhood when she turned World War II bombs into birds—this occurs in a poignant flashback at the beginning of the film—or, if we wish to extend the definition of miracle into a different domain, the fact that Shore has recovered his faith.

This is a slow-moving film but nonetheless an engrossing one. It isn't bitter toward religion; neither is it hagiographic. It combines a healthy scepticism with a grudging nod toward transcendence. Shore's desperation to believe Helen should be beatified, thereby ratifying his sacrifice of Roxanne, is evocatively captured by Harris, and the direction by Agnieszka Holland is thoughtful and restrained.

Ed Norton directed himself as a priest in *Keeping the Faith* (2000), a gentle three-hander about himself and his rabbinical friend Ben Stiller, both of whom are attracted to the same girl, Jenna Elfman. In a normal film such an attraction might prove embarrassing but here no logical rules seem to apply so both young men make plays for her in ways that make it all look more like a Woody Allen sitcom than anything else. It would have worked better as a gross-out comedy directed by, say, the Farrelly Brothers. As it is, the ruminations on celibacy and inter-religious commingling come across as just a mite too frivolous to engage. After a while you forget the two men have received "the call" and just respond to it as a hoary old yarn about the rabbi, the padre and the feisty gal sand-wiched between them.

Early scenes of Norton setting his cassock on fire with an incense con-tainer, and having to douse himself in the baptismal fountain as a result, not to mention Stiller using trendy preaching techniques to bring in the masses, give one to believe we're in for a farce. Later on the film gets thoughtful, perhaps too thoughtful for its own good. It would have made more sense as a triangular love story without the religious overtones, which come with too much baggage, most of it mismanaged. The steady performances of the three main leads make it look a lot more focussed than it really is. It gives away the Woody Allen influence in lines like this from Stiller to Norton after he confesses to seeing Elfman "What do you want me to do—flagellate myself? Jews don't do that. We plant trees." Earlier, Elfman has given Stiller a gift of a mobile phone. "She put God on the speed dial," he informs Norton, "I called it and got the Elvis Presley museum."

There's a happy-ever-after ending where the friendship of all three is preserved, Norton "donates" Elfman to Stiller, and Stiller realizes that, hey, it's cool to date a Gentile, though he does apologize to his congrega-tion for same at Yom Kippur. "I've never seen so much inter-faith danc-ing," he says jovially at his nuptials, "It's like the end of *West Side Story*." It's a pity we didn't get more of the *drama* of *West Side Story* instead of a slick enchilada of mock-ecumenical fervor. The lesson Stil-ler finally learns, i.e., that he has to have faith in people as well as God, is too Capraesque by far.

Mel Gibson played a priest who marries and then becomes widowed in M Night Shyamalans *Signs* (2002). By the time the film begins he's lost his faith as a result of his wife dying in a freak car accident. Unable to come to terms with his grief, he divests himself of his clerical garb, entreats people not to call him "Father," cuts himself off from the Phila-delphia farming community to which he belongs, and refuses to pray. But one morning he wakes up to see his land covered with strange circu-lar patterns. Are they signs from God or evidence of an extra-terrestrial presence? At first he thinks they're the work of pranksters but pretty soon the presence of aliens seems likelier. As the film goes on, such a possi-bility becomes increasingly more ominous as he watches TV reports of similar phenomena in other countries.

With his two children and his younger brother (Joaquin Phoenix) he makes a veritable fortress of his house and prepares himself almost fatalistically to meet his doom. Such aliens, mind you, aren't Steven

Spielberg's cuddly creatures with long fingers and sweet smiles, but beings intent on territorial supremacy—as used to be the norm for sci-fi films of yore. What's strange about Gibson's behavior is the manner in which he engages in little or no communication with the outside world beyond a rudimentary report of his findings to the local police officer. This fact makes the movie, which is shot in dark, ponderous hues, even more claustrophobic than it might otherwise have been.

Gibson usually appears to have matters under control in his films but here conveys fear and vulnerability. He also gets his faith back. This part of the film, combined with a B-movie finale as far as the science fiction is concerned, makes it look like the work of a different director than the one who made *The Sixth Sense*. The suspense is teased out almost tortuously but it's hard not to feel short-changed at the end, where matters are resolved all too tidily in a sugar-coated *Close Encounters* meets *Field of Dreams* hybrid.

Aidan Quinn appeared in *Song for a Raggy Boy* in 2003. This was an indictment of a reform school run by the Christian Brothers in Cork in the 1930s. Quinn himself said he got flogged regularly by the Brothers when he was a lad, but also formed great attachments to some of them. He stressed that he wasn't anti-clerical, despite the fact that he also starred in *This Is My Father*, another hard-hitting tirade against the church in the years gone by. His brief, he insisted, was to expose abuse rather than indulge in gratuitous church-bashing.

When asked how he felt about Ireland now as opposed to when he lived there as a youth, he replied that he was disappointed so few people attended Mass, and also with the rising tide of consumerism, alcoholism and other perils of a post-Catholic country. Rebellion against a flawed church was one thing, nihilism quite another.

The present film, based on the memoirs of Patrick Galvin, deals with an Irish teacher who lost his wife in the Spanish Civil War. He also lost a teaching job in the United States due to his left-wing views. Now repatriated, he's the only lay member of staff in St Jude's school. He soon finds himself at odds with the ultra-strict Brother John, played with chilling conviction by Iain Glen. Glen metes out punishment to the boys on little or no pretext. "The creatures you're about to teach," he advises Quinn, "are not to be confused with intelligent human beings." All they understand is strength, he tells him, and if he doesn't apply that they'll "eat you alive." He addresses the children not by name but inmate number. Quinn, on the contrary, gives them a love of learning, using the carrot rather than the stick to get the best out of them.

Glen becomes even more ferocious when challenged, and when Quinn forms a special bond with a boy called Liam Mercier, played by John Travers, Glen's ire is raised even more. When an allegation of sexual abuse becomes manifest, the stage is set for a dramatic confrontation. There are many violent scenes in the film and also many emotionally draining ones. For some it was seen as yet another example of "death by a thousand cuts" to a severely damaged institution, for others a story of unspeakable cruelty that needed to be told.

Aisling Walsh, the director, had previously made *Sinners*, another indictment of clerical abuse, for TV. She said the script of *Raggy Boy* had landed on her desk many years before *Sinners* and she only made the latter because she feared she would never get funding for the former. Quinn, meanwhile, spoke about his aunt, a 91-year-old nun, and the great work she did for the church. His father he added had also wanted to be a priest when he was young. He said he believed strongly in both religion and the church.

Every barrel had rotten apples, he said, but that didn't mean the barrel itself was bad. We shouldn't throw the baby out with the bathwater. Neither should we shoot the messenger if a film depicted past churchly misdeeds. From an artistic point of view this film was sensitively made and drew strong performances from all concerned. There was a juxtaposition of the events of the Spanish Civil War with those in the reformatory school, though the symbolism was a little too obvious here. The character Quinn played could also be deemed too good to be true.

The Church was maligned more deeply in *The Magdalene Sisters*, as we saw. For too long a culture of silence overhung such matters but now that the toothpaste is out of the tube, as it were, there's a danger of going over the top. Notwithstanding the righteous indignation of all concerned, there are times when a film became so blatantly agenda-driven it lost its credibility. You couldn't say the same for *Raggy Boy*, which is more intent on telling a story, and portrays the members of the reform school—the good, the bad and the ugly—with great conviction and three-dimensionality.

The much-anticipated movie version of Dan Brown's blockbuster novel *The Da Vinci Code* (2006) ignited many storms in tea-cups. The novel dealt with a 2000-year-old church cover-up of Jesus' marriage to Mary Magdalene and other scandals, all of which were hushed up by a secret society called the Priory of Sion. The most malignant character is an albino monk from Opus Dei named Silas and played by Paul Bettany. This murderous character so angered Opus Dei itself that the organization called for the film to be boycotted, censored or, at the very least, have a disclaimer put in at the outset by director Ron Howard stating that it was a fictional piece of work.

As most of the world knows—the novel having sold some 60 million copies—things take off when the curator of the Louvre is found dead with strange symbols carved into his body. The police employ cryptologist Sophie Neveu (Audrey Tautou), the grand-daughter of the dead man, to try and interpret them and she in turn calls on symbologist Robert Langdon (Tom Hanks) to help her out. Together they go on a trail of discovery that leads all the way to the top of a corrupt institution.

Howard wanted to shoot the film in the actual locations featured in the book but this wasn't always feasible. He managed to get into the Louvre, but not Westminster Abbey because of the "theologically unsound" nature of the novel.[95] He felt the scriptural apocrypha were good fodder for an adventurous story that would set tongues wagging, but this wasn't the way the church saw it. Archbishop Angelo Amato from the Vatican Doctrinal Office felt that if the contentious material from the film had been directed at the Koran (or Holocaust) there would have been a global revolt as a result.

The Archbishop's statement is perhaps excessive but let's not forget what happened to Salman Rushdie after he wrote *The Satanic Verses*. In the Catholic world perhaps we could make an analogy between Rushdie and the Martin Scorsese who made a similarly sacrilegious tract in *The Last Temptation of Christ*. Scorsese received death threats, but not official ones like Rushdie, and he never had to go into hiding like the other man. On the other hand, Tom Hanks made a good point when he said that *The Da Vinci Code* arguably helped the church to do its work: "If they put up a sign saying, 'This Wednesday we are discussing the Gospel,' 12 people show up. But if a sign says, 'This Wednesday we're discussing *The Da Vinci Code*, 800 people show up.'"[96] This is possibly true, but raises the issue of "What's the price of controversiality?"

Howard said he didn't see the film as a platform to express personal views on the spiritual. It was really just a suspense story with a quasi-theological scaffolding. He downplayed the outrage it was alleged to have provoked. A newspaper report claimed that 1000 people gathered outside Lincoln Cathedral, which doubled for Westminster Abbey in the film to protest, but Howard says 999 of these were people who came with copies of Brown's book, looking for Hanks to autograph them. The other individual was a nun. Howard didn't meet her, "but everyone said she was wonderful."[97]

Balanced viewers rated the film *qua* film rather than an ideological ground shaker. It was glossily packaged hokum, the Da Vinci "Cod" as some commentators remarked. The protestors, apart from the nun at Lincoln Cathedral, merely swelled Howard's bank balance by their indignation. If the edifice of 2000 years of received theological tradition was this shaky, their demented bleatings were unlikely to stabilize it. Pulp fiction had always been permitted its niche and this shouldn't have been an exception. People read the book, did the tour and now they wanted to see the movie. Those who had negative feelings about the church would have them buffeted while those who hadn't were unlikely to be swayed. Many people got into a flap about the intricacies of Brown's suspect Sherlock Holmesing, but they would have been better advised to put their Bibles under the cinema seat. As Alfred Hitchcock might have said, "It's only a movie, Ingrid."

Angels and Demons (2009), the sequel to *The Da Vinci Code*—though the book was written before it—also followed the potboiler trail. In many ways it was more exciting than its predecessor, and faster-moving.

Beginning with the death of a Pope (was it murder?), and segueing into the kidnapping of four of his possible successors, it also has a terrorist element and (wouldn't you know it) a primitive, ancient sect bent on mayhem.

Tom Hanks again rides over the hill to save the world and Ron Howard again helmed it, and cleaned up at the box office. Spiritual uplift? You must be joking. But within that canvas it told a rollicking good yarn. Even the Vatican gave it a grudging green light. By now the people calling for Dan Brown's head on a plate were at a premium. He had become just another thumping good novelist, and the Da Vinci franchise showed signs of softening.

Another sequel, anyone? By now the church was rocked by yet more pedophilia scandals and had more to worry it than an adventure junkie plumbing the bottom of the barrel for more arcane codes, more convoluted chases and more climactic red herrings.

In a way, the iconoclastic Brown had almost become part of the establishment.

——4——

Reel Spirits

"Movies," according to Ron Base, "are the mythology of the twentieth century, their stars like Gods we worship. We seldom consider how the gods arrived in the movie heavens, and the gods themselves state over and over to an adoring press only too anxious to reinforce the mythology, that they had no wish to be in the firmament but simply woke one day to find themselves there."[1]

Feelings about God have changed markedly since the Golden Age of cinema. Even in films like *In the Line of Fire* (1993), which doesn't have a religious or spiritual theme, we find the psycho-killer John Malkovich coming out with this philosophy of teleological disparity, "God doesn't punish the wicked and reward the righteous. Everyone dies. Some die because they deserve to; others die simply because they come from Minneapolis. It's random and it's meaningless." In a more recent film, *The Island,* Steve Buscemi tells Ewan McGregor, "God is the guy who, when you pray to him for something, he doesn't get it for you."

In a reader survey conducted some time ago by a magazine geared toward 18-34 year olds, 75 percent of respondents said they would rather kill themselves with a steak knife than watch *Touched by an Angel*.[2] Terry Mattingly of the Scripps Howard News Service went one further, declaring that "Legions of Christian consumers who claim to want uplifting dramas about missionaries may, in reality, prefer to watch *Friends*."[3]

It wasn't always thus.

Anyone who didn't believe in God in Hollywood's past, according to the blinkered thinking of the time, was reformed by some spiritual being or a priest, or a child. Even hardened criminals crumbled before figures of moral authority in the last reel. This was a given. Church and state ruled OK, and audiences were glad to go along with the charade vicerously soaking up their punishment. God and His emissaries have also been traditionally well represented on celluloid, ranging from the sublime to the ridiculous.

Topper (1937) falls into the latter category. It starred Cary Grant and Constance Bennett as a vivacious married couple killed in a car accident. Realizing with some understandable shock that they are, in fact, spirits, they wait to be wafted away to heaven. But nothing happens. They then decide that this transition can only take place if they deserve it. Infuriatingly, they can't remember many good deeds they've done in their irresponsible past. To "earn" a place in heaven they decide to liberate their friend Topper (Roland Young) from his battleaxe wife (Billie Burke). Cue lots of frenzied goings-on, and the kind of suave banter Grant could have negotiated in his sleep.

The film proved popular on account of its light touch and a barrage of special effects that were ahead of their time. The shoot was relatively easy for its main leads since they didn't have to show up on set for most of the scenes and they could lip-synch their lines whenever it suited them because they were invisible. Two years later a sequel, *Topper Takes a Trip*, was released, though without Grant. By now Topper had been conveniently dispatched to heaven while Ms Bennett was saddled with the task of reuniting Young with Burke after she sued him for divorce. (Obviously they went too far with his "liberation"). A third installment of the saga, *Topper Returns*, appeared in 1941, opting for a haunted house format this time, but still preserving the fanciful mood. There was even a TV series based on the idea in the 1950s.

Films about spirits were popular during the war years for obvious reasons. People liked to be reassured there was something after death because death was everywhere, and not only among the elderly. Spirits didn't so much cheat death as render it less horrific than it might otherwise be. If they were represented in a user-friendly manner there was money to be made. Films acted as placebos to widows, bereaved lovers and relatives of those killed violently in the trenches.

The Song of Bernadette (1943) won Jennifer Jones an Oscar for playing the French peasant girl who sees visions of Our Lady but as Theresa Sanders remarked in her book *Celluloid Saints*, this is a character many would find difficult to relate to today, a girl who "floats through life untouched by the struggles that plague the rest of us."[4] It hasn't worn well with time, coming to us from an age where a devotional ethos could be taken as read.

Bernadette, whose full name was Marie Bernarde Soubirous, claimed to have witnessed these visions from the age of fourteen. Not believed by many in her lifetime, she was finally canonized in 1933. Early on in the film Our Lady tells Bernadette to dig into the mud of Lourdes to locate a spring. She does indeed find spring water beneath the mud, and a blind man who washes in it appears to have had his sight restored. Bernadette is examined by a doctor but found to have no physical abnormalities. A psychiatrist is then called in to examine her. He suggests that her so-called visions are probably the result of paranoia. Afterward she's sent to a convent where a nun who's as sceptical as most of the other people in the film tells her that in a previous age she would have been burned at the stake.

But as time goes on, her story comes to be believed, and the direction is such that the viewer is won over too. Cinematographer Arthur Miller, no relation to the playwright, won an Oscar for the manner in which he lit up Jones' countenance with reflected light, using a spotlight behind her head to create the effect of a halo.[5] He under-lit the other actors by contrast. This device, combined with Jones' immense sense of self-belief, created an undoubted mystique that drew one into its web.

In 1945 Vincent Minnelli made *Yolanda and the Thief*, a musical fantasy in which a crooked gambler (Fred Astaire) pretends to be the guardian angel of an heiress played by Lucille Bremer in order to gain her fortune. He's exposed when the real angel (Leon Ames) shows up.

Blithe Spirit (1945 also) was an adaptation of a Noel Coward play featuring Margaret Rutherford as a medium who calls forth the ghost of Rex Harrison's dead wife after Harrison, a novelist, asks her to because he's working on a thriller about a homicidal spiritualist. Being of a smug, skeptical disposition, he doesn't for a second believe his wife will appear but she does, as a babbling Kay Hammond. This causes him to exclaim, "I am pained to observe that seven years in the echoing vaults of eternity have in no way impaired your native vulgarity." The pair of them spar, leading to tension between Harrison and his present wife (Constance Cummings) in a witty three-hander. The film was marred by Harrison's almost dandified nonchalance, which was decidedly unspooky, thereby bumping up the comedic element at the expense of the supernatural one, but it's a very polished piece of work. An ensemble effort that exudes professionalism, its theme of "astral bigamy" was certainly original.

One of the most popular films of all time is Frank Capra's *It's A Wonderful Life*, a 1946 offering about a decent, confused man overcome by depression. James Stewart played George Bailey, an architect in a small town whose dreams of career advancement haven't come to pass. He feels worthless and contemplates suicide before an angel named Clarence (Henry Travers) tells him how important he has been to so many people over the years with his kindness. Bailey takes this in and puts all thoughts of ending his life away from him, and cozies up to his wife (Donna Reed) in the cheesy finale.

The manner in which Bailey is saved from self-destruction in this movie is classic "Capra-corn," the scenes that Glenn Hopp refers to as the "unborn" sequence making him realize just how meaningful his life has been.[6] It's roses all the way in the final scene as God's in his heaven and all is right with the world. Clearly, this is a film which could not be made today, or at least not in this way, without being laughed out of the cinema. It's a celebration of ordinariness, the redemption of a man who goes from feeling he's worth more dead than alive to someone who sees miracles all around him.

A "feel-good" film decades before that term was invented, its topsy-turvying of Bailey's circumstances is too simplistic as he goes from the bottom of the valley to the highest peak of the mountain in less than two hours. Could a genuine suicide case empathize with this cathartic transmogrification? Because the film presents us with a coy resolution it's actually a betrayal of the kind of dark feelings Bailey has at the outset, seeing a lining in every cloud. You have to feel that the change of heart evinced by the town's population doesn't ring at all true. If Bailey was aware there was this untapped goodwill in his fellow man he couldn't have been driven to the depths of despair we witness at the outset. Capra ushers in the final felicities with such conviction, however, you hardly notice the film's unwavering falseness until it's well over.

Bailey has actually lived a very fulfilled life and Capra makes no effort to explain to us why he doesn't realize that. He's refused to sell the family business to a tycoon, he saved his brother from drowning, and he prevented another person from being poisoned. Are these things that people actually forget? Are they consistent with the plight of a man who feels so worthless he contemplates hurling himself into eternity because of a financial problem?

We don't tend to analyze the film too much today because it's either loved or hated by Capra enthusiasts or Capra cynics. As such it's untouchable, a relic of an era, as much a part of movie lore as any other minor classic—and as seasonal as Santa himself. To paraphrase Nicolas Kent, it's a film where a heavenly world helps a man to understand this one.[7]

Curiously enough, the man who plays Clarence, Henry Travers, was reformed a year before by Ingrid Bergman when she appealed to his better instincts to part with his cash for her rundown school in *The Bells of St. Mary's.* Capra revealed, "I thought it was the greatest film I ever made. Better yet, I thought it was the greatest film *anyone* ever made."[8] He seemed to be blind to its implausibilities, blind to its sweeter-than-sweet sentiment, blind to the sea-change in a town that goes from narrow-mindedness to Pleasantville without a by-your-leave. And in a way he's right because when you're operating on this level conventional disbelief has to be suspended, or at least postponed. Taken on a superficial level, the film is a joy to behold but the cotton candy life put before us here bears only a tenuous similarity to the real world.

For Capra it wasn't so much a film as a cause. He wrote in his autobiography that for him it expressed his love for "the homeless and the loveless; for her whose cross is heavy and him whose touch is ashes; for the Magdalenes stoned by hypocrites and the afflicted Lazaruses with only dogs to lick their sores."[9]

Is it James Stewart's best performance? It was certainly the one he put most into. The reason for this is probably his great degree of empathy with the character he played. What Bailey was going through in the architectural field as the film starts, Stewart was experiencing in films. He felt disenchanted with them and wanted out. He'd just come back from the Second World War and found the film industry rather trite, an unabashed indulgence in saccharine emotion. He also felt his powers as an actor were waning.

One day on the set, Lionel Barrymore, who played the banker in the film, heard him sounding off in this vein. Barrymore told Stewart not to speak such rubbish, that he was a fine actor and someone who influenced lots of people with his performances. He asked him if he thought it was more decent to "drop bombs on people than to bring rays of sunshine into their lives with your acting talent."[10] He ended by saying that he thought acting was one of the noblest professions in the world.

Stewart took this in and changed his attitude, much like Bailey did after being visited by Clarence. He thrust himself full force into the rest of the film and it paid off in spades.

Having said that, the film lost half a million dollars upon its release. It was critically acclaimed and nominated for a slew of Oscars but there were also dissenting voices. "So mincing as to border on baby talk," proclaimed the *New Yorker*.[11] It was unashamedly treacly but plugged into some need for psychic uplift in a society sorely in need of same. A lot of people list it as their favorite film of all time but a lot also as their pet hate. As such, what we're really speaking about is our own orientations. What it did it did very well but if Capra is trying to tell us every potential suicide can be rescued by a personal Clarence this won't wash. Some problems are insoluble and for some people suicide *is* a way out. This is the blunt fact of the matter. Stewart played a sentimentalist down on his luck, not somebody trying to threaten the cosmic order with dark murmurings. As such, his rehabilitation isn't so much a statement that life is worth living for all men as a slick piece of cutesiness.

"People called me a kind of movie Pollyanna," Capra himself admitted "and I guess maybe I was."[12] He said that because of the war people wanted escape, even slapstick. In such a context his vision of life was too dark by far. Stewart concluded that "Maybe it was just the wrong time to make the picture."[13] Maybe, but time has been kind to it. It's almost a perennial on Christmastime TV, its darkness, in the words of one writer, becoming swallowed up by a kind of "seasonal bauble."[14] In 1974 Sheldon Leonard had this to say, "For a while it was fashionable to dismiss Frank's work as over-sentimental, but now that we're emerging from a dark period the permanent appeal of his pictures is again becoming apparent."[15]

Cary Grant played an angel in *The Bishop's Wife* in 1947, appearing as the answer to a prayer from a bishop (David Niven) suffering from a crisis of faith. Producer Sam Goldwyn wanted Jean Arthur for the female lead but after expressing initial interest she dropped out due to pregnancy. Goldwyn was livid and rang up her husband to say he didn't just "screw" his wife but Goldwyn too. He wanted Grant so much he delayed production for six months until he was free to do it. As soon as filming started, however, he thought Grant's acting was too rarefied. Goldwyn asked him to inject more virility into the role but Grant refused.

"I won't be happy playing it that way," Grant said, "And you want me to be happy, don't you, Mr Goldwyn?" Goldwyn replied, "I don't give a damn whether you're happy or not. You're going to be here only a few weeks, and the picture will be out for a long time. I'd prefer if you were unhappy now and then we can all be happy later." Grant found his character "a rather conceited, impudent, high-minded magician."[16] As a result he couldn't get into the part the way he wanted to.

Goldwyn fired the film's director, William Seiter, after viewing the first week's filming. He canned every scene Seiter shot and rebuilt a whole new set at a staggering cost of $900,000. Grant had to be paid a further $100,000 overtime while the production shut down for six weeks. Henry Koster, the new director, was equally unhappy with Grant and asked him to swap roles with Niven. Grant resolutely refused.

Tension flared on the set, both between Grant and Koster and also with the actress who replaced Arthur, Loretta Young. When it was "sneaked" it didn't look good and Goldwyn, in desperation, drafted Billy Wilder and Charles Brackett to write some new scenes. They did their best but the film flopped anyway. Goldwyn, a man who once said "I'd hire the devil himself if he could write me a good story," was distraught.[17]

The Ghost and Mrs. Muir, also made in 1947 had Gene Tierney playing an impoverished widow who moves into a seaside cottage inhabited by the ghost of a ribald mariner played by Rex Harrison. He first tries to scare her off, as he has done all visitors before, but she's too plucky for this and slowly but surely the pair start a romance. She also makes him lose his boorish personality.

Anxious that she stay in the old house after her money runs out, Harrison suggests ghost-writing a book for her—literally. When it's accepted by a publisher surprise is elicited that it was written by a woman considering its macho nature. Tierney then has a romance with another author (George Sanders).

Harrison is gracious in his acceptance of the fact that she's making her life away from him. "You've made your choice," he tells her, "the only choice you *could* make. You've chosen life and that's how it should be. And that's why I'm going away, m'dear. I can't help you now. I can only confuse you more and destroy whatever chance you have left of happiness. Whether you meet fair winds or foul, make your own way to the harbor."

When it turns out that Sanders is already married Tierney is devastated. Harrison has disappeared from her life so now she has nobody. She can't be with him until she dies. When she does, they're reunited for eternity. The critic Alain Gersault believes the film resembles *Blithe Spirits* in the sense that it posits the theory that a ghost-like state is the only one that results in everlasting love.

It was directed by Joseph Mankiewicz with humor and grace, neatly sidestepping the pitfalls of sentimentalism. Arguably the least frightening ghost story ever committed to celluloid, it bounces along merrily with a leisurely romantic charm. Lee Kovacs described Harrison's character as a kind of Heathcliff figure perched between the eras of eighteenth century Gothic and nineteenth century romantic. He's passionate and full of *bonhomie*, and inexorably welded to the woman who calls him up. She's the catalyst that brings him into existence and she alone fosters his immortality by the book she writes. One writer holds the view that the film is "the only ghost film not to have *believed* in ghosts, in the possibility of their existence, not even from the point of view of dramatic interest . . . In *The Ghost and Mrs Muir* the nature of the phantom is something precise: 'A ghost is the fear one has of it.' The fear or the desire."[18]

Everything is directed with a light touch, especially scenes like the one where Tierney starts to undress in front of a portrait of the captain and suddenly becomes conscious that he's looking at her. She puts a shawl over the mirror where the eyes are reflected to protect her modesty. The film was generally well-regarded, though the critic from *Sunday Graphic* uttered a dissenting voice when he said he couldn't understand the appeal of a film which consisted of a hero who did nothing but haunt and a hero-ine who did nothing but sip milk. Philip Dunne, who wrote the script, felt it would have been more successful if Harrison had been better known in Hollywood and if his "salty" language didn't have to be "bowdlerized" due to the censorial constraints of the time.[19]

In *Here Comes Mr. Jordan* (1949) a boxer played by Robert Montgom-ery is killed and then, when he reaches the Pearly Gates, is given another identity by the celestial gatekeeper (Claude Rains) because he wasn't ready to be received into the hereafter. Hence he has to serve out more temporal time in a new body. *Angels in the Outfield*, made in 1951, dealt with a struggling baseball team that's helped along its way by divine intervention. It was, like so many of these types of spiritual films, re-made in 1994.

Jean Seberg, who would later commit suicide, won the coveted part of Joan of Arc in *St. Joan* (1957). Otto Preminger chose her from over 18,000 other hopefuls in a nationwide search that was the biggest since David O. Selznick went looking for a suitable Scarlett O'Hara for *Gone With the Wind* eighteen years previously. Preminger was apparently taken with Seberg's "special aura of youthful innocence and spontaneous acting ability."[20] She was only seventeen years of age but her parents (reluctantly) allowed her to sign a contract. She was over the moon to have landed the role but it was a poisoned chalice.

"Preminger was ruthless in his quest for perfection," Rona Wheaton wrote, "and he made the film a misery for Joan, bullying and belittling her into timidity."[21] Seberg told *Show* magazine in August 1963, "I was a better actress the first day I auditioned for Otto Preminger than all the time we worked together."[22] He bullied her relentlessly, which destroyed her confidence. The script was written by Graham Greene from George Bernard Shaw's play but she couldn't do it justice, playing down the drama to a point where it was almost non-existent. The "voices" she heard weren't so much those of God as Preminger. Seberg afterward confessed that of her two abiding memories of the film—being burned at the stake and being burned by the critics—the second hurt more.

Ingmar Bergman's *The Seventh Seal* (1957), by contrast, was a masterpiece. The story of an angst-ridden 14th century knight returning from the Crusades to a country decimated by the Black Plague, its most famous scene has the knight (Max Von Sydow) playing chess with Death, his own life hinging on the outcome of the game. It's a film about religious doubt but the very fact of personifying Death seems to suggest the grudging possibility that another kind of absolute, like God himself, might exist. It was before its time in its head-on confrontation with absurdity though the treatment and tone was more in keeping with the medieval setting. The apex of Bergman's achievement, and the film with which he's still most associated today, it forced people to look into their hearts and souls and face the prospect of an eternal abyss and still be somehow uplifted.

In one scene Sydow asks Death, played with crushing starkness by Bengt Ekerot, "Why, in spite of everything, is God a baffling reality that I can't shake off?" He appears to be suggesting that he doesn't actually want faith, that God is an inconvenient albatross on his back. This goes against the grain of his terror of death, and Death. If he carries this "baffling" reality to its conclusion, surely death is the portal to eternity. Woody Allen, a lifelong devotee of Bergman's works, believes that, for Catholics, death is a promotion.

Taking its title from the Book of Revelation, which threatened chaos following the opening of a seventh seal "after which there was silence in heaven about the space of half an hour," the film itself is, in a sense, about silence too. A precursor of Beckettian waiting, it holds us in thrall with its sense of dismal longing.

Corpses abound on Bergman's arid landscapes as his tired knight fights his most daunting struggle of all: the one inside his own questioning self. This is the dark after-teatime of the soul, the last, desperate grasp of a drowning man onto a cliff-face, only to find the very rocks eroding before him. It depicts life as a sick joke and death as an even sicker one. The only real sin is idealism, the only mistake hope. A malevolent deity seems to preside over the carnage He has created, His Stygian emissary like a perverse alter-ego of His own sneering prescience. Antonius Block (Von Sydow) endures the winter of his discontent while Bergman wonders if there's anything behind the veil of mystery other than grim mischief.

The Seventh Seal came out the same year as John Osborne's *Look Back in Anger*, Jack Kerouac's *On the Road* and the English translation of Jean-Paul Sartre's *The Transcendence of the Ego*. With the pre-eminence of kitchen sink drama, "beat" realism and the invasion of a foreign, atheistic culture, society was also vouchsafed the launch of the Russian space mobile Sputnik. It was as if the world of outer space had become people's substitute for heaven. The uppermost reaches of the clouds were no longer celestial havens but rather landmarks to explore with mechanistic technology. The German philosopher Friedrich Nietzsche had told us God was dead. Bergman wasn't going quite that far, but invisibility ran death a close second.

Why, asks the knight, should God "hide himself in a mist of half-spoken promises and unseen miracles?" Why, in other words, is faith so important? He receives no answers to these questions. "Why can't I kill God within me?" he then persists, "Why does he live on in this painful and humiliating way even though I curse him and want to tear Him out of my heart?" It's as if the ultimate mystery is almost cast as a necessary evil for this masochistic interrogator.

"I want knowledge, not faith," the knight cries out despairingly, "I want God to stretch out his hand toward me, to reveal himself and speak to me." That's hardly likely to happen within the film's bleak compass. When he complains to Death that his God is silent, Death replies taunt-ingly, "Perhaps no one is there." "Then life is an outrageous horror," he complains, "No one can live in the face of death, knowing that all is nothingness." Death points out that most people don't consider such absolutes in the normal course of events, to which the knight responds, "But one day they will have to stand at that last moment of life and look towards the darkness." The irony of this exchange is that Death is non-chalant and the knight persistent, a contravention of what one might expect, having been weaned on films where the Grim Reaper seems to delight in reminding mortal beings that "We know not the day nor the hour."

The knight's God has left his phone off the hook, it appears. Man can continue to ring or hang up, but he isn't likely to get a call himself. Faith has to be blind adherence, but this was difficult when the Black Death had decimated everything in sight. How could a "good" God be responsible for the plague, he wonders, in effect enunciating the age-old problem of evil. God had to have foreseen it, so how could he sit by and watch its horrors unfold? If he wanted mankind to be happy, why didn't he cut to the chase and offer us all eternal bliss from the beginning? The Christian answer to this, of course, is that we have to "earn" our reward in this "vale of tears."

Faith would perhaps be easier for the knight were he to take a Kierkegaardian "leap" into it, but he tries to reach it through reason, which is always going to be a forlorn goal. The critic Mary Litch observed that the reason God refuses to announce himself to the knight is because the knight is looking for proof of his existence whereas God would prefer blind faith without any empirical data attached to it. He won't be intimidated.

Philip Strick compared the film to another Bergman classic, *Wild Strawberries*. In both of these films, Strick thought, "The only certainty is death, the only compensation is the family unit, the only unknown is God's ultimate purpose, if any."[23] The most rueful scene is the one where the knight pours his heart out in confession to a man he believes to be a priest. In reality it's Death he's been speaking to all the time.

Bell, Book and Candle (1958) starred Kim Novak as a New York witch who casts a spell over publisher James Stewart to make him fall in love with her. Her scheme backfires when she finds she's in love with him too. As a result she loses her magic powers. This we realize when she starts to cry. It was good fun, but hardly significant. Neither would Stewart be one's first choice of a romantic lead. It's hard to imagine Novak falling for him even as a normal woman, never mind a sorceress, and indeed renouncing her witch-like powers for him. If the film was dependent on the romantic angle to carry it, it would have bombed. It also needed healthy support from Jack Lemmon, Elsa Lanchester and Ernie Kovacs to divert one's attention from such shortcomings. Novak is also so enchanting in that feline way of hers, making her actually resemble her cat, that you find yourself concentrating on her rather than Stewart in their scenes together. She was never a great actress but she had a presence, accentuated by the fact that she seemed to appear in fewer movies than she should have, eventually doing a Garbo on Hollywood. But the film in general is of little worth except for its curiosity value.

Stewart doesn't convince the viewer he's fallen for her in the first place, which makes his subsequent surprise at her sorcery anti-climactic.

The ending is so tame you feel it might almost have worked better as a formulaic drama, with Lemmon and Lanchester getting more of the foreground. When Stewart jilts his lover for Novak with the words "I'm a cad," only the very gullible could buy this. Lemmon himself would have done Stewart's role far more justice.

This is a forgettable film, as were most of those which followed it, both in the sixties and seventies, containing any form of spiritual or religious import. But then in 1977 we had *Oh God!*, a film which made the world sit up: a religious comedy with a difference because it had the veteran comedian George Burns playing God opposite John Denver, who was making his screen debut as the manager of a supermarket.

Denver first hears from God via a letter offering him an "interveiw" (sic). He's surprised that the deity, having created the planet, hasn't mastered the art of spelling. When he meets him, he owns up to some other cosmic errors. "Tobacco was one of my big mistakes," Burns admits. So were ostriches and avocados.

His attitude to life is folksy and capricious. One gets the distinct impression he created mankind on a whim, without much forethought of where it all might lead. Perhaps his mistakes resulted from the fact that he created the world not in six days, but one.

When Denver asks him why he, a mere supermarket manager, was chosen to be the bearer of God's message, he replies, "Life is a crapshoot. The millionth customer who crosses the bridge gets to shake hands with the governor. You're better than some, not as good as others, but you crossed the bridge at the right time." In other words it's all happenstance, not providence. This isn't exactly the theological party line on the nature of existence, but then this God appears to have feet of clay.

Asked whether Jesus is his son, he replies grudgingly in the affirmative, but adds that so is Buddha, Mohammad, Moses, Denver himself, and even the man who said there was no room at the inn when Jesus was born. Pressed on whether he's omniscient, he allows that he's "big" on the past and present, but hasn't the foggiest about the future.

Toward the end of this strangely irresponsible film, Denver exposes a revivalist preacher (Paul Sorvino) as a fraud, Burns himself defending Denver on a slander charge brought by Sorvino. It's a comedy so we permit it its flamboyant flourishes. It's a pity, however, that one of its central lines "If you find it hard to believe in me, maybe it would help to know that I believe in you" has been lifted almost literally from *The Keys of the Kingdom*. Bryan Stone also felt it called into question "at least two of the qualities classically associated with God—omnipotence and omni-science."[24] Listening to God's folksy philosophy in this movie, Pauline Kael contended, was "like sinking in a mountain of white flour." It was hard to disagree, though Burns' *chutzpah* is infectious.

Burns drives a car in the film. He also makes it rain inside it while it's sunny outside, and cleans fallen leaves in a city park. Spiritualist revisionism has arrived in Hollywood. At one point when his Godly status is being challenged in a courtroom, he "proves" it by going suddenly invisible and walking outside, the doors opening miraculously for him as he does so.

The film was a success, so nobody was surprised to see *Oh God: Book II* three years later, or indeed *Oh God, You Devil* in 1984. The third and final outing had Burns playing both God and the devil, which was an original idea—the only original thing about the film really. It's probably fair to say, though, that the new-fangled laidback deity mainlined by Burns paved the way for the kind of contemporary depictions we see in, say, the television animated series *God, the Devil and Bob* and also certain movies like *Bruce Almighty* (2003) where Morgan Freeman is having a hard time up in the clouds after realizing that, even though he's omnipotent, he still can't please all the people all the time.

Warren Beatty jumped on the fantasy bandwagon in 1978 with *Heaven Can Wait*, a remake of *Here Comes Mr. Jordan* in which he plays a Super Bowl quarterback who's whisked into heaven before his time due to a celestial boo-boo, God being only human, as George Burns informed us with some conviction two years previously. The main character was originally a boxer rather than a football player, and Beatty wanted Muhammad Ali to play him, but because Ali wasn't available he changed him to a football player and opted to take the role himself, even if he was somewhat old for that activity. Beatty was forty; his character a mere thirty. It was a frothy vehicle, comedy on gossamer wings, but it was a huge hit, much to the surprise of all concerned, especially Beatty, who did it against most of his advisors' wishes.

Beatty plays Joe Pendleton, who's killed in a car accident just before a big game. On his way to heaven he realizes his demise has been premature. His escort (Buck Henry) and the Archangel Mr Jordan (James Mason) rush his soul back to the scene of the accident, but it's too late because he's been cremated so instead he's transplanted into the body of one Leo Farnsworth, a financier whose wife and her lover (Dyan Cannon and Charles Grodin, respectively) plot his murder while he falls in love with the delectable Julie Christie.

For Beatty, who'd been a Bratpacker before the term was invented, it was a return to safe movie-making. Was this really the same man who had appeared in *Mickey One, All Fall Down* and *Bonnie & Clyde*?

Alexander Walker bristled in the *Evening Standard*, "The direction is so clumsy, some of the heavenly bodies look even more ponderous than the earthly ones."[25] Asked why he took on such an unlikely project, Beatty explained that some of his friends had died recently, which caused him a degree of depression. The film, he hoped, would give him some escapist relief from his gloomy thoughts. When he asked Christie to co-star with him she only consented grudgingly. The pair of them had had a high profile affair which was now over. She really only took the role as a favor to him.

One day she told him she couldn't understand why he was making commercial films like this as opposed to the great continental directors like Fassbinder. Beatty took her point but said a film about the ultimate issues, even a comedy one, might strike a chord. He was right. The public loved the message of *"Amor vincit omnia"* and also warmed to the Cannon and Grodin cameos. Even the poster, featuring Beatty in wings and track suit, with his head lowered and his feet crossed, became famous. Nobody could explain, though, why he called the film *Heaven Can Wait*, thereby confusing viewers who thought they were going to see a re-make of Ernst Lubitsch's 1943 comedy about a man trying unsuccessfully to be admitted into hell.

This, in contrast, concerns transience. As Beatty himself realized, everybody reaches a point in their life when they look at themselves in the mirror and realize they're getting on in years. Defending himself on the charge that re-makes were exercises in plagiarism, he insisted that there were really only five plots; in this sense almost every film was effectively a re-make. This one was beset with on-set rows. Cannon tried to upstage Christie by asking for "alphabetical" billing, while Beatty fell out with Henry and, inexplicably, Christie. Only James Mason, appropriately enough, acted in a civilized manner—as befitted the deity. Beatty had originally wanted Cary Grant for this part but Mason made it his own.

The film earned $77 million at the box office, a figure not to be sneezed at. Beatty and Cannon both received Oscar nominations, Beatty losing out to Jon Voight. From the podium his sister Shirley MacLaine, ironically a vocal spokesperson for reincarnation, tried to console him by calling him "sweet and talented," adding "Just imagine what you could accomplish if you tried celibacy." Beatty smiled at her, perhaps his greatest acting job for a while. His then-girlfriend Diane Keaton was in the adjoining seat. She might have been thinking of Woody Allen's quip, "If I'm reincarnated, I want to comeback as Warren Beatty's fingertips."

Pauline Kael said it wasn't so much movie-making as "glorified piffle-making." It was shot in soft focus, she claimed, "because if Beatty raised his voice or expressed anything other than a pacific nature, the genteel, wafer-thin whimsy would crumble."[26] She referred to him as "an elfin little Jesus" and he never forgave her. In an elaborate bid to avenge the slight, he offered her a movie contract herself to see if she could do any better. Amazingly she accepted and worked on a project for some months before giving up in abject depression and retreating to the relative safety of the sidelines, leaving the movie quarterbacks to do what they did best, and worst.

Heaven Can Wait and *Here Comes Mr. Jordan* weren't the only movies to feature celestial errors. In *A Matter of Life and Death* in 1946, a pilot played by David Niven survives a crash even though he's not meant to. It now sounded like it was time for Hollywood to re-examine Albert Einstein's dictum, "God does not play dice with the universe."

Such a dictum could certainly be applied to *Altered States*, a 1980 offering in which William Hurt played a scientist who's lost his belief in God. He then looks for the meaning of life in a sensory deprivation chamber in the hope that his hallucinogenic experiences here will unlock some primal emotions. The film featured big name actors and was directed by Ken Russell. The script was written by Paddy Chayevsky. A psychedelic amalgam that's far too "sixties" for comfort, it exudes a strong sophomorish vibe when Hurt travels to Mexico to experiment with yet another drug. At times like this one feels back in the era when people read Carlos Castenada as they sat in bedsits with their caftans and their Zen platitudes.

Hurt, as Eddie Jessup, marries Emily (Blair Brown) at the beginning of his research. She's behind him in his ambition until it starts to take over his life. When he starts to change physically it's time for Emily to get worried. Jessup's ostensible brief is to study schizophrenia but his real passion lies further afield. When one of his patients is given a drug to bring on a hallucination that might help him to diagnose her, he asks her how she feels and she replies, "Like my heart is being touched by Christ." Jessup dearly wants to get to the place she's at.

As a child he had visions of angels and saints but he lost his faith at the age of sixteen when his father died of cancer. He believed that his father had gone beyond death and discovered there was no afterlife—the film's first big stretch on credibility. He goes to Mexico to sample some "sacred" mushrooms. A shaman informs him that the experience will return him to his "first" soul, i.e., his primordial identity. "You will be propelled into the void," the shaman says, "You will see a spot. It will become a crack. Out of this will come your unborn soul."

The experience he has isn't quite what he expected. He sees flashing lights, tribal dancing and visions of his wife. Then a snake nearly strangles him. After he wakes up he sees a dead lizard beside him. The shaman tells him he killed it while in his trance. Russell's influence goes into overdrive when Hurt turns into an ape and starts rampaging through a zoo like a demented refugee from a science fiction B-movie. Afterward he does indeed regress to the beginning of time, but almost at the cost of his life. His wife, who's become alienated from him, rescues him—but nobody can rescue the film itself from collapsing under the weight of its own pretensions. Some people took it seriously, to wit one Timothy L. Suttor, who described it as "myth in the deepest sense, a Man-Woman dance where He and She are cosmic forces and the real plot is the theological structure of the visions."[27]

Suttor loses the run of himself completely when he informs us that this dance consists of "a relentless interrogation by the modern scientific worldview of childish Bible-with-crucifix piety." He poses the question, "If the mind travels back through the cosmos of Darwin and Einstein, what ultimate reality will it discover?" He answers it himself: "None at all, of course, because modern science is not the road to God. But neither, apparently, is modern religion, because it's too afraid of philosophy, beauty and science."[28]

Suttor concedes, "Still, Eddie Jessup has something metaphysical going for him—Emily, the timeless enigma-sphinx of his vision, Eve to his Adam. The couple, true to each other by first being true to truth, is a greater theophany than a million visions. Though erotic, their bond transcends the erotic, transcends them, and transcends the universe."

This kind of psychobabble sounds like something concocted by Russell's PR company. He ends by saying, "In Russell's theology, the base of our troubles isn't so much original sin as an almost insurmountable distaste for reality."[29] I would go along with this but it still doesn't make the film any less pretentious.

Not surprisingly, Chayevsky eventually disowned it, feeling Russell had bowdlerized his script, which was in turn based on his own novel, in the editing process. This is most likely what happened. Hurt's final revelation goes, "The final truth of all things is that there is no final truth. It's human life that's real." Could Russell not have given us something more after 103 minutes? It's hard not to feel short-changed by the difficulty of trying to get one's head around Hurt trying to get his head around himself.

You could say the same for the Christopher Reeve vehicle *Somewhere in Time*, which was made the same year. Reeve was high on the hype from his recent role as *Superman* when he took this on but it was one of his more galling career choices and almost sent his career down the tubes. The idea of a man who has "everything" but feels dead inside is hackneyed. It needed more imagination than Reeve, or the director Jeannot Szwarc, can muster up to breathe new life into a tired formula. As lonely playwright Richard Collier, Reeve finds himself falling in love with the portrait of a woman who lived nearly seventy years before so he travels back through time to meet her—as you would.

Reeve knew it was a tearjerker and predicted there would be cynics in the audience who would hate it, the same kind of people who thought the yodelling kids from *The Sound of Music* should have been drowned at the beginning of the picture.

How right he was. Jane Seymour, as Reeve's obscure object of desire, struggles against impossible material. Christopher Plummer is her manager but the miraculous success of *The Sound of Music* didn't repeat itself for him. The film became an embarrassment for all concerned.

Time travel films are hit-and-miss affairs. When they bomb, they bomb big. This had few saving graces. Superman became Superbore, his face too bland to convey genuine yearning. He put it all down to experience and ran back to the comparatively safe terrain of *Superman II*, then in gestation. It took a good man to know what was outside his remit. His bank balance lay somewhere in space, not time.

A third 1980 offering, Bob Fosse's riveting *All That Jazz*, proved a more durable investigation of an epiphany. A blistering take on Fosse's life—and death—it must be one of the most unique biopics of all time, managing to combine stunning choreography with a frenzied editing style that almost nonchalantly takes us into the hereafter when he suffers a fatal heart attack.

To wean him into eternity, his real-life lover Jessica Lange appears as an angel hovering over his hospital bed. Or is she meant to be God? It's all rather ambiguous. She's wearing a bridal dress which she then removes. She's got white underclothes and a rose attached to her wrist. She's erotic, and also strangely comforting. The scene is even more arresting when we consider that Fosse was an atheist. Lange flirts with him, preparing him for the afterlife with some casual repartee. Nine years later, in Steven Spielberg's *Always*, another angel (Audrey Hepburn) will be similarly comforting to a dead man, but without the erotic underlay.

We don't learn her name until the final credits—Angelique. This obviously suggests we're meant to think of Lange as an angel rather than a God (the idea of a female God won't reach the screen until *Dogma* in 1999). At the end of the film Fosse walks toward her, the assumption being that death will bring sexual consummation. Andrew Greeley writes: "Fosse approaches death and God not as a religiously convinced man, and certainly not as a propagandist, but as a thoroughly secular human being trying to make sense out of his own tormented life."[30] The result, Greeley states, "is a daring metaphor for the possibility that God is not merely love, but passionate love, a metaphor elaborated without the slightest concern for its theological orthodoxy, or its basis in scripture and tradition—about all of which matters Fosse could not have cared less."[31]

Douglas Trumbull's *Brainstorm* was released in 1983. The circumstances surrounding this film are almost as eerie as its plot. The story of a man who invents a contraption intended to put him in touch with the Absolute, it ended up achieving that ambition for one of its stars, Natalie Wood, who drowned in the course of filming. Rumors abounded of an affair with Christopher Walken, who plays the inventor, which angered her then-husband Robert Wagner and led to an argument that indirectly resulted in her drowning. Wood had had a pathological fear of water all her life so there was a double irony in the manner of her demise.

Walken's device—a headset which records sensations and then transmits them to the mind of another—proves his own undoing when he puts it on to try and experience death itself after another scientist (Louise Fletcher) has a heart attack while using it. He doesn't only experience death—he dies.

Thereafter he travels to both heaven and hell and is unwilling to return to life despite the protestations of his wife (Wood). He eventually deigns to come back, in a climax that's more laughable than elucidatory. The screenplay was by Joel Rubin, who also wrote the screenplay of two other films extolling the merits of the "death experience," *Ghost* and *Jacob's Ladder*. All three are, in their way, fatuous and half-baked. Trumbull was the man behind the special effects in *Close Encounters* so it was a serious career lapse for him too.

All of Me (1984) had Steve Martin playing an attorney whose body becomes haunted by the soul of Lily Tomlin after her plan to have it lodged inside Victoria Principal goes awry. The right side of Martin's body is controlled by Tomlin but the left by himself, which gives him lots of opportunities to indulge in the kind of idiotic clowning that was vaguely amusing for some years before it became irritatingly mannered.

Ghostbusters, another 1984 offering, was a staggering box-office success. No expense was spared on the production values but the profit margin was still huge. It also went on to spawn a huge number of spin-off products. The concept was pretty simple: three men are employed to rid the Big Apple of its unwanted spirits. Throw in a catchy song, some snazzy special effects and children everywhere went wild over it. Bill Murray's role was originally supposed to have been played by John Belushi before he overdosed and died. Dan Aykroyd and Harold Ramis were his sidekicks. Looking at it now one wonders what all the fuss was about. There was even a sequel made in 1989, the trio temporarily unemployed because of a restraining order prohibiting them from engaging in "paranormal warfare" until an evil spirit accelerates their return to active duty. By now the franchise had become almost a licence to print money.

Maxie (1985) was unique in that it featured a female ghost without a male one in tow—a Hollywood precedent. Feminism had finally found its supernatural voice. Glenn Close plays a dowdy secretary who finds herself possessed by the effervescent spirit of a silent movie star. Her personality becomes more upbeat as a result but as time goes on she gets tired of all the high jinks and wants her boring old self back.

Tim Burton gave a new slant to ghost movies in *Beetlejuice* (1988), mixing gore with a feel-good factor in a film that has Alec Baldwin and Geena Davis playing a couple who are killed in a car accident. Informed that it may be fifty years before they can enter the gates of Paradise, they don't fancy spending all that time haunting their old home because it's now occupied by two insufferable new tenants, Catherine O'Hara and Jeffrey Jones. They employ a spirit, the eponymous Michael Keaton, enjoying himself hugely as a typically repulsive Burton creation to scare them off. Instead he falls in love with their daughter Winona Ryder in her breakthrough role.

Steven Spielberg, who seemed incapable of making a turkey, finally fell from grace in 1989 with *Always*, the tale of a pilot (Richard Dreyfuss) who dies in a crash but returns to earth to act as guardian angel to another pilot (Brad Johnson) on the same base. It was a re-make of 1944's *A Guy Named Joe*, where Spencer Tracy played a pilot who died in World War II combat but returned from the dead to reassure his grieving widow (Irene Dunne) that it was all right to fall in love with Van Johnson.

Always begins with Dreyfuss engaging in some fairly elaborate dare-devil antics in his plane, which fail to impress his girlfriend Dorinda (Holly Hunter). He promises to tone it down but before he can carry through on this—in the ironic tradition of adventure movies—his plane catches fire and he dies. The film now enters its ethereal dimension. He meets an angel, Hap (Audrey Hepburn), who tells him he's dead but can still help the living, i.e., his friend Ted Johnson, whose flying skills he can improve immeasurably by acting as his mentor. When Ted starts romancing Dorinda, Pete is understandably aggrieved and tries to spike the relationship. Hap tells Pete this is wrong; that he must show his true love for Dorinda by letting her go where her heart leads her. In the climax of the movie Pete takes Hap's advice and saves Dorinda's life when she gets into trouble in a plane and thus foregoes the opportunity to be united with him in death. At the film's close he's content to watch her romance with Ted bloom.

Always is Spielberg's only re-make. He adored *A Guy Named Joe* when he saw it as a child. It was, he confessed, the only movie ever to make him cry that didn't have a deer in it. When he was making *Jaws* with Dreyfuss he told him he wanted to film it, whereupon Dreyfuss said he had seen it at least thirty times himself. "If you cast anybody else in Tracy's role," he warned, "I'll kill you."[32] *A Guy Named Joe* warded off any criticism of being melodramatic or far-fetched because of its war context, which acted as a kind of credibility shield for it. Setting the re-make in a time of peace, Spielberg denied himself this privilege with the result that it comes across mawkishly to us with little suspension of disbelief.

The film is smugly Spielbergesque in the sense of everyone living happily ever after but as Pauline Kael asked: "Was there no one among Steven Spielberg's associates with the intellectual stature to convince him that his having cried at *A Guy Named Joe* when he was twelve was not a good enough reason for him to re-make it? Audrey Hepburn delivers transcendental inanities. Where has the actress gone, the one who gave a magnificent performance in *The Nun's Story*? There is no hint of her in this self-parody."[33]

Spielberg's first preferences for the main roles were Paul Newman and Robert Redford, but both wanted to play Pete so Dreyfuss was chosen instead. In early drafts of the film there were many gimmicks that he later jettisoned—incidents like Dreyfuss glowing, putting his hands through things and walking through walls. He decided to do away with special effects for the human story, which he felt was strong enough on its own.

As a weepie it hasn't aged as well as *A Guy Named Joe*, which was marred by military jingoism, but is still regarded warmly. This film, in contrast, has been accused of the Spielbergization of religion, a charge also laid at the door of *E.T.* and *Close Encounters*. Douglas Brode believed *Always* allowed Spielberg to continue his work as an "essentially religious film-maker, one who made moral fables palatable to modern audiences by presenting them within the context of seemingly secular entertainment."[34] Richard Blake suggested that "conservative Catholic theologians" would enjoy the film "but not many other people." He concluded that it was "quite successful as a parable, less so as a film."[35]

Spielberg originally wanted Sean Connery to play Hap but when Connery passed he brought Audrey Hepburn out of retirement for it. She agreed to do it only because time-wise it didn't infringe on the charity work with UNICEF which filled her final years. In fact she donated her $1 million fee to that organization.

The role, sadly, left much to be desired on all counts. This was a different type of angel than we were accustomed to. There were no wings; indeed, no concessions at all to the celestial. "Nobody knows what I am," Hepburn herself admitted, "not even Steven Spielberg. It's just plain old me with a sweater and slacks."[36] The film neatly bookended her career, the original screenplay having been written by Dalton Trumbo, who had made her famous by writing *Roman Holiday* as well. At the end she tells Dreyfuss, *apropos* her visitation, "I'm glad I lived, I am glad I was alive—with a chance to say goodbye." Spielberg also gave Hepburn a chance to say goodbye—but not much else.

Philip French suggested the main consolation the film offered was that we can now look forward to death, safe in the knowledge that our first sight after shuffling off the mortal coil would be the delectable Ms. Hepburn. It could have been another Spielberg classic if the formula worked. Unfortunately, Holly Hunter looking soulful and Dreyfuss administering to her on the sidelines proved embarrassing for all concerned. In the same way as Hepburn looked out of place, so did he. There was no sense of a spirit, just another person on the set. The camaraderie was well done but any film with "Smoke Gets In Your Eyes" as its center-piece song is making a big gamble on the tearjerker front. Audiences don't yield their emotions this cheaply, even diabetics.

Richard Dreyfuss isn't a romantic lead, and there's the rub. He's an adept actor, but he doesn't have the emotive vibe. *Always* pre-dated *Ghost* in the sense of featuring a dead person having to come to terms with his spirit status *apropos* a loved one who's still living, but that's where the comparison ended. Spielberg spent far too much time on the flying sequences to be able to carry the intimate scenes, which meant that this was a movie trying to skate off in two different directions simultaneously. Neither did Dreyfuss' "donkey" laugh help, or Hepburn looking for all the world like a Japanese waiter.

"A better title for *Always* would be *Forever*," wrote Sheila Benson in the *Los Angeles Times*, "which is roughly its running time."[37] Pauline Kael added, "Now that Spielberg is no longer twelve, hasn't he realized there's a queasiness in the idea of playing Cupid to the girl you loved and lost, and fixing her up with the next guy?"[38]

The critics were underwhelmed by the film's undisguised sentimentality but it could have been much worse. In an earlier cut, the final scene had Dorinda plunging into Hades in her plane and then ascending into heaven with Pete in tow. For this relief much thanks.

In *Field of Dreams* (also 1989) director Alden Robinson gave us a latterday *It's A Wonderful Life*, Kevin Costner playing a farmer who hears a voice telling him to dig up a cornfield and turn it into a baseball stadium. As a concept it could have bellyflopped—this wasn't 1946, after all—but it took off, wowing audiences all around America. It's a film about finding oneself, with baseball as a metaphor for larger questions. The mood was austere and enigmatic, which seemed to condone the sentimental fluff, or at least allow it to breathe more freely. Costner takes on a mysterious task on blind faith, building his field with the same kind of zeal Noah used to make his ark, albeit in a more bewildered manner. Only at the end of the film do we realize it's meant to be heaven. "If you build it, he will come," was the film's tagline: it became a mantra uttered by many long after the final credits rolled.

Both *Field of Dreams* and the Robert Redford film *The Natural* (1984) provide baseball stadiums where, as Joel Martin wrote in his book *Screening the Sacred*, "Dreams come true, past meets present, bitterness dissolves into kindness, suffering and loss meet compassion, and faith conquers all."[39] At the end of *Field of Dreams* a son plays "Catch" with his magically reincarnated father. As such, it creates a sacred space and time of mythic proportions. *The Natural*, meanwhile, goes back further to evoke the Arthurian legend of the knight's quest for the Holy Grail. In both cases America's legendary past is united with its most iconic contemporary sport in a package also welded to domestic harmony.

There were an inordinate number of spirit-movies made in 1990. *Ghost* led the pack, but many others tried to capitalize on its success. In this year alone we had *Flatliners, Heart Condition, Almost an Angel* and *Ghost Dad.*

Death remains the big taboo subject in films in any era but particularly our own, which was why *Flatliners* was a brave film for anyone to take on, particularly everyone's favorite girl-next-door Julia Roberts, who was just then beginning her love affair with the world's audiences. Playing a medical student who wants to have a near-death experience she allows herself to have her heart stopped and then be brought back to life. The ultimate fix? Perhaps, but there's a life to be got back to afterward.

The students take turns "killing" and then reviving one another, the pluckier among them trying to stay "dead" the longest. The book on which the film was based was written by Peter Filardi after a friend told him of a near-death experience he'd had while in the hospital. The title refers to the "dead" straight line on an EEG machine which registers clinical death.

There's a kind of Buddhist feel about the film in the sense that the characters aren't so much punished *for* their sins as *by* them. Kiefer Sutherland has treated a child badly in his past and is repaid in kind. William Baldwin has been chauvinistic with women and also gets a dose of his own medicine. And so on. Roberts seems to speak for all of them when she exclaims wryly, "Death beautiful? What a bunch of crap." Despite the experimental plot, the treatment is actually quite traditional, even didactic, the lesson being: don't dice with death or it will come back to haunt you—in this life, if not the next. Because everything has consequences. By the end of the film, they've all become chastened as a result of their "bad karma."

None of them emerge unscathed from the experience. "As the plot develops," one author wrote, "we discover that *Flatliners* is not actually about near-death experiences at all. It is about guilt, forgiveness and the transcendence of personal demons"[40] Put another way, "Questions of religious faith surface precisely at the point where science and technology reach their limits." Which means the film is really about the Promethean price one pays for playing God.[41]

It's not so much a film about death as life, and Joel Schumacher in the director's chair leaves us in little doubt that this is his primary interest. He explores themes like remorse and bereavement, all the buried emotions that have been triggered by this latter day Ivy League initiation rite ballyhoo. Be afraid, be very afraid.

Jerry Zucker's *Ghost* also had death at its core. Putting this title on a film didn't sound like good horse sense from a marketing point of view, but it hit a nerve in the collective psyche. Instead of frightening people it made them upbeat, resulting in a huge career lift for both of its stars Patrick Swayze and Demi Moore. Swayze plays a man who's murdered one night by money launderers soon after discovering some financial irregularities in the firm in which he works. Though his body is moribund, he refuses to let go of his earthly existence. Such is his love for Moore he wants to be with her all the time. Just after he's killed be reaches out his hand to touch her but it just goes through her. He's a reluctant spirit already, suffering the pangs of loneliness.

Swayze isn't threatening, being more like a guardian angel than anything else. He hasn't wanted to die, which makes everyone in the audience empathize with him all the more. Physically he's gone from his lover but his soul won't let go. He's a restless spirit, but with good reason. He has to protect her from the fate he suffered as she could be the next target of the money launderers.

At one point in the film he realizes Moore's cat can sense his presence so he uses this fact to get it to ward off a killer. Elsewhere he consults a mystic (Whoopi Goldberg) to try and make contact with Moore. In the end both of them accept their lots. It's a yuppie parable that just happened to hit the right note and made over $500 million at the box office.

Swayze has to learn to be a "good" ghost in this piece of serio-comic hokum. He has to learn to channel his anger into metaphysical areas instead of purely physical ones. The values here aren't much more subtle than a Disney cartoon. The love is mushy and the villains cardboard but Goldberg rescues it by being the one cast-member who seems unafraid to let us all know it's little more than nonsense. Her best line is when she says to Swayze, who's been pestering her incessantly, "Why don't you just find a *house* to haunt?"

At the end Swayze becomes resurrected, as it were, bathed in a halo of beatific light as the "bad" drug dealer gets carted off to "the other place."

The critic Dan Fainaru said he felt sorry for Swayze, who was used to beating people up in films, being reduced to punching mere air in this one. Iain Johnstone felt the film worked for this very reason, i.e. that Swayze refused to become a feather-headed figure in the clouds but continued on being relentlessly himself, a rather simple, even pathetic person unable to comprehend his new ethereal state. He has sadly died since these words were written but he bore his illness with great grace and courage. He must be looking down at the movie with some amusement, wherever he is, bemused by its beguiling vapidity.

We're not expected to take any of it seriously. A spirit that thinks it can hit a mugger isn't very bright. Neither is it consistent. If Swayze can walk through walls, or fly through the top of a subway, how can he then "stand" in the same subway the same as living people? Either one is of the spirit world or one isn't. You can't have it both ways. Swayze does, especially at the end, where the film totally sells out to the tearjerker element.

It could have been a disaster commercially as well as artistically but it worked. This was even more surprising considering it was reliant on an actor like Swayze, who had limited acting ability, to carry it. Moore underplays throughout, which provides a very necessary contrast to his frenetic sashaying about the place. As for Goldberg, she doesn't try and pretend she's in a film of any significance whatsoever, doing everything but winking at the audience to let us know how she feels about the whole charade.

Writing of the movie in his book *The Haunted Screen*, Lee Kovacs put it eloquently: "The ghost of the 1990s is a pale shadow of his predecessors. Stripped of his castle, or lonely house by the sea, today's apparition is homeless, forced to share the crowded, anxious space of the living. The modern ghost, the ghost of the streets, is no longer a solitary phenomenon but part of a group, a community of ghosts who, as a community, suffer the same anxieties of displacement, fear and loneliness that plague their human counterparts." Speaking more generally of the contemporary ghost, Kovacs claims that he's an uncertain figure, "The old, splendid example of the haunter fades, and merges into the *angst* and collective futility of the end-of-the-century world." Both man and ghost are, in fact, alike because they're both trapped in a "godless, chaotic world." In an inversion of the gothic *zeitgeist*, "Today's ghost must seek help from the living in order to survive." Put simply, the modern ghost isn't so much haunter as haunted.

The film has many parallels to *Always* even if they're not immediately apparent. In both cases the male protagonist has been unable to express his love for the woman in his life while alive. As an extension of this, the plots of both concern the "unfinished business" of the spirit in question rather than the life of the woman left behind. Thus Dreyfuss had to help Hunter get on with her life so he could attain the peace in death that he didn't have in life. Likewise, Swayze has to protect Moore from the fate he suffered and also express his love for her in both word and deed so he can rest in peace forever.

Bob Hoskins played a detective without medical sense in *Heart Condition*. He's just been dumped by his hooker girlfriend Chloe Webb, who prefers dishy Denzel Washington, but when Washington gets murdered in his car, and Hoskins suffers a coronary, he gets Washington's heart in an organ transplant. This isn't just a medical procedure because Washington's spirit enters him as well. He then starts giving him advice on how to win Webb back, as well as some food tips. Washington also helps Hoskins catch his murderer, and to be less racist. The idea was promising but it lacked an edge and flopped.

Paul Hogan tried to reprise the success of *Crocodile Dundee* with *Almost an Angel* that year too, playing a thief who's visited by God (Charlton Heston) while in limbo after being involved in a life-threatening accident. He tries to reform himself by ministering to a wheelchair victim. Like *Heart Condition*, it bombed. As Mae West liked to say, virtue may have had its rewards, but it did nothing at the box office. There was also a bit of nepotism in the production, Hogan's real-life wife Linda Koslowski whom he met on the *Dundee* series turning up as the wheelchair victim's sister.

Bill Cosby even got in on the spirit act with *Ghost Dad*, playing a workaholic father of three children who's about to be whisked out of life unless he can prove to the celestial powers-that-be that he can give "quality time" to his sprogs. He has three days to do so but the film is so boring it seems like as many years.

1991 was also a big year for the celluloid spirit level, with *Dead Again*, *Defending Your Life*, *Truly, Madly, Deeply* and *L.A. Story* all queuing up for attention. By now this kind of movie had almost become a mini-genre.

Dead Again is a *film noir* with a reincarnation theme, surely a first in Hollywood's history. Ken Branagh directed both himself and his then-wife Emma Thompson, each of them playing dual roles. She's suffering from both nightmares and amnesia. When he delves deeper into her subconscious he discovers she's haunted by memories of a past-life murder of a composer and his wife, who also turn out to be herself and Branagh. Branagh was coming off the back of a spate of Shakespearean scripts when he read this one and its novelty gripped him immediately. The story was the real star, he believed. He was also mightily relieved there were no battles or soliloquies in it. He watched Hitchcock movies to help him get into the mood for directing it.

He described himself as "sympathetically agnostic" as far as reincarnation was concerned, but admitted to knowing many people who had
undergone past-life regression therapy with some astounding results so
he kept an open mind on it. As for the film itself, it stumbled between a
few stools and Branagh was never going to be able to carry the Chand-
leresque overtones. But the idea of shooting the 1940s scenes in monochrome, an idea he conjured up in desperation after preview audiences
laughed the first cut off the screen, worked a treat. The critics also
praised its genre-bending ambitions.

Defending Your Life was directed by, and featured, Albert Brooks as
yet another car crash victim who instead of going to Purgatory like all
normal corpses, finds himself in a place called Judgment City. Here souls
are vetted before it's decided whether they're entitled to eternal bliss or
not. He starts watching re-runs of his life and isn't exactly entranced by
what he sees. One of Judgment City's perks, though, is a restaurant
where you can eat all you like without putting on an ounce. He then
meets Meryl Streep, another spirit, and falls in love with her. Now he has
an added problem: What if she goes up to heaven and he's sent back to
Earth? Streep is in a more evolved state than he is and also has a plusher
hotel, Judgment City being very precise about where it places people in
its pecking order. Brooks knows he's in for a grilling from the City's
lawyers, who feel he hasn't showed enough bravery in his life up to now.
Can he remedy this? Or do we really care?

Truly, Madly, Deeply, meanwhile, was almost like a revisionist version
of *Ghost*. It was more thoughtful than that film, and thankfully free from
soppiness as well. Directed by Anthony Minghella, who would go on to
make *The English Patient*, it deals with a cellist (Alan Rickman) who
dies, leaving his pianist wife (Juliet Stevenson) distraught. She can't get
him out of her mind, nor does she really want to. Memories of him flood
her every waking moment. And then one night he comes back to her.
He's dead, but casual about the fact. Other than the fact that he's cold
he's the same as he always was. The problem is that he's also as irritating
as he always was.

As time goes on she starts to remember all of the things that annoyed
her about him and asks him to absent himself from her. Will she, unlike
Demi Moore in *Ghost*, continue to pine for him or move on with her life
and marry Michael Maloney, a man she meets in a restaurant one day
and proceeds to have a relationship with? (Maloney has one decided
advantage over Rickman: he's alive.)

Rickman himself persuades her that this is the path to follow. He does so with a lot more imagination and maturity than Mr Swayze in the other movie, Minghella creating a vision of new life in images like Stevenson holding a baby. More hackneyed metaphors include fleecy clouds but thankfully these are kept to a minimum in a film that charms you with its laconicism.

It's a rom-com, but with more emphasis on "com" than "rom." Anytime it threatens to become sentimental it slaps itself resolutely on the wrists. Rickman comes back to Stevenson merely because he "didn't die properly. It didn't hurt." The manner in which they flash off each other—they're close friends in real life as well, which helps—makes the film work. Things become truly manic when Rickman brings some of his friends from "the other side" around to watch videos, play chess and interpret Bach. He's forcing her to rid herself of him in the kindest manner possible—and also getting rid of the rats that are also "haunting" her.

Steve Martin brought a Woody Allen edge to *L.A. Story*, a film that tried to double as a New Age West Coast send-up. It was moderately witty, featuring a less adrenalized Martin than usual playing a TV weatherman who needs Something Else in his life. Unlucky in love, he finds hippy dippy Sarah Jessica Parker and also intense journo Victoria Tennant. More importantly, a traffic billboard acts as his agony aunt in directing him toward a Better Future.

At this point of the film one could be forgiven for demanding one's money back. The billboard plays linguistic tricks with Martin, asking him to unscramble a fabulously asinine anagram which means, well, nothing. The Lord moves in strange ways, to be sure, and there are more things in heaven and earth than are dreamt of in a weather forecaster's philosophy. Unfortunately, none of them appear in this limp-wristed excuse for a feel-good romp that can't make up its mind if it's a satire, a rom-com or a ditsy allegory about life, love and the whole damn thing. Martin also wrote it so we can pin most of the blame on him. When he gives the billboard a hug, one is tempted to utter the immortal words: "Come out Steve Martin, your fifteen minutes are up." But some people actually grooved to this juvenile claptrap masquerading as a midlife crisis parable.

Groundhog Day (1992) had Bill Murray undergoing the same parabolas of emotion as James Stewart did forty six years before in *It's A Wonderful Life*, the two films neatly bisecting the century. Stewart went from wanting to end it all to learning that there was more to life than his own navel-gazing concerns. Murray learns the same lesson here but his redemption is embraced into a simultaneous career fulfilment.

A good-humored comedy that sees a TV weatherman forced to live through the same horrible day over and over, this sleeper captivated America so much its title entered the language as a new phrase for *deja vu*. A gentle, cathartic film that doesn't take itself too seriously and risk coming across as haranguing the viewer, its light comedic touch and casual chemistry between Murray and Andie MacDowell result in a clever but never cute evocation of smalltown values with a big heart.

Murray is Phil Connors, a man who's utterly contemptuous of the rural town of Punxatawney, Pennsylvania when he's called upon to go there to report on its annual Groundhog Festival. A storm detains him in this despicable place when his job is done and the next morning when he wakes up . . . it's still Groundhog Day. And the next. And the next.

You can guess the rest. After failing to kill himself he comes to an appreciation, nay love of the town's customs and values. He saves the life of a man choking from a bone in a restaurant and also rescues a boy from a tree. He becomes outgoing for the first time in his life and rids himself of his "big city" arrogance.

It's a simple, obvious, Hollywood "message" film. We should all be better people. We must not castigate Palookaville. Certain chores may be dull but we have to perform them. And so on. The boonies have beautiful people in them: try and become one of them. So February 2nd, Groundhog Day, turns out to be Connors' secularized form of redemption. Catharsis in the middle of nowhere. Another field of dreams. A man can live in a seashell and still be king of the universe. Ho hum.

As Audrey Farolino noted in her review of the movie in the *New York Post*, "The movie's premise is rather Kafkaesque, but its message is more Capraesque."[42] In other words, even if you're stuck in the same place with the same people doing the same things every day, you can still find salvation of a sort through little acts of kindness and selflessness. Murray finally professes his love for the woman of his dreams and is then, as it were, redeemed. Richard Corliss felt that the message of the film was that "Most folks' lives are like Phil's on Groundhog Day: a repetition, with the tiniest variations, of ritual pleasures and annoyances. Routine is the metronome marking most of our time on earth. Phil's gift is to see the routine and seize the day." Looked at from another point of view the film gives us the Hindu philosophy that life is "the ultimate guru."[43]

A quite different form of redemption is waiting for Harvey Keitel in *Bad Lieutenant*, Abel Ferrara's 1992 tale of a corrupt New York police officer who's on the verge of nervous collapse due to a lifetime of drugs, sexual perversity and avarice. Keitel isn't given a name, an implication that he has "already lost all sense of humanity."[44] He's also in a moral limbo. He steals coke from crime scenes and re-sells it, spending the proceeds on hookers and booze.

A hooker who provides him with heroin tells him, "Vampires are lucky, they can feed on others. But we gotta eat away at ourselves till there's nothing left but appetite." Keitel is in hell, but a possible heaven awaits as his buried guilt finally manifests itself in a vision of Christ that triggers his odyssey toward self-knowledge, and possible reform. When he meets a nun who's been raped by drug-crazed youths in the sanctuary of a church he's so overcome by her forgiveness of them he cries out to Jesus to help him. He then sees the vision of Christ on the cross and starts to hallucinate. He abuses the image but we sense an imminent catharsis even in his rage.

The nun has had her vagina lacerated with a crucifix by two Hispanic boys but still can't condemn them. "I ought to have turned bitter semen into fertile sperm," is her unlikely reaction, "turned hate into love." Keitel is incredulous when she won't reveal their identities.

In one scene he shoots a car radio when he hears news of a sports fixture that went against his wishes; in another he masturbates against a car as a young woman inside simulates oral sex at his behest. This man is an animal and yet he has an old-fashioned sense of justice. Rapists, particularly violent rapists, must be put away for a long time in his moral calculus. Keitel told *Sight and Sound* magazine: "I believe it is a religious film because hell is here now and so is the opportunity to know heaven."[45] His redemption is so unnatural he howls "like a wounded animal."[46] Jake La Motta isn't far away here.

Steve Martin also went through a novel kind of reform in *Leap of Faith* in the same year, playing a con artist posing as a preacher who can work miracles. At one point he manages to convince a congregation he's made a cripple walk, but the woman in question wasn't crippled at all. His motive is money and he has no conscience about the fact. He's in the business of selling dreams to the gullible. He persistently reassures himself with the thought that they're better off with their illusions than the cold, hard facts of their existence. The film gives us its sucker punch in the last reel when a young boy who's been crippled manages to walk without his crutches. He puts it down to Martin, at which point Martin comes clean and tells him he's a fraud. "What difference does it make," the boy inquires "if you get the job done?" This is the language Martin himself has been using throughout the film but suddenly it doesn't work for him. "Kid" he tells the boy, "it makes every difference in the world." The film isn't so much about the healing of the boy as of Martin himself, by a curious irony. Director Richard Pearce doesn't get into the issue of how the boy was healed, leaving that to ourselves to analyze, if we wish to.

John Travolta was an angel in *Michael* in the same year. The idea was about as innovative as Warren Beatty deciding to re-visit *Here Comes Mr. Jordan* territory. This angel, though it does have wings, doesn't play a harp or utter divine platitudes. No: it smokes, drinks, and swears. If you feel you've wandered back into *Phenomenon* by accident, you could be forgiven for this. Andie MacDowell plays an angel expert drafted in to find out if he's on the level. The audience knows better than even to ask.

Travolta plays George Malley, a mechanic who sees a flashing light in the sky one night when he's coming out of a bar after a night spent celebrating his birthday. His life changes radically from this point on. He develops powers of clairvoyance and telekinesis, and an incredible memory for digesting the material he finds in books, including those written in foreign languages.

The film was used by Travolta as a platform to air his views on Scientology via the character of Malley. Many of the scenes are thinly disguised sounding-boards for this way of thinking, Malley's pantheistic sentiments of becoming one with nature extending even after his death when his presence sways the trees. "We're all made of the same stuff," he says, "living energy." Even the action of eating an apple makes it part of us, and us of it.

An interesting attempt to bridge the dichotomy between science and faith was made in *Contact* (1997), a science fiction film featuring Jodie Foster as a woman fascinated with the idea of communicating with other life forms since she lost her parents at a young age. She feels she's getting signals from a star named Vega but when a plan is set in train to send a person on a research mission to this star she's passed over because she's a religious skeptic. It's technically impressive but fudges the issues it raises so tantalizingly. More *Heaven Can Wait* than *Space Odyssey*, its house of cards implodes in the final cop-out, a misdirected piece of didacticism from Robert Zemeckis.

Matthew McConaughey appears as the white knight who can bring Foster to God via some spurious psychobabble but you can't really get away with merging science fiction and spirituality unless you're a Kubrick. Zemeckis has a way to go before we can speak of him in the same breath. McConaughey also has to struggle with lines like "You could call me a man of the cloth—without the cloth." With dialogue like this, what chance had he, or the film, got? There's a digitally induced Bill Clinton here as well, which is one more cast member than we need in a film that tries so hard to be earnest it falls into a Black Hole of insignificance.

Woody Allen was a spiritually bankrupt author with the appropriate name of Harry Block in *Deconstructing Harry*, a black comedy which won him a Best Original Screenplay Oscar nomination in the same year. Basing itself loosely on Ingmar Bergman's *Wild Strawberries*, it has Allen trying to get various women to accompany him on a trip to collect an award without much success. Harry is a rather unattractive character whose life heretofore has been a disaster zone. Three marriages have gone down the pan and matters haven't been helped by the fact that he's used some of his exes as fodder for his writing.

Allen also namechecks Bergman's *The Seventh Seal* facetiously when The Grim Reaper comes calling in a flashback scene. Tobey McGuire, as the young Allen, is wearing another person's dressing gown so Death has the wrong guy. When he tries to explain that his time isn't up, Death replies grimly, "That's what they all say." Harry eventually ends up in hell, where he meets his father. "Get me out of here," the father implores, "You know I always hated the hot weather." "Let him go to heaven," Woody asks the Devil, played by Billy Crystal. "I don't believe in heaven," the father snaps, "I'm a Jew." "So where do you want to go?" Woody asks. "To a Chinese restaurant!" he replies.

As Woody starts conversing with Crystal, he outlines his sins. He drinks, lies, is vain, cowardly, cheats on his wives and is violent. "Violent?" Crystal inquires. "Yes," Woody tells him, "I once almost ran over a book critic in my car, but swerved at the last minute."

Crystal's hell has air conditioning, which makes the place comfortable for him. He thinks he'll stick it out. While alive he spent two years in a Hollywood studio but "You can't trust those people." Life is a bit like a casino, he surmises. One day you're up, one day down, but "the house always wins." So you have to go for The Main Chance.

At the end of the film Allen sees all of the characters from his books coming to life, as they've done separately throughout. They thank him for giving them existence, including an out-of-focus Robin Williams, playing an actor. As was the case in *The Purple Rose of Cairo*, the distinction between art and reality blurs, the two worlds intermingling.

The film is a hodge-podge but it gives Allen some interesting opportunities to indulge his pet themes. At one point he tells a hooker he suffers from depression and is starting to think Sophocles was right, that we'd have been better off not being born at all. "It's a bit late for that, honey," she chirps. The film is full of these kinds of exchanges. It's an uneven work but fitfully funny. It's also more sexually explicit than anything he's done before, as if he's trying to rope in a younger audience.

If men thought Audrey Hepburn made eternity look enticing, Brad Pitt returned the favor for women in *Meet Joe Black* in 1998. Pitt plays Death but he's had something of a makeover since Ingmar Bergman had him looking all foreboding in his black shroud in *The Seventh Seal*. This Death is quiet and polite, the kind of man you might want your daughter to marry.

In fact Anthony Hopkins' daughter Claire Forlani begins to like Pitt's character. Hopkins is the guy whose time is up, which is why Pitt comes a-calling, but Hopkins makes a deal with him—not on a chess table, mind. He allows the curious Mr Black (Pitt) a couple of days on earth if Black delays his demise by those same few days. Both have something to gain. Hopkins can put his house in order and Pitt use the time to see what peanut butter tastes like—not to mention Ms Forlani's lips. It's all very long-winded and inchoate, a mis-timed movie which mixes the dark message of death's inevitability with a turgid romance in a manner that does a disservice to both.

It steers an uncomfortable path between the sublime and the ridiculous at times, and the subplot dealing with Hopkins' business problems is both unnecessary and overlong. But there's a brilliant last half-hour at Hopkins' 65th birthday party, and a fine sense of muted longing between Pitt and Forlani that underlines the basic theme of transience. It's a pity about the trivial aspects of the plot, and Pitt's puckish inanity, but he's a good enough actor to almost make it bearable.

A re-make of the 1934 film *Death Takes a Holiday*, it tugs at the heartstrings too much overall but one's patience is rewarded finally over the three hours running time. A Reaper who falls in love is quite a novelty but it also strains credibility. In the earlier version the humor was cranked up. Here, the emotional element is foremost, which leads to imbalances no director could overcome. Not even Brad Pitt can sweeten the pill of mortality.

Nicolas Cage and Meg Ryan appeared in *City of Angels* in 1998. This was a re-make of Wim Wenders' beautifully paced 1987 movie *Wings of Desire*, which featured a pair of angels wandering around the streets of Berlin wondering what it would be like to be human, one of them eventually falling in love with a trapeze artist. In this version, which is infinitely more soppy, Cage is the angel and Ryan the heart surgeon he falls for. Renouncing his invisibility, he has to decide if she's more important to him than an eternity hovering over Los Angeles. His obsession makes him follow her everywhere, sneaking up behind her to smell her hair, watching her take a bath, or even have sex with her boyfriend.

He loves her so much he's willing to sacrifice his heavenly state to win her. It's not much of a choice within the terms of the film because heaven here, to be frank, is a rather yawnful place. The other angels, Albert J. Bergeson remarks "mope around much of the time dressed in black, rarely smiling, and almost never laughing."[47] Their dress and demeanor, he suggests, "make heaven seem like East Berlin under communism—lifeless, grey and depressing."[48] Their severe dress would have been acceptable in the original version of the film, he believes, because it was set in "cold northern Germany" but he's bewildered as to why the motif was extended into "sunny California."[49]

When Cage makes the decision, to "fall" to earth, a cruel fate awaits him because the following morning Ryan is knocked down by a truck and dies. Incredibly, Cage doesn't feel aggrieved. "To touch you," he tells her as he cradles her dying body in his arms, "to feel you, to hold you right now, do you know how much I love you?" She then asks him the 64-marker question: Was it worth giving up eternity for this one day? His answer is an unreserved yes. He would rather have had one breath of her hair, one kiss of her mouth, than billions and billions of years with those insufferable old angels up in the clouds.

Cage regarded the part as a huge challenge and sounded off pretentiously about it in interviews. "I'd like to be able to get back to that place I was as a child," he enthused, "when I was awestruck by something that was as simple as a raindrop, or sunlight on my face."[50] The film helped him recapture that innocence, he claimed, because he played a character who was in awe of people: "In that awe I could convey my own feelings about the awe of being alive." From a technical point of view he wasn't sure how to convey such a sentiment. "You can drive yourself nuts trying to interpret the whys and wherefores of angeldom," he said. "I don't blink, I don't have a shadow; it's very trippy. The best choice I could make was to find the most entertaining approach without repeating what's been done of late. I want to maintain some sense of the concept that angels are terrifying." He was looking for "a sense of otherness" even though the film itself was about love.[51] Sadly, for all his ruminating, this remains a one-note performance in a one-note movie. Heaven may be dull here, but so is earth. Put bluntly, Ryan wouldn't justify his choice even if she lived.

Jim Carrey shed his comic, rubber-faced image to play a man trapped in an artificial world in *The Truman Show* in the same year. Somebody is pulling the strings on Truman's life, which is lived in a Pleasantville-style environment. As was the case in *Groundhog Day*, the same things keep happening every day and Truman, like the weatherman in the earlier film, doesn't know why. But one day he stumbles onto the truth. His life is a set-up, his friends are actors and actresses. Even his wife is an actress. The man pulling the strings, played by Ed Harris, is named Christof.

If we were unsure of allegorical ambitions on the part of director Andrew Niccol up until now, they're rapidly dispelled. Truman has had a womb-like existence, his every word and expression captured by a TV network. The ultimate in "24/7" entertainment that goes under the misleading title of "Reality TV," this show has Truman as its unwitting patsy.

What will happen when the worm turns? This is the most interesting part of the film. It doesn't sell out to melodrama like so many similarly themed Tinseltown capers but opts for a more meditative resolution. Peter Finch didn't get off quite so lightly in *Network*.

Robin Williams played one of his "sensitive" roles that year too, in *What Dreams May Come*. It was even worse than its title.

He's married to a painter, Anabella Sciorra. They lose their children in a car accident. Both are devastated and struggling to get on with their lives. Then Williams is killed in another accident. He goes to heaven and meets people like Cuba Gooding Junior and Max Von Sydow. His dog is also there, and of course his kids. What could be more chummy? "If this is where we all go," he blurts out as he surveys the Wordsworthian panorama round about him, "it can't be bad." Sorry, but it is. "Thought is real," Gooding informs him. "The physical is the illusion." How profound. Plato thou shouldst be living at this hour. We all create our own heaven, he continues, or our own hell. And thereby hangs a tale. Where's Anabella? It's not much fun with your easel and canvas in the crepuscular darkness of Hades, is it?

Gooding first appears to Williams in soft focus. He used to be one of his cardiac patients on earth, he tells him as he walks across some water.

When Williams inquires as to the whereabouts of God he's flatly informed that He's around all right but we don't listen to him. Hence the delusion of atheism. "I want to see my children," Williams says. "When you do, you will," Gooding replies, mystifyingly. This knowing cleverness infuses much of the script.

At first everything he sees is a re-enactment of Sciorra's paintings. Gooding explains to him that he's creating his own world, getting to know his wife better than he could on earth. Williams, you see, didn't comfort Anabella in the right way after their kids died. He should have realized she was an emotional wreck and done something about it to prevent a further tragedy. One day as he wanders about the place he's informed Sciorra has taken her own life. He wonders why he can't see her. The answer he gets is that she's in hell. Williams isn't having any of this. He insists on travelling to Hades to bring her back. Max Von Sydow says it isn't that simple. In fact if he's not careful he may end up spending eternity down there too.

What's strangest of all about the film is the casual attitude with which Williams reacts to everything. When he hears Sciorra has committed suicide, he's almost placid. "It's okay because her pain's over," he assures himself. Maybe, but ours isn't.

It would be difficult to describe just how agonizingly insincere this slice of saccharine is. Only Ms Sciorra emerges from it with anything approaching respectability. Its Calvinistic sense of punishment for sins totally flies in the face of the wishy-washy domesticity. Even though we see the grotesqueness of hell, though it's really only purgatory considering Ms Sciorra's ultimate "release," the film has "happy ever after" written over every twee frame.

It's also both confused and confusing. If Williams is truly to blame for his wife's suicide then why didn't *he* end up in "hell" instead? This would have meant Sciorra journeyed downward to *him* and tried to bring *him* back. Maybe they should both have gone down and airlifted one another up. They could have used the rarefied script to give them the necessary propulsion.

What Dreams May Come gives rise to facetious reactions like this. The idea of Williams giving to Sciorra in death what he couldn't in life is old hat, and the dire repetition of the (unexplained) line, "Sometimes when you win, you lose," leading up to the final corollary pay-off, "Sometimes when you lose, you win," is fatuous.

"I just want us to be old together," he tells her at one point, having done the necessary grovelling to this seriously misunderstood artist. The heaven he ascends to is vintage Hollywood: lush scenery that gives off a strong whiff of pedantry. Also, having Cuba Gooding deliver his Sunday School sermons is enough to make anyone pine for a visit to Old Nick downstairs. It has to be more fun than this.

When people commit suicide, we're informed, they lose their mind. This is what hell is: amnesia. If Williams goes down there, he risks that too. But hey, he's up for it. This road to hell is most definitely paved with good intentions. There's a lot of ground to be covered here, a lot of humble pie to be eaten.

He finally learns the truth of the film's dictum: "The real hell is your life gone wrong." To fix it he has to risk everything, to reconstitute himself even as he's in the act of redeeming a woman who's violated the natural order. This is some learning curve. Another of the film's mystifying lines is "Good people end up in hell because they can't forgive themselves." Could Sciorra not? Surely Williams is the man with this problem. In which case, as I said, the roles should have been reversed.

Infinitely more convincing than this gushy drivel was *Stir of Echoes* (1999), which had Kevin Bacon as a blue collar worker beset by demonic forces. Happily married with a young son, one night at a party he allows himself to be hypnotized and in this state he sees dead bodies. He also starts to imagine he can solve murders with his visions. His wife thinks he's losing it and the erstwhile happy household is uprooted to the core.

This had a lot of potential and Bacon gives it his all, but it died at the box office because it was released just a month after *The Sixth Sense*, M Night Shyamalan's masterly tale of the bonding between a child psychologist (Bruce Willis) doing perhaps his first real acting job and a young boy (Haley Joel Osment) in his Oscar-nominated debut. He claims to see dead people. This film truly expanded the horizons of the genre, Shyamalan proving himself a worthy successor to the likes of Kubrick in the manner in which he combines scenes of huge emotional power with horrific visions that flit by almost nonchalantly. The final twist is also mesmeric. The irony is that Willis is as bereft as Osment, and equally crying out to the Lord from his own depths of despair.

Sadly, Shyamalan had less luck with his subsequent projects, *Unbreakable* and *Signs*, where he plumbed more gimmicky psychic terrain that veered toward science fiction while trying to preserve the spiritual elements so conscientiously nurtured here. *The Village* (2004), thankfully, represented a fine return to form with its incredible surprise ending. Though as somebody commented, for this man to make a film *without* a surprise ending would be the biggest surprise of all.

A third 1999 vehicle, *Dogma*, had two fallen angels, Ben Affleck and Matt Damon engaging in various blasphemous pursuits—and a more irascible one, Alan Rickman, questioning God's omniscience. Affleck sees a loophole in divine law which he intends to exploit to threaten mankind's future in this black comedy which was directed by an American Catholic, Kevin Smith. He said he wanted to make a film that would be "entertaining enough" to keep viewers in their seats but also "full of faith."[52] There was a lot of public outrage about the film prior to its release— much of it by people who didn't even know what it dealt with. Smith insisted "It's not anti-Church, it's not anti-God, it's not anti-Christ, it's not anti-Catholic. In fact it's the opposite—a celebration of the need for faith rather than strict adherence to conventional codes of behavior."[53]

This sounded fine in theory but the film itself is a mess, a contrived absurdity that wallows too much in its would-be cleverness and fails to muster up any sort of empathy for its characters. Deserted wife Linda Fiorentino agrees to help Rickman stop Affleck from passing through the arch of a certain church, which would prove God was fallible and thus accelerate a global holocaust, and there's also a character (Chris Rock) who claims to have been the 13th apostle and who is, apparently, owed twelve dollars by Jesus.

"God has a sense of humor," we're advised in a pre-credit revelation, "After all, he created the platypus." This is indicative of the vapid "wisdom" that ensues. As well as being tritely sacrilegious, this scabrous effort is willfully sensationalistic. We're informed at one point that God is female by a feminist angel named Serendipity and we're informed by Rock that Jesus was black. In a previous era such revelations might have raised eyebrows but here they merely come across as jejune.

Alanis Morrisette plays God. Even with an infinitely better director than Smith, it would have been difficult to accept a female pop singer in this role. George Burns got away with playing him as a guy in a baseball cap because *Oh God* was a comedy but *Dogma* has too many intellectual pretensions it fails to deliver on.

Smith justified his blasphemy on the grounds that he was trying to make the Bible relevant for a new generation of Catholics. There was no point in doing a re-make of *The Song of Bernadette*, he contended. This was fine, and nobody could deny that he juggled a lot of theological balls in the air with a view to creating various forums for discussion but the film is tackily put together and evinces a pronounced air of "Look, no hands." Also, any movie relying on Ben Affleck to carry a revolutionary message with credibility is its own worst enemy from the get-go.

Dogma pretends to care about the issues it only purports to raise, its real interest being in pulling down the pillars of any temples ready-to-hand. Its tone is snide and adolescent, which means that whatever theological loopholes it does indeed tap into don't really impress. It can't make up its mind if it's reflective or satirical, which in the end makes it more contemptible than *The Life of Brian*, which at least let us know from the word go what angle we were about to get. *Dogma* tries to serve two masters and ends up serving neither. Basically Smith can't make up his mind if he's angry at the church or amused by what he sees as its contradictions. "Leave it to Catholics to destroy existence," runs one of his lines, "They treat God like a burden."

Elsewhere his labored diatribes on "the failed experience called existence" are yawnfully discursive, guillotining the plot, which is tenuous anyway. The final apparition of Affleck flying over the church where God resides before being plugged by bullets is faintly ridiculous. There's an interesting film to be made about the nuances of Scripture to the thinking mind but sadly this isn't it. All too often it opts for gratuitous iconoclasm instead of profound analysis. A teen sex comedy masquerading as a meaningful examination of intimations of immortality, it persists in inconsequential juvenilia instead of taking its controversial precepts to their conclusions.

Fiorentino, playing the great, great, great grand-niece of Christ tries to look curious but merely comes across as jaded in her interrogations of the apocryphal angels. The parts dealing with voodooism and mythology are also highly ludicrous, as indeed is the fundamental premise of the expelling angels trying to get back to heaven and thus proving God fallible.

Smith doesn't even cut it as the celluloid *auteur* of *The Idiot's Guide to Paradise Lost*. He gives Affleck lines like "All the time I've been down here I've felt the absence of the divine presence." Damon, who's somewhat less intent on leaving Wisconsin forever for the celestial delights he's seen slip by him, looks even more uncomfortable as his sidekick.

When Rock tells us "A black man can steal your stereo but he can't be a saint," it's time to squirm in your seat and pray for the end of this meretricious movie. The end doesn't come half quickly enough, Morrisette answering Fiorentino's question "Why are we here?" by tweaking her nose. Every dogma, one is tempted to say, has its day.

The film, as Theresa Sanders noted in *Celluloid Saints*, is predicated upon a fundamental misunderstanding of Catholic precepts. The two angels, for instance, imagine that a plenary indulgence means that one's sins, even one's mortal sins, are automatically forgiven. "What a plenary indulgence offers," Sanders writes, "is simply a remission of any temporal punishment that a person's sins might have incurred. It cannot change the decision on whether or not someone goes to heaven; it merely removes any penance that a heaven-bound person must perform before entering paradise."[54] Such a fundamental oversight, or rather misinterpretation, destroyed the overall credibility of the project for her.

Another film made that year, *Stigmata*, is also pretty ropey in its theology. This is the kind of thing that shows us just how excruciatingly trite Hollywood can be when it really puts its mind to it. It's the fluffy tale of a freewheeling, laidback Pittsburgh hairdresser (Patricia Arquette) who's chosen to be the bearer of the eponymous wounds by dint of the fact that she's basically a kindly soul and . . . well not much else really. The villain of the piece is one Cardinal Houseman (Jonathan Pryce) looking familiarly oleaginous. He's willing to go to desperate lengths to prevent Frankie (Arquette) from spreading a secret gospel. This is the gospel of Saint Thomas, which the film seems to think the Vatican regards as heretical. This isn't true but why spoil a good plot with the facts?

Anyway, Cardinal Houseman is one of the few people in the world who knows about this and he's raging that Frankie seems to have got wind of it. Is it possible that the spirit of a dead monk who also knew about a secret gospel chose Frankie to spread the good news for a forthcoming era? If so, she has to be liquidated, and soon.

Houseman sends Father Kiernan (Gabriel Byrne) to interrogate this strange young woman who finds herself writing in Aramaic when she goes into her trance-like states. She also finds herself quoting from the said gospel, and saying things like "Split a piece of wood and I am there," which is not, presumably, the way the other hairdressers in Pittsburgh speak, even those who don't pay their bills.

Fr Kiernan doesn't really want this job because he's heard Frankie is an atheist, and atheists don't usually have bleeding palms, do they? Presumably not, unless they've become so depressed by their lack of faith that they slit their wrists. The hapless priest is even more discommoded when, after meeting Frankie, she offers to pierce his nipples for him. One can safely say that this isn't an oft-asked saintly request. But we know Frankie, a female version of Francis of Assisi, presumably is "holy" because a lot of pigeons tend to flutter around her in the film. Father Kiernan is a reluctant priest, his commitment half-hearted. He became ordained to run away from commitment. Frankie, on the other hand, is deeply committed. She's generous, kind and loving. She also has an active sex life without being married, but this doesn't disqualify one from sainthood in good-old liberated 1999.

In the end, after dealing with Houseman, Frankie and Fr Kiernan get it on. He realizes the seminary doesn't really do it for him so it's far better to canoodle with the pigeon woman, who might even give him a free make-over after they go to the altar together.

The message of the film is that just because one wears a soutane, this doesn't necessarily mean holiness. Ask Saint Francis, who was probably also very good with pigeons, and who was also chosen to be the bearer of stigmatic wounds. He wasn't a hairdresser, of course, but you can't have everything. Neither could he have cozied up to Fr Kiernan in the final reel, unless we were to have a gay stigmatist. This will probably have to wait until the new millennium, where audiences might be even more "liberated."

What Lies Beneath (2000) out-Psychoed *Psycho* as director Robert Zemeckis used a slow dripfeed of tension to work up to his final surprise. Michelle Pfeiffer is alone in her rambling New England mansion when things start to go bump in the night—and day. You think she's going crazy until the pieces of the jigsaw start to coalesce. A whodunit with a difference, this supernatural thriller is like *Fatal Attraction* meets *The Others*, Zemeckis creating almost unbearable tension before secrets from her husband's past start to emerge.

Kevin Spacey won an Oscar for playing Lester Burnham in *American Beauty* later that year. A poignant and often hilarious look at suburbia, midlife crisis and the possibility of psychic redemption through regression to a state of simplicity, Lester tells the story from beyond the grave.

Unhappily married to a realtor (Annette Bening) whose God is material comfort, his libido is awakened by an infatuation with a friend of his daughter from school. This sets in motion a series of events that result in his rejuvenation and revitalization. He chucks his white collar job to work at the local hamburger joint and also starts to exercise and smoke pot, going back to his adolescence in the 1960s for stimulation. Meanwhile, his daughter is having a relationship with a strange drug-dealing neighbor Ricky (Joaquin Phoenix). Ricky has a film which he keeps playing over and over again, featuring a plastic bag blowing in the wind. He's fascinated by its ordinariness. If Lester achieves liberation by building up his body to "earn" his Lolita, imagining her enwreathed in roses, so does Ricky by watching the free flight of the bag.

Lester, in the words of Robert K. Johnston, is "shrivelled of soul" until he "literally begins to smell the roses."[55] He realizes the American

Dream is really the American Nightmare. Like Robin Williams in *Dead Poets Society*, he wants to seize the day. His infatuation with his daughter's friend may smack of being a dirty old man but he sees it differently. She's awakened not only his libido but his concept of, yes, American beauty. If he has to die as a result of his brief euphoria, so be it. As he puts it after having informed us that masturbating in the shower is the highlight of his day, "In a way, I'm dead already." The Nicolas Cage of *City of Angels* would know the feeling.

There are many subplots here as well: the voyeuristic neighbor, the closet gay man, Bening's hilarious affair and so on. They're all welded together seamlessly in a film that inhabits a wickedly piquant dreamscape of the heart as it summarily dissects a vapid culture, placing us instead in a twilight zone of recaptured bohemianism—even if only for a day.

American Beauty is a film about rebirth and understanding. It's a film about the absolute necessity of knowing oneself and pursuing one's vision wherever it may lead. Paul Coates wrote in his book *Cinema, Religion and the Romantic Legacy*: "It preserves the idea of an afterlife while voiding it of religious otherness and judgement. Instead, there's a pure acceptance of all that has been and will be—an almost Nietzschean eternal recurrence within the mind."[56] If structuralism, he argues, is correct to attribute the force of myth to the reconciliation of opposites, *American Beauty* achieves its mythical impact "by satisfying both the widespread modern inability to credit an afterlife, and the desire for one. It will come, but will not involve anything potentially disturbing. It will be, as it were, another version of Ricky's playing and replaying of the film archive: a stream of apparently banal moments seen in the true light of transcendence, earthly beauty become sublime."[57]

Spacey gave an equally astounding performance in *Seven* in 1995, playing a serial killer who kills people he regards as guilty of the Seven Deadly Sins. It's an Agatha Christie type of idea taken to a subliminal level in a film that chills one to the marrow, especially in the final scene, which contains one of the most grotesque surprises in mainstream cinema.

Set in a *noirish* city where, as one critic observed, nobody seems to pay their electricity bill, the darkness is underlined by a fairly constant rain to copperfasten the bleak mood. Spacey plays John Doe, a Travis Bickle figure subsumed with self-righteousness over his gruesome acts. In the end, his mission accomplished, he wants to die, and Brad Pitt falls into the trap of killing him. Now we have a new protagonist, and a new "sin." David Fincher, the director, said he shot the final scene in daylight out of a mischievous sense of irony. When the characters finally see the light, his thinking ran, they're still in hell.

Doe sees his murders as "sermons." His first victim, an obese man adjudged to be guilty of gluttony, is forced to almost literally eat himself to death. A second, epitomizing greed, suffers a similar fate. He continues on with sloth, pride and lust, which leaves us with the terrifying final couplet of envy and wrath. Fincher holds a mirror up to a Dante-esque inferno transposed from medieval to modern times, with Pitt and Morgan Freeman, an elegiac philosopher-cop on his last case, being dangled like marionettes by the draconian, Bible-thumping protagonist whose miasma of slaughter almost inevitably leads to his final, electrifying shock.

The Others (2001) had Nicole Kidman very effectively playing a religious mother of two children in an England mansion as she waits for her husband to return from World War II. When her daughter starts seeing ghosts, the film gets just as spooky and atmospheric as one would wish.

Dragonfly (2002) is like an amalgam of *The Sixth Sense* and *Field of Dreams*, a mystical tale of a man who reaches faith in an afterlife through unusual means. Joe Darrow (Kevin Costner) is a Chicago surgeon who's just lost his wife Emily (Susanna Thompson) in an accident in Venezuela when the bus in which she's travelling gets caught in a landslide. Inconsolable in his grief, he throws himself into his work with a vengeance but can't get her memory out of his head. More portentously, she seems to be trying to communicate with him from the grave, using her former patients—she was a pediatrician—as conduits. Shaken to the core by these signs, he concludes she's trying to speak to him through a dead kidney donor who's just been admitted to the hospital where he works.

Darrow is further disturbed by the predominance of a dragonfly motif. Emily was always fascinated by these insects and they crop up with alarming frequency. So also does a design he likens to a crooked crucifix. Feeling he's losing his mind he agrees to take a sabbatical from work. At the urging of his kindly neighbor Miriam (Kathy Bates) he also decides to go on a white water rafting trip with some friends. Before he does so, Darrow realizes that the crooked crucifix design is actually a waterfall symbol for map-readers. Remembering that one of the last photographs he took of Emily had a waterfall in the background, he forms the notion that she survived the bus accident and is in a coma somewhere near such a waterfall.

He frantically tries to re-trace her footsteps and travels to the scene of the crash. Here an intriguing revelation awaits him. Part psycho-drama and part thriller, the film draws you into its eerie web almost against your will. While the ending is upbeat it's not overly smug.

In the fantasy comedy *Bruce Almighty* (2002) Jim Carrey plays Bruce Nolan, a TV reporter who seems to have it all: a successful job and a beautiful girlfriend (Jennifer Aniston). However, he spends a lot of his time venting his spleen on God, giving out to him about the way his life is going.

After a particularly bad day at work, who else but God himself, played with quiet authority by Morgan Freeman, appears and tells him just how demanding a job it is being the Almighty. Carrey isn't convinced so Freeman decides to hand over his supernatural powers to him for a week to let him see for himself. In his new role Carrey is like a child in a candy store and both he and the film's director Tom Shadyac, who previously worked with him in both *Ace Ventura* and *Liar Liar*, have fun as Carrey finds himself able to indulge all his fantasies at a whim, much to the bewilderment of Aniston. But power comes with a price tag. On the sixth day, God reminds him that, despite all his exertions, he hasn't done much to improve the world. He gives him an extra day to, as it were, clean up his act. The film now goes into a different groove as Carrey learns how difficult it is to be God. One is reminded of the old Jewish dictum: "God is like an Italian waiter—he has too many tables."

Surely this is theologically suspect and flies in the face of God's omnipotence. Hollywood has given us the depiction of the deity as a top-grade magician who nonetheless fails to pull all the rabbits out of his hat. Or is this to take it all too seriously? As God Mark Two, Carrey is still the same as ever, i.e., intensity personified. Except now he's intense with power: a dangerous combination. The only thing he can't manipulate is people's freedom to make choices. "How do you get someone to love you without affecting free will?" he asks Freeman after a tiff with Aniston, to which Freeman gives the classic response, "Welcome to the world! If you get an answer to that one, let me know." The point, of course being that not even God can make Aniston love Carrey if she doesn't want to. Otherwise there would be no point in Creation at all.

As well as being a theological parable, this is a very funny movie that gives Carrey ample opportunity to indulge in all manner of face-pulling, verbal and visual gymnastics and whatever you're having yourself. The manner in which he out-scoops his rival at the TV station is also ribsplitting. There are also some laugh-out-loud lines, as when Bruce says to God: "Thanks for the Grand Canyon. Good luck with the apocalypse."

This is almost as good as Shadyac using a bowl of tomato soup to give us a microcosm of the Parting of the Red Sea.

At the end of the day what the film really concerns itself with is the concept of gratitude for past favors. Carrey said he took the role because he felt most of us live unfulfilled lives and as a result blame God for our shortcomings. Unfortunately, it becomes preachy in its last quarter. With prayer one can become a better person. Patience is a virtue. Love means letting go. The poor need help—and so on. All fine precepts, but do they belong in a Jim Carrey movie—particularly one that begins as zanily as this?

One wonders if Carrey, a talented actor, can continue to have it both ways, i.e., having a jolly old time being irreverent and then going all solemn on us and finishing up by sounding like the James Stewart of *It's A Wonderful Life* with an angel at his shoulder. When he finally surrenders to God's will you feel you're in a different movie, a mature one where everyone can't win the Lottery because that would create chaos. And, well, God is trying his best under very difficult circumstances.

Freeman's God harks back to the George Burns of *Oh God* in 1977, who appeared to John Denver on the 27th floor of a 17-floor building (on "Hope" Street) in a golfing cap, as mentioned already. He also comes out with the same post-Capra platitudes, as when he says to Carrey, "If you want to see a miracle, *be* the miracle." One imagines the young Steven Spielbergs of the world cooing at this.

Angelina Jolie was an ambitious newscaster in *Life or Something Like It* in 2003. This came to us with the hardly earth-shattering message, "Live each day as your last, because one day it will be." Lanie (Jolie as a peroxide blonde) looks and dresses impeccably and is engaged to be married to a handsome baseball player. In the past she had a brief fling with her colleague Pete (Ed Burns), a dishevelled guy who looks as if he sleeps in his clothes. She doesn't like him anymore but he carries a torch for her. He feels there's more to her than she's letting on—even to herself.

One day Lanie meets a psychic who makes some weird predictions about sport and the weather. Then he adds the cruncher: "You're going to die next Thursday." She brushes it off, but she still has a niggle. Then the longshot sporting prediction comes true . . .

Is she really going to die on the following Thursday? Whatever happens, she decides to change her image and become more offbeat and goofy. Her boyfriend doesn't like her makeover, which makes her wonder if they're really suited. Has their whole relationship been a sham?

On a televised broadcast concerning a bus strike Lanie really flips. Instead of just doing a straightforward interview with a striker she launches into a frenzied rendition of the Rolling Stones' "I Can't Get No Satisfaction" on air.

She thinks she's going to be fired but instead the TV ratings go through the roof for her show and she's offered the promotion she's always wanted, to a major New York network. Will she take it? And is she still going to die? With all the excitement of the promotion she seems to put that little detail into the back of her mind.

This is a mildly enjoyable date movie with a wafer-thin plot and some "surprises" you can spot a mile off. We all know the "real" Lanie is tailormade for Pete but Burns and Jolie fail to muster up the necessary chemistry to make this believable on screen. You also feel that, off-screen Jolie would be way out of Burns' league altogether as a girlfriend. Thirdly, are there really any psychics out there who tell you things like "You're going to die" (I doubt they'd stay in business very long)?

The point is, considering his strike rate of predictions coming to pass—he even gets an earthquake right—he should be engaged in saving lives, or cleaning up at bookie's offices.

But maybe we shouldn't ask questions like that about a film that has few pretensions beyond being a feel-good fable. If you don't believe me, check out the climactic interview between Jolie and Stockard Channing, a hardnosed journalist who turns on the waterworks at the drop of a hat. Is this life? No, not even something like it.

Another curious movie, *The Man Who Sued God* (also 2003), is a Billy Connolly comedy that plays around with the term "act of God" as applied by insurance companies to denote events like earthquakes, flash floods, tornadoes and bolts of lightning. It's the latter that strikes Connolly's boat one day when he's out lobster-fishing. It's utterly destroyed but the insurance company won't pay up, which leads him to perform the act of the title. It's all something of a joke at first but after he meets journalist Judy Davis she manages to mobilize the media and he becomes a celebrity of sorts, which is supremely irritating to a primate, a cardinal and a rabbi who sit muttering smart-alecky platitudes on the sidelines. We even get a cameo appearance by the Pope, who's no doubt highly excited by Connolly's prowess.

The film adopts a light tone on the question of faith, as in exchanges like when the primate says to the rabbi, "I think we can take it as read that God exists," and the rabbi replies, "I hope so. I spend half the morning praying to him." Connolly isn't so much interested in money as justice, as he proves by turning down a generous out-of-court settlement by the insurance company. The company becomes increasingly worried that his case could set a precedent and open the floodgates to a barrage of similar claims stretching back to God knows when—if that's not the wrong expression under the circumstances.

When the film gets to the courtroom stage we get a lot of clever dialogue. "The church can only win this case," Connolly expounds at one point, "if it can prove God doesn't exist." Insurance companies, he argues, say the term "act of God" is just a figure of speech, but if the church complies with this it's tantamount to a corroboration of the taking of The Lord's name in vain, which would be to break one of its own Commandments. There's a lot of mock-Jesuitical logic going on here as Connolly, a former lawyer, whimsically explores the philosophical ramifications of a legal precept with religious overtones.

In the latter stages it goes soft, Connolly opting for a "moral" victory instead of a financial one. The "Love conquers all" message kicks in here as well, making it all rather saccharine-tinted, which is in marked contrast to the plethora of expletives characterizing the script up to this.

It isn't a film about religion, or even a religious term, as much as an onslaught against the ruthless methods big firms are prepared to use to safeguard their interests. This includes the bribery of Connolly's brother with a career promotion if he's willing to say Connolly is a scam merchant, and also a dirty tricks campaign against Davis, who's alleged to have an ulterior agenda.

In one scene Connolly taunts a priest by saying that the combined wealth of the churches could pay off the entire Third World Debt, implying that they're in collusion with large financial institutions and thus unsympathetic to his cause. The priest turns the tables on him by suggesting that maybe his boating accident was indeed an act of God in the literal sense, i.e., a reminder to Connolly not to become too attached to material possessions. This doesn't really need to be said as Connolly's main love in life is his daughter.

Connolly's final speech in the courtroom encapsulates the film's basic message: "If God exists, I don't think he sits around sinking people's little boats. I don't think he causes earthquakes and landslides, or dreams up ways to make people's brakes fail. If there is a God, surely he's everywhere. He's in the sea, in a lobster, in a line of a Robert Burns' poem, in a woman's thigh." He's also in the smile of his daughter—and in the courtroom itself. As if to underline this, a cockatoo bursts through the window and lands on the judge's bench. We seem to be momentarily in a different kind of film during this scene.

More pointedly, Connolly concludes that the "act of god" term is a lie insurance companies use to rob and con the public. By the end of the film we're supposed to be heartened to know that its days are numbered. Insurance stocks crash at the Stock Exchange and irate customers demand refunds. Connolly, meanwhile, goes boating with Ms Davis. She asks him how long it's going to take him to pay his legal bills. "About twenty years," he replies. Whereupon she tells him that she's been offered £350,000 to tell their story. So they all live happily ever after. It's a pity about this soft-centered finale as the film has a lot of bite in its earlier stages.

The conclusion is that God does indeed exist. He did, after all, send Connolly Ms Davis, and also his daughter. And he taught him that there's more to life than boats. "Even in this globalized world," we're informed, "love is still a powerful player," the film fizzling out on this cheesy note, as if to distance itself from the vulgar irreverence of the foregoing ninety minutes.

The spirit world infused an animated film that year too, *Brother Bear*, in the form of a North American Indian, Lithka, who has been killed by a bear he was chasing for running off with his fish. Lithka's fiery young brother Kenai, enraged by this, kills the bear to avenge his brother's death. Lithka is unhappy as a result and changes Kenai into a bear to teach him a lesson. The film basically concerns Kenai's "Road to Damascus" experience via an odyssey he takes to the bear equivalent of Shangri-La. Here, in the Mecca of the bear kingdom, he bonds with a cub, Koda, who accompanies him on his journey.

Koda's father was brutally killed by a hunter, a story he relates to the other bears. As he gets to the end of it Kenai suddenly realizes the cub's father was the bear he killed. Distraught, he apologizes to Koda, but he's inconsolable. As the film progresses, Kenai starts to see life from the bears' point of view, something he couldn't do at the beginning, fired up as he was with macho ideas of dominance. The irony is that he has been humanized by an animal. At the end, Lithka comes down from the spirit world to change him back into an Indian again, but Kenai refuses to leave Koda. "He needs me," he says, continuing life as a bear and surrogate father to the cub to atone for killing his real one.

Tim Burton toys with our emotions in *Big Fish* (2004) by never telling us for sure if the magical world he conjures up has a basis in reality. By filtering it through the reminiscences of an incorrigible spinner of yarns (Albert Finney) we're confused about the veracity of the reminiscences, becoming increasingly more skeptical about them as they become more far-fetched. In Finney's mythical past we meet giants, dwarfs, witches and werewolves, and enter an idyllic town called Spectre which is reminiscent of the toytowns of *The Truman Show* and *Pleasantville*. Burton also inserts gothic and surreal elements into the mix to unsettle us just in case we become too comfortable. The result is a film that repeatedly throws us curve balls until in the end he persuades us there are different forms of truth that can be attained, and also different forms of immortality.

The Harry Potter phenomenon finally has domesticated the spirit world, making it user-friendly and taming the gothic into a form of amiable hocus-pocus. Its outrageous success seems to dissolve the makers of any responsibility to expand its horizons. The books have sold an obscene amount of copies worldwide and they're steadily closing on that other best-seller, "The Bible," which perhaps says it all about the age we live in.

Enid Blyton on broomsticks? Perhaps, but J.K. Rowling has been unfairly blamed for promoting a kind of voodooism as her general values are strictly Christian. John Lyden correctly said *Harry Potter and the Goblet of Fire,* the fourth book of the series to be filmed, "deals largely with a conflict between those who would use magic for good and those who would use it for evil, so that its morality is quite traditional."[58] C.S. Lewis' *The Chronicles of Narnia*, also recently filmed, falls into the same barrow for Lyden, the overtones of the occult leavened by a strongly Christian message. He even goes so far as to state that the battle between Moses and the Pharaoh's magicians in the Bible negotiate the same ethical trajectory. Conservatives, he argues, refuse to see such similarities "in their zeal to criticize popular culture."[59]

The late lamented Michael Jackson cozying up to E.T. (Courtesy of Photofest.)

Ingrid Bergman and Bing Crosby in a scene from *The Bells of St. Mary's*. (Courtesy of RKO / Photofest.)

Mary Tyler Moore and Elvis Presley from *Change of Habit*, Presley's last film. (Courtesy of Universal Pictures / Photofest.)

Raf Vallone and Tom Tryon share a scene in *The Cardinal*. (Courtesy of Columbia / Photofest.)

Otello Sestili (Judas) whispering to Enrique Irazoqui as Jesus in Pier Paolo Pasolini's *The Gospel According to St. Matthew*. (Courtesy of Continental Distributing Inc. / Photofest.)

Myriem Roussel in a scene from Jean-Luc Godard's *Hail Mary*. (Courtesy of Photofest.)

Publicity poster for *I Confess*. (Courtesy of Warner Bros / Photofest.)

Donna Reed and James Stewart having a swinging time in *It's A Wonderful Life*.
(Courtesy of RKO Films / Photofest.)

Willem Dafoe as Jesus in the crucifixion scene from Martin Scorsese's controversial *The Last Temptation of Christ*. (Courtesy of Universal Pictures / Photofest.)

The climactic scene from *On the Waterfront* where Marlon Brando as Terry Malloy has just been beaten up by the mobsters and is being comforted by Karl Malden and Eva Marie-Saint. (Courtesy of Columbia Pictures / Photofest.)

Michael Palin playing Pontius Pilate in Terry Jones' satirical *The Life of Brian*. (Courtesy of Orion Pictures / Photofest.)

Publicity poster for *Oh God You Devil*. (Courtesy of Warner Bros / Photofest.)

Audrey Hepburn as Sister Luke in *The Nun's Story*. (Courtesy of Warner Bros / Photofest.)

Jim Caviezel as Jesus in Mel Gibson's unlikely hit, *The Passion of the Christ*. (Courtesy of Newmark / Photofest.)

Publicity poster for *The Robe*. (Courtesy of 20th Century Fox / Photofest.)

Peter O'Toole suffering from (or rather enjoying) a messianic complex in *The Ruling Class*. (Courtesy of United Artists / Photofest.)

Tom Hanks and Audrey Tautou in a publicity shot from the outrageously successful *The Da Vinci Code*. (Courtesy of Columbia Pictures / Imagine Entertainment / Photofest.)

Alan Ladd in his most famous role as the charismatic gunslinger *Shane*. (Courtesy of Paramount Pictures / Photofest.)

Elissa Landi surveys the decadence around her in *Sign of the Cross*. (Courtesy of Paramount / Photofest.)

Gina Lollobrigida looking suitably alluring in *Solomon and Sheba*. (Courtesy of United Artists Corporation / Photofest.)

Publicity Poster for *The Song of Bernadette*. (Courtesy of 20th Century Fox / Photofest.)

Charlton Heston as Moses in Cecil B. DeMille's second version of *The Ten Commandments*. (Courtesy of Paramount / Photofest.)

—5—

Real Spirits

Just as today's films are questioning old verities and throwing out many sacred cows, so are the stars and directors going on record with their skeptical attitudes toward things spiritual. Peter O'Toole once defined himself as a "retired" Catholic, saying "All I believe is that the No. 11 bus goes along the Strand to Hammersmith—but I know it isn't being driven by Santa Claus." (*Daily Mail*, June 16, 1972)

In 1963 Richard Burton told *Playboy* magazine, "The weak rely on Christ, the strong do not."[1] He went on to describe fervent churchgoers as moral cowards looking for the bromide of "fire insurance" through prayer. Burton also remarked, "The more I study religion, the more I'm convinced that man never worshipped anything but himself. He created God in his image." Alec Guinness converted from Anglicanism to Roman Catholicism, feeling this religion was the "crack unit" of spirituality, i.e., the most daunting and challenging discipline. He also felt something "Waughish" in his conversion. He attended the Sacraments until his death.

His conversion took place in 1956, partly as the result of a pact he made with God to do so if his son Matthew recovered from poliomyelitis, a form of infantile paralysis he fell prey to in 1952, which resulted in him being paralyzed from the waist down. He also said, "Let him recover and I will never put an obstacle in his way should he ever wish to become a Catholic."[2] There were fears he might be permanently disabled for life but he made an almost full recovery and his father made good his vow.

He admitted he had many faults, but stressed that he would have had many more without religion. He had contemplated becoming an Anglican priest once. The idea of being a Catholic one appealed to him also, but celibacy would have been a bridge too far for him.

In his youth he had a devotion to many saints, particularly the two Teresas—of Lisieux and Avila. He had an ambition to be a saint himself too, one that went the way of all flesh as the muse took hold of him. Lyndall Gordon believed he was someone who wished to be a saint more than a poet, but became all the greater as a poet for his failure to attain sainthood.

He experienced feelings of almost mystical ecstasy in the presence of the Blessed Sacrament, writing once in his diary that he was walking up Kingsway in the middle of an afternoon when an impulse compelled him to start running. With a state of almost sexual excitement he ran until he reached the little Catholic Church there which he'd never entered before. He knelt down, and for ten minutes was lost in his thoughts.

On another occasion he said he got very put off by people who looked at the afterlife—if it exists—as a cocktail party attended by one's dead friends and billions of others, where one waves happily to Mary Queen of Scots, Shakespeare, Socrates and a few Catholic saints. It must have been very exhausting for the VIPs to be continually on show. The vision of God, whatever that may mean, seemed to get bypassed. Perhaps he was expected to just put in an appearance now and then as some giant genial host." He believed in heaven and hell, but not in the traditional sense. He believed time ceased for the individual at death, so there could be no afterlife as there was no before-life, but he believed the personality lived in God's keeping. He wondered why eternity was always thought of as a length of time when what it really represented was a state where time no longer existed.

He didn't like the post-Vatican II reforms, which saw the Mass reduced to a kind of social meal in which the laity performed the Consecration. He hadn't especially liked Latin at school but missed its sonority in the "essential and unchanging parts of the Mass." He winced at congregations intoning Introits etc. in dull English, slowly and badly, while the reading of the Epistle in a plummy voice by some inarticulate speaker was unbearable to him. He preferred the priest to stand with his back to him rather than facing him like, as the author Piers Paul Read put it, "a jovial scout-master serving orangeade and cupcakes in a village hall."

He felt the church was bending over backwards to please the young, but that they themselves were bored with such compromises. Why else would they be rushing to alternative religions in such numbers? Guinness himself flirted with Buddhism for a while, but preferred the rigorous discipline of Catholicism, which sat better with his scrupulous nature. Why, he wondered, did the Church ever abandon the Latin liturgy, which contained words ladened with 2000 years of devotion? The new Mass was so banal and vulgar, it reminded him of being in a supermarket of the heart: "Hand-shaking and embarrassed smiles and smirks have replaced the older courtesies—kneeling is out; queuing is in, and the general tone is rather like a BBC radio broadcast for tiny tots."[3]

Guinness was also psychic. He warned James Dean that he would die in the car that killed him just a week before Dean's tragic accident. "If you get into that car," Guinness said to Dean, "you will be found dead in it by this time next week." And he was.[4]

Gabriel Byrne's feelings about religious matters have changed quite dramatically since he was a boy. He's a non-believer now, as he revealed on TV recently,[5] but used to serve Mass as a child, loving the sound of the Latin, of which he learned large chunks. He even became addicted to candle grease at this time and also wine and some hosts. A priest told him his hand would wither if he ever ate a host. This wasn't the only thing a priest told him that didn't come to pass.

Byrne thinks of the church as his first theater. He found the incense seductive, and the candle-light and flowers. One day when he was eleven years of age a mission priest came to his school and showed him slides of Ecuador and Bolivia, where his Order was stationed. Byrne was entranced and six months later he found himself on a boat for England intent on becoming a priest. At this junior seminary he had his first taste of real drama when he appeared in a production of *Oliver*.

He spent three years there in all but was too young to know what he wanted. He had unreleased sexual energy which he channelled into athletic events. He discussed marriage with some of the other seminarians, unsure of where he stood. It was an unreal time for him. Eventually, and perhaps inevitably, he got into trouble for smoking. The rector told him he'd been observing his behavior for sometime and it was obvious to him that Byrne had no vocation so the best thing for him to do would be to pack his bags.

The rest is history. Byrne went on to become a famous actor. Today he thinks that putting a large amount of men together in an institution is unnatural, and a breeding-ground for perversion. He sympathizes with pedophiliacs and is a strong advocate for the abolition of celibacy.

Martin Sheen was raised as a devout Roman Catholic but fell away from practicing his faith in his late twenties. He said he became alienated from Catholicism in the 1960s because it wasn't politicized. He grew away from it because it wasn't strong enough to hold him.

Sheen suffered a heart attack on the movie *Apocalypse Now* and it transformed his life. The attack, he felt, was a manifestation of a spiritual as well as a physical illness, a "recompense for a life improperly lived."[6] Up until now he'd made fame his God and the chickens were coming home to roost. As he recovered he gave up cigarettes—in the past he had smoked up to eighty a day—began to exercise and eat healthily and, more importantly, started to look inside himself for the root cause of his discomfiture.

He came to the conclusion that in the race for movie success he had neglected his family and other things that should have been closer to his heart. Up until his attack, he confessed, "Only my career was important to me. But our careers are just projections of our egos. We're not careers any more than we are our hair, clothes, or whatever. Who we really are is something far more substantial than an image."[7]

After *Apocalypse Now* wrapped he tried to distance himself from it, even withdrawing his name from an Academy list of nominees for the Best Actor Award. "I'm not interested in any violent pictures," he said.[8] He felt the character he played had entered his DNA, giving him dark thoughts and emotions which he couldn't quite deal with.

There followed four years of torment. "I was a miserable man, and miserable to be around," he confessed. "My family couldn't live with me and I don't blame them." For three months he separated from them, and from his wife. "It was the craziest I ever felt," he told an interviewer from *Vanity Fair* magazine in 1987, "I was at sea, really adrift. I would stop perfect strangers on the street and ask them if they believed in God."[9] One night in a restaurant he got drunk and took a swing at a police officer in anger after being robbed. He ended up in jail.

From that night on he vowed never to drink again. He also became reconciled with his wife. A few years later he appeared in the film *Gandhi* in India and reached a higher form of reconciliation with himself. He came to the conclusion that we were all united in life after finishing that film, that we were all from the same father and an endemic part of the mystical body of Christ. In the poor children of India he saw his own children, realizing that all of mankind was interconnected.

After he returned from India he became a practicing Catholic again. He also sounded off about his belief in reincarnation, claiming that until the third or 4th century the Church believed in it too. He found it hard to believe he wasn't Adam. He believed we were all still in the Garden of Eden, trying to get back to God.

His work he sees as conducive to that aim, creativity being really a manifestation of the spirit of God's presence in us. It's a conduit and we have to grab it. In the next film he made, *Man, Woman and Child*, he insisted on $1\frac{1}{2}$ hour lunch-breaks during which he could do yoga to get in touch with that spirit. At the moment he's integrated his Catholic beliefs into a fascination with Indian mysticism, where balance of mind, body and spirit is paramount.

Sophia Loren describes herself as a witch with an acute extra-sensory perception. She says she wears a red garment at some point of every day "to keep the demons at bay." When her grandmother died, she believes the woman's spirit entered her body.

She was once invited to a gala charity ball in Brussels but refused to take the plane that would get her there because she had a premonition about it crashing. The girl who replaced her, a former Miss Italy, was killed in a plane crash on her return. On a lighter note, Loren once shared a plane with the Irish rock singer Bono, of U2. Agitated when she spotted lightning outside, Bono reassured her by saying, "Don't worry; that's just God taking your photograph!" (*Hollyweird*, Michael O'Mara, p. 191)

John Wayne was also deeply superstitious. He felt a hat on a bed led to lack of work and freaked if anyone put one there. He also hated anyone opening an umbrella indoors. If he was playing poker and anyone accidentally dealt a card face up, he made them stand up and circle his chair three times to break the spell.

Barbara Stanwyck always wore a gold medallion round her neck for luck. Fred Astaire felt a plaid suit he owned brought him good omens. Edward G. Robinson carried an old silver dollar. John Garfield wore the same old pair of shoes in each film, and James Stewart the same hat.

Vincent Price claimed to have had a vision of the death of Tyrone Power on November 15, 1958 when he was flying from Hollywood to New York and saw written in the clouds the words "Tyrone Power Is Dead." Power had collapsed on the set of the film *Solomon and Sheba* at the exact sale time Price said he saw the message.

Zsa Zsa Gabor believed that if a mirror broke, you had to stand on the Pont Alexandre Bridge in Paris and throw the pieces over your shoulder into the Seine or you'd have bad luck all your life. Director Gillo Pontecorvo always wore the same overcoat for the first scene of a film. He never allowed anyone to wear purple on his sets, and wouldn't answer questions put to him on Thursdays. If someone spilled salt in his presence he ran round a table throwing more salt everywhere to keep demons at bay. If someone spilled wine he made them dip their finger in it and daub it behind the ear of everyone in the room.

Glenn Ford became a believer in reincarnation in the 1970s when he underwent hypnosis and regressed to five previous lives, among them a Christian in 3rd-century Rome where he was thrown to the lions. He also believed he was a guard in the court of King Louis XIV who was killed in a duel, a 19th century Scottish music teacher and a Denver cattle baron in the late 1800s. Sylvester Stallone, meanwhile, believes he had a previous life during the French Revolution.

Shirley MacLaine is Hollywood's best-known believer in reincarnation. Some of her books get up people's noses but she would want to be an extremely talented writer of fiction to have made it all up. She believes she was reincarnated at least three times and has gone into trance-like states through what she calls "spiritual acupuncture" to recapture memories of these past lives, one of which ended by her being crushed to death by an elephant.

Peter Sellers said he allowed himself to be visited by the spirits of dead people in order to draw inspiration from them for characters he was playing in his movies. He was using them, he admitted, but they were also using him because he gave them a shot at another life through him. Gina Lollobrigida claims she saved her family from being killed towards the end of World War II when she had a premonition one day in her Roman home that it was going to be bombed by the Nazis. She told her sisters to move away from the place they were sitting by the window and within seconds a bomb exploded, shattering the area they had just vacated. Robert Mitchum's son Chris also claims to have psychic powers which caused his father to defer to him in time's past.

Other stars have had near-death experiences. Liz Taylor suffered an acute viral infection on the set of *Cleopatra* in 1961 and slipped into a coma. She says she felt herself drifting out of life in a manner that was painful but also beautiful—like childbirth. She had an out-of-body experience of dying before an emergency tracheotomy brought her back.

(Peter Sellers is also alleged to have died and come back in 1964, over a decade before his final, fatal heart attack.) Taylor recently remarked that she felt heaven didn't want her and hell was afraid of her. She went on to state that the latter destination was where she expected most of her friends to be.

Richard Gere has been devoted to Buddhism and the Dalai Lama for many years now, his commitment to Tibet, a country he aids financially, helping to keep his feet on the ground. Buddhism, he claims, has made him less lustful for the oxygen of fame. It's given him serenity and a sense of his real identity. The Gere Foundation channels millions of dollars to Tibetan causes annually as well as raising money for AIDS research.

W.C. Fields believed that more people were driven insane through religious hysteria than by drinking alcohol. Towards the end of his life Fields, an agnostic, was espied reading the Bible. Asked why, he replied acidically, that he was looking for loopholes. Orson Welles used to say that he didn't pray because he didn't want to bore God, an unusual statement from a man deemed to be possessed of a gargantuan ego.

Lily Tomlin said that when we talk to God we're praying, but when he talks to us we're schizophrenic. Mel Brooks saw the main problem with God being that he can't keep everyone happy. He was like a Jewish waiter in that he had too many tables. Charlie Chaplin once spoke of his wish to play Jesus on screen. He was a logical choice, he argued, because he was a Jew and a comedian—and he was also an atheist, so he would be able to look at the character objectively.

Phyllis Diller expressed an unusual take on Genesis: "God created Eve when He had finished creating Adam," she announced. "Then He stepped back, scratched His head and said, 'I think I can do better than that.'"

Frank Sinatra didn't believe in a personal God (except, some might joke, himself). Marlon Brando joked that he was the type of guy who, when he died, was going to heaven to give God a hard time for making him bald. Sinatra said he believed in nature, the birds, the sea and the sky, and didn't look further than this for miracles. He didn't believe in relying on a *deus ex machina* for a favorable roll of the dice. He had a respect for life in any form, he told *Playboy* magazine in the mid-1970s, like Albert Schweitzer, Albert Einstein, or Bertrand Russell.

He was covering all the angles here, as was Bob Hope when he confessed that he did benefits for all religions. He said he would have hated to blow the hereafter on a technicality.

Alfred Hitchcock, as we saw in his approach to *I Confess*, was Catholic to the core. In fact when he married his assistant director Alma

Reville, he insisted she convert to Catholicism. He attended Sunday Mass for most of his life, particularly when his mother and daughter were visiting him. (His daughter married the grandnephew of a Cardinal.)

Part of the reason *I Confess* failed at the box office was due to the fact that Hitchcock imagined its Catholic elements, in particular the idea of the sacred seal of the confessional, would appeal to audiences. This was a poor judgment on his part as most viewers couldn't imagine how Montgomery Clift, his tormented priest, would risk his life to protect that of a murderer. For once, the "McGuffin" failed, as I said already.

As Richard Blake wrote in *Afterimage*, Hitchcock wasn't as interested in theology as in directing a good thriller. To this end he created "a fine secular protagonist who happened to be a priest caught in the demands of his profession, and loyalty to a woman he once loved and may love still."[10] From this point of view Clift might as well have been "a captured spy facing torture and death rather than revealing state secrets to the enemy, or a lawyer choosing personal ruin rather than incriminating a loved one."[11] The director Eric Rohmer said of Hitchcock, "His works are of a profane nature, and though they often deal with questions relating to God, their protagonists aren't gripped by an anxiety that is properly speaking religious."[12]

Clift *was*, of course, but either due to the constraints of the script or his own neurotic reticence, he didn't make this manifest. To quote Blake, "He never articulates his motivation as fear of losing his soul or committing grave sin by violating the sacred trust of the priesthood. In his conflict he doesn't balance his eternal salvation against his earthly life, nor does he pray for divine guidance. Specialised Catholic knowledge adds little to the understanding of his dilemma." As a result, the bottom fell out of the plot, thin and all as that was.

Hitchcock's Catholicity fuelled many of the plots of his films, whether he realized it or not. In *Psycho* we can deduce that Marion Crane (Janet Leigh) must suffer for her sexual dalliance at the beginning of the film, and indeed her larceny. Similar notions of crime and punishment are threaded through many of his other thrillers without him appending overt didacticism to them.

One may surmise that Hitchcock was both attracted to and repulsed by sexual philandering. He remained faithful to his wife, apart from minor flirtations, during their fifty four-year marriage, but seems to have been driven to distraction by sexual desires which, for one reason or another, he couldn't put into practice. He was strongly attracted to Grace Kelly but could only express this desire vicariously through his camera lens.

Likewise for Kelly's successor Tippi Hedren, a woman he did make some sexual overtures to. When they were rebuffed, he played some cruel pranks on her, giving her a toy coffin on one occasion. During the filming of *The Birds* he subjected her to immense pain, at one point almost being responsible for her eye being gouged out by a seagull. He also tied him self to her contractually without giving her film roles, thereby killing her career by default. If we're to be Freudian about all of this we could see that his anger was partly at Hedren and partly at himself for desiring her. Such schizoid confusion is of course at the heart of his most famous character, the Norman Bates of *Psycho*, another conflicted soul torn apart by sexual guilt.

Toward the end of his life, Hitchcock stopped attending Mass and developed a resentment of priests. He felt paranoid about the fact that they hated him and were chasing him.

James Dean, like his Method contemporary Clift, was also riven by neuroses. He famously said that he wanted to "live fast, die young and make a good-looking corpse," quoting the famous John Derek line from *Knock On Any Door*.[13] A more relevant quote, from *James Dean: In His Own Words* (Omnibus Press, 1989, p.75) was, "If a man can bridge the gap between life and death, I mean if he can live on after he dies, then maybe he was a great man."

Elsewhere he remarked, "Death is the only thing left to respect. It's the one inevitable, undeniable truth. Everything else can be questioned, but death is truth. In it lies the only nobility for man, and beyond it the only hope."

At his funeral pastor Xen Harvey remarked, "The career of James Dean has not ended. It has just begun. And God himself is directing the production."[14]

David Thomson believed Dean knew there was a darkness somewhere, as awesome as the planetarium in *Rebel*, and that if he looked into it, then he would be resolved, happy and unhappy, evil and benign, Thomson believed he needed audiences in the same way a ghost needed a house to haunt.

There wasn't an opportunity for greatness in this world, he wrote once to a priest-mentor he had, Reverend James DeWeerd. On the contrary, mankind was basically conditioned to behave in a streamlined manner. If one tried to break out of that mold, like a fish trying to swim in the sand, he would drown.

Dean formed a strong attachment to a woman fascinated by the occult who went by the name of Vampira, though she was actually born Maila Nurmi. He wanted to find out if she was obsessed by a satanic force, he told Hedda Hopper in an interview, but he found that she wasn't interested in anything except her make-up.

Nurmi believed Dean possessed what she called "morbido," which was the opposite of libido: an impulse toward death. He'd always been fascinated with death, she knew, and didn't think he'd live to see thirty. On his wall he had a photograph of a man being struck by a bullet. He also liked to have photos taken of himself in funeral caskets. In his apartment he had a noose hanging from the ceiling. One day when Nurmi was there he asked her to read him a Ray Bradbury story about a boy who'd hanged himself in his garage. He informed Nurmi that he believed he would also die of a broken neck. This did happen, though not with a noose.

According to Warren Newton Beath, who wrote the book *The Death of James Dean*, Dean never fully recovered from his mother's painful death from breast cancer when he was nine. "With her loss," Beath hypothesized, "it seemed that the underpinnings of his universe were knocked out. No horror was beyond possibility." Beath contends that Dean sought out a quick and violent death for himself to avoid the lingering torture of his mother's disease.

The author John Gilmore, who wrote the book *Live Fast, Die Young*, claims Dean told him, "My mother wasn't afraid of death. You know what scared her? Losing life, losing what she had." Asked how he felt about death in general, he told Gilmore it was like going into a darkness as black as a dirty river. "There isn't any heaven," he added, "no matter what they tell you. There's no hell either. There's nothing before you're born and nothing after you're dead." Gilmore then asked him what kept him going if these were his beliefs. "Fear," he replied. "Fear of being nothing and fear of having pain."

Shortly before he died, Dean made a road safety commercial for television with the actor Gig Young (who would shoot both himself and his wife some decades later). In one part of the ad, Young asked him if he had any advice for young drivers. "Take it easy," Dean replied, a slight smile playing about his lips, "the life you save may be mine."

On the set of *Giant*, his last movie, the director George Stevens prohibited him from racing during the shoot because, he surmised, he was afraid he'd break a leg.

Dean suggested—presciently—that it was probably his neck that Stevens was more worried about.

After he died, Jack Warner reflected ruthlessly that it was irresponsible of Dean to die after Warner had worked so hard to build him up into a star. One is reminded that after Elvis Presley died, his manager

Tom Parker insisted that Elvis Presley Enterprises would continue as if nothing happened.

Parker wore a florid shirt to the funeral.

The Spanish film director Luis Bunuel often satirized religion in his films. He was an avowed atheist despite (or because of) a pious youth. Frequently such a youth results in an inversion of the original devotion. Bunuel was similarly skeptical of science but loved mystery, dreams and the surreal—all of which are present in his films in greater or lesser degrees.

Bunuel claimed to have lost his faith after reading Darwin's *The Origin of Species*. Around the same time he lost his virginity. The church's revulsion of things sexual confirmed him in his animosity towards it. In his autobiography *My Last Breath* he wrote, "Saint Thomas Aquinas went so far as to affirm that the sexual act, even between husband and wife, was a venial sin, since it implied lust." As far as religion was concerned, "Desire and pleasure may be necessary, since God created them, but any suspicion of concupiscence, any impure thought, must be ruthlessly tracked down and purged. After all, our purpose on this earth is first and foremost to give birth to more and more servants of God."

This line of thinking made the forbidden fruit of sex even more tantalizing for the young Bunuel: "Wicked pleasures became all the more to be savoured because they were mortal sins." In his autobiography he explained how his philosophy came into being: "If we could imagine there is no such thing as chance, that the history of the world is logical and even predictable, then we'd have to believe in God. We'd have to assume the existence of a great watchmaker, a supreme organiser. Yet by the same token, if God can do anything, might he not have created a world governed by chance? No, the philosophers tell us, chance cannot be one of God's creations. The two are mutually exclusive. Since I myself have no faith, which is also a matter of chance, there seems to be no way to break out of this vicious circle, which is why I've never entered it in the first place."

He went on to say that, presuming God exists, "What am I to him? Nothing, a murky shadow. My passage on this earth is too rapid to leave any traces. It counts for nothing in space or in time. God really doesn't pay any attention to us, so even if he exists, it's as if he didn't." These sentiments suggest Bunuel didn't even study the rudiments of Christianity, which emphasizes the fact that God has numbered every hair on the head of each of his beings.

In Bunuel's film *The Milky Way* one of his characters exclaims, "The fact that science and technology fill me with contempt forces me to believe in God." He himself disagreed with this viewpoint, "because one can also choose, as I have, simply to live in the mystery." This to me sounds more like agnosticism than atheism proper. "If we could only find the courage to accept the fundamental mystery of our lives," he argued, "then we might be closer to the sort of happiness that comes with innocence. Fortunately, somewhere between chance and mystery lies imagination, the only thing that protects our freedom, despite the fact that people keep trying to reduce it or kill it off altogether."

Bunuel was fascinated by religion even though he disagreed with most of its precepts, and right up to his death he engaged in robust discussions about it with a Dominican priest of his acquaintance. "Before I knew you, Luis," the priest remarked to him once, "my faith wavered sometimes, but now that we've started those discussions, it's become invincible." Bunuel replied that he could have said exactly the same thing about his own unbelief, adding that his surrealist friends would have been amused by him engaging in all these *tête-à-têtes* with an ideological adversary.

He was also intrigued by the idea of death, and even hell. "In these modern times," he declared, "the flames and pitchforks have disappeared, and hell is now only a simple absence of divine light. I see myself floating in a boundless darkness, my body still intact for the final resurrection, but suddenly another body bumps into mine. It's a Thai who died 2000 years ago, falling out of a coconut tree. He floats off into the infernal obscurity and millions of years go by until I feel another body. This time it's one of Napoleon's camp followers. And so it goes, over and over again, as I let myself be swept along for a moment in the harrowing shadows of this post-modern hell."

As he approached death, this mischievous director imagined a final joke he could play on his equally atheistic friends. He could summon a priest to his deathbed and, to their horror, make a confession of all his sins before asking for absolution and receiving the Last Rites. He wondered if he'd have the strength to play the joke. Nobody knows if he did, but judging by the puckish nature of many of the concepts in his films, and his childlike penchant for pulling people's legs, he would have made every effort to do so.

Ingmar Bergman, another skeptical director, struggled all his life with a "tormented and joyless" relationship with God. In his autobiography *The Magic Lantern* he wrote: "Faith and lack of faith, punishment, grace and redemption, all were real to me, all were imperative. My prayers stank of anguish, entreaty, trust, loathing and despair. God spoke, God said nothing." Life doesn't have a purpose, he believed, and when we die we're extinguished: "From being, you will be transformed to non-being. A god does not necessarily dwell among our increasingly capricious atoms."

A priest in his film *The Serpent's Egg* outlined Bergman's desolate alienation: "We live far away from God, so far away that no doubt He doesn't hear us when we pray to Him for help. So we must help each other. We must give each other the forgiveness that a remote God denies us."

Woody Allen's homage for Bergman is apparent from as far back as *Interiors* in 1978, his first "serious" film. He interested him, Allen confided, because he dealt with themes that were enormously significant—death, the meaning of life, the question of religious faith.

Bergman's influence on Allen can be seen in films like *September* and *Another Woman* as well as *Interiors*. He felt Bergman found a way to show the soul's landscape, says Allen of his hero. By rejecting cinema's standard demand for conventional action, he allowed wars to rage inside characters that were as potent as military operations.

Allen still sees death as the central issue affecting everyone. We can do something about everything else—love problems, money problems and so on, but this is the one unsolvable mystery overhanging us all. Bergman had the perfect metaphor for it in *The Seventh Seal* with the Black Plague. Allen admits he hasn't been as successful. He can't go beyond what he did. Sometimes He makes fun of death but it's always there, gnawing at us in the same way as it did Antonius Block. In that sense, nothing has changed and it never will. Nobody can go beyond Bergman. If we appear to, it's just old wine in new wineskins.

Woody once confided that his parents' values in life were God and carpeting. One of his favorite hobbies is putting incongruous concepts together like this to trivialize the more profound one. Elsewhere he wrote that in youth he was sadistically beaten by boys of all races and creeds. Of his first wife he emoted that have these deep philosophical discussions and she always proved he didn't exist.

In *Love and Death* Allen speaks of God as an "underachiever." Elsewhere he has a bewildered character emote, "Not only do I not believe in God, but try getting a plumber at the weekend." (*The Guiness Dictionary of Poisonous Quotations*, compiled by Colin Jarman, 1991, p. 191.) And elsewhere again, "If this world is really only an illusion, then I definitely paid too much for that carpet."

With somebody like Allen, eschatological curiosity is always tinged with quirkiness, as when he trilled, "I'm what you call a teleological existential atheist. I believe that there's an intelligence to the universe, with the exception of certain parts of New Jersey." In more solemn

mode, he informed *Time* magazine as far back as 1979, "My real obsessions are religious—to do with the meaning of life and the futility of
obtaining immortality through art."

He was in frivolous form again when he reflected that the silence of
God was a problem, but a bigger one was getting man to shut up! The
first part of this reflection shows his influence by Bergman, the second
his Groucho Marx persona. Whenever he threatens to get profound he
usually pulls the carpet from under himself. It's as if humor is a safety
valve to stop him confronting huge issues baldly, without any regress.
Like most comedians he wears a mask.

Allen directed *Love and Death* in 1975. This centered on a cowardly
Russian soldier in the era of Napoleon, the plot acting as a hook upon which
he could hang his customary fusillade of quasi-philosophical meanderings.

In one scene he pines: "If only God would give me some sign—a
burning bush, a parting of the seas . . . or having my uncle Sasha pick up
a check." The profundity of the first two Biblical concepts and their
funny upending is his stock-in-trade.

At another point of the film a character looks out at an array of dead bodies
on a battlefield and exclaims, "God is testing us." Allen replies, "If he's
going to test us, why doesn't he give us a written?" He argues over the justifi-
ability of killing Napoleon with Diane Keaton in screwball fashion, the scene
a mixture of farce and theological rigor. "If I don't kill him," he exclaims
heatedly to her, "he'll make war all over Europe. What would Socrates say?"

Allen told *Esquire* magazine the film implied God didn't exist, or, if
He did, He wasn't to be trusted. "After coming to this conclusion," he
added, "I have twice been nearly struck by lightning, and once forced to
engage in a long conversation with a theatrical agent."

"I don't want to achieve immortality through my work," Allen admitted once, "I want to achieve it by not dying." (*The Times Quotations*,
Times Books, 2006, p.135.) And in his book *Without Feathers* he confessed, "I don't mind dying; I just don't want to be there when it happens." His quips have become instantly quotable in the manner of a
latter-day, soul-searching Oscar Wilde.

Basically he defines himself as an agnostic. "I don't believe in an
afterlife," he's quoted as saying in Fred Metcalf's *Penguin Dictionary of
Humorous Quotations,* "Although I am bringing a change of under-
wear." A Jew who was bored by most Jewish things in his childhood,
including the synagogue, he suggested baseball and movies were much
more important to him than religion during his formative years.

He didn't think he was lucky or unlucky to be Jewish; it was just the
way things were. He didn't envy Catholics, regarding them as a breed

who couldn't see interesting movies "because the Legion of Decency wouldn't permit them."[15] He also found the Catechism boring "and I felt the same thing about Hebrew school, my mind drifting out the window, not learning anything, just counting the minutes until it was over."[16]

Ethical and eschatological issues, however, are in his DNA, all the way from comical asides in his early movies to *Crimes and Misdemeanours* in 1989. This film explores the concept of justice gone awry. How can a man commit murder and get away with it while decent, law-abiding folk suffer the slings and arrows of outrageous fortune? In many seminal scenes the problem of evil, which is an issue as old as time, is captured by Allen with an intensity many thought beyond his range.

In the earlier *Manhattan* he's asked how quitting his job is going to affect him. "I'll probably have to give my parents less money," he replies, adding, "This is gonna kill my father. He's not gonna be able to get as good a seat in the synagogue. He's gonna be in the back, away from God, far from the action." Such irreverent lines don't always mask his genuine concern for issues like the hereafter, though a lot of this is based on fear—a very Catholic emotion.

Hannah and Her Sisters (1986) is generally regarded as the best film of his middle period, Allen winning an Oscar for his screenplay. He plays a hypochondriac who constantly imagines he's on the way out, either through a brain tumor or some associated terminal condition. At one point, after hearing the good news from his doctor that his immediate concerns are unfounded, he does a dance of delight down the street. But his joy is short-lived.

Having received momentary relief from the immediate fear, he now starts to think: He may not die today, but he definitely will someday, so no matter how many times his fears are quelled, no doctor in the world can quell his ultimate one. Relief, therefore, is suddenly transformed into an inconsolable despair over "the human condition." The scene is a mixture of fun and panic, leading to Allen's hilarious forays into Catholicism and being a Hare Krishna, albeit with stringent reservations in each case.

Desperately searching for some belief-structure to shore against the ruins of his terror of mortality, his rent-a-creed persona comes at us in its full hilarity as we see him unpacking a crucifix from his shopping bag with the same perfunctory air as he does a loaf of bread.

At another point he considers suicide seeing as his life has no meaning. He then decides that even if it is indeed absurd and we "only go round once and that's it," it might still be worth the ride. He decides to live for the moment because that might be all we're vouchsafed. There's fun to be had even if it doesn't extend into a new guise in a putative here-after. Or, as contemporary parlance would have it, "We're not here for a long time, we're here for a good time." This isn't so much a rationaliza-tion of hedonism on Allen's part as a survival mechanism, a way of hold-ing on to his sanity as he stands on the edge of an abyss.

Elvis Presley was always a spiritual person despite a life of bingeing on junk food, prescription drugs and fifth-rate movies. His love of music was forged in the churches he attended as a child and gospel singing remained his first and truest love. He also liked studying Eastern mysti-cism, and dipping into Kahlil Gibran's book *The Prophet* when the tin god of fame failed to fulfil him.

Elvis, the surviving member of twins, always felt an emptiness at his core that all the success in the world couldn't fill. He never understood why he was pitch-forked to stardom from a two-room shack in a forgot-ten town in the poor end of Memphis. There had to be a plan, he felt, and some divine intervention.

He sometimes saw himself as a kind of reincarnated Jesus. On the night he was conceived, his father, Vernon, said he saw a blue light in the sky. This fed into the biblical idea of the star in the East. Elvis was also an only son who would, in his pre-teen years, move to a larger place and gather round himself many disciples, some of whom would finally betray him. He would then be crucified on the altar of success.

In April 1964 he met his spiritual guru, Larry Geller, a part-time hairdresser who introduced him to a brace of eclectic literature on every-thing from yoga to transcendental meditation. He met him at a time when Elvis was sorely disenchanted with the no-brainer movies he was making for the likes of Hal Wallis and Norman Taurog. He had, as it were, sold his soul to the devil in aligning himself to canny shark Tom Parker, the man who put his name in lights at a horrendous price to his artistic integrity.

He had always felt this unseen hand guiding his life since he was a little boy, he told Geller, had always felt something big was going to happen to him even if he couldn't say exactly what it was. And then it happened and he couldn't understand why he was plucked out of all those millions of people.

Elvis felt he understood most of the books Geller had given him from an intellectual point of view but hadn't had the profound spiritual experi-ences they described. Geller said that wasn't a problem. What was important, he emphasized, was to surrender his ego to God. The small country boy in Elvis, which had never really gone away no matter what heights of grandeur he reached in the music and film world, found this easy enough to do.

Geller tapped into Elvis' disenchantment with the goldfish bowl of Tinseltown, opening his mind to a world of ideas that Elvis, right-wing thinker that he was, had previously shied away from. He'd never bought into the hippie cult or any of the baggage that went with it but Geller talked to him about his mother—the woman he would love more than any of his girlfriends, or even wife—and how his life had, in a sense, been freeze-framed since that woman died. Other women since then had satisfied him sensually but he had an insatiable yearning for the one who bore him. In a sense, the umbilical cord had never really been cut.

Geller introduced him to a Self-Realization Fellowship run by a woman named Daya Mata, who actually reminded him of his mother. He even started a Meditation Center in Graceland, his home, and did readings from the Bible, Timothy Leary and Gibran. Afterward he usually gave his own idiosyncratic take on them, much to the amusement of the self-styled "Memphis Mafia," his slew of gofers who knew him only as The Hillbilly Cat. They felt Geller was tampering with his mind and told Parker to get rid of him.

At this point Elvis had been living with Priscilla Beaulieu for many years and she wanted to marry him. In March 1965, at a time when both Priscilla and the rest of Elvis' entourage were getting seriously worried that he was drifting away from them, he had a vision one day while out walking with Geller. He looked up at the sky at one point and saw what he believed was the figure of Joseph Stalin emerging from it. In a frenzied state he rushed up to Geller and told him what he'd seen.

After a few moments, he said, the Stalin vision turned into one of Jesus. To him this was a sign. Stalin was his own dark side and Jesus his chance of salvation. What the vision was telling him was to ditch the dumb movies he was then making and seek a richer path to fulfilment. He told Geller he wanted to be a monk.

As soon as Elvis saw the vision he knew what Geller meant about surrendering his ego.

He admitted to Geller that the Stalin vision was like a lightning bolt that went through his body, transforming him completely and making him see God as a tangible being directing his life.

Geller told him there was no need to give up the movies to be a monk, which seemed to appease Elvis. He told Geller he would have had difficulty raking leaves in a monastery with Priscilla watching him.

It didn't seem to occur to him that joining a secluded order would mean giving up his wife too.

The monk idea was laughed off by everyone at Graceland and Elvis soon found himself back in the movie groove. He decided to steer a middle ground, to be in the movies but not of them, as it were, and to use his fame to spread his message wherever he could.

Afterwards he started to believe he had God-like powers himself. He felt he could affect the weather, change cloud formations and even heal the sick. He saw angels and UFOs and did additional readings from the Bible to anyone who would listen. (Only brave souls chose not to, as they were all on his payroll.) Some of these readings were more Elvis than the Bible. He would say things like, "Moses was this white-haired son of a bitch who came down from the mountain. The burning bush directed his ass on down." (*Elvis Aaron Presley: Revelations from the Memphis Mafia*, by Alanna Nash, HarperCollins, 1995, p. 405.)

In May 1966, not long before he gave up movies forever and returned to live performing, Elvis recorded a number of gospel songs in Nashville, including "In the Garden," "Farther Along" and the favorite of his whole repertoire, "How Great Thou Art," the latter earning him a Grammy Award.

Shortly afterward he married Priscilla and Parker had Geller dismissed from Graceland. Priscilla persuaded Elvis to burn most of the books Geller had given him. He did so, but carried their messages inside him until the day he died. Years later he re-employed Geller and told him he'd never forgotten the lessons he'd taught him. He felt he was a version of Christ, he said, entrusted with carrying His word to his fans. On the day he died, in fact, the book he was reading was Frank Adams' treatise on the Turin Shroud, *The Scientific Search for the Face of Jesus*.

Elvis always claimed his first, and truest, love was gospel music, and that he was most himself when singing it. This is evident right up until the end of his life when he sang "How Great Thou Art" in concert. The strains of "Thus Spake Zarathustra," which preceded his entrance at such concerts, copperfastened this effect. It was as if a divine being were about to enter. When he himself did, dressed up in his elaborate jumpsuits, audiences went into raptures of frenzy. Those who touched the hem of his garment felt privileged. He threw sweat-drenched scarves to others. One was reminded of Veronica wiping the face of Jesus at the crucifixion.

Since he died, many people have claimed to have had psychic contact with him. A "Presleyterian" church was even established in his name in Denver in 1990. The Church of the Risen Elvis was set up at the same time in the same city.

In 2002 an Anglican priest from Ontario started a breakaway church called "Christ the King, Graceland Independent Anglican Church of Canada." As "Elvis Priestly," Fr Dorian Baxter went onto the altar to croon Elvis' melodies with a clerical twist. "Well it's one for the Father," he crooned, "two for the Son, three for the Holy Spirit and your life has just begun."

Like Presley, Marlon Brando was an intuitive person who believed he contained inside himself the ability to influence outside events. He also felt he could control pain, and even his blood pressure, by a Hindu practice wherein he attained a state of what he called "satori," which is the state Zen masters describe as "sudden enlightenment." Such a state enabled him to keep calm in moments of crisis, and also deal with the curses that visited his family in recent years, such as the suicide of his daughter Cheyenne, the killing of her fiancé, Dag Drollett, by her brother, Christian, and Christian's subsequent incarceration in jail.

Brando found his spiritual side excited by Polynesian culture, which he fell in love with while filming *Mutiny on the Bounty*. Afterward he bought the island of Tetiaroa, near Tahiti. He found Tahitians to be the happiest people he ever met, and the ones most untouched by materialism. America, on the contrary, had bigger cars, bigger houses, etc. and yet produced more miserable people than almost any place on earth. Consumerism, the urge to own more and more, left holes in the soul.

When Brando was young he embraced the Judeo-Christian concept of good and evil and also its corollary, i.e., that all of us were responsible for our lives. In his autobiography, *Songs My Mother Taught Me*, he said he changed his mind about this. "Epicurus said that God was either uncaring," he wrote, "and chose to ignore evil, or else he was unable to prevent it and therefore wasn't omnipotent. Augustine, trying to resolve the paradox that Christians face about how a supposedly benevolent God could allow evil to exist, rationalized it by arguing that evil wasn't a product of God but rather the absence of good."

In this context, Brando argued, events like the Holocaust and the slaughter of Native Americans (a favorite cause of his) were explained. He refused to buy into this, believing that the roots of the behavior we comfortably dub "evil" are genetic. Man's predilection towards violence, avarice and self-aggrandizement can't be suppressed by any philosophical or religious system, he believed. Further, more people were killed in the name of religion and the defense of dogma than any other single cause. As a result of this he felt terms like good and evil were outmoded Biblical archetypes.

"Catholic priests," he said, "may order their parishioners to say ten Hail Marys after confession, but in Africa and other places, religious masters put their followers into trances." Such trances helped him to achieve states of tranquillity amidst the chaos of his life, so much so, in fact, that he once asked a doctor to circumcise him without an anaesthetic because he felt enabled to kill the pain of the procedure by his heightened state of satori. The doctor refused, but Brando did manage to bring his blood pressure down by twenty points as a result of his meditation.

Brando saw the spiritual struggle essentially as a search for the self. "When one stops seeking to find out who one is," he said, "one has reached the end of the rope." He himself spent his life trying to do this, soliciting the help of analysts to help him, though many of these, he complained, just took his money and ran. (Some of them, he joked, seemed to need psychiatric treatment themselves.)

Some years before he died he said that he accepted the prospect of his imminent demise philosophically. He was calm about partaking his leave of the earth. In fact he made the preparation for old age and death into a goal that he felt he should embrace with stoicism and good grace.

Other Hollywood celebrities have had more traditional attitudes to things spiritual. Martin Scorsese was a pious youth who grew up in Little Italy. As a boy he refused to eat meat on Fridays, and believed that if he missed Mass on Sunday he'd go to hell.[17]

When he received his First Communion, he was "fascinated by images of the crucifixion and drew endless pictures of it, which I gave the nuns at school."[18] At that time he saw his religion as a violent affair, even a bloodlust. This was "domesticated," he felt, in the Mass. The twin themes of blood and devotion would go on to infuse his work from *Mean Streets* through *Taxi Driver* and even to *Raging Bull*.

Scorsese has always drawn a line between Hollywood and religion. He remembers his father taking him to see *Quo Vadis* as a child: "I was just fascinated by the beautiful three-strip Technicolor, and what looked to me like the artefacts of ancient Rome. The next one was *The Robe*. It was the first film in Cinemascope. The curtain opening at the Roxy Theatre for that new kind of image, and then the music coming up, was quite extraordinary. The ancient Roman world became in my mind part of the church and part of the ritual of the church. The music of the church became completely mixed into the music of *Quo Vadis* and *The Robe*."[19]

When Scorsese was in high school he went on a retreat where he was subjected to a fire-and-brimstone sermon from a priest. This had a traumatic effect on him, resulting in a spiritual crisis. As a result of it he wrote a memoir of the occasion which he called *Jerusalem, Jerusalem*. He was so shook over the sermon, which focused primarily on sex, that he was advised by the priest to seek psychiatric attention. He found it difficult to reconcile the Old Testament God of fear with the new one spreading love and forgiveness. The subject obsessed him and he decided he wanted to be a priest to try and work it out. At the age of thirteen he entered a preparatory seminary in New York but was expelled from here as a result of his poor grades. (He put these down to the fact that he had fallen in love shortly after enrolling.) In the next few years he still felt he had a vocation but then it trailed off. He ended up trying to work out the spiritual contradictions in himself through film, becoming "a priest of the imagination."[20]

"I believe there's a spirituality in films," Scorsese has been quoted as saying in the book *The Century of Cinema*, "even if it's not one which can supplant faith. Over the years many films have addressed themselves to the spiritual side of human nature, from Griffiths' *Intolerance* to John Ford's *The Grapes of Wrath* to Hitchcock's *Vertigo* to Kubrick's *2001*, and many more. It's as if movies answer an ancient quest for the collective unconscious. They fulfil a need that people have to share a common memory."[21]

Scorsese is fascinated by masochism, all the way from the Johnny Boy of *Mean Streets* to the Travis Bickle of *Taxi Driver* and the Jake La Motta of *Raging Bull* to the Jesus of *Last Temptation*. Only through suffering, the Catholic in him seems to be suggesting, can we see the light. It's arguable he took the dark Catholic iconography of his childhood too seriously and barracked his films with it as a kind of expiation.

He once described the feeling he got in church as being "the same type of feeling someone else might get from taking an acid trip."[22] Asked why he stopped practicing, he replied, "I had some problems with sex and mortal sin, but what really did it was sitting in a church in Los Angeles and hearing a priest call the Vietnam War a holy one."[23]

He said elsewhere that he had really wished to become a priest "so that I'd be saved." He eventually wound up "finding a vocation in movies with the same kind of passion."[24] This wasn't too difficult since he was a cinemaholic since youth. Recurring attacks of asthma had left him bedbound through most of it, so when other children were out at play he was either reading or watching films on television. Screen characters became his friends, his other-self. He watched films voraciously, accruing an encyclopedic knowledge of their diffuse coordinates. No detail escaped him, and many of these would find their way into his own works in the years to come.

Perhaps his most loaded religious metaphors occur in *Mean Streets*, his 1973 evocation of racketeering, uneasy camaraderie and dubious salvation. At the beginning we hear Charlie, played by Harvey Keitel, say "You don't make up for your sins in church; you do it in the streets; you do it at home. The rest is bullshit and you know it." But the streets, as we learn, only serve to extend his sins, not minimize them.

Charlie is conflicted, unable to reconcile the two sides of himself which are spurring him variously towards crime and the church. "I was raised with priests and gangsters," Scorsese said once, "and now, as an artist, I'm both a gangster *and* a priest."[25]

"Most mornings on the way to school," he informed an interviewer, "I'd see bums fighting each other with broken bottles. There was blood all over the ground, which I had to step over. Or I'd be sitting in the derelict's bar across the way. We'd watch guys get up and struggle over to another table and start hallucinating and beating up someone."[26]

Richard Blake analyzes the influence of Catholic liturgy in many of Scorsese's films in his book *Afterimage*. "To prepare for his bloody mission of redemption," Blake writes, "Travis Bickle in *Taxi Driver* adopts a Mohawk-style haircut, a form of tonsure, and carefully encases his body in weapons, checking the mirror to see that his lethal vestments are in place. Similarly, Max Cady in *Cape Fear* decorates his body with tattoos, one of which is a large cross that covers his back, much like the cross on the back of a priest's chasuble. *Raging Bull* opens with Jake La Motta doing a slow motion dance alone in the ring with his hooded leopardskin robe, much like a monk's cowl, and with the billowing cigarette smoke that's suggestive of clouds of incense. In *Kundun* the monks in their cinnamon robes perform their religious duties in a way that could be a stylised version of a Catholic monastery."[27]

Today Scorsese is no longer a practicing Catholic but he realizes Catholicism is in his DNA, in the marrow of his bones. He knows it's impossible to outgrow or disown it, that it encompasses everything about a person quite apart from religion.

John Huston was as fascinated by religion as Scorsese, but much more inclined towards atheism. Once when he fell ill in Galway and was being cared for by nuns in the local hospital he admitted as much. Their reaction surprised him. Instead of contumely he actually received extra-special attention. All he could conclude was that they thought he was basically a good person but nonetheless condemned to hell for his beliefs, or rather lack of them, so they decided to give him some temporary comfort while he was alive.

Huston had a unique view of the deity. "In the beginning," he announced, "the Lord God was in love with mankind and accordingly jealous. He was forever asking mankind to prove our affection for Him. But then, as aeons passed, His ardor cooled and He assumed a new role, that of a beneficent deity. All a sinner had to do now was say he was sorry and God forgave him. The fact of the matter was that he had lost interest."[28] Lack of interest then led to total indifference for Huston, leading him to believe that God had taken up, maybe, with life elsewhere in the universe, on another planet.

This was no doubt fascinating but also evasive. So did he actually believe in a deity? Here's his answer: "I don't profess any beliefs in an orthodox sense. It seems to me that the mystery of life is too great, too wide, too deep, to do more than wonder at. Anything further would be, as far as I'm concerned, an impertinence."[29]

He also had humor. Dogged by bad weather on the set of *Moby Dick*—one particular storm almost saw Gregory Peck going up to that big studio in the sky—he joked that he originally imagined his problems in directing the film were caused by a conspiracy by his assistant director. Eventually he realized they came from a more obscure source—God. He claimed it was the most difficult film he ever made.

Donal McCann, who worked with Huston on *The Dead*, was an actor who kept very much to himself so not many people knew how he felt about religion but he had strong spiritual leanings. Towards the end of his life he was "re-baptized." Before every stage performance he would nominate somebody who had died or was sick and dedicate the performance to them. "The stage," as his friend and colleague John Kavanagh put it, "became a sacred place." (*Donal McCann Remembered*, edited by Pat Laffan, New Island Books, 2000, p. 49.)

The director Bob Quinn felt McCann had a darkness at the heart of himself which was caused by a fundamental insecurity, both with himself and the world around him. This perhaps caused his spikiness.

Sadly, most of McCann's best work was theatrical so therefore lost to posterity, but he did produce some marvellous cinematic performances. He worked for Bernardo Bertolucci in *Stealing Beauty* but his greatest work was in the Huston film *The Dead*, which was based on James Joyce's famous story of the same name. I interviewed him during the making of it and he spoke to me of the "haunting" beauty of Joyce's intimations of mortality as perceived by the two main characters in the story: Greta (Anjelica Huston, John's daughter) and Gabriel who played himself.

He often quoted the last lines of *The Dead* when he was in a morose mood: "His soul swooned slowly as he heard the snow falling faintly through the universe and faintly failing, like the descent of their last end, upon all the living and the dead." In a strange way they seemed to give him solace. It was almost as if he saw the snow washing away all his own past mistakes in one fell swoop.

"Joyce's metaphor of the snow makes the idea of death very comforting," he confided to me, "almost a consummation devoutly to be wished." It put him in mind of Keats being "half in love with easeful death." But Joyce's story, of course, is about a different kind of death: the spiritual death of the two characters.

Gabriel is immersed in his own world so much that he's never given himself totally to Greta, while she carries a torch for someone who died of consumption as a young man. Her hidden secret emerges at the end of a long night, leading to the elegiac voiceover of the finale.

Huston died shortly after making the film and McCann was shocked at his passing, despite Huston's great age at the time. His death put McCann in mind of the larger issues in life. He had a cerebral intelligence undercut by a simple, even pious faith.

It wasn't his only contradiction. A gentle person who could also be brutal, he seemed to reserve most of his sensitivity for his work. Interviewers were often terrified of him, including this one. The first time I met him he was nursing a pint in a bar, alone with his thoughts. "You're Donal McCann, aren't you?" I hazarded, which drew the reply, "I used to be." He gave a wry laugh at this. An hour later he behaved as if I were his long-lost brother. But a few days later his irascibility returned.

This was the way he continued to behave, and misbehave, any time we met. He was like litmus paper, like mercury. In his quiet moments, of which there were many, you were never quite sure if he was contemplating the meaning of life or the fate of a horse he backed in the 2.30 at Doncaster. Such was his mien; it could easily have been both.

I once asked him what meant most to him in life. It was a long time before he answered. "I get little shafts of happiness from knowing I've done my work well," he revealed, "but I also have a sense of dismay at the universe and my place in it." This made him snatch at moments of magic because they were so transient. He got a "cathartic" sense of elation from the applause of audiences. It became like a drug to him—almost as great as the other two drugs of his life: alcohol and gambling.

When McCann was "on the bottle," as I learned, he was rude and crude. He could insult and embrace you within a minute. Out of such instability of temperament sprung many of his creative juices but he was a difficult man to live with. One morning I visited him and he bore scars on his face, having fallen into the fireplace of his home the night before, too worse the wear for drink. He was also violent with the woman he lived with at this time when he had imbibed too much.

I said to him once that when I watched him play the character of Mulhall in *Strumpet City*, a television drama in which he co-starred opposite Peter O'Toole, I felt he looked like he wanted to kill everyone he looked at. "Maybe it was myself I wanted to kill," he answered. He said no more on the subject but he had that darkness about him that was intensified with alcohol. Cancer took him from us too early but he achieved a peace in his last months that didn't look possible for such a volatile man. He also gave up the drink, which most people would have imagined impossible.

It would be difficult to imagine two more contrasting stars than McCann and Christopher Reeve but if we look beneath the surface we can see the similarities. When Reeve was paralyzed from the neck down in his horrific 1995 equestrian accident he wanted to kill himself. He didn't have a traditional faith to tide him by, just a grudging agnosticism. As time went by, though, and the love of his wife and children continued to sustain him, not to mention the support of friends, medical people and his own iron will, he came to a partial acceptance of his lot which was buttressed by a flinty determination to one day walk again.

He wrote movingly at the end of his book *Still Me* that he felt like the captain of a damaged boat cast adrift at sea. "Off in the distance is a flashing light," he said. "It could be a buoy, another ship, or the entrance to a safe harbour. We have no way of knowing how far we have to go, or even if we have to stay afloat until we get there." But he was still willing to fight the good fight, even if the cards were stacked against him. Ingmar Bergman's medieval knight wasn't quite so determined.

Reeve's father was an atheist and he himself had no religion to speak of before his accident. He flirted with Scientology for a time and eventually attained a kind of spiritual peace. "When the unthinkable happens," he wrote in his book *Nothing Is Impossible*, "the lighthouse is hope. Hope must be as real and built on the same solid foundation as a lighthouse. In that way it's different from optimism or wishful thinking." He tried to resist what he calls "the numb zone," a state of mind where you don't feel depressed but not excited either. In 1995 he had to confront the fact that he was basically a 42-year-old infant. What happened since then proved him to be much more a Superman than when he had full command of his faculties and was flying through the air on a studio lot. Sadly, he died in 2004.

Bob Dylan couldn't be called a Hollywood film star in any strict sense, though he's appeared in films like *Pat Garret and Billy the Kid* and *Hearts of Fire*, as well as "rockumentaries" like *Don't Look Back, Eat the Document* and the experimental movie *Renaldo & Clara*.

Of the latter he said, "It's about the essence of man being alienated from himself and how, in order to free himself, to be re-born, he has to go outside himself. You can almost say that he dies in order to look at time, and by strength of will can return to the same body."[30]

Renaldo, he revealed, "needs to hide from the demon within, but he discovers that the demon is in fact a mirrored reflection of himself."[31] He lives in a tomb, Dylan explained, and spends the movie trying to transcend that, to break out of his own soul through dreaming, "but sometimes the dream is so powerful it has the ability to wipe him out."[32] In another sense Renaldo is Everyman, whereas Clara is the symbol of freedom.

Dylan went through a "born again" phase in the late 1970s.[33] "Jesus put his hand on me," he said in Dayton, Ohio in 1980, "It was a physical thing, I felt my whole body tremble. The glory of the Lord knocked me down and picked me up. There was a presence in the room that couldn't have been anybody but Jesus."[34]

He released three Gospel albums round about this time, *Saved, Shot of Love* and *Slow Train Coming*. Many of his old rebel adherents felt he'd sold out, but there was no gainsaying the quality of the music. "You Gotta Serve Somebody," sang the man who once warned "Don't follow leaders." Almost in an eyeblink he went from self-styled messiah of rock to servant of the Lord.

His Christ, he explained, wasn't "some dead man who had a bunch of good ideas and was nailed to a tree."[35] He was a living, vibrant entity. "We know this world is going to be destroyed," he pronounced in San Francisco, "and Christ will set up his kingdom in Jerusalem for a thousand years, where the lion will lie down with the lamb."[36]

He went on to say that he knew it wasn't fashionable to think about heaven and hell "but God doesn't have to be in fashion. He's always been fashionable. My ideology now is coming out of the Scripture. I follow God, so if my followers are following me, they're gonna be following God too, because I don't sing any song which hasn't been given to me by the Lord to sing."[37]

This was either a "road to Damascus" experience for the rock icon or the most cleverly orchestrated career move in history, engineered to re-motivate interest in flagging record sales. Or maybe it was just Dylan being Dylan, the perennial chameleon. As he once famously sang, "He who's not busy being born is busy dying."

When I interviewed Leonard Cohen in the late 1980s I asked him how he felt about this phase in Dylan's life. "I believe he was being sincere," he said, "nobody could write music that powerful unless it came from the heart, and soul."

Cohen himself re-discovered his love of Zen mysticism around this time. "It's like scraping off the rust," he told me, describing the way he meditated. "Zen is a religion for the truly lost, a concerted effort to work out the rambling intoxications of my mind. There's a crack in every experience, and that's how the light gets in."

A man who's been going to Tibet since the mid-1970s to meditate, he says, "I've always found myself drawn to the voluptuousness of austerity." He also likes the "empty" quality of Zen: "There's no prayerful worship, no supplication, no dogma. I don't even understand what my teachers are talking about a lot of the time. But I like the questions they're asking. If you keep your mind sharpened, you'll summon things from places you don't understand."

After I met him, Cohen went to a meditation center 6000 feet up in the Californian hills where he got up at 3 am in the morning to shovel his way through the snow that blocked his path to the center. Once there he tried to hammer his thoughts into unity, seeking some form of epiphany that would make sense of his eclectic past.

He's seventy-five now, but no closer to absolute answers than he ever was. I asked him if he believed literally in the line from his song "Suzanne" where he says only drowning men could see Jesus. His reply was slow and considered.

"I think you have to surrender, and surrendering often involves going down on your knees, or on your back or on your belly. In those moments you have to forget about the things that have held you up. You have to let them go. When you do that, something comes into your heart that's your true mainstay. Your deepest resources are called into activity when you let the weaker ones go. In the morning we sprout as flowers, in the evening we are cut down and withereth. Therefore, teach us to number our days. Nobody has the whole picture."

Cohen doesn't lie on beds in the Chelsea Hotel with Janis Joplin clones anymore, or indeed the Hollywood actress Rebecca de Mornay, with whom he also had a fling. Neither does he have himself fed tea and oranges by enigmatic ladies down by rivers. In latter times he's found something far more fulfilling in the knotty shards of his own convoluted psyche.

In *Endgame*, the playwright Samuel Beckett has his main character scream out about God: "The bastard—He doesn't exist!" Such a contradictory attitude sums up many people's contrapuntal attitude to faith, oscillating as they do between rage and incredulity. "I don't believe in Mary," Charlie Sheen likes to joke, "but God was her mother." In the recent Jack Nicholson movie *About Schmidt* we have a jolly undertaker tell Nicholson, who's devastated about losing his wife, "God doesn't mind you being angry at him."

Luis Bunuel epitomized a contradiction like Beckett's in his much-quoted epithet, "I'm still an atheist, thank God." The writer Georges Duhamel said he respected God as a concept too much to hold him responsible for the absurdity of the world. Alfonso X suggested that if God had consulted him before he created the world he would have advised him to go for something simpler.

It may surprise some people to learn that Mae West, who's primarily regarded as an earthy, even pagan soul, had a fascination with the supernatural for most of her life. She felt the hand of spirits guiding her through all of the seminal decisions of her life, and was a devout Church-goer as well.

She often held séances to try and get in touch with her mother's soul after she died, and also believed that she once made contact with her dead father through "spirit tapping." She dabbled in astrology and numerology as well, and liked to attend fortune-tellers.

In 1941 West attended a spiritualist convention in Los Angeles that focussed on extra-sensory perception. After it was over she consulted a spiritualist who instructed her on techniques she might use to tap into this part of herself. With this in mind, she locked herself away from everyone she knew for three weeks in an attempt to connect with her inner self.

In the third week of her sequestration she claimed to hear voices coming from her solar plexus, first that of a girl and then a boy. Finally she received a visitation from her mother. Such visions, she contended, stayed with her off and on throughout her life. She even held ESP sessions at her house after filming *Myra Breckinridge*.

After West's brother died she claimed his spirit hovered over her bed at night, his eyes filled with tears. She asked a psychic what this might mean and was informed it was probably her brother expressing guilt for making some bad decisions in life. West did her best to assure him he shouldn't fret about such matters in subsequent visions.

Was she pulling people's legs with all of this? Arguably, but whatever else her sins, she didn't usually lie about matters of such moment. After her mother died she seemed to lose faith in the occult, telling people there was no afterlife and she would never see the woman again. Such a reaction hints at the fact that her belief in eternity did indeed exist, as one can't turn against something that wasn't there in the first place.

She once said she imagined religion was for different types of people, i.e. ultra-serious ones, but in time she realized that one can be upbeat and still spiritual: one can still have a good time in life, can party and sample life in the fast lane of Hollywood's glitter. Without concentrating too much on spiritual matters one can still eat, drink and be merry. She certainly did the latter. As for the former, few could deny that she lived her life according to her lights, and it's doubtful if her conscience kept her from sleeping at night—alone or accompanied.

I met Tony Curtis, West's co-star in *Sextette*, when he was in Dublin to promote his autobiography. "I don't look for the meaning of life any more," he told me, "I just try to pick my way through it. I nearly over-dosed a few times, and I once held a gun to my temple intent on ending it all. Those kinds of experiences shape you. When the absolute becomes negligible, the opposite happens too. You sacramentalize the moment." Curtis has been doing that for many years now, nightclubbing with women young enough to be his grand-daughters. The victim of a mother who bullied him incessantly and a father who never achieved his life's dreams, this son of disaffected Hungarian immigrants was always going to be a man to snatch at instantaneous thrills, be they sex, drink or drugs—or all three together.

The eldest of three sons, his middle brother was killed in a street accident and his younger one was schizophrenic. Such grim details have also made him grab at what scraps life threw at him and make them count.

His philosophy, or rather non-philosophy, of life is that it's all in the throw of the dice: "Albert de Salvo, the killer I played in *The Boston Strangler*, could have been Harry Houdini if the fates dictated otherwise. Sidney Falco, my *Sweet Smell of Success* character, could have been Fred W. De Mara, the con man I played in *The Great Impostor*." When I asked him how he felt about religion, he replied, "Not much. Did it ever strike you as odd that roughly 90 percent of the people on this planet have been killed due to religion?"

Fame almost killed him too. It came too fast and too furious, sending him from New York's Lower East Side to Hollywood in a streetcar named desire. "Those whom the Gods despise," he says, quoting the famous line, "they first make famous. It's a greased tightrope." As well as having been involved in a string of failed marriages, Curtis also had to contend with the death by drug overdose of his son Nicholas but he's rolled with the punches. "I feel younger now than I did when I was twenty-one," he told me.

The ageing Lothario has had a second incarnation as a painter. "I've beaten the fucking odds," he said, "how many can make that claim? I should have been dead ten years ago. I could have been a Marilyn Monroe. There are no laws, no plans. You have to make your own. I free-based cocaine when my movie career started to go down the toilet, and my marriages, but I picked myself up out of the gutter. I went into the Betty Ford Clinic. Elvis Presley—the man who stole my haircut— couldn't do that. It's why I'm here today."

Curtis, who looked death in the face more than once, believes in taking one day at a time, and not only where substance abuse is concerned. "Life is all in the blink of an eye," he says, "the beat goes on, the baton passes, and while you've got it you enjoy it." Human beings, he believes, have great arrogance as well as great ignorance. "We fret and fuss and pontificate, while that good-old earth just keeps on going from green to brown and back again. The sky is what it looked like 5,000 years ago, but here we are, worried from day to week to month because the wraparound is so brief for us."

At eighty-four, Curtis says he still doesn't know what he wants to be when he grows up. He doesn't have much truck with Hamlet's "To be or not to be." For him it's just "be." He's been on the brink more than once, his fingers clawing at the cliff-face of life, which makes him see the infinite in a blade of grass.

He likes to dream and sometimes wonders if the dreams are his reality and reality his dream. "In the morning I go to the bathroom," he says, "and then I take care of business. I eat. I work—because you can't sleep 24 hours a day. You take care of business. You get married, you get involved in a career. You have kids. But you always go back to your own head at night and dream. Dreams were the first movies a guy ever made. You go to a movie and buy a ticket and you get two hours of a dream. That's all you walk away with. Dreams are how we connect with our subconscious selves, our better selves, our real selves."

Life itself is also a dream for the ageing legend. It only seems like yesterday when he looked at Cary Grant on the screen and thought, "I want that." Films are his immortality. He fantasizes about a time "1,237" days from now when people will wonder what their ancestors looked like, "and they'll have a little machine that lets them summon up this dark-haired, blue-eyed guy named Tony Curtis."

His life has been a series of U-turns: "At twenty you say, thank God I didn't get hit by a car, thank God I didn't die from an overdose, thank God I wasn't murdered, thank God I didn't go to jail. At thirty it's thank God I got a job, thank God I'm getting laid, thank God that pain in the ass wasn't something serious, thank God it was him and not me that died, thank God I don't have to support my parents anymore."

Later on, says the man who was born as Bernie Schwartz, you think of your mortality. What has life been about? What comes after? Does anything? And how have you conducted yourself? Faithfully sometimes, other times not so. But you did your best in a given circumstance, and who could judge you for that?

People can be anything they want in life, he told me, they just have to be hungry enough for it: "It's all in the mind. Mario Lanza once lost 40 pounds for a role. If Danny de Vito is in a movie, he wears lifts. Napoleon was four foot eleven and yet he had these generals who were six foot one. You're as big as you think you are."

He didn't want to be trapped in Bernie Schwartz's body, didn't want to be a displaced Hungarian-American Jew. So he became an actor. "Once my career took off, I became 120 different personalities."

He compares it all to "that ivory ball the Chinese used to cut," explaining how such multiple personalities entered his soul without any retrograde effect: "After they cut it they made another one inside and then another one inside that again. But they never took it apart. I believe the human condition can drive in and out of itself like that too—like the layers of an onion peeling away to reveal everything or nothing."

Asked about the purpose of living, he refuses to be drawn. "I live one blink at a time. I see what I see. I don't draw conclusions. The sky is blue at two, at twenty-two, at eighty-two, that's all I know. Each of us is a module, a process towards something else, but I don't profess to know what that is. All I know is that somebody up there seems to like me because he took me from nothing to everything. God knows why."

He'll be remembered for a half dozen movies, in any case, and at least two of them (*Some Like It Hot* and *Sweet Smell of Success*) are classics. "I never had time for any of that Method bullshit," he told me. "You just went in there and hit the marks. I don't go in for *schools* of acting. If it feels right, is my philosophy, do it. The secret of art is artlessness. Larry Olivier once gave me a little tip about acting. Clothes make the man, he told me. 'When you look in the mirror' he said to me, 'dress as the person you want to be.' It's something I've been trying ever since. And it works."

Curtis' brother, Julius, who died in the street accident, was only nine at the time. Curtis himself had to identify him in the hospital after he died. Has he ever recovered from this ordeal? "I can't say for sure if I have. In many ways I blame myself for Julius being knocked down because he wanted to play with me earlier that day and I told him to get lost." As regards the identification—was he near death at the time? "He was unconscious, but I felt he could hear what I was saying to him. I learned later that the sense of hearing is the last thing to go from a dying person. I felt he even heard me standing there when I was saying nothing. The thought of that makes me feel a little bit better."

Curtis' other brother Bobby was an even more tragic case in many ways. At an early age he developed chronic schizophrenia and spent most of his life in sanatoriums. Tony visited him off and on over the years but finally it became too painful to confront him. "I don't even know what circumstances he died in," he told me when I expressed surprise that the date of his demise (1992) only appears as a footnote in his autobiography. "It was too much to take in," he whispered, his eyes filling up.

The Schwartz family in more ways than one have been like an albatross round his neck—before and after fame. His mother all but destroyed his youth, and then, after he hit the stellar heights, she tried to jump on that bandwagon too, importuning him for money and joining the celebrity set, even guilt-tripping him about the fact that Bobby should have been allowed climb aboard too. "Do something for Bobby!" she kept saying; it tore me apart."

I asked him how he felt about spirituality as therapy when things got rough.

"Frank Sinatra said he was for anything that got you through the night—prayer, a woman, or Jack Daniels. I've tried all three. Different things work at different times. Religion for many people is like the one-armed bandit at the casino. You want the three cherries all the time. Then when things are going well, you forget. You get back to the mean s.o.b. you always were . . . until the next time you're in trouble. What's that quote? 'There are no atheists in the trenches.' I've been there." So is he an atheist now? "We don't know what's down the pike. You just grab the moment. Your life is the sum of all your experiences and out of that maybe you deserve eternity. Maybe."

He's been lionized by the critics more often than not—probably as a result of those chocolate box looks—but the affable star who wasted many years in drugs, alcohol abuse and woeful movies feels that if he were taken more seriously as an actor (he showed just what he could do in *The Boston Strangler*) it could all have been very different. But if Curtis has only put his talent into his work, he's put his genius into his life. It's a long way from East 78th and First Avenue in Manhattan to the upper stratosphere of Hollywood but he made that odyssey against all the odds, and made it count. Having been beaten up by local hoods on these streets, and then again at home by his mother, the minefield of Tinseltown was, by comparison, a walk in the park.

A graduate of the old school of movie-making when stars were larger than life, Curtis is still painting at his age—and good luck to him. His personality is as infectious as his laughter, and he seems to embody a *joie de vivre* that's all too rare among superstars nowadays. Such an upbeat attitude seems strikingly at odds with the kind of life he's led, and the thousand natural shocks fate has dealt him, but the ever-buoyant actor has never been one to moan. He's made it to the top in a jungle where only the fittest survive, and has no intention of winding down until they put him in a box.

He may not sniff cocaine anymore "The only drug I take nowadays is my blood pressure tablet," he quips, and he insists on diet Coke with his vodkas, but he can still entrance pretty girls from under the noses of the Bratpackers, and is an object lesson to anyone who has descended to the depths of alcoholic or, indeed, narcotic despair. He who endures the most pain rather than he who inflicts it, finally conquers.

—6—

The Symbolic Mode

It's often claimed that we live in a "post-Christian" world. If this is true, perhaps the closest we can come to a religious experience is through images on a screen. John W. Martin contends that religion today manifests itself through cross-cultural forms that include "myth, ritual, symbols of purity and gods." Hollywood has filled these forms with "a tremendous variety of contents."[1] One of these is science fiction. According to Douglas Turnbull, creating a UFO is "like photographing God."[2]

Geoffrey Hill puts it slightly differently: "We pay our votive offerings at the box office. We buy our ritual corn. We hush in reverent anticipation as the lights go down and the celluloid magic begins. Throughout the filmic narrative we identify with the hero. We vilify the anti-hero. We vicariously exult in the victories of the drama. And we are spiritually inspired by the moral of the story, all the while believing that we are modern techno-secular people, devoid of religion. Yet the depth and intensity of our participation reveal a fervor that is not much different from that of religious zealots."[3] In April 1975, while addressing the Arts Club of Chicago, Pauline Kael remarked startlingly that almost every interesting American movie in the past few years had been directed by a Catholic.

The Irish journalist Mary Kenny, commenting on George Bush's 2004 pledge to land a man on Mars by 2020, expressed the view that the strange fascination with Mars was a form of pseudo-religion. There was nothing on it, she contended, and it was pitiful to see grown men cry because of the loss of the Beagle spacecraft sent there. But over-secularized scientists must believe in something so they transfer their God-shaped hole to the empty and meaningless Red Planet. She did concede that pictures from Mars had an ancillary function. They make us realize how surprisingly beautiful is our planet Earth.

Because of the decline in conventional religious belief, people have turned to genres like science fiction to fill the gap left by a dead Christian God. They've also turned to movements like Scientology, whose adherents include such celebrities as John Travolta, Tom Cruise and Elvis Presley's daughter, Lisa-Marie. The explosion of interest in UFOs may also be put down to this crisis of faith. Religion started out with heaven in the clouds before Darwin and other scientists precluded such superstitious beliefs, but now we seem to have returned to this mindset with the profusion of sci-fi films which find, if not God, at least some highly evolved beings in ethereal realms—or distant galaxies.

If our heroes have changed, so also have our villains. We don't need to see dragons slain anymore, or magic swords being cast into the sea. The Stygian darkness of hell can be replaced by a man in an office opposite a laptop. Neither does insanity have to be roaring patients in a snake pit; it might just as readily be an ostensibly normal man or woman gazing into space on a motorway, or in a phone booth. Heaven and hell are within us and we don't necessarily need objective correlates. The gothic has become the mundane, which is why film-makers now operate mainly on the symbolic level when they wish to proselytize: They know that nothing else would be accepted by agnostic audiences.

Neil Hurley, in his essay *Cinematic Transfigurations of Jesus*, even makes a case for the fact that Ernest Hemingway conceived *The Old Man and the Sea* as a Jesus story, and that John Sturges' film of the book, made in 1958 with Spencer Tracy in the lead role, carried the theme onto celluloid. He cites Tracy's bleeding hands as examples of stigmata, the fish as the cross "resisted, reluctantly engaged, yet finally accepted in death" and the final scene in front of a church as similar to the crucifixion.

The messianic figure in films used to appear in everything from swashbucklers to Knights of the Round Table films to westerns. Ever since the demise of the western genre, science fiction has supplanted these forms. Thus from *Star Trek* to *Star Wars* to *The Matrix* we have iconic saviors of the galaxy, as opposed to the frontier, or fiefdom, or garrison town. In a sense such variations don't really affect the plotlines. Whether the Christ figure is dressed in buckskin (as in, say, *Shane*) or a black leather jacket (as in *The Matrix*) what we're watching is the same general polarities of good and evil playing themselves out. The explosion of relativism in ethical thinking has led to a profusion (if not ubiquity) of "grey" areas in such films. Such greyness first appeared in the phenomenon of the "anti" hero.

In recent decades the distinctions have become so blurred that we have vigilante murderers in films like *Taxi Driver* being cheered by audiences even as they engage in gratuitous blood-letting. Is this a sign that we've become desensitized as cineastes? John Wayne once said he'd never play a character who shot someone in the back. A more contemporary figure like Clint Eastwood mightn't be as taciturn in such matters. "Dirty" Harry wasn't so called for no reason. The goalposts have shifted so far that sometimes it's difficult to know who the good guys are any more. It's a long time since villains were distinguishable by black hats, a bad complexion and designer stubble. Heroes, meanwhile, may be slightly manic, like the cop Mel Gibson plays in the *Lethal Weapon* series.

The character played by Michael Douglas in *Falling Down* (1993) makes the point abundantly clear in the finale of that movie. A white collar man who flips out and begins a campaign of wanton destruction, he's eventually cornered by tired policeman Robert Duvall and taunts him by suggesting Duvall ought to be mighty pleased with himself. "How did I get to be the bad guy?" he asks. To which one might reply: Society is the real bad guy. It's society with its consumerist goals and pigeonholes that has turned Douglas from a straight arrow conformist to a deranged sociopath. There but for the grace of God—or domestic stability—go we all.

The bottom line is that symbolism today is compromised. Saviors can be stained and villains have redeeming virtues. They may even be juxtaposed even in the one genre. Arnold Schwarzenegger can negotiate the transition from ruthless executioner to being on the side of the angels in the *Terminator* series and we accept this as read. Cyborgs don't have to go through the same dark nights of the soul as the rest of us mortals when it comes to shifting our allegiances.

Maybe the main thing to beware of is over-analyzing movies, or strangling them into a format that will readily accommodate our own cozy presuppositions. We can stretch any film to breaking point by seeing its main protagonist as a Christ figure, all the way from *Rambo* to *The Matrix*. Doing this robs a work of its individuality and imposes contrived constraints on it that war against its nuances. When ethics supersedes aesthetics we wind up with a dead art form that works to the detriment of both.

Most films can be interpreted as symbolic in some form or another but perhaps Mara Donaldson stretches it a bit in her essay *Love and Duty in Casablanca* where she argues that the development of Rick (Humphrey Bogart's character) "from self-love to self-denying purity needs to be interpreted in its theological context as the redemptive transformation of Rick's sinful narcissism" into a "salvific sacrifice."[4]

In his essay *Descent into the Demonic*, George Garrelts posits the theory that even *Citizen Kane* can be interpreted as a metaphor for the Genesis story. "There's no room for God in the film," he writes, "because Kane has presumed to take on the role of God."[5] He has disowned an edenic childhood in his self-aggrandizing search for power, the only thing connecting him to that world being his beloved sledge Rosebud, which gets burned in the final reel in the poor man's Dante-esque inferno, symbolizing, in Garrelts' mind, the demonic state into which Kane has descended.

We can view Billy Wilder's *Sunset Boulevard* (1950) in this manner too, seeing faded diva Norma Desmond (Gloria Swanson) as a woman who achieved her reality, her God-like status, through the illusory medium of film. "But the price mere mortals must pay for this deification," writes Michael Thomas Morris in his essay *Twilight of the Gods*, "is that the camera also practices spirit theft."[6]

Desmond loses control of her essence once she goes over the hill in a career sense. She's had no inner reality all through the years of her fame. It wasn't she who got small, she tells William Holden in one scene, it was the pictures—but does it really matter? Because in a sense they're one and the same. In the end, madness is her only answer to the unbearability of being on the celluloid scrapheap; this is her comfort blanket against a built-in obsolescence. Only then, as Morris puts it, can she "soften the blow she suffered in falling from the cinematic Olympian heights and safely enter her own private world of myth and magic."[7]

Desmond belongs to a world of Hollywood Babylon, living in a tawdry temple with stained glass windows and archaic paraphernalia where dead rats patrol a swimming pool that's decayed and empty, like everything else about her. Her life is like the aftermath of one big party she doesn't realize has ended. As Joe Gillis (the equally failed screenwriter played by William Holden) knows, it's dangerous to wake a sleepwalker so he doesn't, perpetrating the myth that her butler and former husband Erich von Stroheim is also a party to, i.e. that she's still a force to be reckoned with.

All of her whims are pandered to, right down to penning fake fan mail to keep the dream alive. The burial of a chimpanzee even acquires reverential overtones in this perverse dream world. Desmond wishes to make a screen comeback—as Salome, fittingly. To this end she visits Cecil B. DeMille, a man who could have overseen such a project way back when. Is Gillis about to be her real-life John the Baptist? Will she have his head on a plate when her little dance of death has run its course and he fails to succumb to her anachronistic charms?

Gillis is a gigolo, a kept man. He trades his body and his writing talent, such as it is, for the blandishments of her musty mansion, an accomplice after the fact. He watches her re-spin the spools of her life both verbally and visually in a rash of home movies screened for his, and her, delectation. These movie shows almost resemble séances in their calling-up of a bygone era before sound "infected" the movies. She gleefully watches him fabricate a forced enthusiasm as he wonders how he'll get back to his "other" life outside these gothic gates.

Desmond's stardom, as Morris points out, is awash with religious overtones. It was, after all, her generation which gave rise to the gods and goddesses of the silver screen "making the very act of movie-going a quasi-religious experience."[8] Her generation "also built the gigantic cinematic cathedrals with all their architectural splendour. They were baroque, Moorish or Egyptian sanctuaries with row after row of seats arranged pew-like before the magnificent tabernacle curtains which veiled the holy of holies. Popcorn and cola became the ritualistic meal as the lights dimmed and the faithful watched those curtains part. The cinematic deities played out their mythic tales amidst all the numinous trappings of a cultic experience."[9] Even the studio posters got in on the act, proclaiming "more stars than there are in heaven" to the salivating voyeurs who trooped through the portals for a rub of their favorite relic. They watched their demigods on thirty foot high screens in Holy Communion with them, empathizing with their predicaments, dreaming their dreams with them and/or sharing their fall from grace if and when it came.

When this era ended, as it had to eventually, it was, ironically, the hardnosed cynics like Gillis who were the catalysts. They saw through the pomp and *faux*-splendor and screamed "Enough!" They wanted to be done with convoluted histrionics, with blasphemous chimpanzee obsequies. There was a different kind of life to be lived outdoors, different kinds of ideals to be seized. Gillis' pragmatic breed, as Morris points out, "would usher in the money grabbers who would desecrate these temples, tear down or hide their glorious detail, rip away the tabernacle curtains, and divide their sanctuary into a multiplex." In cultic terms then, this screenwriter *manqué* is a "liturgical spoiler."[10]

There are also Biblical echoes in George Stevens' *Shane*, where Alan Ladd, as the buckskin-clad outsider, purges a Wyoming valley of evil as personified by the cattle barons and the serpentine Jack Wilson (Jack Palance), who cuts a decidedly Luciferesque figure in the film's latter half.

Shane is a Christ figure—mysterious, stately and enigmatic. He "came from nowhere and is going nowhere," wrote Donald Richie, "like Jesus Christ."[11] He also sacrifices his life for a cause. As Ryker, Emile Meyer's flowing beard silhouetted against the sky suggests Moses. Viewed another way, the Starrett household, as personified by Van Heflin, Jean Arthur and Brandon de Wilde, could be seen as the divine family writ small and transplanted to another era. Significantly, Heflin is cutting wood when we first see him: like Joseph the carpenter. His name is Joe; his wife's Marian—close to Mary.

It can, of course, also be appreciated on the level of straight-up western, or even pastoral, or epic. Some have even viewed it as a socialist parable, where the "redeeming angel" idea is sidelined. Pauline Kael interpreted it as a medieval allegory, with Shane as the "chivalric" Galahad and Wilson the Prince of Darkness. It's a testament to Stevens' breadth of vision that children could be enthralled by it while adults advanced revisionist theories about its motifs. These are still going on. Rarely has a classic of the genre had this many ripples and yet such disarming simplicity.

In the penultimate scene we get a Pauline conversion of one of the villains (Ben Johnson) and thereafter Shane himself becoming a kind of superhuman figure as he appears to ascend to the clouds in the atmospheric finale.

Is he an Old Testament figure or a New Testament one? He arrives with the olive branch of peace but ends up bringing the sword. He has to leave the valley in the same way Christ had to leave the world. Their natures exclude both from harmony within an existing milieu, but for radically contrasting reasons.

In general I'm inclined to agree with David Jasper, who argues in his essay "On Systematising the Unsystematic," that this was George Stevens' "greatest story" rather than the film that carried that moniker. *The Greatest Story Ever Told*, Jasper remarks, even at three hours and ten minutes (cut down by Stevens from its original four hours and twenty minutes), still proved to be too daunting for the concentration span of the average cinemagoer, especially since it was already told much better twelve years before. Alan Ladd in buckskin, in other words, was a "more acceptable" savior for cinema audiences than the rather "unctuous"

Jesus of Max Von Sydow in the later film.[12] Put another way, *The Greatest Story Ever Told* is a "gnostic" form of the American myth, whereas *Shane* is an "apocalyptic" version of it.[13]

Shane, according to Jasper, doesn't try to pretend that the Holy Land is really the American West; instead it portrays that epic landscape "in its own colors and with its own mystery and story."[14] Such a story, he concedes, is "simple and moralistic, undeviating in its imagery and utterly without irony," but precisely for those reasons it allows its images to work as myth. Put another way, "It fulfils the viewer's fantasies without disturbing the longings which underpin them." In the darkened cinema, or living-room, the film offers "an undemanding and non-liturgical hope of redemption, the specific fulfilment of a generalized dream."[15]

Ladd often described himself as a small boy's idea of a tough guy. This may well have been true for he had a choirboy look and was of diminutive stature. (His female leads had to stand in trenches opposite him, or he himself on a box.) But in a strange way this gentleness made him more of a romantic figure in *Shane*. Only when he drew his gun did a hard look come into his face. If Jesus threw the moneylenders out of the temple, Shane dispensed with the Rykers in Grafton's saloon. He may not have sacrificed his life at the end, but he was willing to, which is what counts. (It's also a possibility he's dying at the end. "You're bloody!" Joey shrieks outside the saloon. Shane clutches his side as he rides up the mountain.)

Jack Schaefer, who wrote the book, didn't intend it as a Christian parable. His character, he allowed, "may qualify as a savior, but not as a Christian one. He's more an alpha primate male fulfilling his genetically ingrained obligation to his kind."[16] Stevens saw him in the knight errant mode Kael alluded to, but also with the other echoes we've mentioned. In any case, as Robert Banks pointed out in the book *Explorations in Theology and Film*, the medieval knight is "already in part a Christ-figure, so speaking of Shane in this way still leaves us with the question of whether he's a compromised Christ-figure or rather a legitimate blend of types appropriate to his context."[17]

We can almost "read" the Bible into every frame of this movie. When we first see Shane he's coming down from a high place—heaven? He then crosses a river, a possible allusion to his baptism in the river Jordan. When he arrives at the Starrett ranch he meets his "disciple" Joey (Brandon De Wilde). He accepts his ministry, sloughing off his "divine" robes (the buckskin) for "store-bought" clothes to live among mere mortals for a time. But his destiny beckons.

Shane is a God who dearly wants to be a man. He tries to escape his fate but, as he tells Joey outside the saloon at the end, "I tried it and it didn't work. You can't break the mould. A man has to be what he is." Translated into salvific parlance, perhaps we should change that to "a God has to be what he is."

Before his final act of cleansing the valley, he has to make the hard decision not to let Starrett meet the gunslingers. Starrett wants to but Shane knows he's "no match for Wilson." Starrett counters by claiming that, while he may not be faster on the draw, he could outlast him: the brute force of nature pitting itself against the hardware of technology.

Starrett was in a similar mood when he told Shane earlier, *apropos* pulling up the stump of a tree, "There are some things you gotta do with your bare hands." Significantly, Starrett beats Shane in the final fight at Starrett's ranch, Shane also having to resort to hardware to knock him out by hitting him on the head with his gun.

"You hit him!" Joey shouts. "You hit him with your gun—I hate you!" Here we have Brandon De Wilde swapping his "exciting" role model for a "domestic" one, much in the way he would disown the Paul Newman of *Hud* some years later for Melvyn Douglas. Afterward comes Shane's poignant farewell to Marian, the woman with whom he's fallen in love. She asks him if she'll ever see him again and he replies, "Never is a long time, Marian," as he gives her an extremely poignant handshake.

Shane resembles Jesus, or at least Hollywood's depiction of him, in the sense that he's shy and taciturn for most of the time but when he puts on his guns—which we may take as a loose parallel for Jesus preaching—he turns into a forceful character. Stevens amplifies the soundtrack on more than one occasion to carry this transformation, Ladd's deep voice compensating for his small stature and gentle features to earn him "tough guy" chops.

In the climactic ride into town, Stevens superimposes him over shots of a cemetery cross. Earlier, he has him riding between three trees, two of which stand together (the Starretts) and the third a little distance apart (Joey). He's fractured the family unit and can have no future here. When he kills Wilson, the film's sneering Lucifer, clad in black, he must go back from whence he came, i.e., the place on high. In the final shot of the film, instead of riding into the sunset like most cowboys, he rides instead into the sun *rise*.

The clouds part and a hint of sun creeps through, like sanctifying grace. This is his resurrection. The stone has passed from the tomb. A new era dawns, the evil exorcised and paradise regained.

Federico Fellini's masterpiece, *La Strada* (1954) has also been analyzed for Christological echoes. Fellini was castigated for blasphemy in *The Miracle* and his priests are usually caricatures (*Roma, Amarcord, 8½*, etc.) but some critics have made reference to the fact that the character of Gelsomina in this film (she was played by his real-life wife Giulietta Masina) was a female Christ-figure. Such critics also saw the road of the title as a metaphor for life's journey. Her friendship with The Clown (Richard Basehart) leads to a discussion about the importance of all things, however small, like a pebble. When the brutish Zampano (Anthony Quinn) kills The Clown she falls apart and dies alone. Only after her death does Zampano realize he loves the woman he's treated so badly. His punishment is to have to live the rest of his life without her.

Gelsomina saves Zampano by dying because her death is the only thing that could have brought him to an awareness of his own weakness. In this sense she's a martyr.

Marlon Brando played a Christ figure (Terry Malloy) in *On the Waterfront* (1954) as we've already seen. (In the original version of the script he also died.) What's interesting is his conversion from crime by the waterfront priest Fr Barry (Karl Malden).

Malloy begins the film as a dumb but lovable lug, a patsy to a corrupt organization. His boxing career has gone west and he's slotted himself into a commodious rut, taking the easy jobs and the easy money as the years slide by him. "Wanna hear my idea about life?" he asks his girlfriend Edie (Eva Marie Saint). "Do it to him before he does it to you." This is an inversion of the biblical edict, "Do unto other as you would have them do unto you." It's only when his involvement in the killing of Edie's brother moves him into an awkward crisis of conscience—Edie is the "prize" for him confronting mobster Johnny Friendly (Lee J. Cobb) that he's galvanized to pull down the pillars of this particular temple of chicanery.

Malloy's brother Charlie (Rod Steiger) doesn't want him to "sing" to the Crime commission and thus end up like Edie's brother, "falling" from a rooftop. That's why he threatens to take him to "River Street," a den of execution, unless he "wises up." "If I spill," Malloy tells Fr Barry, "My life ain't worth a nickel." Barry replies, "How much is your soul worth if you don't?" Earlier, Malloy has told Barry his guilt is "like carrying a monkey on your back," a clear reference to the cross of Jesus.

At the end, Malloy/Jesus staggers to the entrance of the Hoboken waterfront, standing in for Golgotha. He falls, also like Jesus, and rises

again. Edie stands in for Mary, or Veronica. By this time Johnny
Friendly has been thrown into the water—like Satan cast into the pit.

The Jesus figure here has come from the other side of the ethical
divide, having attained something of a Pauline conversion in the course
of the film, due to the good graces of both Edie and Fr Barry. His "mutilated body can shuffle away through the conformist crowd, a loser of the
20th century whose passion burns through the spectator's heart with a
purer fire than was ever kindled by Hollywood representations of
Calvary."[18] Once again, love has found a way.

East of Eden (1955), Elia Kazan's masterly adaptation of John
Steinbeck's novel—though it only covers the last third of it—is the film
that brought James Dean to the world, playing Cal Trask, a character
based on Cain from Genesis. It also has Abel in the form of Richard
Davalos and Raymond Massey, his father Adam, as the God figure.

The film basically concerns Cal's wish to win his father's love.
Imagining the old man cares more for his brother Aron, he, in a sense,
"kills" Aron by bringing him to see their mother, who's a prostitute. The
sheriff of the town subsequently quotes a verse from the book of Genesis
to Cal, citing the fact that "Cain rose up against his brother and slew
him. And Cain went away and dwelt in the land of Nod, on the east of
Eden." This quote wasn't in Steinbeck's original novel.

Later on, Adam makes Cal read a verse from the Book of Psalms about
free will. Cal doesn't appreciate the profundity of its lesson (that we can
all change) until his father is about to die. Kazan doesn't labor the Biblical parallels and they're all the stronger for that. Jo Van Fleet won an
Oscar for playing the bordello madam—Kazan's arguable snake in the
edenic garden. "The punishment of Cain is a strange and perplexing
one," Steinbeck wrote in his book *Journey of a Novel: The East of Eden
Letters*. "Out of Eve's sin came love and death. Cain invented murder
and he is punished by life. The mark put on him is not placed there to
punish him but to protect him." Steinbeck wanted this duality preserved
in Kazan's film.

The book was never meant to be a straight allegory. This would have
made it, and the ensuing film, too simplistic. His main brief, as he said,
was: "The battleground between good and evil, the sorry man."
Cal Trask is that man but he takes a leap Cain never could, or would.
If he carries the birthmark of "original sin," he's not alone. Where he
differs from Cain is in his attempts to love, and to procure a different
kind of love in return. His odyssey is one from desperation to muted
epiphany.

If Adam is God, then Cal's desperate struggle for his love acquires added ramifications. It is, in effect, his allegorical pitch towards transcendence: To quote Ernest Ferlita from his essay *Film and the Quest for Meaning*: "The mythical journey of Cal—Cain is superficially between the brooding coast of his mother's sin and the sunlit valley of his father's righteousness, but only to adjust our vision to the coexistence of good and evil in each of us."[19] He may choose either option, but one will lead him "east" of Eden.

Paul Newman appeared in an Oscar-nominated role in *Cool Hand Luke* in 1967, playing a sacrificial martyr challenging the authorities in a prison compound, with allegorical parallels to Jesus that weren't picked up on by most reviewers of the film when it was first released, despite the fact that the film contains many gospel songs.

What appears to be rebelliousness in this "convict Christ," to use an expression of Newman's biographer Elena Oumano, is, in Luke's mind, pure logic.[20] More than once he tells his captors, "You're going to have to kill me," which is eventually what happens.

Luke is a chain gang convict who, like Jesus, lays down his life for his friends. Resisting authority with a vengeance (and some wry humor) he succeeds in instilling revolt among his fellow jailbirds, but only after paying the ultimate price.

He's a forerunner of the R.P. McMurphy of *One Flew Over the Cuckoo's Nest*, i.e. a man regarded as dangerous by the authorities because of his influence on a group of people they formerly had under their thumb. As such he must be exterminated, and, as in the gospel, it's a friend (George Kennedy) who turns him in at the end. Kennedy is more St Peter than Judas, however, giving him up to the prison officers on a plea bargain.

"What we got here is a failure to communicate!" the ruthless warden keeps telling him, in the film's most quotable line: What he means is that he's unable to submerge Luke's will. This is a rebel with a cause, part Jesus, part Mary Magdalene. Luke also has a comical side, eating fifty eggs at one sitting as a challenge, which causes his stomach to distend to enormous proportions.

Daniel O'Brien, investigating the film's symbolic import, notes that Luke spends a lot of time in a white robe. He also adopts a crucifixion pose after eating the eggs, his legs even placed like those of Jesus on the cross. His prison number is 37, which is probably a reference to Verse 37 of Luke's gospel: "Now there is nothing that God cannot do."[21] O'Brien also comments on the fact that in one scene Luke challenges

God to strike him down with the words "Love me, hate me, kill me, anything. Just let me know it." Overall he finds the film "a blatant, if fuzzy allegory."[22] The symbols aren't strident. They're not cymbals. But they're there nonetheless.

Luke soaks up all the punishment the compound throws at him until he can't bear it any more. He eventually cracks. Or does he? We're not sure. Kennedy believes he doesn't but Luke shows something of a death wish at times. He can hardly be blamed for this as his life is one long trek up the hill of Calvary. Many scenes are reminiscent of Jesus' scourging at the pillar.

Luke is killed, significantly, in a church, after he gives a modern slant on Jesus' "My God, my God, why hast thou forsaken me" speech. His dying words are a backward taunt to the warden: "What we got here is a failure to communicate." O'Brien, referring to him as "God's own son or holy fool," notes that he faces martyrdom with a smile.[23]

He's done what his fellow jailmates, his "disciples," didn't have the courage to do but his death inspires them. In the film's last scene these laborers in the vineyard, as it were, toast his memory, elevating this "natural born world-shaker" to near-mythic status. Neil Hurley wrote in his essay "Cinematic Transfigurations of Jesus, "A kind of resurrection is implicit in the scene. As the Christ of faith lives on in his followers and, for many Christians, in a glorified state, so too has Luke a timeless place in the hearts and minds of those who knew him and would keep his memory alive."[24]

Newman also played a criminal who invites his own death in Arthur Penn's *The Left-Handed Gun*. In the last scene here, playing Billy the Kid, he allows Pat Garret (John Dehner) shoot him dead while pretending to go for his gun. But he's taken the bullets out. As he falls he puts his arms out in part-cruciform mode. James Dean also used this "crucifixion pose" in *Giant*. It's come to be seen as a Method contrivance which seems to suit the victim guise of so many graduates of this school of acting. In Dean's case, a rifle standing in for the cross, he even had Liz Taylor at his feet like Mary Magdalene to complete the triptych.

Stanley Kubrick made what's perhaps the most astounding science-fiction film of all time with *2001: A Space Odyssey* (1968). In a way it's not fair to call it sci-fi because it's so much more than that. Maybe *2001: A Metaphysical Odyssey* would be a more appropriate title.

Starting in a pre-historic era and going from *homo sapiens* to a nuclear age in a matter of seconds in what has been dubbed the most extensive flash-forward of all time, this is the *auteur* film to end all *auteur* films, the actors mere figures on Kubrick's mind-bogglingly original tapestry.

It was a truly audacious device of narration—or should I say lack of it. Nobody before had ever gone from past to future with such a blunt disregard for the present. But then there were a lot of things in this psychedelic movie that nobody had ever done before.

The point he's making in the flash-forward is that not too much, really, has changed. Hairy apes have been replaced with naked ones now clothed in space garb, but their communication with one another is hardly more insightful, reduced to monosyllabic clichés and glad-handing oneliners. The thighbone is now a computer: the "one-eyed Polyphemous" named HAL, who's finally blinded not by brute force but the futuristic alternative of having his memory-banks disconnected.

HAL is the enemy in the camp, a Trojan horse whose pathetic plea for mercy falls on deaf ears. He's unable to move but from his immobile perspective he oversees the whole operation like a corrupt supernatural force. In this Garden of Eden the serpent doesn't so much hiss as drone in self-piteous fashion. He tries to tempt the astronauts to partake of the forbidden fruit but they resist. Their prize is the space embryo, a harbinger to a future era that may or may not be better.

In this sense Kubrick's finest movie is a search for the ultimate that coils in upon itself tantalizingly. Everything changes and yet nothing changes essentially. It's like the Nietzschean idea of eternal recurrence. The astronauts travel through galaxies, but their minds remain moribund.

Pauline Kael believed that the film had "the dreamy, over-the-rainbow appeal of a new vision of heaven. It says man is just a tiny nothing on the stairway to Paradise."[25] Something better may be coming, but whatever it is we have no control over it: "There's an intelligence out there in space controlling your destiny from ape to angel, so just follow the slab."

Shakespeare said it another way in *The Tempest*: "As flies to wanton boys are we to the gods; they kill us for their sport." Kubrick's gods are less threatening, but vouchsafe just as few answers. They yield the secret of space travel and hint at a future apotheosis but beyond this all we have is the iconography of a slab that doesn't even contain the outline of a human (or saintly) form. This slab is ultimately as flat and infuriating as the smug bromides of the astronauts' dialogue. Kubrick has seen the future and it's . . . silent.

Kubrick was an atheist, as was his screenwriter Arthur C. Clarke, but together they postulate "the existence of aliens who are so far advanced that they've become God-like."[26] That's as far down the religion road as the film, or its director, was willing to go.

An audio-visual delight from the moment the strains of "Thus Spake Zarathustra" are struck up, *Space Odyssey* asks more questions than it answers, and therein lies much of its appeal. The only constant between past and future is a monolithic edifice that could represent anything from technology to God. The pace of the film is dour and downbeat, which makes the apocalyptic scenes all the more alluring. When we segue from apes playing with thigh bones in the "Dawn of Man" sequence to a space-child acting as an ethereal harbinger of the future in its mystifying closing stages we're made frighteningly aware of never having had a cinematic experience quite this visceral before.

In the final shots the star-child looks directly at the screen as if to say, "This is yourself you're staring at, some aeons on. I am you and you're me. One day the cycle will be complete." Gerard Loughlin comments, "The star-child looks directly at us from the screen, across the divide between stage and auditorium, between cinematic and real space. We're confronted with the eye of the cinema itself, with the god-like gaze it bestows on the viewer. If *2001* is a religious film it is the religion of cinema itself, the transcendent vision of the camera's eye."[27]

Kubrick lets the film tell its story with a minimum of fuss but leaves hints a-plenty that he's working on a very suggestive canvas. It predated Neil Armstrong's walk on the moon by only a year but in a sense transcends it in the manner in which it enriches our understanding of the origins of the cosmos and man's ever-changing place in it.

For his astronauts he chose two actors, Keir Dullea and Gary Lockwood, who would disappear into the woodwork, leaving him free rein to dazzle us with his camerabatics—especially a phantasmagorical sequence lasting many minutes where we're made to feel we're zooming from one galaxy to another.

Attempting to explain the opening sequence he said, "Man is the missing link between primitive apes and civilised human beings. We're semi-civilised, capable of cooperation and affection but needing some sort of transfiguration into a higher form of life. Since the means to obliterate life on earth exists, it will take more than just careful planning and reasonable cooperation to avoid some eventual catastrophe. The problem is essentially a moral and spiritual one."[28]

Mankind, he seems to be saying, takes a step backward every time it takes one forward. The learning curve *is* a curve. The primeval grunt of the ape becomes sophisticated into space-speak but there's just as little fellow-feeling in the bland future as the hairy past, maybe even less. This is a world characterized by "the exchange of banalities, outmoded forms of politeness, hollow speechifying, reciprocal suspicion, the Howard Johnson lounge, the souvenir snapshots taken by the moon explorers, the ridiculous 'Happy Birthday' intoned thousands of miles away by parents proud of their astronaut offspring, the father who no longer knows how to talk to his little girl."[29]

From a visual point of view all this was never meant to be analyzed to the death. It's the closest a film can come to replicating the experience of actually being in space. If such a wondrous sensation means religion to us then Kubrick seems to be saying, so be it.

"Sometimes," he once surmised, "I think we're alone in the universe and sometimes I think we aren't. In both cases the idea makes me dizzy."[30] We experience the infinity of space and perhaps, by extension, that of time—and our own minds—as well. But the intimations of immortality are filtered through the visual convolutions, which sometimes renders them ambiguous, as was Kubrick's intention.

Michael Herr contended Kubrick "always acted like he knew something you didn't."[31] John Brosnan notes that the director was often accused of being "deliberately enigmatic in order to disguise the fact that the film wasn't really about anything." Brosnan himself described it as "nothing more than a secular movie about God."[32] In the end, like the director itself, it leaves a sensation of null wonder.

In one way its God is technology itself. John Simon described it as "a shaggy god story." Other critics panned it for self-indulgence but this is one film where a director may be permitted such a luxury. Indeed, were it absent, much of its hypnotic magic would have gone by the board. The refusal to have any truck with aliens, in any case, brings the sci-fi genre into a radically different era than the "Put a monster into the movie and we'll make a profit" mindset.

In a *Playboy* interview he did shortly after it came out, Kubrick put his eschatological cards clearly on the table by saying, "All the attributes assigned to God could be the characteristics of biological entities that have evolved into something as remote from man as man is remote from the primordial ooze from which he first emerged." This is Darwinism with a particularly strident skeptical sting.

In another interview he refused to give a "verbal road map" of the movie for fear any viewer not seeing it the way he did might feel he'd missed the point. We shouldn't try to explain it, he advised, any more than we should try to "explain" a Beethoven symphony.[33] Art wasn't a signifier but rather the thing itself.

Just before it went on release, Kubrick let his mask slip a bit. "MGM don't know it yet," he joked, "but they've just footed the bill for the first

$6 million religious film."[34] The remark was tongue-in-cheek but he was wily enough to know what he was promulgating.

Speaking of the monolith, he teased, "The truth of a thing is in the feel of it; not in the think of it." Clarke spoke of it as a sort of Swiss army knife—it does whatever it wants to do. It's as mysterious as it is ubiquitous. It confronts us daringly, but just as daringly refuses to yield up its secrets. Like HAL it doesn't move, but unlike him it doesn't speak either. Is it a force of good or evil? We're never told. Derek Elley called it "a cold technological equivalent of Homer and Virgil—for the Space Age is not concerned with personality."[35]

The film covers a wingspan of no less than three million years, going from tribal unrest among the apes to the famous "Star Gate" sequence where Dullea sees himself die and be reborn due to the power of the monolith. The dialogue throughout is almost non-existent, a mere 46 minutes in a total of 139, which focuses the attention almost totally on how the film looks.

Dullea evolves from astronaut to angel, and then back to space baby in the film's cyclical pattern toward a new dawn, but there's nothing schematic or contrived about this. We're not sure what Kubrick is at and we're not sure he is either. He hints at immortality but won't commit. The slab tantalizes us with its ubiquitousness as the only connecting thread between the film's widely fractured time-frames but it refuses to yield up its secrets, if indeed it has any. Is it the sign of a superior intelligence? Is that intelligence God? Does it matter?

We shouldn't over-interpret Kubrick's visual fantasy. One code-breaker even wrote to him asking if he chose the name HAL because each of the three letters were just before the ones in IBM in the alphabet. Kubrick was amused at the coincidence but denied any intent. Maybe we should be similarly circumspect about seeing sermons in every frame of his astral journey.

Alexander Walker believed Kubrick reinterpreted religious experience as transcended intelligence. The sense that we're not alone in the universe hints at a supernatural presence but doesn't posit it. Bob Gaffney thought, "People would read anything into it. Kids on acid trips were just looking for the meaning of life."[36]

In his book *A Cinema of Loneliness*, author Robert Phillip Kolker argues that the monolith, far from representing a benign force, is actually a harbinger of violence. "After all," he points out, "the first result of contact with it is killing. The ape touches it and learns to use a bone as a weapon. The widescreen close-up of the ape's arm crushing down his new-found club is a prophecy of human savagery to come."[37]

Kolker is even leery about the famous transmogrification of bone to spaceship in the flash-forward. "The ape showed a manic joy in its discovery," he notes, "but the space travellers show neither joy nor sorrow. They're mere receivers of the data flashed on the various screens that surround them. The territory they conquer seems to offer no excitement. The ape used his tool but now the tools and the men are hardly distinguishable."

One of the tools, HAL, rebels, but even HAL seems to have more humanity in him than the astronauts. One critic went so far as to say that the best things in the film were the machines "which are more splendid than the idiotic humans." The astronauts, put another way, are "mechanized," whereas HAL is a "fascinating neurotic."[38] If the former have had personality bypasses, as Kubrick seems to suggest, HAL, in contrast, is a rather endearing character, particularly as he makes his final plea to Dullea for mercy. He uses every ruse in his armory to stave off his extinction, even with a tinge of humor. It's as if he's trying to browbeat Dullea by saying, "You wouldn't do this to a friend, would you?" before succumbing to the inevitable with some grace. But before this point, the instinct of self-preservation seems more prominent in HAL than it does in the astronauts.

The dying astronaut seeing the monolith at the end prompted another viewer to ask: "Has an old man gotten religion on his deathbed or has Dave seen his next incarnation?" Man, he concludes, has reverted back to his primitive essence and has then come back, his odyssey over, in a higher form to witness the second millennium.[39]

In the transition from adulthood to senescence and then sudden embryonic status, Kubrick would seem to be suggesting the possibility of reincarnation, or maybe he's throwing various images at us in a playful kind of "mixed grill" fashion. His Future Shock world is almost one of nullity, a world where the humans have submitted to being ruled not by apes or dinosaurs, but machines, the de-programming of HAL a rather feeble attempt to reverse the trend.

But Future Shock is also Future Numbness, an air-conditioned nightmare of vacuous platitudes and synthetic sandwiches. Playing chess with HAL (who can lip-read) is vaguely reminiscent of the knight in *The Seventh Seal* trying to bargain with The Grim Reaper. A different form of second-guessing is going on here as this smarmy Frankenstein plans a clever lock-out so he can wrest control of the mothership from these earthling upstarts.

At the end, as Kolker put it, "Old Mankind is catapulted by some force back into the cosmos as a wandering foetus, presumably ready to start anew." Oh bland new world that has such people in it.

Kubrick warned us that people who didn't believe their eyes wouldn't be able to appreciate his film. But there weren't many of these. In the main, young people tripped themselves out on acid for the ultimate celluloid fix as it opened worldwide. At one showing, a man ran down the cinema aisle and crashed through the screen screaming, "I see God!" Kubrick's reaction was: if the film had stirred the emotions then it had succeeded.

He once said he didn't know what the monolith was meant to signify himself, just as Samuel Beckett claimed he didn't know who Godot was in his most famous work. (If he did, he claimed, he would have said so in the play.) Kubrick allowed that the religious implications were inevitable because all the essential attributes of such extra-terrestrial intelligence are the attributes we give to God.

Most people wanted reductive answers to the significance of it all but Kubrick left this to the chattering classes at the trendy parties. He did, however, concede that "On the deepest psychological level, the film's plot symbolized the search for God, and finally postulates what is a scientific definition of Him. The realistic hardware and the documentary feelings about everything were necessary in order to undermine your built-in resistance to the poetical concept."[40]

For today's audience, the film is widely seen as an exemplar of druggie New Age-ism, but this is to disavow its perennial origins in man's search for an icon, arguably religious, upon which he can hang his hopes and fantasies.

John Boorman, an avid admirer of it, pointed out that the success of the movie was down to the fact that, since the western genre was on life support, our need for mythic heroes was first passed onto the spy film, and then science fiction. Kubrick was the deserved beneficiary of the need for iconic figureheads.

Not for long, though, because in the same year we had Mia Farrow giving birth to the devil's child in Roman Polanski's *Rosemary's Baby*. The following August, in real life, Charles Manson and his army of dissolutes brutally murdered Polanski's friend Sharon Tate, then seven months pregnant, smearing her blood and that of others on the walls of her luxurious Hollywood home. Manson's brutality seemed to usher in a decade that saw an obsession with satanic overkill.

In *The Godfather* (1972), religion is used as part of the family business of killing to, as it were, legitimize it, whether it's the baptism of the first film of the trilogy, neatly intercut with forensic executions, or the procession of *Godfather 2* that follows Vito Corleone's murder of a rival.

As the film begins, Don Corleone (Marlon Brando) is almost invested with God-like status as an undertaker comes to him asking him to dispense rough justice to an enemy because the legal system has failed. We're made to feel this dark don is hearing confession, or sitting in some kind of divine judgment. Soon afterwards, director Francis Ford Coppola intercuts scenes of Brando's daughter getting married with one of his own underhand deals.

In the baptism scene Brando's son, Al Pacino, is asked by the priest performing the ceremony, "Do you renounce Satan?" "I do renounce him," he replies, whereupon the camera cuts to a Mafia hit. "And all his works?" the priest continues, as we flash back to the church. "I do renounce them," Pacino declares, whereupon we cut to another bloody execution. The point is obvious but nonetheless impressive.

The great force of the film, of course, resides in the manner in which violence is perpetrated under the guise of "business." We frequently hear characters tell somebody, "It's not personal." But what could be more personal than killing someone? In this moral twilight zone the Corleones, and their warring factions, go through their motions. Such motions also involve the sacrosanct unit of the family. Betraying this, even in a minor way, apparently ranks a notch higher than slaughtering a stranger.

As alluded to already, these people don't seem to have any problem reconciling wanton destruction of their enemies with the pleasant rituals of marriages, baptisms and luxurious banquets. Perhaps this is why one wag suggested the film should be re-titled *Four Funerals and a Wedding*.

Coppola was denounced for this, but not as much as he was for putting a horse's head in a gangster's bed in an early scene. "There were thirty or so people killed in the film," he protested, "but everyone said, 'You killed a living animal to get the horse's head.' I didn't, of course. 'The horse was killed by the dog companies to feed your little poodles.'"[41]

In the final analysis, as Carlos Clarens writes in his book *Crime Movies*, Don Corleone is the upholder of natural law, God's law, separating good from evil: "By intent, religious ceremony is used repeatedly to counterpoint some of the most violent deeds of the Corleones: the preparations for a massacre are intercut with the christening of Michael's firstborn; a procession is in progress as the young Vito stalks his first victim across the roofs of Little Italy. Rather than implicating the church in the underworld, as the Marxist observer might have it, these parallels serve to turn the violence into a sacrament."[42]

To reinforce the impression of justified sacramental violence, some vaguely Biblical references are scattered throughout: the hand-kissing, the "kiss of death" with which Michael (Pacino) casts off his treacherous brother Fredo, and some prescient lines such as "Whoever comes to you at the Barzini meeting, he's a traitor," or, "Before I get to my hotel, I'll be assassinated," which sound like parodies of parables.

Brando saw *The Godfather* as a parable of corporate crime in America, and another indictment of his country's doublethink. "If Cosa Nostra had been black or socialist," he claimed in *Songs My Mother Taught Me* (Random House), "Don Corleone would have ended up dead or in jail, but because The Mafia patterned themselves so closely on corporatism and dealt in such a hardnosed way with money and politics, it prospered." The Mafia is a quintessentially American institution, he asserted. Not quite as wholesome as cheerleaders or Mom's apple pie, of course, but personifying all the classic mores of white collar crime writ large.

Brando did a famous cameo in *Apocalypse Now* three years later. Robert Duvall's "I love the smell of napalm in the morning" has entered the language, and Brando's mesmerizing portrayal of Kurtz, the disaffected green beret colonel gone native—and mad—in his cavernous lair still resonates with grim foreboding. Coppola again directed.

This is an all-stops-out, full frontal assault on the Armageddon-like insanity that was Vietnam as well as a fascinating glimpse into the eclectic turmoil of Kurtz's mind. A loose re-working of Joseph Conrad's *Heart of Darkness*, it has a hypnotic, surreal quality to it as we watch a burned-out Army Intelligence officer engage in his obsessive mission to destroy Kurtz in the jungles of Cambodia during the rainy season.

Martin Sheen, as Willard, represents the cleansing agent in the film. He's the assassin who hunts down Kurtz, the embodiment of raw appetite let loose to reign in a Godless kingdom. By killing him he can carry on his mantle, become the new lion king in the jungle. But Willard stops one step short of this. After the ritual sacrifice of Kurtz—intercut with the slaughter of a water buffalo in the editorial style we've already seen Coppola show a preference for—Willard drops his machete, renouncing the kind of life Kurtz epitomized. Instead, with the tribesmen at his feet, willing to accept him as their new guru, he leaves it all behind, going back to his boat. His job has been done just like Shane's was. George Stevens gave us a corrupt valley but Coppola's poison brew is a jungle. As Willard leaves it starts to rain, as much a symbol of imminent purification as Stevens' dawn light.

To quote Richard Blake, "Kurtz has eaten of the fruit of the knowledge of good and evil and made himself equal to God, the author of a new code beyond the petty categories of unimaginative men." In his "ruined Eden decorated with skulls and decaying corpses, he has constructed a new moral order for himself."[43] This is the nub of the issue. He can't be evaluated by conventional moral terms. He's not a fallen angel or a latter-day Adam. He's more like Emily Bronte's Heathcliffe, an indefinable force of nature. Coppola's alliance of him with the buffalo isn't accidental from this point of view.

He's Conrad's "heart of darkness" in human form, a man who is both terrorized by, and himself represents, "the horror, the horror"—his own dying words that capture his final descent into the seventh circle of hell.

An ever-spiralling budget—costs were estimated at $150,000 per day—turbulent weather conditions that often turned the sets into flotsam and jetsam and Brando's insistence on turning John Milius' script inside out—and thereby creating a Kurtz who would have ominous parallels to his own troubled soul—threatened to up-end the shooting of the movie many times. Sheen even suffered a heart attack at one point, but somehow it got made.

Looking back on it now over a quarter of a century later, maybe some of the Kafkaesque kudos that greeted its release may be deemed over the top (screenwriter Robert Towne snootily dubbed it *Apocalypse Now And Then*) but it still stands as a coruscating indictment of military violence as well as a moodily Malthusian porthole into the mind of a rogue colonel gone off the rails.

You can almost taste the tension as we await the appearance of Brando amidst the rotting bodies and squawking carrion birds of his decadent empire. When he finally appears, bald and Buddha-like, stroking his pate as he reads the poetry of Auden, speaking sparingly but with the authority of his own inner agony ("You're only an errand boy sent by grocery clerks," he tells Willard prior to being executed) the film enters a unique dimension that lifts it onto the mythic level.

This was a bruising production for all concerned, a journey into a different kind of darkness for cast and crew alike, and one which took its toll on many people's health, lifestyles and financial circumstances. Steve McQueen, Al Pacino, Robert Redford and Jack Nicholson had all turned down the role of Kurtz before Coppola offered it to Brando at a fee of $1 million a week for three weeks work as well as 11% of the gross. Did he deserve it? The jury is still out on that one. The overall budget was over $35 million—astronomical for the time—for the 238-day shoot.

A susurrating, psychedelic epic conceived in chaos, it's a film people either love or loathe but can't be immune to, especially in these war-torn times where Kurtz may be seen as pre-dating somebody like Osama bin Laden in his demonic conviction. It's also, sadly, Brando's last great mini-performance, acting as a seismic coda to a career that might have been more fondly remembered had it ended with his symbolic execution in this nightmarish compound.

Jack Nicholson is an unlikely candidate for canonization, but in an essay entitled "A Salvific Drama of Liberation," Charles Ketcham makes a case for the fact that Nicholson's film *One Flew Over the Cuckoo's Nest* (1975) has him cast as a Christ-figure, liberating the other members of the mental institution he inhabits for most of the movie while making himself into a sacrificial lamb.

Ketcham believes that in Ken Kesey's novel, upon which the film is based, the hospital stands for the "Evil Empire, which, if we are to be saved, must be challenged and reformed by the forces of the Good."[44] In such a "titanic and religious" struggle, Nurse Ratched, played by the Oscar-winning Louise Fletcher, epitomizes that evil. Before R.P. McMurphy, the Nicholson character, is about to undergo shock therapy he asks significantly, "Do I get a crown of thorns?"

McMurphy's psychological tussle with Ratched forms the nexus of the film. She finally succeeds in "crucifying" him by dint of a lobotomy, but his friend Chief Bromden, representing redeemed humanity, escapes in his place. Ketcham quotes David Graybeal in the final paragraph of his essay. "The History of Jesus Christ," Graybeal wrote, "has taught us all that the non-conformist, the questioner of certified authority and established procedure, the lover of persons and life, will be killed. God's story in Christ has also taught us that not even death will be able to stop the liberator's empowering effect."[45] This may be to superimpose on the movie certain motifs Kesey or Milos Forman, its director, weren't aware of, but it doesn't mean it can't be viewed as an allegory of some sort, with or without these emphases.

McMurphy, writes Ketcham, is a Christ-figure because "It is he who brings to the patients their sense of worth and dignity, it is he who stands up against the Evil One who has tyrannized the 'crazies', and it is he who finally suffers and dies so they may be free."[46] This is as apparent in the movie is it is in Kesey's novel, a straightforward utilization of the "Christus Victor" theme in traditional Christian thought.

The station where Ratched dispenses her pills, what one author refers to as the "Holy of Holies" almost takes on the status of an altar as the film goes on.[47] In one scene, as the patients queue up for their medication, one of them sticks out his tongue and she puts the pill on it as if it's the Host.

There are further Biblical allusions. When the director of the hospital asks McMurphy who he "really" is, McMurphy looks at his referral sheet and says, "What does it say there?," a line that's an almost direct parallel to Luke's Gospel where Jesus asks, "Who do the crowds say that I am?" in rhetorical response to the same question. When McMurphy takes the inmates out for a day he brings them fishing, another significant echo of the apostles. Finally, there's the "last supper" with his friends before Ratched (the Judas figure) hatches her plan to "crucify" him. After his lobotomy he's described as being "as meek as a lamb," another Christological echo. When Chief Bromden escapes from the "cuckoo's nest" at the end, a cry of "He is risen" goes up from those left behind.

The film ultimately begs the question: Are the really mad people in society *patients* in mental institutions or actually running them? The inmates take over the asylum for a while but their jollity is short-lived. When McMurphy is lobotomized, not so much because he's deemed sick as dangerous, the status quo is regained. One man does fly over the nest in the film's life-affirming finale but the lingering mood is one of tragedy in this searing indictment of a world gone mad at the top, with the Nurse Ratcheds holding most of the aces.

Network (1976) offered us a different kind of prophet: the one played by newsreader Peter Finch, who proselytizes and prioritizes through a TV show. In an industry that prioritizes audience ratings above all else, his Malthusian prophecies, no matter how off-the-wall, can't be ignored by the network bosses because he's pulling in so many viewers.

They use him until he becomes too dangerous and then plan to liquidate him. This is a novel form of martyrdom. Finch is "mad as hell and won't take it anymore." He's a televangelist in work clothes, a secular priest, a certifiable goon, but he makes dollars—the new religion. When he threatens to blow his brains out on live TV, thereby making it dead TV, what we're witnessing is hara-kiri with attitude. Meanwhile the background Pharisees speak about him as a piece of meat. Pontius Pilate is alive and well in Paddy Chayevsky's explosive script, which sees a demented man crucified on a totem pole of inane voyeurism, eccentricity being prized only as a temporary *divertissement* before "the suits" get back to worshipping the Golden Calf of Mammon.

The TV executives are the devils here. Stranded in the middle of the two poles is William Holden, a fundamentally decent man caught in the throes of an affair with Faye Dunaway, a woman who doesn't know, or want to know, the difference between reality and fantasy. When Holden tells her she can't change the channels on life like she can on TV she remains unperturbed. This is a woman who has grown up on Bugs Bunny, confronted with somebody suddenly terrified by his own mortality. Death is a palpable thing for him, he tells her; he's nearer the end of his life than the beginning. But not as near it as Finch.

Also that year Martin Scorsese directed *Taxi Driver*, the film that made Robert De Niro famous. Richard Maltby described it as a horror movie, not because of the presence of a psychopath in it, but rather because the psychopath in question is the only perspective it offers on its narrative.

In a film like *Halloween*, Maltby points out, we also witness the subjective perception of a character we know to be mad and dangerous, but Donald Pleasance at least told us what was going on. In *Taxi Driver*, on the contrary, the subjectivity is rendered more frightening by the fact that the sole agent of its narrative, Travis Bickle (De Niro), is unable to explain himself to anyone, least of all himself.

As far as Maltby is concerned this is the most effective way for a director to create true fear in his audience. *Halloween* does it to a lesser extent because we don't see the madman. In this way the notion of pure evil is sustained. But eventually we do see him, which mitigates the terror for us. It's like somebody coming at us from behind and saying "Boo!" The fright we get is from the surprise. Afterwards we can deal with it. The problem with Travis Bickle is his uncertainty about who (or why) he wants to kill.

Bickle is alienated man writ large, spiritually dead, and only roused to life by killing others. Scorsese describes him as a "false saint" who "sets out to save people who don't want to be saved and ends up hurting them."[48] This is a perverted Jesus who achieves a rare form of hero-worship by ridding the streets of sludge in a vigilante-style operation that stems more from the shellshock of war (he's a Vietnam veteran) than the urge to purify. He falls in love with the near-divine vision of Betsy (Cybill Shepherd) in the film's early stages but blows it by leading her into the very *demi-monde* he will soon eradicate. Later he meets his very own Mary Magdalene in the twelve-year-old hooker Iris (Jodie Foster). Her name is a flower, but this one has never had a chance to bloom, deprived of oxygen in a city which strangles purity at birth.

When Bickle first sees Betsy he compares her to "an angel in a white dress." He wants to save her as he later wants to save Iris. If Iris is being destroyed by street life, Betsy is having her purity sucked out of her by the mechanics of the political process. He tells her he thinks she's lonely. Perhaps this is a projection of his own alienation. He sees a higher self for her as he does for himself. But when this becomes impossible he goes to the other extreme.

We could even draw a strange parallel to the Norman Bates of *Psycho*. Bates, like Bickle, is an inhibited idealist who becomes psychotic when the world doesn't conform to his wishes. When we first see Bates it's in the guise of helping Marion Crane (Janet Leigh) atone for her sins, not murder her. Bickle goes through the same parabola of emotions. At times, De Niro's voice even seems to mimic that of Anthony Perkins, who played Bates, in its dreamy boyishness.

Bickle comes to us without a history apart from a brief reference to the war. What's important to note is that he's a fallen angel living in a post-edenic world. There's a pestilence abroad, filth and slime on the streets, and he's been delegated by some unseen authority to clean it up. We don't see his family, his friends, anything of his past. When the film begins, so does his life.

From the metal prison of his taxi he surveys the human species at work and play: the bland political candidate, the elusive beauty who campaigns for him, the neophyte hooker he must redeem, the blood-thirsty passenger (played by Scorsese). Bickle seems to be taking it all in coolly but in his casual asides about hoping that a rain will come to wash away all the slime we know that he's just marking time before he embraces his destiny as a vengeful saint. The wrath of Jove will descend upon this pestilence and eradicate it and afterward there will be peace again, if only for a short while. Then it might be time for another foray into murky alleyways and brothels where twisted old men exploit the Irises of this world.

Steam rises from manholes which, in the words of Lesley Stern, "hints at a rotting universe beneath the streets, a decay that is barely contained."[49] Marina Connolly likens it to the "yellow smoke and fog" of T.S. Eliot's *Waste Land*, or even Dante's *Inferno*.[50] Bickle tells the politician Betsy is canvassing for that he wants him to clean up the city. He welcomes the rain that washes the garbage off the sidewalks but he him-self has to remove the *human* garbage.

Part redeemer and part executioner, Scorsese sees Bickle as being "somewhere between Charles Manson and St. Paul."[51] The film seduc-tively draws us into his perverse mind, implicating us in his "fetishistic handling of guns, his holding his hands over the flame to prove his will, his obscene monocular vision of the city and its evils."[52]

Scorsese captures the solitude of this urban psychopath with an array of gentle vignettes which makes the final explosion of latent energy leap off the screen like a cannonball. De Niro cultivated a bow-legged walk to catch the crab-like nature of his character, his feet turned inwards just as his head is.

Bickle tries to take Iris out of the sewer but for some strange reason he dumps Betsy *into* it by bringing her to a pornography cinema. In each instance he mixes the normal world and underworld together. Put another way, he comforts the afflicted and afflicts the comfortable.

When Betsy breaks it off with him after he brings her to the porn movie—he's brought her there not so much to shock her as because it's his own preferred habitat—he tells her she'll "burn in hell." The Madonna has suddenly turned into a devil in his eyes.

Paul Schrader wrote the screenplay after reading Albert Camus' absurd novel of senseless slaughter and its nonchalant aftermath, *The Outsider*. Bickle and Meursault, Camus' equally offbeat narrator, are soulmates in this regard. He also based it on a 1963 French film, Robert Bresson's *Pickpocket*, which told the story of a petty criminal who is as obsessed with his criminal activities as is Bickle. Neither of them fully understand their motivation. They see the world through a glass—or windshield—darkly.

New York, Schrader once suggested, is a place where you come to be lonely. In *Taxi Driver* that loneliness attains horrific proportions as the walking time-bomb that is Bickle eventually erupts into an orgy of violence. In the end he seems to be saying to us: In order to kill something you have to become it. So he descends into the hell around him, embracing it. What makes this even more chilling is that audiences find themselves cheering him on as he does so, much as they cheered on the Clint Eastwood of *Dirty Harry* or the Charles Bronson of *Death Wish*.

"On every street in every city there's a nobody who dreams of being a somebody." Thus ran the billboard tagline to promote the movie. One man, John Hinckley, took it literally and shot Ronald Reagan—after seeing it fourteen times. He wanted to impress Jodie Foster. Life—and death—imitated art.

De Niro refused to discuss Hinckley in interviews about the film but he was embarrassed about him. Schrader contended that *Taxi Driver* didn't create Hinckley; in fact it probably stopped other Hinckleys, because it deals with suppression of emotion, suppression of sex, suppression of natural instincts. Until they finally explode.

Bickle can't relate to Betsy, his "Virgin Mary" in Scorsese's eyes, on a sexual level. Instead he brings her to a place where she can watch a perverse fabrication of sex. His world upended by the war and its grim aftermath, he retreats into his own private cauldron to morph into his new identity. He becomes what Scorsese called "a commando of God," the man who can rid the Big Apple of its human pollutants. It doesn't matter if he kills a pimp or a political candidate, or both. What's important is that he kills something, anything, to release his demons.

Working the graveyard shift in his yellow coffin he reveals that he thinks he has stomach cancer. It's as if the city's disease has entered into him too. The only way to cure it is by his nihilistic exertions. So the young man with the boy-next-door looks and the Charles Manson edge does what he has to do to make himself into a new kind of anti-hero, a purveyor of insane justice who kills without an ounce of sadism, or glee. He's really just doing his job. A pre-Schwarzenegger Terminator, perhaps. Clint Eastwood crossed with Dostoevsky as directed by Bergman.

"All the animals come out at night," he tells a passenger in his cab, "whores, skunk pussies, buggers, queens, fairies, dopers, junkies." By the end of the film he's reduced himself to their own level, the spiritual pollution that cascades over New York's mean streets finally entering his own devolved soul. He doesn't wallow in his heroic status nor is he disgusted by it. Instead he seems cool, even lobotomized, as he surveys his grim handiwork, the deranged angel of death finally learning how to hate.

"I am God's lonely man," Bickle writes in his diary, the slightly formal tone masking the underlying terror of a man teetering on the edge of a terrible fate. It's as if he's using the Almighty as a benchmark for his bloodlust, as if He has conveyed him with the authority to clean up the mess. If New York is Sodom and Gomorrah then Bickle, in his own dead head, is the prophet called upon to demolish it single-handedly.

The taxi and his claustrophobic apartment are the twin prisons where he spends his days and nights. Together they conspire to unhinge him, transforming him into a one-man army. His only connections are to his firearms, his mirror, and the television he watches from almost point blank range, tipping it back and forward on a table with his foot until he knocks it over and it explodes.

It's a small gesture in the circumstances but he seems unaware of what he's done. He shows no reaction to the destruction of the set. It's a precursor of things to come, this removal of the last item that spoke to him. Relieved of its banter, he's now free to express himself on his own terms with his new Mohawk haircut, his battle fatigues, and his urge to seek out those pulling the strings of decadence.

Bickle doesn't seem to want to engage in life at the outset, merely to observe it. He doesn't suggest any physical intimacy with Betsy or indeed Iris. Buying a Magnum could be a phallic symbol but this is the level he's at. It's as if he has an ascetic streak which applies to other aspects of his life as well. As he puts it himself, prior to his attempted assassination of the politician, "No more pills, no more bad food, no more destroyers of my body."

The veteran home from the war is in some ways like the Arthur Block of *The Seventh Seal*. Here Max Von Sydow was "God's lonely man" too. Was Scorsese using the scum of New York as an analogue to the Black Death? Bickle doesn't expect to survive the bloodbath. He writes in his diary to Iris, "I'll probably be dead when you read this." Instead he becomes a hero, and at the end of the film checks himself in his car mirror much in the way he did in his apartment in the "Are you lookin' at me?" scene. The implication is that even more blood is on the cards, another mini-Armageddon. This killing machine has other Everests to conquer.

In a few years another victim of shellshock, the Christopher Walken of *The Deer Hunter*, will engage in similarly self-destructive behavior by playing Russian roulette until he puts a bullet through his head.

In the meantime, though, George Lucas awaited, his business being to reinstate the family audience.

The famous line from *Star Wars* (1977), "May the force be with you," has obvious echoes of the Christian blessing "May the Lord be with you." Indeed, Sir Alec Guinness, who appeared in that film as Obi-Wan Kenobe, said that when he was at Mass one time, a fellow worshipper intoned the former greeting to him rather than the latter. He was obviously being jocose, in deference to Guinness' fame, but he made the older man feel awkward. The term, according to Lucas, came from Carlos Castenada's story *Tales of Power*, in which the Native American shaman Don Juan talks of a "life force."

Obi-Wan can be compared to either a wizard or hermit, or both. His desert lifestyle, as David Wilkinson pointed out in his book *The Power of the Force*, puts him in the tradition of prophets like John the Baptist. A monastic figure who becomes both mentor and surrogate father to Luke Skywalker (Mark Hamill), we don't have to look too far to see the messianic parallels.

Lucas grew up on a diet of Flash Gordon comics. He said he had a mystical experience at the age of six which involved him questioning both the nature of God and reality and where he fitted into the overall scheme of things. His parents were Methodist but he saw this as a self-centered religion. He resented Sunday school, preferring church ceremonies.

As a teenager he lacked direction in life but in 1962 a strange thing happened to him. His car overturned when he was driving along a country road. It was about to burst into flames when his seatbelt broke and spun him out of the vehicle. Afterward he became convinced this stroke of luck saved his life. He saw it as providential. In this incident we have the reason he refused to join his father in the world of business, immersing himself in the study of philosophy and sociology before enrolling in the University of Southern California Film School.

Obi-Wan describes the Force as "an energy field created by all living things. It surrounds us and penetrates us. It binds the galaxy together." If we want to read a New Age God into this then the corollary, Darth Vader, is our corresponding Devil. Vader has been influenced by the dark side of the force. He wants to destroy the Jedi but is redeemed by trying to save his son.

These polarities are very simplistic. *Star Wars* is like Kubrick's *Space Odyssey* for kids. There's nothing thought-provoking in its simplistic ethical polarities and bog standard adventure sequences. And yet it has probably had more impact on audiences than any movie before or since, as well as spawning a raft of sequels. *Premiere* magazine tried to explain why: "Movies, like religion, have an uncanny ability to make people believe things that are directly contradicted by their everyday experience. And that ability sometimes enables movies to, in a weird way, replace religion. *Star Wars*, anyone?"[53]

Lucas has always claimed he never intended the mythology of the film to be a replacement for religion but rather an adjunct to it, a kind of "generalized spirituality" in which people of various persuasions could share. He created the religion of *Star Wars*—if such it could be called— by taking "all the issues that religion represents and trying to distil them down into a more modern and easily accessible construct."[54]

Jacques Peretti, in an article in *The Guardian* in 1999, wrote, "We live in a largely godless culture. The Manichean mumbo-jumbo of *Star Wars* makes it a perfect faith-light for a soft-brained world." Its mass hypnosis, he felt, was reminiscent of the outpouring of grief that followed upon the death of Princess Diana: "Just as we are now all capable of fake sentiment, so we are now all capable of fake deep."

Lucas is reluctant to say God and the Force are one and the same thing for him, preferring to work in a speculative framework whereby things mean what audiences want them to mean, i.e., that they create their own gods, or non-gods, from the arabesque of experience that is their lives up until the moment they see the director's moving images in front of them.

John Brosnan railed against Lucas' cheesy, California-style, New Age mysticism in his book *The Primal Screen*, accusing him of inventing "a safe religion that doesn't step on any theological toes, and is just as absurd as any of the existing religions in the world."[55]

Brosnan also has a problem with Obi-Wan Kenobi's comparison of the Force to an energy field binding the galaxy together, as mentioned. What, he asks, was binding this galaxy together before life evolved? And if there was nothing to bind it, how did life evolve?[56]

Lucas' friend Steven Spielberg put his mystical head over the parapet in 1977. His theme was ordinary people in extraordinary situations and his movie, *Close Encounters of the Third Kind*, was just what audiences reeling from the overkill of such as *The Heretic* needed by way of wondrous antidote.

An introverted child, Spielberg retreated into movie-making to find a higher truth. Celluloid became his mealticket to a kind of legitimized hallucination and he embraced it with every fiber of his being. He had hit the box office jackpot three years before with *Jaws* but this was virgin territory, the film that would take him from a standard issue genre to a novel one.

He knew he was flying blind with the present film, understandably tense about a movie that involved a grown man leaving his wife and family because he believed so fervently in UFOs. Richard Dreyfuss plays Roy Neary, an electrical worker who becomes obsessed by the vision of a mountain. He builds a model of it out of soil he shovels into his living-room, which causes his family to walk out on him.

Spielberg is being self-indulgent here, in no hurry to tell a story in the conventional manner, so intent is he on getting us to empathize with Dreyfuss' obsession. "As a narrative," wrote Richard Maltby in his book

Harmless Entertainment, "the film is incomprehensible; as a story it spends twenty-four hours getting to the point at which a 1950s science fiction movie would begin."

Paul Schrader wrote the original screenplay, describing it as "a metaphysical update on the life of St. Paul."[57] He explained that Dreyfuss' main journey wasn't to outer space but rather inner space. In his script Dreyfuss eventually reaches the conclusion that UFOs "are not out there, but up there"—i.e., in the head. Spielberg hated the script and binned it, substituting his own one with the "spiritual encounter."[58]

In one of the early scenes the Nearys sit watching Cecil B. DeMille's *The Ten Commandments* on TV. "It's four and a half hours long," the mother (Teri Garr) complains, adding that there's "nothing in it" for her children. Dreyfuss is upset by her reaction and begs to differ, saying "It would be good for them." What he's really articulating here is his need for something else besides the creature comforts of consumerism. He needs a spiritual dimension in his life but he can't get it in the way other people do. He has a yearning for comic book fantasy delivered in intergalactic fashion.

The end of the film, where Dreyfuss finally sees the aliens, was described by the critic Pauline Kael as "savior-like." "They're sunburnt Gods," she wrote in the *New Yorker*, "arriving through Blakean Old Testament clouds. This isn't nuts-and-bolts Popular Mechanics science fiction; it's beatific technology—machines from outer space deified." Ray Bradbury likened the sequence to a "religious experience."[59]

One scientist gasps "Oh my God!" when the mother ship is first viewed. "On the one hand," wrote critic Douglas Brode in his book, *The Films of Steven Spielberg* (Citadel, 1995), "this is a commonplace utterance of amazement; on another, he has no idea how right he is, for the spiritual religious quest Dreyfuss has embarked on is about to reach its happy conclusion."

John Brosnan wrote in *The Primal Screen* that *Close Encounters* appeals to the child within us that still wants to believe Somebody Up There likes us. It's the Walt Disney version of Kubrick's *Space Odyssey* for him, a "giant cinematic security blanket."

Showing the aliens at the end of the film was, to his mind, a huge mistake. Not only because it took away the element of mystery that enshrouds Kubrick's film but also because they're rather boring. "I suspect," he writes, "that a species of aliens that journeys all those long light-years across the coldness of space just to play silly games with the human race hasn't got much to teach us." *Touché*. And nowadays, he adds, in a reference to the 2002 Mel Gibson film *Signs*, "They've enlarged their repertoire of pranks to include leaving funny patterns in our cornfields."

The moment a man stepped on the surface of the moon, people often argued, science fiction could never be the same again because it would be replaced with science *fact*. In 1969 we learned finally that there was no man on it, contrary to legend, and neither was it made of green cheese. Would lovers ever be able to write poetry about it again, or film directors mythologize it, or indeed other planets? Spielberg proved they could.

He was a breath of fresh air to the sci-fi genre from the point of view that he relieved us of green blobs with ridiculous-looking antennae which had been the staple of B-movies of this ilk for a generation. He was also wise to point out that we shouldn't assume extraterrestrials are going to be aggressive. The very fact of their arrival on earth, he has always argued, suggests a superior intelligence.

"I'm sorry," he suggests, "but I just don't believe that anyone smart enough to construct the technology to travel hundreds of light years through space would come to earth with hostile intentions."[60] Of course he rescinded that view for his more recent *War of the Worlds*, a reversion back to the B-movie stereotype of aliens. It's also eminently reasonable to argue that aliens could be both intelligent *and* aggressive. Future movies should perhaps adopt an open mind on the orientations of aliens, whatever their appearance, or IQ levels.

Michael Phillips, the film's producer, was actually the person who suggested Spielberg make the aliens friendly. Spielberg wasn't convinced that he could market a movie based on friendly aliens. Phillips argued that a superior race of beings would most likely come to earth to help us, as indeed we would to another planet peopled by beings less intelligent than us, if such an eventuality transpired. His point is well taken but it still didn't allay Spielberg's fears. One can see why because, even if he was right, a film of earthlings being touchie-feelie to "lower" Martians wouldn't necessarily put bums on seats. It's also important to note that "intelligent" earthlings being kind to lower Martians doesn't automatically presuppose the corollary of this scenario.

Spielberg knew that if the film was a hit it wouldn't primarily be because of its dramatic potential but rather because UFOs were a "seductive alternative for a lot of people who no longer have faith in anything."[61] Is this, as suggested already, a kind of backlash against a post-Nietzschean "God is dead" society? Or a manner of dealing vicariously with same? In his 1959 book *Flying Saucers*, Carl Jung posited the theory that "modern man appropriates machine images to his own magical purposes and turns the stuff of science into myth and religion."

Spielberg's biographer Philip Taylor suggests that nobody does this better on screen than Spielberg himself, "a suburban animist with a tinge of Manichaeism."[62] Jung thought that a belief in UFOs was caused by an emotional imbalance resulting from either trauma or pining. We're close to a Freudian thesis here, the oedipal search for a father figure.

You leave the cinema wondering what's going to happen to the aliens. Will they be coming back? What's their purpose? But it's so visually splendid you're more likely to take it on its own terms, as a study of wonder and obsession that may or may not hint at absolutes.

From Spielberg's personal standpoint we can almost draw a line from the introverted child whose parents split up to a young man looking to fill that paternal gap with a quasi-religious substitute for the God of yore.

In a larger context, we can also point to the huge numbers of Americans today who fervently believe they've been abducted by aliens and returned safely to their homes afterward. Is this also a sublimation of a religious need? Even the profusion of people who attend psychiatrists today would appear to evince similar yearnings. In a former era, the confessional (or the "undivorced" father) performed this "listening" role.

Spielberg's obsession with UFOs can very easily be seen as a sublimated search for God. "I would love to see something that can't be explained by science or magic," he revealed once, almost making the point himself.[63]

His biographer Joseph McBride is in little doubt that the film has a religious subtext. In proposing a seductive alternative for a lot of people who no longer have faith in anything, he argued, Spielberg countered the growing cynicism of the post-Vietnam, post-Watergate era with a myth of transcendence, expressed in the secular idiom of the modern world. Skeptical of organized religion, Spielberg managed to posit a different form of idealism for a disaffected generation. Tony Crawley makes a comparison between *E.T.* and *Whistle Down the Wind*, where Alan Bates in mistaken for Christ by quite a different set of children.[64]

The public's reaction to it all was mixed, some viewers adopting a sour attitude to what was deemed to be a tabloid sense of awe. Once *Jaws* became a hit, the director complained, people went after *Close*

Encounters with a vengeance. That's the price one pays for success. Critics adopt a retrospective perspective toward it, imagining that fame was the spur all along, not love of the craft. Pauline Kael's review was predictably sardonic: "God is up there on a crystal chandelier spaceship, and he likes us."[65]

Molly Haskel, of *New York* magazine, dissed it totally, claiming Spielberg's "pseudo-religion" was "as phoney as the pseudo-science on which it rests."[66] Rex Reed went further, describing it as "a gooey marshmallow of a movie with nothing more at the core than more gooeyness masquerading as godliness."[67] I doubt this is fair to Spielberg, who leaves godly issues to the viewer to decipher. He accepts the fact that his films, including *Close Encounters*, have "bubblegum" elements in them, but they're still a step above date movies. Because he clouds them in topical domestic set-ups he escapes a charge of intellectual pretentiousness. It's up to us to add whatever we like to his commodious givens.

Another "bubblegum" movie to attract attention at this time was *Superman* (1978). The symbolism here can't really be credited to director Richard Donner but rather the man who created the comic strip that inspired all of the Superman films. This outing is bigger on special effects but it tells the same timeworn story in the same timeworn way.

Christopher Reeve is the "chosen one" who escapes death on Krypton as a baby. He falls from the sky like an asteroid. He grows up with foster parents, works miracles by stealth and has a dual identity and also an adversary who tries to tempt him or, failing that, to destroy him. The adversary's name is Lex Luthor, which sounds a bit like Lucifer. Nobody needs to wonder why.

After all the hoopla from *Superman* died down, Spielberg came back with a movie that would make his name immortal. Its title would also enter the language: *E.T.*

It was an unashamed weepie, but a top-grade one. Big men broke down and cried at the cute dreams of this turtle-like creature with the long finger and the drawly voice. It was a love story wrapped in a sci-fi package, and a poignant ode to the child inside all of us. "The first screening," Spielberg remembered, "was truly like a religious experience. It must be a little bit like the way people feel when they think they've seen God."[68]

There are many religious echoes in *E.T.*, particularly in the scene where we first see him in Elliott's outhouse, which has distinct reverberations of the stable in which Jesus was born. Ted Koppel, a former host of the ABC show *Nightline*, said "It's essentially the Christ story. Christ was the ultimate extra-terrestrial."[69] Spielberg was clued-in enough to know that the best way to deliver such a spiritual message was in a secular manner. As Marta Tarbell of *McCall's* observed. "Like Christ, E.T. can heal the sick and perform miracles. He also dies, is resurrected, and finally leaves earth for home, which is somewhere above."[70] In this sense "the other planet" is the next life.

Even the "sub-Michelangelo graphics for the film's poster," as Neil Sinyard points out, "have a religious dimension."[71] Gaye Ortiz feels that E.T., like Christ, is a "pre-existent entity." Also, his early life has been hidden from us, he came to little children, he suffered a death and resurrection, and then ascended to his original home. More significantly, his was a message of unconditional love, much like that seen in the crucified Christ.[72]

Dr Phil Lineberger, a pastor of the Metropolitan Church in Wichita, said it wasn't until E.T. was dying, and Elliott started to get stronger as a result, that he saw the full metaphorical force of the atonement theme. "Christ died for our sins so that we might live," Lineberger wrote, "just as E.T. was doing. And when he was resurrected at the end, and ascending, being watched by all the kids who had become his disciples, it all started lining up for me."[73]

If this is Jesus, it's a Jesus who gets drunk and also wears women's clothes. The reason we don't find all of this ridiculous is because of Elliott's empathy with him. Both of them are marooned, one on a foreign galaxy, the other trying to come to terms with an absent father.

Spielberg claimed he "never anticipated religious parallels with the Immaculate Heart which people found E.T.'s glowing heart to be, or the fact that E.T. comes back to life."[74] It was never his intention, he went on, to "draw myself into sainthood. I thought I was making a little film that only a few of my closest friends would enjoy."[75] He's being disingenuous when he suggests that the Christ parallels aren't obvious. No director, Jewish or gentile, puts a glowing heart into a character without expecting its meta-significance to be picked up on. He's being coy here because the whole mood of the film is reverential, even if undercut by the whimsical humor.

Universal Studios weren't averse to exploiting such parallels, using the shot of E.T.'s glowing finger touching the hand of a child as one of its promo brochures, which was a direct throwback to God's finger touching the hand of Adam in Michelangelo's famous fresco.

Spielberg, a "nice Jewish boy from Phoenix," was slightly embarrassed by the analogy. He knew he'd let himself in for it but was leery about the prospect of going to his mother and telling her he'd made a Christian parable.

John Lyden feels we should be cautious about "baptizing" the film as if it simply repeated the Christian message because Spielberg, for starters, is Jewish rather than Christian. His use of Christian motifs, for Lyden, "reflects his ability to utilize images that are familiar to our culture, and to appropriate them for his own purposes."[76]

E.T., like *Close Encounters*, gives us an alien who's pre-eminently benign. Spielberg invested his character with human characteristics: intelligence and not a little humor. It was as a result of this that the poignant edge intruded when he became ill, or had to go away. (When did we feel sentimental about an alien departing the planet in a film before?)

He described the first screening of the film as being almost like a religious experience, as mentioned, audiences afterward turning out in droves to hail a movie that worked both as adventure story, children's film and symbolic text. But not everybody gushed about it. Derek Malcolm, to name one eminent critic, was underwhelmed by its gushy philanthropy. He found it maudlin and manipulative, and decidedly lacking in passion. These were comments that could be applied to his entire *oeuvre*.

With the exception of *Schindler's List*, many people feel Spielberg prettifies life from his twee soapbox, indulging his comfortable illusions in a manner that would be unthinkable to, say, Robert Altman or Francis Ford Coppola. He appeals more to Middle America, lacking the other two men's edge. It isn't only his aliens who are overly user-friendly but his humans as well. Because he's such a good technician he gets away with this. Even hardened cynics like Martin Amis were bowled over by *E.T*, and almost reduced to tears by it. Amis confessed that he was "barely able to support my own grief and bewilderment by the end of it."[77]

The religious dimension in Spielberg's work is more symbolic than anything else. He describes himself as a religious theist but a political atheist. Whatever that means, it allows him free rein to be as indulgent as he likes and still cloak his work in the raiment of a higher truth. This is fine but he rarely delves into anything like grey ethical areas, the grand spectacle being his forte, with any message safely hidden inside the glossy marshmallow texture of suburban *anomie*. This is mythmaking without an intellectual conscience, a kid playing with trains that never go into dark tunnels without at least a fighting chance of seeing light at the end of them that isn't another train coming the other way.

Put simply, the good guys always win in Spielberg's films. It's no secret that his biggest hero is none other than Walt Disney. Which is no doubt why *Time* magazine once began a profile of him with the words, "Once Upon a Time there was a little boy named Steven, who lived in a mythical land called Suburbia . . ."

Variety magazine called *E.T.* "the best Disney movie Walt Disney never made."[78] Dave Kehr of New York's *Daily News* said that Spielberg had fought off the "movieisation of television by the televisionisation of movies."[79]

Martin Scorsese's *Raging Bull* (1980) is another tale of spiritual redemption, though it hardly appears so at first glance. Telling the story of middleweight boxer Jake La Motta, it earned Robert De Niro a thoroughly deserved second Oscar for playing the embattled protagonist.

Between the years 1949 and 1951 La Motta enjoyed relative success but he's more noted today for being the Nearly Man of the sport, a man who was destroyed both by his demons and a training regimen that was both too extreme and short-lived to be effective. He was also the victim of such a ferocious temper that for a lot of the time he didn't seem to know where the boxing ring ended and real life began. What's important, though, is that De Niro plays him as a sheep in wolf's clothing, a man forever searching for acceptance but cutting off the very people who could provide him with this through a series of brutish exercises in misplaced venom. At the end, premature retirement mollifies him.

The film opens with a quotation from the Gospel of John, "So for the second time the Pharisees summoned the man who had been blind and said, 'Speak the truth before God. We know this fellow is a sinner'. 'Whether or not he is a sinner, I do not know,' the man replied, 'All I know is this: Once I was blind and now I can see.'"

Placed in this context it falls neatly into a spiritual trilogy also encompassing *Mean Streets* and *Taxi Driver*, the two other seminal De Niro/Scorsese collaborations about men trying to straddle the brutal dictates of street life with a tenuous pitch toward purgation. In the first two films the purgation is filtered through crime and horrific murder; in the present one it comes laden with blood. The fact that Scorsese followed it up a few years later with Catholicism's iconic blood martyr, the messiah of *The Last Temptation of Christ*, adds an intriguingly revisionist coda to the theme.

Paul Schrader, who wrote the screenplay for the film, didn't insert the Biblical quotation into his script. It was tagged on later by Scorsese, who was obviously interested in making a different kind of film than Schrader envisaged.

For Schrader, La Motta is "the same dumb lug" at the end of the film as he is at the beginning. He felt Scorsese "imposed" salvation on him in a manner that was untrue to the character he himself had created.[80] This is unfair because every script goes through an osmosis from page to stage and anyone who's seen *Raging Bull*, which was voted the Film of the Decade by *Time* magazine at the end of the 1980s, will be cognizant of the fact that it's much more than the story of a slugger who beats up his wife, abuses his brother and ends up as a down-at-heel comic mainlining sophomorish banter with drunks in his run-down Miami club.

It's ironic that such an inarticulate man would, in retirement, become a kind of after-dinner speaker. That said, his pronouncements in his Copacabana club would hardly rank as high poetry. He's inarticulate, but hardly dumb. He displays a marked sense of humor (mostly scabrous, but humor nonetheless), which is usually the sign of at least a basic intelligence. He also has his own code of honor. Even in the La Motta canon there are some things one doesn't do—like throw a fight, or rat on a friend. He's not quite the Noble Savage but he might say, to use a phrase of Leonard Cohen's, "I have been faithful to thee in my fashion."

Schrader's reading of La Motta's life was that he welcomed the batterings he took in the ring as so many purgative offerings to whatever gods ruled boxing to atone for his extra-curricular sins. He sees the film as being about "a pseudo-religious masochism" and "regeneration by blood."[81] It's also about misplaced Calvinistic guilt.

Looked at from the inside out, and invested with the almost Manichean intensity De Niro brings to the role, and Scorsese to the direction, what it really is is a parable about a man who tortures himself to achieve a perfection in the ring that's always one step beyond his compass. More sinned against than sinning, he absorbs so much punishment he's reminiscent of the martyrs of medieval times. "You never got me down, Ray, you never got me down," he says to his nemesis Sugar Ray Robinson at one point, leering at him after losing yet another significant bout, his face dripping with blood and his eyes half closed. Some critics read an allegory of La Motta's "fall" from grace in this exchange, but this is perhaps to over-analyze it.

The film has many parallels to *On The Waterfront*. La Motta even has a Brother Charlie in Joey (Joe Pesci), the man he abuses so vehemently as paranoia about his wife's perceived infidelity takes root. "Did you fuck my wife?" he asks Joey in an early scene, his mind becoming diseased as a result of frustration over the way his career is going. Vickie (Cathy Moriarty) is like the Edie of *On the Waterfront*, the "good" girl who can stave off certain disaster in her man if only he develops enough street smarts to realize that fact.

Jake expressed the same awkwardness with her as Terry Malloy (Marlon Brando) did with Edie in the earlier film, the macho man in him intent on "telling it like it is" in the big bad world of boxing. When Malloy tells Edie to "Do it to him before he does it to you," this isn't so much a philosophy as a bruised soul's exercise in survival.

Jake carries it through to a new era. Both Edie and Vicki are aware that such posturing is little more than transparent bravado trying unsuccessfully to camouflage vulnerability. They let it play itself out, secure in the knowledge that both pugilists are soft at the core.

Malloy shows his softness by becoming a turncoat against his former allies to win Edie's love; La Motta in the prison scene where he breaks down after being arrested for statutory rape, slamming his fists against the brick wall until the agony is too great. Afterward he starts using his elbows and finally his forehead in a defining piece of purgative masochism. This scene, which probably won De Niro his Oscar—the original script had him masturbating instead but Scorsese couldn't get away with this in a mainstream movie—ends with him breaking down in tears, the bull become baby as he finally realizes the slough of despond into which his life has fallen.

So does the blind man see at the end? Well there's no outright epiphany so perhaps we should just call him partly reformed. When he gives Joey a placatory kiss in the closing stages—a most uncharacteristic gesture for the Bronx Bull—he's begun his process of recovery, searching inside himself for the tenderness nobody ever knew how to tap into, least of all himself.

In Scorsese's book we're all Jake La Mottas, all gambling in the ring that is our life. We hardly use violence on our loved ones as he did, or suffer from paranoid delusions, but we battle, boats against the current, or like Camus' Sisyphus, rolling a boulder up a hill and having it tumble down again—repeatedly.

Scorsese never felt this was a boxing film. It's more a story about a man regressing to his mother's womb through a brutal regime of violence in the ring and outside it.

He suppresses sexual urges before fights by pouring ice cubes down his shorts. At another point he asks Joey to hit him as hard as he can in the face, without his gloves on. "Harder!" he screams as Joey delivers punch after punch, "Harder!" Everywhere he looks he sees people out to betray him: Joey, Vickie, the people who hang around them, the promoters, the pimps, the gofers taking backhanders. Everytime he loses a fight he goes into a dark despair, obsessing about his weight or any other topic that springs to mind, beating himself up both literally and metaphorically as he strives for illusory dreams.

It's interesting that La Motta quotes Marlon Brando's famous speech from *On the Waterfront* in the last scene. The comparison between the two greatest actors of our time doesn't end there as they also, coincidentally, essayed the same character in *The Godfather*, Brando playing Vito Corleone as an old man in *The Godfather* and De Niro playing him as a young turk in *Godfather II* in a flashback sequence.

De Niro is here issuing a valentine to his hero by rendering the famous "Brother Charlie" speech in front of his dressing-room mirror before he goes out to do his stand-up routine. What's surprising is that he puts so little feeling into it, running the lines off in perfunctory fashion as he chomps on a cigar. This is in marked contrast to Brando himself, who invoked such passion with Rod Steiger some three decades previously.

Is this De Niro trying to lay the ghost of his idol or La Motta simply sloughing off the loser tag of Terry Malloy? Morris Dickstein put it well: "A good actor (De Niro) plays a bad actor (La Motta) imitating a good actor (Brando) as he played a washed-up ex-fighter (Terry Malloy) who talks like a bum but isn't."[82]

Both men were boxers, and both of their careers were cut short for different reasons. Malloy took a dive in Madison Square Garden because "the price was on Wilson," his opponent. "Brother" Charlie placed some bets on the side for his crime boss Johnny Friendly, while Malloy got a "one-way ticket to Palookaville."

La Motta never dived, but ended his career prematurely because of his self-destructive behavior. And yet both are "redeemed," if that's not too strong a word. Brando saves himself by exposing the Friendly syndicate (the name is rife with irony) to the Crime Commission, while La Motta sheds his bullish demeanor in his transformation into family-man-cum-nightclub-host, reciting doggerel poetry to himself before going through a mock warm-up routine for his gig by pummelling his fists in air-punches and telling himself humorously "I'm the boss, I'm the boss."

In the end, as Michael Bliss stated, this is the story of a man neither saved nor damned, rather "pitifully poised on the brink of self-awareness without the sensitivity or intelligence to pass over into enlightenment."[83] But we can't blame him for this. He came as far as he could, given the emotional equipment at his disposal.

Religious symbolism was much more obvious in Jean-Luc Godard's *Hail Mary* in 1985. This drew a lot of publicity for most of the wrong reasons. It was meant to be a contemporary re-working of the Mary-Joseph story, a great idea in theory, but in Godard's hands it became little more than self-conscious posturing underscored by a lot of prurient camerawork.

In this telling of the tale, Mary is a gas station attendant who also plays basketball. Joseph, her boyfriend, drives a cab. When she finds herself pregnant he refuses to believe she hasn't been "with a man," as he's perfectly entitled to do. "I sleep with no one," she tells him, "I touch no one."

Later on she wards off his sexual advances with the formalized, "The hand of God is upon me and you can't interfere." The dialogue gets even more stilted when she asks her doctor, to whom she goes for a gynecological examination, "Does the soul have a body?" "The body has a soul," he replies. Mary goes on to ruminate, "Let the soul be the body. Then no one can say that the body is soul, since the soul shall be body."

By now patrons are entitled to leave the cinema if they wish, having withstood such a tirade of gobbledygook, but the reason most of them left wasn't so much from boredom as outrage caused by the gratuitous nudity. The Pope condemned the film and many protest groups rowed in behind him. At its initial showing at the New York Film Festival, holy water was scattered outside the cinema and a rosary said in reparation for the sins of those going in.

Such people gave the film attention it didn't deserve. If it were made by some (s)exploitative novice it mightn't have been so surprising, but this was Godard. Why did he dwell so long on Mary's pubic regions? By all means have her attend her gynecologist. Any woman who conceived without having sex would have done this. But does it give him the right to then treat her like a sex object?

The "angel" Gabriel is represented by Mary's unsavory uncle, and there's a subplot involving a science professor who gives thinly disguised theology lectures to his lover Eva. She has a tryst with him in Paradise Villa where she, perhaps inevitably within the film's direly unimaginative remit, eats an apple. The critic Eleanor Ringel, in a review published in *The Atlanta Journal*, said the whole package gave off an aura of kitschy reverence, "like a day-glo Jesus on the dashboard of a yellow cab."[84] It left viewers wondering not so much why God made Mary as why Godard made *Hail Mary*.

Robin Williams played a much more impressive Jesus figure in *Dead Poets Society* (1989), opening the minds of his pupils at a New England prep school in such a way that he leaves an indelible impression on them. He also inspires them to challenge tradition. His revolutionary pedagogy is a danger to the established order so has to be removed, like the R.P. McMurphy of *One Flew Over the Cuckoo's Nest*. He doesn't die in the end but he's given life to many by rocking the boat of the institution he inhabits all too fleetingly.

Williams, as John Keating, liberates his pupils from staid academia by becoming their spiritual guru. "Seize the day," he advises, but when one of his pupils, Neil Perry, tries to break out of the straitjacket his father has groomed him for, it doesn't work. He ends up killing himself. Is this act one of desperation or rebellion? Significantly, the boy puts a crown of victory on his head even as he goes to his death. Maybe he sees himself as a symbol, a wake-up call to his classmates to resist their own fathers. This theme of the teacher as savior was also taken up more recently in the Julia Roberts movie *Mona Lisa Smile* (2004), the slant here being more feminist-oriented.

Four years later, as if to exonerate himself from his syrupy past, Steven Spielberg made the film he said he'd been steeling himself all his life to do, the one that would finally silence all those naysayers who accused him of perpetrating "blancmange infantilism." It was, of course, a disaffected Jew's damning indictment of the Holocaust, *Schindler's List*. Centering itself on the unique philanthropic actions of a World War II entrepreneur who acted out of character in saving a thousand Jewish factory workers from almost certain death in the concentration camps, it was a monochrome *tour-de-force* refreshingly free of any Spielbergesque excrescences.

There are no pat answers here. He deleted scenes that could have been construed as sentimental or bathetic in favor of a grim vision of an era most Jews wanted to forget. The film is his blooding, a return to an era he had perhaps airbrushed out of his subconscious because it was too painful for him to deal with.

In his youth he'd heard all of the revolting stories of der Fuehrer but had chosen dream rather than nightmare to express his perspective. He had made films that showcased soft emotions. The ones on view here were more unrelenting. To Liam Neeson he confided that he wasn't going to be the traditional Steven Spielberg on the movie, replete with his bag of fluffy tricks, but rather a bona fide film-maker who would let the story unfold osmotically in its own stark time.

All through his youth he'd felt his Jewishness isolated him from Gentiles and had subdued it to avoid loneliness. But now the time had come to launch a full frontal assault on the greatest mass murder in recorded history. That he chose to do it through the story of a former capitalist made it all the more tantalizing, though David Mamet rubbished it when he wrote in *Make-Believe Town* (Back Bay Books, 1997) "It's not instruction, but melodrama. Members of the audience learn nothing save the emotional lesson of all of melodrama, i.e. that they're better than the villain."

Mamet concluded that the audience isn't superior to "those bad Nazis." Any of us, he asserts, has the capacity for atrocity, just as each of us has the capacity for heroism. The film as he sees it rewards the audience for merely seeing that the villain is bad and, as a result, "feeling this perception is a moral accomplishment." The overall mechanism of it all is merely this: "If you can't pay the rent, then I will tie your daughter to the train-track." In such a scenario the Nazis are the "waxed moustachioed" villain and the Jews the daughter. The film itself is "as far from philo-Semitism as concern for the girl on the tracks is from feminism."

What he's really saying here is that the Holocaust is too easy a target for our righteous indignation, which to his way of thinking makes *Schindler's List* yet another exploitation film. As far as Spielberg was concerned, he just couldn't outgrow his Bambi overtones. Old habits died very hard with Mamet, if not like-minded gurus of the screenwriting world, who felt patronized by a parable that, in its way, was almost as obvious as Spielberg's previous attempts to convey Savior-like status on one-dimensional heroes.

Fearless (1993) brought us back to the area of gritty drama in a non-political context, featuring Jeff Bridges as an architect who always had a fear of flying. After surviving a horrific plane crash he undergoes a dramatic life-change.

Director Peter Weir shoots the crash scene in a semi-surreal manner, portraying it almost like a graveyard where Bridges' soul leaves his body. He wanders through a cornfield holding a baby, a serene expression on his face. Has he passed through death or "merely" had a near-death experience? Weir leaves it open to conjecture but Bridges will never be the same man again.

He helps other survivors but doesn't hang around for gratitude. He doesn't even tell his wife (Isabella Rossellini) he's survived. Instead of returning home to her he goes to a motel. The FBI eventually track him down, finding him relaxed, even debonair. A psychologist (John Turturro) tries to talk to him about Post Traumatic Stress Disorder but his advice is lost on him. He feels neither stressed nor disordered.

Relieved of past phobias, he even manages to eat a strawberry in a restaurant, having been allergic to them all his life. He seems to be reinventing himself in every detail of his life, attaining a kind of Buddhist calm. Strawberries are a symbol of "forbidden fruit" in the film.

Tom Hulce plays a lawyer who wants him to claim financial reimbursement for his ordeal but he isn't interested in this. He just wants to focus on the moment, the immediacy of being alive. Instead of dying in the crash he's been born. But this comes with a price: He becomes alienated from his wife, forming instead a deep friendship with another survivor of the crash (Rosie Perez) who lost her baby in it.

He tells her his father died when he was thirteen, playing softball in the garden. He couldn't understand why this man, who was devoutly religious, was taken from him so young. "Why did God kill him?" he wonders. He lost his faith afterward.

"People don't believe in God as much as they think," he tells Perez; instead they choose not to believe in nothing. It's as if they're conning themselves to avoid having to face the abyss of atheism. They tell themselves things like, "We'll die if we rob banks, or eat red meat," filling themselves up with bromides and placebos to steel themselves against the kind of shock he himself experienced when he was thirteen.

"You're safe with me," he tells Perez as he drives her down the road in his car. "I've never been in an accident yet—at least when I've been behind the wheel." This causes her to say, "What are you telling me—there's no God but there's you?" He laughs at her riposte. "We're safe because we're dying already," he remarks, which upsets her. He looks out of the car at the people walking by on the street. "We've passed through death," he assures her. "We know more than the others."

He feels Perez and himself are ghosts. They've shared a cathartic experience and that makes him closer to her than he can ever be to his wife, or child. When she becomes hysterical about the fact that she feels responsible about not clutching her baby tightly enough on the plane he re-enacts the crash for her in his car, giving her a toolbox to hold onto as he lunges into a wall at breakneck speed, endangering both of their lives. The toolbox goes flying, proving to her that no matter how tightly she held onto her baby it would have flown from her arms.

In another scene he persuades her to buy gifts for her child while he does likewise for his father. "Where will we go?" she asks afterwards. "We could always disappear," he suggests. In a sense, he's disappeared already. Having performed a healing role in the plane, and now acted as her "angel" his new life is one that has no baggage. He was ready to die when the plane crashed. Having survived, his old one means nothing to him.

"Follow me to the light," he had said to the other passengers, the figurative ramifications to Jesus blindingly evident. Turturro likens his feelings of invulnerability to that of certain Vietnam veterans who felt that, since they'd cheated death in the trenches, they could virtually take any chances afterwards and come through. (Bridges stands on the ledge of a skyscraper with his arms outspread at one stage, almost looking like he thinks he can fly.)

Rossellini pleads with him to let her in to his new life but he can't, at least not until the final scene where he eats another strawberry and almost dies. In his mind he sees the crash again, and the tunnel of light, before "resurrecting" himself with the words "I'm alive!"

Weir adopts a mystical directorial style that succeeds adeptly in immersing us inside Bridges' altered attitude. The "tunnel of white light" symbolism is somewhat old hat, and the strawberry/forbidden fruit motif all too obvious, but this is a film that's so spellbindingly seductive you can forgive it its occasional indulgences in hackneyed imagery.

Tom Hanks appeared as a kind of "holy fool" in *Forrest Gump* in 1994, winning an Oscar for plagiarizing Dustin Hoffman's performance as the idiotic *savant* in *Rain Man*. The editing was clever, making Gump a part of various epochal events, and the episodic storyline had a kind of picaresque appeal, but this was wildly over-praised.

Everybody quoted the line "Life's like a box of chocolates; you never know what you're gonna get" as if it had some kind of profundity. In fact the film itself was like a bar of chocolate. We may not have known what we were going to get but when we did get it it proved somewhat saccharine and lacking in depth.

The whole farrago is little more than a self-congratulatory indulgence in clever camera-tricks that succeed in super-imposing Gump over famous figures in history. At the end he wonders if we have a destiny "or are we just floating about, accident-like, on a breeze?" His conclusion, "Maybe it's both" is fairly typical of the muddled nature of the entire venture.

Peter Sellers played a similar kind of dignified simpleton, gardener John Chance, much more endearingly in *Being There* in 1979. He also brought humor to it, something Mr Hanks isn't too good at. Elevated to God-like status in Washington's political corridors due to a disingenuous misinterpretation of everything the simple man says, it's a gentle satire on both media spin as well as psychobabble, and also the way we've lost touch with nature. Basically what it proved was that Chance wasn't stupid, but rather the world was. Nobody seems to have commented on the fact that his celebrity status is achieved with little or no effort on his part. What does that say about the gullibility of everyone else? Sellers epitomizes innocence here. When he's put on a soapbox he takes it in his stride. The image he seems to be imparting is one of Zen tranquillity—a marked contrast to Inspector Clousseau & Co.

He perfectly conveys a man totally at ease with himself, whose every innocent remark is given an added significance by his auditors. The film displays the perennial truth of the lesson behind "The Emperor's New Clothes." In other words people will believe what they want to, regardless of the evidence. Or, put another way, "Both Chance and Jesus teach that God is found exactly where most people wouldn't have thought to have looked—in a garden or on a cross."[85]

The Shawshank Redemption (also 1994) was less popular than *Forrest Gump* at the box office despite earning a slew of Oscar nominations. It got a second wind in its video life and is now warmly regarded as one of the most moving movies of the nineties. Chronicling twenty years in the life of a banker (Tim Robbins) wrongly convicted of murder, it concerns itself with the manner in which he uses his banking skills to stop himself being destroyed by the cruel prison regime. His relationship with fellow inmate Morgan Freeman is well handled by Frank Darabont, making his directorial debut, but there's something a bit obvious and heavy-handed in the manner in which the film (based on a Stephen King short story) attempts to entreat our empathy.

A redemption theme is also central to the much-hyped *Terminator* series, which involves the struggle of two people (Sarah Connor and her son John) to avoid being destroyed by cyborgs from the future. Arnold Schwarzenegger is the guardian angel figure in *Terminator II* and *Terminator III*, though not in the original, where he's a villain.

The Matrix (1999) has obvious Christological echoes. Keanu Reeves is Neo, an anagram of "One," as in "The One" and if you look you can find representations of Judas, Mary Magdalene, Moses and John the Baptist as well.[86] But you would probably just be better off to sit back and enjoy the camerabatics. Reeves is impressive as a computer programmer in the same way Arnold Schwarzenegger is as a cyborg.

The Phantom Menace (1999) was the long-awaited *Star Wars* sequel and it came trailing clouds of glory. The set was guarded like Fort Knox to prevent "leaks" from this precious celluloid vault but after all the hype, the spin-offs, the subterfuge and the astronomical budget it all proved rather a damp squib. The religious overtones were more pronounced—Anakin's virgin birth, the title of "Chosen One," etc.—but the formula was tired. We'd been here before. Everybody oohed and aahed at the special effects and the outlandish creatures but it was hard not to stifle a yawn at the stylized language and repetitive props. Here was a project all dressed up with nowhere to go.

The antinomy between good and evil is so bald we're almost back in the era of films from the thirties and forties. Nowhere is there any attempt to make characters look real or behave in what we might call a credible manner. We're in the milieu of paradigms, and any diversion from absolutism would seem to tarnish that.

Kiefer Sutherland, whose face we never see, is responsible for educing a symbolic confession in *Phone Booth* (2003), a film light years away from *The Phantom Menace*. Once an upwardly mobile publicist (Colin Farrell) enters a phone box in New York just as he's about to cheat on his wife he's pinned to the spot by Sutherland, who tells him if he leaves the booth he'll be shot.

Farrell spends the next hour or so pouring his heart out over a number of calls in this tale of character reformation through emotional striptease in front of a veritable circus of New York onlookers, including both his girlfriend and wife. That's the price he must pay for his redemption. In this sense Sutherland is reminiscent of the Kevin Spacey of *Seven*: a vigilante moralist with a bit missing. Let's not forget Spacey ritualistically killed those he imagined guilty of the Seven Deadly Sins in the earlier morality fable.

It's a claustrophobic film, a quick fix parable that doesn't lay on its message with a trowel, combining elements of the thriller with Farrell's reluctant purging, thereby downplaying the central metaphor of the phone booth as confession box.

Nothing, sadly, is downplayed in *The Good Thief* (2003). "The thought that there was a place for a thief in heaven always made me cry," says Nick Nolte here, alluding to the words of Jesus to the man being crucified beside him in the Bible, "this day thou shalt be with me in Paradise."

Nolte is a gambler and a drug addict but he goes cold turkey while planning a heist. It involves stealing art treasures from a Monte Carlo casino. There's also a waifish Bosnian hooker for whom he becomes a kind of father figure, and a policeman who wants to save him from himself. Neil Jordan both directs and writes. There's a lot of jazzy camerawork and slick dialogue as he tries to create a smoky, atmospheric ambience but it really adds up to nothing more than a hill of beans.

A re-make of a 1955 French thriller (*Bob le Flambeur*), it strives too much after effect. Nolte speaks in a kind of bronchial grunt. We needed a

Robert Mitchum or even a De Niro to convey the would-be Hemingway hero down on his luck that Jordan no doubt had in mind when he wrote his pretentious script. Nolte looks the part all right, his face ravaged with the effects of any substance abuse you care to mention, but you can always see him acting—the ultimate sin for an actor. As for the heist, he orchestrates an ingenious twist to evade capture but the acting and direction are so self-indulgently hammy it's hard to care how it pans out. (Rule One for heist movies is to keep the interest in the heist alive.)

If Jordan stopped trying to impose himself on his material and let it speak for itself he might get back to the kind of movies he used to make. *The Good Thief* is yet another classic example of him using a celluloid sledgehammer to crack a very vacuous walnut.

7

Hell Can Wait

Samuel Butler once wrote, in tantalizing vein, "The Devil tempted Christ, but it was Christ who tempted the Devil to tempt him," an interesting observation on free will. Contrast that with Ronald Knox's statement, "It is stupid of modern civilisation to have given up believing in the devil when he is the only explanation of it." (*The Pan Dictionary of Contemporary Quotations*, Compiled by Jonathon Green, 1982, p. 21.)

Satan is almost like an affectionate character from movies, an old friend we recognize immediately from his array of beguiling tricks. This is probably because we've seen him depicted in as many comic guises as horrific ones. Things were much more ominous in the time of Dante's *Inferno*, Milton's *Paradise Lost*, Goethe's *Faust*, and George Bernard Shaw's *Don Juan in Hell*.

In his essay "The Problem of Evil in Contemporary Film," Reinhold Zwick examines the manner in which the devil in cinema has changed so dramatically. In Derek Jarman's *The Garden* (1990) he's a sado-masochistic man in leather. In the apparently immortal *Omen* series he's everything from boy-child to girl. He's also a female in Martin Scorsese's *The Last Temptation of Christ*, and in *Highway 61* (1991) he's a "poor gullible soul-hunter" who makes the viewer almost pity him. Clearly, as the incarnation of evil, Zwick contends, the devil has lost a lot of his horror. In *The Witches of Eastwick* he proves easy meat for three women after letting his lechery get the better of him.

Nikolas Schreck reminds us that movie devils have been portrayed as being in league with such "divergent scarecrows" as Saddam Hussein, the President of the United States, Kaiser Wilhelm II, Nazi Germany, heavy metal music and even the 1960s hippie counterculture.[1]

According to Schreck, the huge success of family-oriented fudge like *Star Wars* and *Close Encounters of the Third Kind* resulted in the demise of genuine Satanic films. Hollywood had been going soft since the seventies, he felt, Lucas and Spielberg cranking out "unchallenging fantasies of Manichean simplicity—a dreary 12 year old boy's vision of the universe where machines are neat, girls are icky and everything moves really fast and explodes."[2] The brave new world of these movie icons was "strangely devoid of any eroticism" in his view, "as squeaky-clean and wholesome as a 1950s TV show." It was like a slap in the face to the likes of Bunuel and Polanski, who had dug deep into the surreal, subversive underbelly of the genre. For Schreck, this was indicative of a new world order where conservatism ruled OK. The crucifix and garlic hadn't killed the devil, but rather yellow-streaked cowardice.

All that Money Can Buy (1941) had a mischievous devil played by Walter Huston persuading an indigent farmer (James Craig) to sell his soul for seven years of wealth. He subsequently becomes corrupted by this wealth and turns into a manipulative moneylender. When Huston returns to collect his due desserts, Huston employs a lawyer to plead his case before a jury of the damned and ends up winning back his soul.

The Devil With Hitler (1943) is a comedy wherein the devil (Alan Mowbray) is about to get sacked because he isn't recruiting as many sinners as he used to. Anxious to prove that he isn't losing his touch, he approaches his board of directors with a plan. They're threatening to replace him with Hitler but he claims he can get Hitler to perform a good deed within forty-eight hours. If he can bring this about, the directors agree to let him keep his job.

Mussolini, Herman Goering and Joseph Goebbels also turn up in this harmless piece of satirical fluff, which sees Mowbray eventually impersonating Hitler and trying to do the good deed himself, der Fuehrer proving himself highly resistant to virtue. It was a brave undertaking considering the fact that it was made just after America was becoming involved in World War II, but some of the satire, particularly that involving concentration camps, is in poor taste. Charlie Chaplin, of course, had paved the way for such a satirical spoof with *The Great Dictator* two years previously.

The Picture of Dorian Gray (1945) had a moodily distant feel to it, no doubt enhanced by the voiceover. German expressionism meets drawing-room comedy in this strangely effective adaptation of the Oscar Wilde evergreen. We don't see a devil as such, and George Sanders isn't really a Mephistopheles. Neither is Hurd Hatfield, who sells his soul for the elixir of eternal youth as personified by his own portrait, a blatantly evil man. Sadly, he more resembles a foolish one in above his head.

The film begins with Sanders spouting Wildean witticisms far too off-handedly to give them their full weight but when Hatfield appears he makes us sit up to attention, looking like a cross between Dracula and Louis Jordan. His face is like a mask, all the better for the part he's playing. He seems to have no trouble getting women like Angela Lansbury or Donna Reed despite the fact that he acts like he's just had a personality bypass. Are good looks really this much of an aphrodisiac?

It isn't long before he realizes that eternal youth comes with a price. Under Sanders' world-weary urging he plays a cruel trick on Lansbury which causes him to dump her and she in turn commits suicide. A murder follows, and another suicide, as he lives in terror that anyone will see the portrait that ages while he remains permanently twenty-two. The net seems to be tightening on him at every turn but it's he himself who finally ends his life.

There are many effective touches: the brothel scene where Lansbury's brother finally finds Hatfield, the descent into the underworld, a lamp-shade that swings back and forth over the head of the man he kills, throwing shadows onto the toy he used to play with as a child.

It was virtually Hatfield's only notable performance but he was ideal for it. He wears a look of rueful forbearance as he drags himself deeper into depravity, causing one to wonder repeatedly: Is youth worth this? Because he never seems to have much fun, nor indeed to be capable of it. He appears to be motivated by curiosity rather than lust, a cold dandy who takes an almost masochistic delight in contemplating how deeply he's sunk into the abyss. A smidgeon of decency prevents him from marrying Reed, the same decency that calls him back to Lansbury, only to realize she's died by her own hand.

There was no melodrama, which was unusual for this time—and this genre. Director Albert Lewin is sympathetic to his main protagonist even as he consigns him to his inevitable nemesis. He doesn't judge him any more than Wilde did. A human tragedy has unfolded, that's all we can say for sure, and Lewin captures it reflectively in his gothic chiaroscuros.

If there's a criticism to be made of this, it's the casualness with which Sanders & Co. accept the fact that Gray manages to look so young. Not even 21st century facelifts could achieve this, and yet they greet him with the kind of laconicism one might reserve for a friend who's keeping himself trim by going to the gym three times a week, eating all the right foods and staying away from beer and cigarettes.

Hatfield was stereotypical of characters who consorted with the devil in films at this time. To quote Schreck again: "In the mass psyche's wish-fulfilment fantasies, the unbridled erotic decadence presumed to typify the upper class leads directly to consorting with Satan. A standard location in almost every film concerning Satanism is the opulent chateau concealing unholy rites behind its civilized facade. In keeping with this well-heeled undercurrent, there has been a surprising number of celluloid Satans played by actors with upper-class British accents. This trend, particularly evident in Hollywood productions, seems to symbolize some archetypal recognition that the Devil, despite his poor reputation in some circles, is essentially a gentleman."[3]

Angel on my Shoulder (1946) is a fantasy about a murdered convict (Paul Muni) who makes a deal with the devil to come back to life in another form, i.e., as a law-abiding judge. Claude Rains stole the film as the devil, playing him as an urbane gent worried about the fact that judges sometimes make moral decisions and, equally pressingly, that the temperature of hell has fallen below 180 degrees.

Damn Yankees (1958) featured a middle-aged baseball fan (Robert Shafer) who makes a deal with the devil, a chirpy Ray Walston, whereby he gets to be transformed into the body of a promising young player of the game so he can help his team, the Washington Senators, improve. He morphs into the body of twenty-two-year-old Tab Hunter and wins an important match for the Senators but afterward wants out of the deal, courtesy of an escape clause he's built into it which Walston does his damnedest to nullify. Walston sends his lubricious assistant Lola (Gwen Verdon) to earth to seduce Hunter but he resists her redoubtable charms, silly man.

This is a film which has everything: sports, dance routines, music and diabolical charm. Walston gives the performance of his life and Verdon isn't far behind. Hunter has all the excitement of a wardrobe but then this was hardly surprising. Trainspotters may be interested to see Bob Fosse do a cameo as Verdon's dance partner during her mambo number. We also get Walston essaying a parody of Al Jolson's "Mammy," transmuted into "Those Were the Good Old Days." Truly, the devil has all the best tunes—but Verdon runs him a close second. The pair of them did it all on Broadway to much acclaim and they reprised it here with irresistible mirth.

Santa Claus (1959) was a gimmicky Mexican film giving us a Santa that didn't reside in the North Pole but preferred to orbit the earth in search of children he could get to do naughty things like steal dolls and suchlike. It was an interesting concept but died of imaginative bankruptcy.

Ingmar Bergman departed from his trademark soulful meanderings to make *The Devil's Eye* in 1960. In this subtly impressive movie the devil, an urbane Stig Jarrel, discovers a stye in his eye which has been caused by the fact that Bibi Andersson refuses to relinquish her virginity. He reincarnates Don Juan (Jarl Kulle) to seduce her but Kulle falls in love with her instead. She doesn't reciprocate his ardor, having eyes only for her fiancé, so he fails miserably in his task. Jarrel is outraged and as a punishment forces Kulle to listen to Andersson's wedding night pillow talk with her new husband.

His stye disappears when Andersson tells her husband she's never been kissed. As he puts it himself, "A tiny victory in hell is often more fateful than a great success in heaven." This remark, like many in the film, is addressed to the audience, Bergman actually employing a narrator, Gunnar Bjornstand, to take us through the various scenes. The film begins with the words "Dear Frightened Audience," but Bergman's non-Satanic films are much scarier than this quirky evocation of a sometime Lothario past his sell-by date.

Luis Bunuel directed *Simon of the Desert* in 1965. This is the story of Saint Simon the Stylite, a 5th-century hermit who spent thirty-seven years on top of a pillar in the desert. He eats frugally, denying himself food to test his resolve. He has no time for personal property and doesn't even understand what the word "mine" means. On the negative side, he lacks emotion. When his mother comes to visit him he refuses her embrace. He invites her to live near the pillar but not inside it. The devil tries to tempt him three times: firstly as a sexually enticing woman, secondly as Jesus and thirdly, as the film enters its surreal Bunuelesque mode, as a woman who emerges from a coffin and then appears on top of the pillar, asking him to go on a plane with her to what turns out to be a modern-day discotheque.

This is the most unsatisfactory part of the film and one, by all reports, Bunuel himself didn't want. But his money had dried up by this point so he had to rush matters toward a conclusion.

The film is better when it's being ironic, as in the scene where Simon provides a thief with a new pair of hands after his old ones are chopped off and he immediately proceeds to slap his child with the replacements.

Theresa Sanders believes the film "strategically resists" giving us a message but nonetheless seems to be saying that if Simon's life is indeed useless, "the alternatives that we've found for ourselves since his time aren't much better."[4]

We were proffered a Satanic western in 1966 with *The Devil's Mistress*, and in 1985 a diabolic pornography movie, *New Wave Hookers*. Both were fifth-rate attempts to exploit dual genres and ended up doing a disservice to both.

Richard Burton played the title role in *Doctor Faustus* in 1967, investing the role with all of his sepulchral moodiness, but little else. Most people were familiar with the manner in which Christopher Marlowe's morality fable ended and it needed more originality and feeling than Burton could muster to build on that. (There are those who would say Burton himself had sold his soul to the devil of Hollywood mediocrity by this time too.) A brief respite from tedium is provided by his wife Liz Taylor, who plays three different cameos in the film, including an amusing one as a female Mephistopheles, underscoring the real one, essayed with sure-footed clearness of purpose by a bald and ruthless Andreas Teuber.

The venture came about as a result of Burton doing it in play form with the Oxford University Dramatic Society two years previously. He filmed it at his own expense—suggested to be in the region of £1,000,000—flying the entire cast to Rome in a vanity project to end all vanity projects. It might have worked as an Old Boys exercise in sophomoric nostalgia but Burton tried to invest it with more *gravitas* and it imploded.

The play version had been panned by the critics and they were no more merciful with this. "Burton and Taylor travel down to hell on a moving staircase," wrote *Time* magazine, "a journey enlivened by the writhing of intertwined torsos, at whom Mr Burton furtively glances as if they were corset advertisements on the London underground." As for Taylor: "When she welcomes Burton to an eternity of damnation, her eyeballs and teeth are dripping pink in what seems to be a hellish combination of conjunctivitis and trench mouth." Taylor cancelled her subscription to this magazine in a fit of pique instead of laughing heartily. Did she seriously believe she was making a work of art?

Bedazzled, in the same year, had Dudley Moore as a lowly cook selling his soul to Peter Cook, a devil with a lot of wit and charm. He gives him seven wishes which he proceeds to waste with unwise choices. He asks to be made into a millionaire, a rock star, an intellectual, etc. but all of them go wrong because Cook puts a catch in each. Moore would have been much better employed to wish for happiness, but then of course there would have been no film.

All he really wants is the love of Eleanor Bron but he goes the wrong way about it, being a man. When it comes time to send him down to hell Cook shows a human side and decides to let Moore off. His motive all the while has been to get a billion souls into hell, at which point he can put in a claim to get himself back into heaven, but his gesture of goodwill to Moore scuppers that, as he learns to his chagrin. So he has to go back and buy his soul all over again. Except this time Moore won't play his game any more, which causes God to emit a huge roar of delight in the film's last scene.

Raquel Welch does an interesting turn as Lust, though she didn't have to do much to get into character. At this point in her life she was arguably the sexiest woman on the planet. Fearing he would become "aroused" during their bed scene, Moore wore three pairs of underpants. In a later scene she does a bump-and-grind routine on a bar counter as Moore, in a nun's habit, sits beneath her smoking and drinking. The incongruity was choice.

Moore always regarded this as his favorite film. Selling one's soul was never meant to be quite this much fun. Moore and Cook had to restrain laughter during many scenes. Unfortunately the public didn't agree and it opened to poor reviews, most people feeling that the pair failed to repeat their success on the small screen with this wacky venture.

Cook captures the world-weariness of his lifestyle extremely well, however, bemoaning the amount of work he has to do to corrupt people, whereupon they then have the audacity to make deathbed repentances and cheat eternity. He also does things like tear out the last pages of books to frustrate readers, scratches LPs, and flicks traffic meter switches so that they read "Expired."

In *Rosemary's Baby* (1968) Roman Polanski's inspired direction and Mia Farrow's elfin fragility made some very shocking scenes like her rape by the devil just about watchable. Adapted from Ira Levin's best-seller and executed with a taut sense of menace, it expanded the scope of the devil possession movie to include "normal" people, in particular pregnant normal people. Polanski also makes Satan's witch and warlock, played by Ruth Gordon and Sidney Blackmer respectively, more jovial than demonic, in contrast to the portrayals in Levin's novel.

The plot involves Farrow's husband (John Cassavetes) being induced by his neighbors to impregnate her with his satanic seed. The Faustian deed will, he's promised, advance his career. Anybody that was contemplating reproducing might have been sharpishly persuaded to desist as a result but this psycho-drama packs a real punch, not least because of its apparent lack of interest in gratuitous jiggery-pokery. In fact we don't even see the eponymous baby. All we see is the reflection of his cat's eyes in Farrow's face at one point.

Polanski is an agnostic so his interest in diabolism was purely academic, even skittish. He was more intrigued by the human story behind the subhuman circumstances, and distanced himself from empathy with such circumstances by having the film seen totally from Farrow's viewpoint, thereby sidestepping any involvement in her experiences.

The National Catholic Office for Motion Pictures (formerly the LOD) gave it a C rating, which was hardly surprising. It wasn't only the devil worship that was problematic, the Office stated, but "the perverted use the film makes of fundamental Christian beliefs, especially the events surrounding the birth of Christ, and its mockery of religious persons and practices."[5] It gave Polanski a left-handed compliment by adding that the "technical excellence of the film seems to intensify its defamatory nature."

In Britain fifteen seconds were cut from the rape sequence because of its conjunction of black magic and kinky sex. Polanski was outraged, fuming to the *Evening Standard*, "The censor's attitude belongs to the Inquisition."[6] But when audience attendances hit the roof, all this seemed to be somehow irrelevant. The Condemned rating probably accentuated the film's desirability for filmgoers rather than detracted from it.

Polanski worked hard on the aforementioned technical excellence. For one scene in which he wanted the Sistine Chapel replicated he had his crew spend six weeks getting the effect he wanted. In another scene he sent Farrow across Fifth Avenue during rush hour traffic without any protection, telling her nobody would knock down a pregnant woman. Farrow herself, in a scene which called on her to be jabbed with a needle, had a real doctor give her a real injection.

The shoot dragged on so long that Farrow's husband at the time, Frank Sinatra, became furious. He wanted her for his own film, *The Detective*, and wasn't too impressed with her diabolical ambitions—or indeed with Polanski. He eventually issued her with an ultimatum: She was to finish the film or the marriage was over. She decided on the latter option.

A film like this, in which the forces of evil defeat those of good, would have been inconceivable a decade before but many cataclysmic events took place in the sixties to dent people's confidence in an omnipotent, omni-present God. First we had the assassination of John F. Kennedy, then Martin Luther King and finally Robert Kennedy. Crime was on the increase, as was abortion. Divorce had become commonplace. In a few more short years the humiliation of Vietnam and Watergate would act as further nails on the coffin of stability.

Rosemary's Baby, in a sense, made Satanism respectable. Diehard devotees sniffed at it and MOR audiences avoided it like the plague, but those with a passing interest in the subject, or indeed in well-made movies, gave it their undivided attention.

In his autobiography Polanski says he no more believes in Satan as evil incarnate than he does in a personal God. For the sake of credibility he decided there had to be a possibility that Rosemary's "supernatural" experiences were "figments of her imagination."[7]

Farrow, despite the fact that she claimed Catholicism was "tattooed on her soul" as a result of her upbringing, didn't have a problem doing the film. She gave it her all, no doubt aware that it was probably going to launch her career in "exciting new directions."[8] This despite the fact that she saw the plot as little more than a "childish sketch of evil right out of a Catechism book."[9]

There's an ironic postscript to the movie. When Polanski made it he hired Anton LaVey, who'd started a Church of Satan in the 1950s, as technical advisor. A year afterward Charles Manson and his band of "devil's representatives" had Polanski's wife Sharon Tate brutally murdered alongside a number of friends. They were all savagely mutilated.

After the death of Tate people began to surmise that it had something to do with Polanski. Polanski himself thought this an eminent possibility too but there's nothing to suggest Manson had ever flirted with Satanism in any way so it's probably just a sick coincidence that the murder had overtones of occultism. (Jayne Mansfield *was* a member of LaVey's church and when she died in a horrific car crash that all but decapitated her he wasn't slow to draw a connection to the fact.)

Polanski was enraged about the fact that some people felt he brought these tragedies on himself by the kind of life he led. There was a perception that, "These were the films you made, so this was the life you led— and the death you died."[10] There was even a suggestion in *Newsweek* that Tate was involved in black magic the night she was murdered, a totally unfounded (and subsequently discredited) allegation.

The Devils (1971) was based on a real-life series of events in the French town of Loudun in 1632. It deals mainly with the demonic possession of a group of nuns. Dubbed *Carry on Witches* by some critics as a result of its farcical depiction of sexual excess, it had Oliver Reed as a lusty priest who's finally burned at the stake after being accused of sorcery. It was hard to take any of it seriously, especially with Ken Russell on helming duties. He wallowed in the self-indulgent nature of the material, which included everything from anal exorcism to masturbation by crucifix. The film isn't so much about witchcraft as sexual repression.

In September 1632, Ursuline Prioress Jeanne des Anges (played by Vanessa Redgrave) claimed to have seen visions of a dead priest, and also a living one, Urbain Grandier (Reed). Other nuns had similar visions. The devil was adjudged to be present in such visions, and Grandier himself somehow complicit in it all.

In one of Jeanne's visions she saw Grandier as Christ on the cross. When he came down from it she kissed the wounds on his hands and licked those in his side, tasting his blood with her tongue. She then imagined herself having sex with him, the vision ending with her driving a crucifix into the palm of her hand until she bled profusely.

Grandier was arrested in December 1633. The nuns, meanwhile, were taken to various churches to be exorcised. Grandier, who had earlier advocated marriage for priests, was burned at the stake.

Russell has never exactly been renowned for his restraint and here he hyped up the flimsy anecdotal pretext of his film to boiling-point. He actually shot a further scene where a life-size figure of the crucified Christ is "raped" by the nuns while another priest, played by Murray Melvin, masturbates as he watches the debauchery unfold.

This scene was rejected by the censors, which caused Russell some dismay. "It was really central to the whole thing," he protested, "intercut as it was with Grandier finding both himself and God in the solitary simplicity of nature." He saw his overall vision as one of "over-ripe, perverted religion going as bad and wrong as it can possibly become, with the eternal truth of the bread and the wine and the brotherhood of man and God in the universe."[11] Unfortunately, this wasn't how the finished film looked, and most audiences surmised that the director seemed to be enjoying the decadence too much for comfort.

Russell defended himself by saying, "I didn't set out to make a cosy religious drama that would please everyone, but a true film about the horror and blasphemy perpetrated against human beings by their fellow men in the name of Jesus Christ. This is an eternal theme, as a glance at the horror in Northern Ireland will remind you.[12] The film was a political statement, he insisted. "Although the events took place over 400 years ago, corruption and mass brainwashing by church, state and commerce is still with us, as is the insatiable craving for sex and violence by the general public."[13] He admitted his film was "harsh," but wished that the people who were horrified by it had read the book on which it was based, "because the bare facts are far more horrible than anything in the film."[14]

The British film censor John Trevelyan also made Russell cut out Vanessa Redgrave saying the word "cunt." It had taken him a decade of fighting, he told Reed, to get "fuck" accepted, and the British public weren't yet ready for the stronger expletive.[15]

The film was a hit at the Venice Film Festival but didn't do well in the U.S. The general critical reaction was that Russell, once again, was content to wallow in unashamed decadence under the auspices of purporting to make a sociological statement about restrictive attitudes to sexuality. In Britain Alexander Walker thought it "a garish glossary of sadomasochism" with a taste for visual sensations that made scene after scene look like "the masturbatory fantasies of a Roman Catholic."[16]

Both Reed and Russell denied it was meant to be horrific or outrageous, but perhaps their definitions of such terms were different from those of the average viewer. Reed took the film more seriously than most of his others and it showed in his performance. He earned this accolade from Julian Upton: "[He] held together a riotous feast of shrieking pyrotechnics with a performance of such control, emotion, pain and sensitivity that the scenes of his torture are still difficult to watch thirty years on."[17]

Hammersmith Is Out (1972) was another one of those Richard Burton/ Liz Taylor collaborations that seemed designed to keep them working together at all costs in a vain attempt to keep their shaky marriage together, and to hell (oops) with the viewer. Melvyn Bragg likened the pair of them to "two heavyweight champs who had fought each other to exhaustion but still cannot quit."[18]

A loose re-working of the Faust story, Burton plays an asylum inmate who promises the world (and the flesh) to the asylum's intern (Beau Bridges) if he helps him escape. Bridges agrees and they go off on the road together, creating mayhem with Taylor (a waitress) in tow. Bridges gets juicy executive positions and has an affair with Taylor but then tires of her and asks Burton to kill her. Burton tells her he'll spare her life if she agrees to have his child—the good old anti-Christ staple directors use when they run out of other ideas.

It's a pity the once promising Burton was reduced to this. He does his best to make the devil look bored, but only ends up making him boring.

Taylor, on the other hand, is content to ham it all up, as if she knew something her husband didn't (i.e., that the only way to rescue it was to recognize the fact that it was ridiculous and behave—or misbehave—accordingly). Bragg joked that she "slipped in and out of character like a loose kneecap."[19]

Intended to be a black comedy, it ends up being merely grey. It was directed and narrated by Peter Ustinov, who also appears in it as the man running the asylum. How was his radar so much on the blink? Perhaps he took it on merely to work with two legends. Whatever his reasons, wearing three hats makes it very much a vanity project. And like most vanity projects it was destined to malinger in celluloid Hades—or rather limbo.

Burton was now showing the effects of a self-destructive lifestyle in his pot belly and bloodshot eyes. In some of the scenes he actually looked under the influence, as if he hadn't even accorded the production the courtesy of remaining sober.

The Devil in Miss Jones, which was both directed and produced by Gerard Damiano, hit the screen in 1971. It concerns a depressed virgin who killed herself. Because suicide is regarded as a mortal sin she ends up in hell. She's upset about this, not having done anything particularly damnable in her life, so she asks for permission to return to earth to, if you like, "earn" her eternal punishment.

Resurrected, she pursues a lustful path, engaging in various orgiastic delights, including masturbation with a bathtub hose. When she goes back to hell, her punishment isn't fire but cohabitation with a frigid man. The devil that has been unleashed in her must now be relegated to a redundant state.

It's a playful concept which gave Damiano many opportunities for X-rated frolics involving most bodily apertures as Miss Jones makes up for lost time. The public flocked to it in droves. Though some American states banned it, it continues to enjoy cult status even today, being one of the few films to successfully make the transition from hardcore porn to mainstream morality fable with equanimity. Having said that, the lion's share of its viewers have been more engrossed by its aggressively erotic content than the mischievous irony of the *denouement.*

In the same year William Friedkin made *The Exorcist*, a work that was about to change forever the way religious films would be approached.

He'd mixed with drop-outs and vagrants in his youth, apparently on course for a life of crime. (He was arrested for armed robbery on one occasion.) He was saved, he told people, by his mother, who had exerted a "saintly" influence on him. It was hardly she who inspired—if that's the word—his fascination with the satanic.[20]

"There's a darkness in my soul," he confessed once, "a profound darkness that is with me every waking minute."[21] This was certainly apparent from the type of movies he made even before *The Exorcist*. His all-time favorite film was Orson Welles' *Citizen Kane* and his ambition was to revise it in some form. His latest work was hardly likely to do that but nobody could have predicted its supersonic success both with the Academy and the public.

The plot was ingenious enough. A priest named Father Merrin, played by Max Von Sydow, discovers an evil spirit in the course of an archaeological expedition in Iraq. The said spirit subsequently enters the soul of Regan McNeil (Linda Blair), and thereby hangs a tale. Manic events ensue, all the way from levitation and head-swivelling to vomiting green slime.

It became Warner Brothers greatest hit of all time, much to the amazement of those who thought it would result in walk-outs or, worse, becoming a work of satiric derision. It may have, but most people were too terrified to laugh at the outrageous events on display. A lot of that was down to Von Sydow's *gravitas*. It was a long way from *The Seventh Seal* to this. Playing chess with Death was one thing; trying to banish the devil from an invidious twelve-year-old quite another, but he discharged the responsibility with some distinction.

Friedkin had a nervous breakdown on the set and afterward declared that he believed in possession by the devil as a result of working on the film. It had no central message, he claimed; it was simply meant to be the record of a case history—the last recorded exorcism in America, which formed the basis of the William Blatty novel that was its source.

Blatty revealed that his "obsession with 'the evidence of transcendence' had its roots in a youthful terror of death, and a desire to subdue the waking dream of obliteration."[22] For him the tangible evidence of a "force of evil" is itself, ironically, "a reaffirmation of the existence of divinity."[23] From this point of view, as Mark Kermode points out, his work can be seen as "evangelical entertainment in which shocks provide the emotional charge, while the intellect edges towards an acceptance of faith."[24]

One scene has Blair masturbating with a crucifix; another one features a statue of the Virgin Mary transmuting into a naked prostitute with an erect penis. Nobody could accuse Friedkin of holding back.

As we saw, he wasn't the first director to portray masturbation by crucifix, but rather Ken Russell. Before giving Blair the role, Friedkin
inquired if she even knew what masturbation was. She assured him that
not only did she know what it was, but she practiced it, adding, "Don't
you?"[25] At this point her would-be director realized that even if the law
forbade her from seeing the film, her gentle years would hardly result in
her being corrupted by its venal material.

The shooting was plagued by a plethora of mystifyingly eerie accidents and mishaps. A fire destroyed the set early on. On Von Sydow's
first day on the set his brother died. Blair's grandfather died in the same
week, and the son of Jason Miller, another cast member, was knocked
down by a car and almost died. Ellen Burstyn also wrenched her back,
and a gaffer cut his toe off. Jack MacGowran, who played a film director,
died a week after doing his death scene. Strange images also showed up
on some of the footage: double exposures of Blair's face and so on. No
wonder Friedkin had a breakdown when it all finally ended.

Blatty's book was based on a sensational exorcism which had taken
place in 1949. It was of a 14-year-old boy who had allegedly started
speaking in a voice—and language—not his own. His bed shook up and
down and furniture moved to block his way as he left it. An invisible
hand slapped him, leaving an imprint on his face. When a priest came to
exorcise him, the boy broke his arm. The furniture in the room then tried
to "attack" the priest. A bottle fell off the wall sometime afterward and
shattered the tiles but remained intact itself. The boy then started vomiting strange fluids but doctors could find nothing medically wrong with
him. He went on to marry and have three children, remembering nothing
of his ordeal.

Many people fainted, and even threw up, at the first public showings
of the film but they kept coming to it in droves, either out of a misplaced
fascination or some kind of masochism. Others believed themselves to
be as possessed as Blair was and sought out Father Merrins of their own
to cure them.

A Church of Scotland spokesperson said he would rather take a bath in
pig manure than see the film. Peter Biskind said it was "drenched in a
kind of menstrual panic," comparing it to Brian de Palma's *Carrie* in the
sense of being "filled with disgust towards female bodily functions."[26]
Vincent Canby called it "a chunk of occultist claptrap," adding that its
$10 million budget would have been better spent "subsidising a couple
of beds at the Payne-Whitney Clinic."[27] Nonetheless, it swept the boards
at the Oscar ceremonies, no mean achievement in a year that also had

Marlon Brando's *Last Tango in Paris*, *American Graffiti*, *Serpico* and *Cries and Whispers* to contend with.

Evangelist Billy Graham contended there was evil in the film itself, not just in the events it chronicled. This theory would seem to have been borne out by the number of freak events that surrounded its screening.

In Toronto, four women went for psychiatric treatment after seeing it. A West German teenager shot himself. In England a 16-year-old boy died from an epileptic attack after coming home from the cinema. In 1974 the murderer of a 19-year-old girl put his action down to what he had recently seen on the screen. "It wasn't really me that did it," he argued in his defense. "It was something else inside me."[28] It wouldn't be fair to say Friedkin welcomed these developments but they certainly swelled his bank balance.

Certain priests felt it was authentic, in particular a Father Kenneth Jardoff, who wrote in New York's *Catholic News*: "Most of the reviewers who disliked the movie used a kind of egocentric reasoning. They had never heard of demonical possession, therefore the film is a fantasy. Yet one of its strong points is its authenticity. The guttural sounds used as part of the soundtrack were recorded at a real exorcism."

Other church authorities praised it for portraying a struggle between good and evil where the forces of good finally prevailed, and for giving us in Father Merrin a credible priest who was himself assailed with doubts about his faith. Few argued with the fact that no matter how horrific or manipulative it appeared to be, it was an engrossing piece of film-making, even if for most of the wrong reasons.

The film's exorcism, by definition, is its *piece de resistance*. The wheel has come full circle. No longer does Moses lead the Israelites to the Promised Land. Instead, Fr Merrin struggles to keep snivelling demons at bay. A new benchmark has been reached in "spiritual" movies at the expense of general profundity. This is all too true, but since when did we have the right to expect anything else of Hollywood, a town that prides itself on dumbing itself down to its lowest common denominator time and again, because that's where it knows its audience lies? If we wanted profundity we wouldn't have been at the movies in the first place.

The devil's choice of a victim is also disingenuous. As Jeffrey Burton Russell wisely remarked, he should really be credited with more intelligence than to possess a harmless little girl rather than a national government. Her evil, grotesque and all as it is, doesn't go beyond the room she inhabits. Her danger is empty and self-indulgent. There's no

Armageddon threatened here, just bilious excrescences. Nikolas Schreck added, "The Devil could come up with something more threatening to the social order than pissing on Mom's rug, playing with herself, throwing up, or saying 'fuck.'"[29]

Schreck saw the film as the ultimate misogynistic tract, a demonization of female sexuality that went right back to the Middle Ages. John May agreed. In his essay "The Demonic in American Cinema" he wrote, "The film makes the regrettable neo-Puritan assumption that sex is at least reductively demonic, since practically all of Regan's symptoms are portrayed as sexual aberrations, spoken or otherwise."[30]

Schreck elaborated on this neo-Puritanism. "While it's never stated officially," he wrote, "the implicit Catholic code of the film suggests that the mother may be partially responsible for drawing the devil into her home. As a sexually active divorcee, she's technically guilty of sin. Female sexuality is portrayed as an unholy aberration, which must be chastised and expunged by the celibate male figures."[31]

This is a perfectly valid interpretation of the events as they unfold, but somewhat reductive. I doubt either Blatty or Friedkin suffer from Puritanism or misogyny. Neither are they pillars of Catholic orthodoxy. Maybe we should remember that at the end of the day what we're talking about here is an escapist horror film. The connection between profanity and possession is admittedly a tired cliché but we should see it as just that rather than evidence of a covert sexist manifesto.

Friedkin also dismissed the idea that the reports of the accidents and tragedies that attended the shooting were publicity gambits. Nobody would deny that he pumped them up to make the tills ring more sweetly for him, and Von Sydow made a good point when he said that the film's lengthy shooting schedule (fifteen months) made such accidents and tragedies more likely, but there were still an inordinate amount of them.

For this actor the film could be seen as the third instalment of an eclectic trilogy. He appeared in the screen's most intense study of religious doubt in *The Seventh Seal*, went on to play Jesus in *The Greatest Story Ever Told* and now here he was expelling demons. (He added one final twist to the screw by playing the devil in *Needful Things* in 1993.)

There are as many viewpoints on the film as there are viewers of it. Harry Ringel wrote in *Cinemafantastique*: "*The Exorcist* has done for the horror film what *2001: A Space Odyssey* did for science fiction: legitimised it in the eyes of thousands who previously considered horror movies nothing more than a giggle."[32] A contradictory opinion held that it "wasn't the first bad movie to be a hit, but it is a new kind of blockbuster. It represents a new extreme in the cinema of cruelty. What is it that makes people pay to be abused? Are their emotions so deadened that they need sledgehammer blows to make them respond? The film offers perverse sexual kicks that make ordinary porno movies look wholesome."[33]

Needless to say, *The Exorcist* bandwagon wasn't going to stop with this one outing, Hollywood not being noted for bashfulness when it came to milking A Good Thing. It wasn't a question of *whether* there would be a sequel, but *when*.

John Boorman was consulted to take it on. Boorman had already been approached by Warner Brothers' head of production John Calley to direct *The Exorcist* itself but had demurred, finding it repulsive. "You're such a snob," Calley taunted, reminding him that the book was a best-seller and the film of it likely to be one too.[34] Clearly, they were coming from different sides of the consumerist fence. Boorman made *Zardoz* instead, a gothic extravaganza set in the future, which bombed. Obviously Calley's box office sense was more focused.

Calley then offered Boorman *The Heretic*, aka *Exorcist II*, and this time Boorman peaked his ears. He realized to his cost that he'd missed the boat with its predecessor. He also felt the latter script had more intriguing potential, carrying elements of the thinking of Teilhard de Chardin in it in the manner in which it tried to marry science to religion by dint of a creative explanation of Darwinism that also embraced God. Written by William Goodhart, the script Boorman received depicted Regan as an instrument of benign clairvoyance that had been hijacked by evil forces. When you dressed this down into plain English, it wasn't a million miles away from full-on devil possession. But Boorman was intrigued.

By now Blair is an adolescent attending a psychiatrist (Louise Fletcher) who feels she's suppressing the memory of her childhood trauma. In a bid to bring it all to the surface, she plugs in a machine to link her own subconscious to that of Blair and see what pans out. Bad call! When chaos ensues, Richard Burton (as a priest) is drafted in to try and salvage the situation. (This is Mistake Two.)

Exorcist II gives us a New Age devil movie, an elaboration of its predecessor rather than a re-tread, but the golden rule of sequels is: If it ain't broken, don't fix it. Intellectuals should stick to intellectual fare rather than flirt around with commercial genres in the vague hope of inserting some metaphysical juice. The result was a flat and flaccid hybrid that did nobody any favors. Judith Crist said it for most viewers when she expressed the opinion that Burton deserves all he gets when attacked by a swarm of locusts.

Burton told Boorman he wasn't sure what the film was about, to which Boorman replied, "Neither am I." Almost a dozen endings were mooted, and Burton said he'd agree to any of them to get the damn thing finished, beaten down as he was by the Californian smog and sunshine. The one they chose found him collapsing on a bed with Blair.

Boorman has Burton trying to get his head (and mouth) around turgid dialogue like, "Evil is a spiritual being, alive and living, perverted and perverting, weaving its way insidiously into the very fabric of life." One imagines he would have preferred a Shakespearean soliloquy of the most labyrinthine kind than this stodgy *shtick*.

What audiences wanted was an elaboration of the first movie, not a revisionist parable awash with thought-provoking concepts. Friedkin cut to the chase and afterwards extrapolated, which made for better drama. Boorman tried to present the Thinking Man's horror movie, imagining those who flocked to the original might want a stronger dose of background material. In actual fact all they wanted was a stronger dose of bodily functions gone horrifically wrong. He tried to squeeze too many ambitious ideas about spiritualism into a film unable to cope with them. Eventually the structure tenuously holding them together in their half-baked form collapsed under all the mumbo-jumbo.

Boorman took himself far too seriously, trying to go up a rung on the scarefest totem pole and still keep the cash registers tinkling. Alas, it didn't work out like that and the film grossed a mere $14 million (as opposed to the original, which totalled a cool $82 million).

In the end he was undone by his own intellectual pretensions. Trying to make a pitch of misdirected virtue rather than vice was always going to be a non-starter. Stanley Kubrick advised, "the only way to do a sequel to *The Exorcist* is to give them even more gore and horror than before."[35] Nobody, he said, was really interested in goodness. And so it came to pass.

The film strangled itself in a welter of aimless meanderings, Boorman's attempt to flesh out the character of the priest, despite Burton's best efforts, falling flat on its face. (He even gave him a crisis of faith, and also tried to interject a sexual element into his relationship with Blair.) Sydow refused to reprise his role, as did Ellen Burstyn as Regan's mother, so this was always going to be an uphill project.

Pauline Kael savaged it with criticisms which Boorman, a man brave enough to recognize that his visceral intellect sometimes warred against his box office appeal, took on the chin. "It might have been a horror classic if it had a simpler, less ritzy story," she said, "but it's too cadenced and exotic and too deliriously complicated to succeed." She conceded that there was enough "visual magic" in it for a dozen good movies but what it lacked was judgment, "the first casualty of the movie-making obsession."[36] She also rubbished Burton's mannered playing, reminding one of Boorman's own observation that if you took away the Welshman's fathoms-deep voice, there was really very little left.

The Exorcist has a lot to answer for as it began a trend that's still going on today. Its mish-mash of scatological (rather than eschatological) gore, its vomit-spewing excesses, its pretend earnestness undercut by special effects that were the real *raison d'etre* behind the exercise—all these would be used and abused by succeeding generations of film-makers anxious to cash in on Friedkin's inventiveness.

Gregory Peck became part of the horror craze in 1976, with *The Omen*. The reason he accepted it was because he hadn't had a hit movie for a while and had become "exasperated with producing movies that lost money."[37] The idea of having the child as the demon of the piece harked back to *Rosemary's Baby*.

It's all based on a highly unlikely pretext. The wife of diplomat Robert Thorn (Peck) gives birth to a stillborn child. Not wanting to tell her this he accepts a substitute, Damien, from a priest. Damien will turn out to be the Antichrist, his ominous nature first telegraphed to us when his nanny hangs herself at a party in front of all the guests. He later becomes hysterical near churches.

Peck doubted this would have happened. "The script read like a good pulp thriller," he hissed dismissively. He also felt Thorn would have been "too intelligent to accept a substitute child without question, and without asking to see the body of his own dead son, or researching the background of the substitute child." Neither was he convinced that Thorn would have deceived his wife. But he allowed that it was "a sort of rollercoaster thrill ride for the audience."[38]

When Peck is warned about the kind of child he's raising by another priest, the latter is dispatched to that big seminary in the sky. It now falls to Peck to fill in the blanks. After some research in Rome he discovers that a birthmark on Damien's skull carries the devil's number: 666.

Lee Remick played Peck's wife. On the first day of shooting he sent her two dozen roses and a note with this message. "At last we get to work together on such a jolly little subject."[39] Humor, once again, was the safety valve "respectable" stars needed to keep their focus.

After Damien murders Remick, Peck realizes he'll have to kill his son. But as he attempts to do so he himself is shot by police who don't know what's happening. Damien is then adopted by the President of the United States. Suddenly, things don't look too promising for the future of the country. And so the film ends. But already we know a sequel will be in the offing.

As was the case with *The Exorcist*, many freakish real-life tragedies coincided with *The Omen* shooting. As Peck was flying from L.A. to London to start filming his plane was struck by lightning. Eight hours later a different plane carrying David Seltzer, who wrote the script, was also struck by lightning. Shortly afterwards the hotel in which the film's director Richard Donner was staying was ripped apart by an IRA bomb. For a scene in Israel a private jet was hired to collect Peck but he wasn't ready to board so postponed his journey. The plane crashed, killing all on board. After the film was finished both the special effects man, John Richardson, and his assistant were hit by a truck in the Netherlands. The assistant died and Richardson himself suffered severe head injuries. Amazingly enough, this accident occurred outside a small Dutch town named Ommen.

Donner splurged out a massive $6 million on advertising the film, which was more than twice what it cost to make. Over 13,000 copies of the trailer went out to cinemas, and a novelization was written to make up for the fact that, unlike *The Exorcist*, it hadn't been developed from a best-selling book. The gambit paid off and it earned $4.3 million in its first three days. It became the most successful film of Peck's whole career against all the odds. Its success he described as nothing short of "obscene."[40] Charlton Heston, who'd said no to it, must have been tearing his hair out. Almost before the week was out, opportunistic directors started vetting other satanic scripts. The devil once again was having all the best tunes and they wanted to be a part of it.

Church authorities were divided in their reactions to it. Some felt it recaptured the sense of evil that was lacking in most revisionist thinking about religion while more circumspect viewers recognized it for what it was: an unadulterated money-spinner.

The critics were also divided. *Variety* liked it, alleging that the "satanic suspense melodrama, fallen into artistic disrepute after *Rosemary's Baby* and *The Exorcist*, resumes its class status again with *The Omen*."[41] But Vincent Canby wrote in *Time* "William Friedkin's *The Exorcist* seemed pretty dreadful at the time, but alongside *The Omen* now looks like a work of cinematic art."[42]

Seltzer was man enough to admit he'd written it as pure escapism without any religious pretensions—as if we needed to be told. Donner felt the church should have been glad he was informing people about the fact that the Devil was "alive and well on the planet Earth," a rather lofty phrase used in conjunction with a rather lowbrow movie. Could he not have agreed with Seltzer that it was B-grade hokum dressed up with a respectable star to make it look like a metaphysical investigation into a lurking nefariousness? Whatever his attitude, he was laughing all the way to the bank alongside his fellow-pillagers of erstwhile untouchable terrain. It was open season on Old Nick and they all had Billy Friedkin to thank.

The sequel hinted at in the film's final moments arrived promptly the following year. *Damien: The Omen II* was about as imaginative as its title. It had another Hollywood veteran, William Holden, at its helm, but it totally wimped out on the Armageddon-style climax of its predecessor.

Instead we see the little tyke wreaking havoc in the upper echelons of the business world. Holden tries to do what Peck couldn't, i.e., quell the savage beast, but he's thwarted in his efforts by no less an adversary than his own wife, who's actually one of Damien's colleagues.

Holden plays the boy's uncle, but it takes five murders before he starts to feel All Is Not Right. (And we used to think Mr Holden had insight.) This might have been acceptable if the deaths were in any way imaginative but slipping through ice, plummeting down an elevator shaft and being pecked by a raven (a la *The Birds*) before being knocked down by a truck don't quite cut it. Neither does the boy in question inspire any kind of real fear, walking about the military compound where he's been primed with a smug grin on his face that's supposed to pass for grim portent.

The last instalment in the *Omen* saga was reached in 1981 with *The Final Conflict*, which had Sam Neill in a very tame effort that tries to inject a romantic subplot into a political milieu with drastically uneven results. The series, which had been steadily self-destructing since the Gregory Peck effort, went out on a whimper rather than a bang.

The Devil's Son-in-Law (aka *Petey Whitestraw*) was a 1977 blaxploitation flick that was so bad it was good. Unashamedly kitschy, it had Rudy May Moore as a dismally poor stand-up comic who's gunned to death by gangsters. The devil (Tito Shaw) offers to bring him back to life if he impregnates his daughter. Moore agrees, but when it comes to performing the dreaded deed he refuses, the lady in question being no oil painting, to put it mildly. He tries to deputize an alcoholic in his place but his plan fails, the film ending with Shaw getting ready to walk the embattled Moore up the aisle.

Alongside the ridiculous plot there's a plethora of bad taste gags, prefiguring the kind of fare the Farrelly Brothers and their ilk would negotiate a generation on. We also get slapstick mixed in with martial arts in a *melange* that has acquired much appeal with time. It's all so much deliciously scabrous nonsense with nary a redeeming virtue in sight.

Tony Curtis appeared in *The Manitou* in 1978. "That movie wasn't released," he told me, "it escaped. I would class it as the cruddiest piece of work I've done—and that's saying something. They tell me it has a kind of cult following now. That only happens to really great films or really terrible ones." This was one of the latter variety.

The plot concerns the evil spirit of an ancient Native American shaman that becomes resurrected through a fetus on Susan Strasberg's neck. It takes a particular type of genius to dream up a storyline this excruciatingly outlandish. Curtis, along with other veterans like Burgess Meredith and Stella Stevens, did their best to look as if they wouldn't dearly prefer to be somewhere else.

The director, William Girdler, was killed in a helicopter crash in the Philippines a few months after the film was made in yet another one of those life-meets-art tragedies that seems to bedevil such films.

In 1980 we were back to diabolical frenzy again courtesy of Stanley Kubrick's masterly version of Stephen King's novel *The Shining*, though King himself thought it was flawed.

He was flattered that the great Kubrick adapted one of his books but he felt the finished product was an aberration of the novel he wrote. He likened it to a Cadillac lacking an engine. Many people feel the same way about King's own writing. The criticism is, in any case, off-kilter. What Kubrick did was re-mold a horror story into a reverberative psychodrama which hinted at celestial/infernal dimensions. This was a step further than King's more limited coordinates.

Nicholson played demented author Jack Torrance, becoming the caretaker of a Colorado hotel that's built on an ancient Native American burial ground. As the film goes on and Torrance becomes increasingly unhinged, ghosts from the past emerge.

In King's novel, as Alexander Walker noted in *Stanley Kubrick, Director*, Torrance is a pawn of the past, incited to kill by those whose own lives are extinct, but in Kubrick's version he *becomes* his past.

At times Nicholson seemed to be camping it up in slasher movie mode, all teeth and smiles as he croons, "Heeeere's Johnny," a reference to the

TV talk show host Johnny Carson, but the overall impact of the film was to chill you to the marrow, even as you marvelled at Kubrick's special effects: blood-filled corridors, a hotel lounge that goes from emptiness to festivity, Torrance entering the empty Gold Room which becomes transformed into a ballroom packed with jolly 1920s guests and so on.

Henry Bromwell's view was that Jack was simply an "exaggerated, highly stylized boogeyman rising from the shadows to frighten children."[43] Nicholson asked Kubrick at one point if he was playing it "too broad" but the director allayed his fears, assuring him that he wanted a "semi-comical villain who was also very evil."[44] Nicholson remarked, "When the material is as unusual as it is in *The Shining*, dealing with ghosts and spirits, the acting has to be larger than life."[45]

This is probably why he revelled unashamedly in the gore. For him it was a trip back to the scarefests of Roger Corman, albeit with a subterranean, psychedelic edge. He was accused of going over the top by critics but a closer appraisal of his performance sees a slow build-up of frustration segueing into mental collapse triggered by writer's block. The ghosts that haunt Hotel Overlook are like the ones in *The Sixth Sense*, or Nicole Kidman's *The Others*, being emanations of Torrance's unnerved psyche. In the latter stages, of course, what with the "Heeeere's Johnny" scene and so on, it became comedic. Or perhaps audiences laughed at it merely to release the previous hour's unbearable tension.

Morris Dickstein wrote in *American Film* that, "For all its brilliance of execution, *The Shining* comes to grief on the problem of motivation."[46] Kubrick de-emphasizes the theme of the "evil house" which linked King's novel to the gothic tradition. *The Shining* becomes the first horror film which blames it all on writer's block. This, to his mind, is a cop-out which makes "inordinate demands on Jack Nicholson's mobile face and leering satanic grin as a substitute for motivation." Surely this is to miss the point. Wasn't it Nicholson's unhingement that created the block rather than vice versa?

Critic Jack Kroll thought of it as the first epic horror movie, saying that it was to other horror movies what *2001: A Space Odyssey* was to other space movies.

Speaking of the supernatural element in it, Kubrick said that ghost stories appeal to people because they had spirits and gave credence to another world, and the hereafter. If we were afraid of them, that fear was offset by a hope that death wasn't the end for mankind. This isn't logically correct because we can be afraid of things that don't exist—that's what imagination is—but it explains this agnostic's fascination with the horror genre.

Kubrick told Kroll that King's book struck an extraordinary balance between the psychological and the supernatural in such a way as to lead you to think the latter would eventually be explained by the former. This was hardly likely considering we were speaking about Torrance's derangement.

When Kubrick phoned King to say he wanted to film his book he told him he thought the whole notion of ghosts was "optimistic" in the sense that they seemed to presuppose life after death. "What about hell?" King countered, to which Kubrick replied, "I don't believe in hell." This (rightly) sounded to King like wanting to have your eschatological cake and eating it too. He concluded that Kubrick didn't seem to want to get behind the concept of the ghost as a damned soul, which was unusual considering he was filming such a dark and gothic work.

The Shining is probably the first truly intellectual horror movie Hollywood witnessed. There was none of the conventional melodrama, with maidens-in-distress fretting over slowlyturning doorknobs in the middle of the night. The immediate *ambience* may have been surreal, but the acting and direction were so mesmerizing it conduced toward psychological realism, or even super-realism.

Was it "the best horror movie ever made," as Kubrick hoped, or merely the tale of an "exaggerated, highly stylised boogeyman rising from the shadows to frighten children," as Bromwell observed? Maybe the answer lies somewhere in the middle.

Steven Spielberg produced a pale reflection of it in 1982 with his ghost story *Poltergeist*. (Craig Nelson was the named director but the word on the street was that Spielberg had a huge input.) The film centers on a family set upon by spirits that abduct their daughter. It was a fairly schlocky affair with a ghostbuster also in tow. The real-life ghostbuster upon whom this character was based, Beatrice Straight, was bemused by its "snake oil" overtones. She didn't deny that events like those that took place in the movie could have happened in real life but she knew Hollywood had a reputation for cranking up their sensationalist element. The idea of whirlpools stealing children or trees swallowing them up was pure (or impure) melodrama in her eyes. In fact she said that usually when she was called upon to visit a "haunted" house, her first impulse was to advise the callers to submit themselves for psychiatric analysis.

The Devil and Max Devlin (1981) came from the Walt Disney stable, thereby breaking an age-old tradition by coming with a PG rating instead of the familiar G one for the first time in its illustrious history. God alone knows why they bothered. Elliott Gould is the nasty landlord killed in a car crash. Consigned to hell, he meets a most unlikely devil in the form of Bill Cosby, offering him his life back if he can find three people willing to sell their souls within three months. Both Gould and Cosby bear all the hallmarks of two stars who would dearly like to be released from this juvenile nonsense, as would the audience. It wears out its welcome long before the end.

Oh, God! You Devil (1984) was the third instalment in the George Burns canon of religious films, except this time he got to be both God and the devil together. Ted Wass plays a down-at-heel musician who meets him in the guise of an agent (no prizes for guessing which role this is). Wass realizes there's something funny about him when he lights his cigarette with his fingertips—as you would.

He's willing to sell his soul because he's broke and unfamous. Also, his wife is pregnant. Burns offers him seven years of fame and fortune in exchange for it. This is indeed expedited but (surprise surprise) Wass is unhappy afterwards. He wants to go back to his old life and his old wife (whom he loses in the transition to superstar). He's so desperate he attempts suicide. God comes in at this stage, willing to forgive him his lapse. Later on, God and the devil (i.e., Burns and Burns) play poker for his soul, God winning by a bluff (which one would have imagined to be the other man's prerogative). Wass can now go back to his old identity. It's mildly amusing, Burns relishing lines like, "If I didn't exist, God would have to make me up. I make him look good."

Crossroads (1986) has frustrated musician Joe Seneca selling his soul to the devil (who still has all the best tunes), so that he can emulate the genius of blues guru Robert Johnson, who died in 1938. The plot was apparently borrowed from the canard that the legendary violinist Nicolo Paganini sold his soul to the devil so he could play with the eccentric virtuosity he was noted for but it rambled too much to engage.

Jack Nicholson played the Devil in *The Witches of Eastwick* in 1987. This was a "bizarre, not always coherent" comedy.[47] He joked that it was a part he'd been "practicing for all his life."[48] Anjelica Huston gave her old lover a wry grin when she heard that. More than anyone else, perhaps, she knew what he meant. To research it he read voraciously: Dante's *Inferno*, Thomas Aquinas and witchcraft tomes from the Dark Ages.

"One of the things I came across," he revealed, "is this big long debate about the definition of God. And the only thing they could come up with is that anything definite you can say about God must be supported by its paradoxical opposite."[49]

Nonetheless he was in his element playing the menace with such glee—and doubly so since he was surrounded by three beautiful women as the witches: Cher, Susan Sarandon and Michelle Pfeiffer. (Huston tested for one of them but wasn't cast, despite having won an Oscar for *Prizzi's Honor* the very day before.)

As Daryl Van Horne, Nicholson is faced with the job of providing sexual liberation for these New England sorceresses, a task he undertakes with some relish in a racy adaptation of John Updike's book. The film went on to make a fortune, characterized by fine ensemble playing. Cher had a few bouts of nerves but Nicholson, who had the image of being a male chauvinist prior to the shoot, proved an unlikely ally to her. The witches in question feel that the men they know can't accommodate their wild fantasies and dream about one who can. Enter Mr Nicholson. He proceeds to seduce each of them in turn, but in so doing disempowers them, which means the cure for their original predicament, if you like, is worse than the disease.

Van Horne brings their witch-like powers to the fore, resulting in the death of a newspaper editor, after which they become struck with remorse, which confuses him. Obviously they're not as committed to sorcery as he is, which kick-starts the reverse action of the film's last quarter.

It's now revenge time, which means doing things like sticking needles in a voodoo image of Van Horne to make him suffer for his sins. As for Van Horne himself, he remains bewildered about the fact that they've turned the knife on their liberator. It's now time for him to chew the scenery in a manner that's like Jack Torrance crossed with The Joker from *Batman*.

Nicholson's devil is more comical than scary, but no less potent on account of that. His mischievousness, in a sense, humanizes Van Horne, which is either refreshing or disastrous, depending on which way we view the film's intent (i.e., as polemic or entertainment). "I don't want to play him safely," he warned before shooting began. "I want them to be worried."[50] He hardly achieved that, but his larger-than-life qualities more than compensated.

The role gave him a lot of leverage for farcical playing. If he melodramatized psychosis in *The Shining*, here he did the same with his sub-angelic powers.

The "horny little devil" even got a chance to indulge in some classic misogyny toward the end of the film where he rants against women in Nietzschean vein as "just another one of God's minor mistakes, like tidal waves, earthquakes and floods." "You don't think God makes mistakes?" he asks rhetorically. "Of course He does. We all make mistakes. Of course if we make mistakes they call it evil, but if God does, they call it nature." He goes on to speculate about whether a "cure" or "vaccine" could be found to protect mankind from these unwished-for vermin, "Maybe we could do something about it—build up our immune systems, get a little exercise—you know, twenty push-ups and you never have to be afflicted with them again."

George Miller, the film's director, wanted his devil to be as alluring to the three women as he was threatening to them. "To a degree," he averred, "Christian concepts of chastity for women were created by a male-dominated society to protect themselves from such a presence."[51]

It would be over-egging the omelette to interpret Adrian Lyne's *Fatal Attraction* (1987) as a Satanic film, but the manner which Glenn Close meets her end (her last gasp rise from the dead harks back to everything from *Deliverance* to *Dressed to Kill*) changes it from a thriller about a guy who has casual sex to a chiller about a mad bitch who's apparently indestructible. Her eyes also give her something of a possessed look in some of the scenes. Michael Douglas played the male lead.

In the original version, Close commits suicide listening to "Madame Butterfly." This was more realistic. She had attempted suicide earlier in the film in similar circumstances. The act also had a kick: She stabs herself, and leaves Douglas' fingerprints on the knife. This was clever, but failed to jibe with a Medea clone invading the sanctity of the family house refusing to go down for the third time when Douglas' wife finally gets in on the act. Lyne smelled money in the "wow" ending so shifted the emphasis from feminism to *grand guignol*. Close wasn't too pleased about this and her frustration is understandable. In the finished cut she's like the human—if she is human—incarnation of AIDS. Douglas, who gets her into this pickle, would suffer further recrimination from feminists a few years down the road with *Basic Instinct*, a film that was, to them, too "Close" for comfort.

In the same year Robert De Niro played Louis Cyphre, a rather unsubtle soundalike for Lucifer, in Alan Parker's *Angel Heart*. A dark, unsettling thriller, it has Mickey Rourke as 1950s gumshoe Harry Angel, hired to track down a missing singer. After various sojourns through Harlem's occult underbelly he discovers that he himself is the missing man, having sold his soul to the devil years ago in exchange for fame in the music world.

To avoid paying his debt to he of the cloven hoof, Rourke killed a soldier and took his body, having a psychic erase his memory of that fact. The Faustian overtones of the film rankle but Parker hasn't stinted on the special effects and De Niro is a smug, self-satisfied devil, pumping up the mischievous element but hardly stretching himself to Nicholson-like proportions. Lisa Bonet rides shotgun with some *elan*.

There's a lot of blood and sex combined, leaving the film open to charges of gratuitous overkill in a pulp fiction kind of way but the high-wattage cast rescues it from the level of pantomime, a pit it could easily have descended into with lesser talents. In the view of Rourke's biographer Bart Mills, the reviews focussed too much on the film's "alleged salacity" to the detriment of its overall intentions.[52]

De Niro, as ever, conscientiously chose the outfits he wore and eased himself into the part as one would into a comfortable armchair. Having said that, he was still a standard issue Mephistopheles, and probably could have phoned in his performance as he never threatened to break into a sweat. Rourke, on the other hand, did enough sweating for both of them, especially in the final scenes where Mr Cyphre collects his unpaid-for debt courtesy of a voodoo priestess named Epiphany Proudfoot (Bonet) who gets shot through the vagina on Rourke's bed while Cyphre sits on the sidelines filing his pointed nails.

"You'll burn for this," says a policeman standing over Proudfoot's dead body, the pun obvious, which renders Rourke's reply "I know—in hell" rather superfluous. All that remains now is for Rourke to plummet down through a squeaky elevator as the final credits roll.

With narrowed eyes, ponytailed hair and a goatee, De Niro certainly looked the part, but in a sense he let all of these accoutrements do the acting for him. His preparation for the role was meticulous (he agonized so much about doing it, it took him three months to finally say yes to Parker) but the execution was perfunctory.

Despite this, Parker was generous in his praise of De Niro: "I've never met an actor who put so much into a part, and such a small part at that."[53] Andy Dougan felt he looked "suitably Mephistophelean with his long hair, beard and impossibly long fingernails, which he drums on his Malacca cane."[54]

Dougan felt the overall enterprise was juvenile, however, and De Niro a "comic book Satan" whose role demanded little of him but to "smile sardonically in a variety of shadowed locations, hands folded on his cane to display his lengthening nails, and bounce oneliners off a deadpan Rourke."[55] He also felt the final image of the freight train descending "interminably, presumably into hell, belonged in a thirties Broadway revival of *Faust*."[56]

De Niro afterward confessed that he preferred playing villains to heroes because they gave him more scope for artistic expansion. Virtue was often bland, or boring. People tended to identify more with vice because we were all flawed.

For Ms Bonet, previously known to U.S. viewers for *The Cosby Show*, the transition was mind-boggling: a bit like *I Love Lucy* crossed with *The Devil in Miss Jones*.

"Selling out can happen in a lot of different ways," Mickey Rourke is quoted as saying in Bart Mills' *Mickey Rourke* (Sidgwick & Jackson, 1988, p. 66), "You make deals not with the devil, but within yourself. You do sell your soul in a way." If this is true, Hollywood got a Luciferean revenge on him in the following years by sending him on a different kind of elevator to celluloid obscurity.

There were no less than four different representations of the devil in Martin Scorsese's *The Last Temptation of Christ* (1988). The first was as a serpent speaking with the voice of Mary Magdalene. This was an obvious throwback to the Garden of Eden. The second was as a lion, Scorsese name checking The Book of Daniel. It was also a pillar of fire (The Book of Exodus was the source here) and finally a beautiful woman.

Jeff Goldblum played the devil as a serial-killer in *Mr. Frost* (1990). Arrested after having been discovered with multiple mutilated bodies to his credit, he proceeds to give the shocked detective (Alan Bates) a videotape of his crimes. Incarcerated afterward in an asylum, he refuses to speak to anyone except psychologist Kathy Burke, to whom he reveals that he is in fact the devil himself. "I am the extreme case," he says, lamenting the fact that so many misdeeds in the world are put down to dysfunctionality instead of good old-fashioned evil.

He continues to kill from the asylum, using mind control to possess people's souls, but the one he's really after is that of Burke herself, which he eventually manages to get after she shoots him. In a chilling finale, we realize Burke has actually *become* Frost. This was a fascinating, under-appreciated film which refused to wallow in its violence, concentrating instead on Goldblum's subtle strategies to secure scalps.

Exorcist III was also released in 1990, a jaded amalgam of the other two. By now the franchise had totally outlived its usefulness and despite the efforts of a quality cast (George C. Scott, Nicol Williamson, and Brad Dourif) it failed to re-heat the *soufflé*.

There were corpses a-plenty and a token effort to analyze why such horrible things were going on, but by now the satanic cult had begat more imaginative devil's children and this was where the future lay. Friedkin had let the genie out of the bottle and seventeen years later nobody had quite emulated him.

Scott's presence in itself was almost enough to carry the film, which did rouse genuine fear in the manner of its dispensing of corpses—in particular that of a priest whose entire blood supply is impeccably bottled *a la* Hannibal Lecter—but Dourif's Machiavellian prognostications and Scott's final crucifixion pose against an asylum wall, followed by his redemptive line "We won" after he shoots the sacrificial lamb, made you feel a certain element of shock fatigue.

The original *Exorcist* had a surprise factor, and a lengthy lead-up to the gore which gave it genuine drama, but sequels have a habit of jumping in head first without any respect for viewers' intelligence. Such was the case here, which made you doubly frustrated that the undeniable talents of both Scott and Dourif didn't have a more productive tableau upon which to express themselves. *Exorcist III* was a brooding threnody that did few favors for itself. After the disaster of *Exorcist II* so many years before one might have been entitled to expect something more than this tired rehash of routine mania, we won? No, sorry. We lost. Again.

Linda Blair turned up in *Repossessed* that year too, returning to what she knew best after failing to make a film career since *The Exorcist*. Playing a character who'd been possessed seventeen years earlier (just in case we forgot), she's now in the clutches of Beelzebub once again, Leslie Nielson's exorcism failing to hold. The latest effort to rid her of her demons is performed by a rookie priest on TV as a fundraiser, this being the televangelical age. But, wouldn't you know, it all goes wrong and Nielson, who's been recalled to help out, gets himself transmuted into various guises, among them a rabbi, Groucho Marx, Rambo and The Singing Nun.

A rock band that recruits the help of the Pope and the Dalai Lama is then called up to trill "Devil in a Blue Dress." This is enough to finally get rid of him—and us. The film was an unmitigated disaster but pre-dated the spate of horror-comedies that would infest our screens with alarming frequency right into the new millennium. It also set Nielson up for the *Naked Gun* trilogy in its scabrous chutzpah.

Stay Tuned (1992) built itself around the idea of television junkies being imprisoned inside the TVs they loved so much from the outside, essaying a number of doughty tasks in endurance game show mode to stave off eternal damnation. This is the flipside of the *Pleasantville* coin, a film in which "Reality TV" acquires horrific ramifications.

John Ritter and Pam Dawber are an average suburban couple but she's concerned that he's spending too much time watching the goggle box. When "Spike," the devil, offers him the ultimate satellite system he's an easy victim but no doubt he would have preferred *I Love Lucy* to Spike's preferred *I Love Lucifer*. Other genres are covered too, all the way from sci-fi programs to cartoons, thrillers to historical dramas and sport to sitcoms. A black comedy that's guaranteed to cure television addicts the world over, Jeffrey Jones as the devil gets the best line, as he advertises his attractive multi-channel package: "People would give their souls for a system like this." They do too.

Robert Vaughn played the devil in *Witch Academy* that year as well. This was a juvenile comedy featuring a bunch of scantilyclad sorority girls who spend most of their time playing wicked practical jokes on one another. The fun begins when Vaughn offers to change one of them, the put-upon Veronica Carothers, into a beauty when she expresses the wish to be rich, beautiful and powerful one night after she's had enough of their cruel japes. You don't make a deal with the devil without paying the price, though. In addition to helping her get revenge on her frat pals, Vaughn wants her to kill people and then marry him so he can populate the planet with his little grandchildren.

As well as calling the shots he gets most of the film's best lines as well. The reaction to his first appearance is "Oh my God!" to which he replies tartly, "Not quite." Later on Carothers says to him, "If you really are the devil, where are your horns?" "Gone," he tells her, "the wonders of cosmetic surgery."

Max Von Sydow played the devil in *Needful Things* (1993), one of the few actors to have been both God and the devil on screen. (Rex Ingram and George Burns shared the honor.) Based on a Stephen King novel, it has him as a small town shop-owner who offers his customers items they desperately want without charging them. All they have to do to earn their purchase is play a practical joke on one of their neighbors. This may sound harmless but it opens a Pandora's Box of acrimony, eventually leading to murder.

Ed Harris is the town sheriff but he's not much of a match for Von Sydow, who tells him, "You can't win. I've got God on my side. He tolerates my little shenanigans. A famine here, a flood there, a little blood-lust, a broken heart . . . So get off my case, I'm just a fall guy." When another customer in the shop exclaims "Jesus Christ" in surprise after being impressed by a gun, Sydow cuts in with, "The young carpenter from Nazareth? I knew him well. A promising young man. He died badly."

Being a Stephen King adaptation it was tailor-made for such acerbic wit but the most amusing line of all came from a crew member. One day he spotted the director, Fraser Heston, giving some tips to Von Sydow. Aware that Heston—Charlton's son—had played the baby Moses in *The Ten Commandments*, and also that Von Sydow had been Jesus in *The Greatest Story Ever Told*, he chirped, "Now you don't see that often; there's Moses telling Christ how to play the devil!"[57]

Viggo Mortenson was the devil in *The Prophecy* (1995) but the film is really about the Angel Gabriel, played with uniquely spooky appeal by Christopher Walken. This was a new take on celestial malevolence. Walken is annoyed that God is spending too much time thinking about humans, leaving him to do thankless tasks. He rebels like Lucifer, embarking on a quest to find the soul of an evil general to help him corrupt the planet. Eric Stoltz, meanwhile, is the "good" angel who's "hidden" the said soul in the body of a Native American girl. There's also priest-turned-cop Elias Koteas. If all this sounds ridiculous it's because it is, but Walken would look good even reading the phone book and he gives it a crazy kind of credibility.

The Mephistolean theme was transmuted into a legal context (lawyers generally being soft targets for demonization) in Taylor Hackford's *The Devil's Advocate* in 1997. This begins with small-town attorney Keanu Reeves defending a guilty-as-sin child molester after some momentary soul-searching in mid-trial.

His wife, Charlize Theron, who's just as ambitious as he is, eggs him on. There's also a journalist who taunts him in the men's room, and a mysterious ring. At the celebration party to toast his success at winning yet another difficult case he's approached by a lawyer from New York who hands him a juicy check to up sticks and move to the Big Apple. Theron is overjoyed.

They move into a lush apartment with all the creature comforts and a commanding view of the city. The only problem is that Reeves is out a lot. Theron soon gets bored decorating. Neither is she over the moon about her female "minders," particularly when one of them asks her to feel her bare breast to prove that it's real. A moment later the woman's face turns grotesque and her body starts to deform itself horrifically. Is she hallucinating?

Reeves meets his boss, the charismatic John Milton (Al Pacino). The fact that his is also the name of the man who wrote *Paradise Lost* doesn't register with Reeves, his main reading material being arcane law books.

Pacino brings Reeves onto the roof of his office. It has a crucifix-shaped path surrounded by water. "You're killing me with kindness," Reeves remarks—significantly. Pacino says that's company policy. Reeves looks over the edge and nearly falls. "It's different when you're looking down," Pacino remarks. Satan usually has a worm's eye view of life. When we first see him he's going down into a subway. This is reminiscent of the penultimate scene from *Jesus of Montreal*, the underground standing in for Hades there as well.

Pacino's living quarters are standard gothic. Only someone as dim as Reeves could fail to react to their excesses. "Where does he sleep?" is all he can say, having noted the absence of a bed. "How do you know he sleeps?" one of his associates responds. Reeves then asks, "Where does he fuck?" to which Pacino answers deliciously, "Everywhere!"

Reeves' career goes on the up and up. More bad cases, more big payouts and an ever-growing reputation for never losing. One of his clients is an O.J. Simpson-style character with a dodgy alibi. Reeves runs with it and the man is acquitted. Theron, meanwhile, starts to go round the twist.

Pacino is so entrancing in the part you start to feel that if you were indeed to sell your soul there's nobody you'd prefer to sell it to than this man. He hams it up in the last quarter but this is his prerogative. He plays the hard-done-by fallen angel to perfection. "Maybe God threw the dice once too often," he complains, "maybe he let us all down." And elsewhere, "I'm the hand on the Mona Lisa's skirt; they don't see me coming." Hackford has made him as ugly as he can with his slicked-back hair, nefarious smile and piercing eyes. He even gives him a cloven hoof effect by having him wear Cuban heels. But none of this is over-insistent. We're still watching Al Pacino all the while.

Some of his lines are overly suggestive. "I see the future," he announces at one point, and then, after a pregnant pause, "of this firm." We also get the inevitable, "Speak of the devil." The scene where he persuades Theron to put her hair back—changing hairstyles become almost a motif of unhingement—is vintage Pacino. Who could resist this kind of persuasiveness?

There's not much logic in the unfolding of events. The big surprise, though many will guess it, is that Pacino is actually Reeves' father. When his Bible-thumping mother comes to visit him in New York she meets Pacino in an elevator and it all comes back to her. This was the man who impregnated her, who subsequently walked out. But obviously he's been watching his son's progress through the legal profession with some interest.

In another type of film the woman would have run to Reeves with this revelation immediately. But this isn't another type of film. Instead she just broods quietly about it.

Equally hard to fathom is Reeves' reaction to Theron's incarceration in a psychiatric ward. Okay, so he gets a bit upset when she slits her throat with some broken glass but he's over it in a few minutes, concerning himself instead with his relationship to Pacino.

When Pacino finally reveals who he is—duh—the man helping Reeves to win all these unwinnable cases, Reeves allows himself some mild surprise.

Pacino's dialogue is choice here. "Let me give you a little inside information about God," he enthuses. "God likes to watch. He's a prankster. He gives you this extraordinary gift, and then, for his own amusement, his own private cosmic gag reel, he sets the rules in opposition. It's the goof of all time. Look but don't touch. Touch but don't taste. Taste, don't swallow. Ah ha! And when you're jumping from one foot to the next, what is He doing? He's laughing His sick fuckin' ass off. He's a tight ass. He's a sadist. He's an absentee landlord. Worship that? Never!" Here we have the Luciferean pride that goes all the way back to the other John Milton.

But now comes the nub of the issue. To repay his father for services rendered Reeves is requested to impregnate his half-sister (a lady in whom he has evinced a pronounced sexual interest) so Pacino can increase the satanic population of New York. Reeves begins the necessaries but then hauls back and blows his brains out. (The audience may be forgiven for having doubted he had any in the first place.)

"Free will," he mutters to Pacino before he dies. One is almost disappointed to see the "bad guy" scream "No!" as his plan is thwarted. Reeves has decided it's better to be a slave in heaven than to reign in hell, unlike his Daddy. "Behold," his mother had warned, "I send you out as sheep among the wolves," a quotation Pacino repeats. Reeves became a wolf himself for a time, but now he's reverted back. The manner in which he commits suicide, thereby saving the city, and his own soul, is reminiscent of the last scene in *The Manchurian Candidate* where Laurence Harvey, an equally brainwashed victim, perpetrated a similar martyr-like act. At this point we get the expectable fireball, falling frescoes and whatnot. His half-sister is also dispatched to Hades.

As a reward God reincarnates him, sending him back to the trial of the child molester whom he's defended so immorally.

Will he do so again? No. The new and improved Reeves, having presumably seen how the whole soul-selling thing would have panned out after taking a long hard look at himself in the mirror, decides to go the virtuous route instead. He refuses to defend the child molester, deciding a small-town life with his lady-love, financially restricting as that might be, is the best way forward.

At which point the journalist who'd taunted him before tells him the idea of a lawyer following his conscience would make a great newspaper story. He's willing to pay him handsomely for the exclusive. "Call me in the morning," Reeves says after thinking about it for a moment. At which point the journalist morphs into Pacino. The old devil is up for more mischief.

"Vanity," he exclaims as the film fades out, "my favorite sin." In other words, there's more than one way to skin a cat.

Pacino does a choice imitation of Reeves at one point, and even of Frank Sinatra singing "It Happened in Monterey," letting us know in no uncertain terms that he doesn't take any of this hokum seriously, which means we react to the black humor with more humor than blackness. Would that Reeves could be so cavalier.

There were no less than four Satanic films made in 1999: *South Park: Bigger, Longer and Uncut*, an outrageous animated effort in which Satan even gets to cozy up to Saddam Hussein; *Bedazzled*, a forgettable comedy, *End of Days*, an even more forgettable drama, and *The Ninth Gate*, a welcome return to form for Roman Polanski, the man who really started it all.

Bedazzled was a re-make of the 1967 film of the same name discussed earlier. In this version Liz Hurley, who was more noted for wearing (or should I say almost wearing) spectacular dresses than her acting ability, was cast in the role of the devil, with Brendan Fraser playing the man she toys with.

She offers him "seven utterly fabulous wishes for one piddling little soul," which does sound like a good bargain the way she puts it. "I can't give you my soul," Fraser counters. "What are you—James Brown?" "Souls are over-rated," Hurley replies, "It's like your appendix. You'll never miss it."

His first wish is to be rich and powerful and to be married to Frances O'Connor, the woman he loves. She grants this but makes him a

Colombian drug dealer who gets caught. O'Connor, meanwhile, sets her sights on another man.

Hurley tells him women aren't necessarily attracted to wealth, but rather emotional sensitivity. He goes for this next but overdoes it, getting sand kicked in his face at a beach as he weeps over a beautiful sunset. O'Connor makes off with the man who kicks the sand. And it's hard to blame her.

For his third wish he asks to be a huge and famous basketball player. O'Connor is the journalist trying to get off with him until she sees he isn't sexually well endowed. He's also a birdbrain.

His fourth wish is to be made into a rich and famous intellectual who *is* well endowed. This is arranged, but when he brings Ms O'Connor back to his apartment for some rumpy-bumpy he's somewhat disconcerted to see his lover there before him . . . a man.

By now he should be asking for brain cells from Hurley. Instead he asks her to make him into somebody who did something important for mankind. Fine. She turns him into Abraham Lincoln—on the night he's about to be assassinated.

He's now informed he has just one wish left, Hurley having sneakily counted a desire for a Big Mac earlier on as one of the seven. Realizing he's up against the stops he decides to go to confession. He tells a priest everything and the priest, a man of eminently more sense than he, calls the police. In jail he meets God, a black man who tries to give him some good advice. When he gets out he tells Hurley he's had enough of this wish business and she throws him into hell in a temper. While there he makes a wish that O'Connor will be happy. The attack of virtue makes Hurley redundant but she takes it like a man. Back in the real world he tries to get off with O'Connor but fails. Nonetheless, another woman materializes so there might be hope for him after all. At the end of the film he sees God playing chess with Hurley in the park. Ingmar Bergman it's not.

Fraser doesn't have much star appeal but he acts his socks off in his various incarnations. Hurley's nonchalance, on the contrary, makes hers a one-note performance. She lacks Peter Cook's charm from the original. (Raquel Welch was such a hit as Lust in that film, maybe they got the idea for making the devil into a sexy woman right there.)

On the credit side, she gets most of the film's best lines. When Fraser tells her he thinks she's "hot" before he knows who she is, she replies, "Baby, you have no idea." In the restaurant ordering the Big Mac she asks him to pay because "I left my purse in the underworld." After she meets him first she says, "You can ask me anything you like except is there a God—I get that one all the time." She then concedes that there is, and that he's male. "Most men think they're God," she expounds. "This one just happens to be right." In a more frustrated mood she reveals that she's "stuck in this horrible job for eternity. Everybody hates me. My life is a living hell."

Bedazzled didn't use the fact that it was made in the last year of a millennium to any effect, unlike the frenzied *End of Days*, which threatened an almighty retribution if Arnold Schwarzenegger, a security man who's on the side of the angels for a change, tries to fight off the demonic threat of Gabriel Byrne, a most unconvincing devil. The film would possibly have worked better if the roles were reversed but even then it would have been little more than an excuse for a barrage of millennial mumbo-jumbo.

Byrne wants to "blood" himself as an earthling by finding some suitable woman to walk up the marital aisle with so he can birth an anti-Christ, just to get the new century off to a good start. There are lots of fireballs and suchlike, not to mention Rod Steiger as a priest who's in the unfortunate position of having to say lines like "There are forces at work here that you couldn't possibly comprehend."

Roman Polanski gave us a female devil played by his real-life wife, Emmanuelle Siegner, in the 20th century's last great satanic movie, *The Ninth Gate*. In fact it makes his earlier *Rosemary's Baby* look almost quaint by comparison. It's a luscious, literary film, Johnny Depp playing a rare book dealer employed by rich bibliophile Frank Langella to ensure that his copy of the 17th century book *The Nine Gates of the Kingdom of Shadows* is the real deal. There are two other copies of it in existence and Langella also wants Depp to check if these are forgeries or not.

The man who sold Langella his book commits suicide at the start of the film. Depp then interviews his widow, Lena Olin, who proceeds to seduce him so she can get the book for herself for her own devious purposes. He asks a friend (James Russo) to mind it for him and Russo is murdered, hanged upside down in the manner of one of the book's engravings. Depp now decides he wants out but Langella ups his fee. Thereafter he gets sucked into the riddle of the authorship and the engravings on the book, turning from mercenary to a genuine acolyte of the Prince of Darkness.

It's a gory film but never gratuitously so. It's richly textured, deliriously decadent. Not so much a film to make your flesh crawl as to have you sit up in wonderment as Depp gets entranced by the chase. It doesn't sell itself out for the cheap shock and is doubly shocking for that because we really feel these cultists mean business. In the autumn of his career one might have feared that Polanski would "go" Hollywood on us but instead of that he's become even more counter-cultural than of yore, biting away at the gothic underlay of his moody canvas.

What a pity, then, that 2000, the first year of the new millennium, dragged us back to the kind of clichéd formulas lazy directors always used to appeal to the lower end of the market. Instead of the imaginative fervor of *The Ninth Gate* we got *Little Nicky, Lost Souls*, and *Bless the Child*, each more reprehensible than the one before.

Maybe the last depths of ridicule for Beelzebub were plumbed in *Little Nicky*, where Harvey Keitel contemplates retiring from the infernal throne before deciding to stay on for another 10,000 years—presumably for the enhanced pension plan. This decision outrages his two elder sons, who decide to go from hell to New York—Travis Bickle didn't see much of a difference—to subvert his authority. Adrian (Rhys Ifans) is the eldest, with Cassius (Tiny Lister) the next in line.

Keitel tries to scupper their plan by sending his youngest son Nicky (Adam Sandler in familiarly gawky, baby-voiced form) to bring them back in a magic flask. By the time he gets there, Cassius has already possessed the Mayor, who's lowered the drinking age of the city to ten and changed its motto from "I Love New York" to "I Love Hookers." Adrian, meanwhile, has got into the Cardinal's soul and has him saying things like "Let the sin begin."

Sandler eventually gets them both into the flask, which Keitel proceeds to stuff up the anus of Adolf Hitler and Nicky goes back to earth to marry a design artist he's fallen in love with. He's allowed do this because he's really half-angel, as one might have guessed from his gentle, stuttering ways. As Ifans says to him in the film's best line, "Even the voice inside your head has a speech impediment."

Lost Souls was a supernatural thriller featuring Winona Ryder as a character who latches on to a scheme whereby the devil is about to invade the body of an atheistic crime writer and terrorize the earth. Winona has to get to the writer first and make him believe in God in this post-*Omen* slice of tosh.

Winona was herself possessed as a child but now works with a priest (John Hurt) performing her exorcisms. It's when she's having trouble trying to get rid of a devil from a murderer that the crime writer Ben Chaplin, in a woeful piece of miscasting, pops up. It's all about as

credible as the fact that a rich actress would find herself accused of robbing a department store in broad daylight.

Satan's School For Kids also came out that year. A re-make of a 1978
TV movie with Pamela Franklin, it had Shannen Doherty enrolling at a
prestigious college in the attempt to learn what drove her younger sister
to suicide the year before, only to discover a coven of witches in residence, with the ambition of (what else) taking over the world.

Bless the Child was another assembly line product cranked out in by-
numbers mode, Kim Basinger playing a woman who tries to protect her
daughter from Rufus Sewell. The film fires a lot of salvoes without being
even vaguely scary, a unique achievement. Basinger's grand-daughter, it
turns out, was born on a date that qualifies her for "Slaughter of the Inno-
cents" status (the director feels the need to explain that term to us) and
other children with the same unfortunate birthday have been abducted by
Mr Sewell and his cadre of equally bloodthirsty souls so they can eradicate good from the world. The little mite is autistic but has paranormal
powers which could threaten Sewell's ambition to—whisper it—banish
virtue from the world forever.

The film starts off as a family drama with Basinger looking after Cody,
the child, because his mother Angela Bettis, Kim's sister, has a drug
problem. Bettis is out of sight for six years and then turns up at Kim's
house, Rufus in tow, and says it's time she had the little girl back, she
being the mother and all. Kim has worries about the drugs but then realizes the problem goes a bit deeper. She doesn't really like Rufus, who's a
bit pushy about the custody thing. She doesn't know about his demonic
nature at this stage but you sense these things, don't you?

After Rufus kidnaps Cody he tries to get her to jump from a big building, saying things like, "Tonight you could be reborn for my Lord: or die
for yours," and "Does God even exist? Maybe he's just a nice idea—like
the Easter bunny." This is all fiercely interesting, but we just know she
won't fall for his evil machinations.

In the end, we feel this horrible man isn't going to be able to use her to
fulfil his ambition of taking over the world, or whatever, so it's time to
reserve all the hosannas for herself and Kim, who goes in hot pursuit
with an FBI agent (Jimmy Smits) who knows a thing or three about the
occult. He doesn't stop Kim getting shot dead by Rufus but the spiritual
power guiding herself and Cody brings her back to life. Nice trick.
She should thank Cody as well. Who wouldn't be without a daughter
like that? Christina Ricci co-stars as another druggie who loses her

head—literally—in this godawful piece of claptrap where the good/evil dichotomy is far too bald and the special effects aren't very special.

The Sin Eater (2003) starred Heath Ledger as a member of an arcane order of priests sent to Rome to investigate the death of the head of the order. The body of the dead man has strange marks on the chest which are those of the eponymous sin eater, i.e., a renegade spirit that effects absolution on corpses by sucking their souls out and taking their sins into themselves. The less said about this the better.

In *The Passion of the Christ* (2004), Mel Gibson's controversial take on the last twelve hours of Jesus' life, we had a rarefied, androgynous Satan. Only when the final credits roll does one realize it's a woman. There are no cloven hoofs here, or raging fires of hell, just touches like a child in his/her arms suddenly morphing into an old man, and an insect crawling up his/her nose. The manner in which (s)he drifts through the film owes something to *The Ninth Gate* where Emmanuelle Siegner did likewise. His/her question, "Do you think that one man can take the full burden of sin?" is also reminiscent of Scorsese's devil in *Last Temptation*, who posed a similar conundrum.

After Jesus is crucified, there's an effective aerial shot of the diabolical reaction. Humanity has been saved—for a few millennia anyway.

Two-thousand nine saw a re-make of *Dorian Gray* which souped-up the gothic element. Ben Barnes played the dandified cad who sells his soul to the devil amidst much gore and debauchery under the auspices of an eventually disapproving Mephistopheles in the figure of Colin Firth, whose daughter Barnes romances before the climactic bloodbath as the picture in the attic wreaks a truly gruesome, if inevitable, revenge.

Old wine in new bottles? Indeed, but sometimes the well-tried yarns outdo the more contrived contemporary ones. Oscar Wilde knew what he was talking about when he prophesied that man would always lust after youth. It's just a pity he didn't live to see the Botox generation.

Notes

CHAPTER 1

1. *Hollywood Wit*. Rosemary Jarski, Prion, 2000, p. 68.
2. *Bloomsbury Dictionary of Quotations*. 1991, p. 1.
3. *Oxymoronica*. Ed. Mardy Grothe, HarperCollins, 2004, p. 150.
4. *Reading the Gospels in the Dark*. Peter Fraser, Trinity Press, 2003, p. 2.
5. *Ultimate Wit*. Des MacHale, Mercier, 2002, p. 84.
6. *Charlton Heston: A Biography*. Michael Munn, Robson, 1986, p. 18.
7. *Cecil B. DeMille: The Man and His Pictures*. Pete Gabe Essoe and Raymond Lee, Castle Books, 1970, p. 219.
8. *The Hollywood Tycoons*. Norman Ziebold, p. 177.
9. *Movie Talk*. Ed. David Shipman, Bloomsbury, 1988, p. 54.
10. *The DeMilles: An American Family*. Anne Edwards, Collins, 1988, p. 85.
11. *In the Arena*. Charlton Heston, HarperCollins, 1995, p. 109.
12. *Ibid.,* p. 103.
13. *The Movie Book*. Don Schiach, Acropolis, 1992, p. 12.
14. *Ibid.,* p. 169.
15. *Autobiography*. W.H. Allen, 1960, p. 235.
16. *Cecil B. DeMille*. Charles Higham, Charles Scribner & Sons, 1973, p. 61.
17. *Yes, Mr. DeMille*. Phil A. Kovary, Putnam, 1959, pp. 280–281.
18. *Cecil B. DeMille: The Man and His Pictures*.
19. *Ibid.,* p. 208.
20. *Hollywood Censored*. Gregory Black, Cambridge University Press, 1994, p. 29.
21. *People on People*. Ed. Susan Radcliffe, Oxford University Press, 2001, p. 103.

22. *Reading the Gospels in the Dark.* p. 12.

23. *Cecil B. DeMille.* Charles Higham, Charles Scribner, p. 160.

24. *Divine Images.* Roy Kinnear and Tim Davis, Citadel, 1992, p. 43.

25. *The Epic Film.* Routledge & Kegan Paul, 1984, p. 45.

26. *Hollywood Babble On.* Boze Hadleigh, Birch Lane Press, 1994, p. 12.

27. *Movie Talk,* p. 54.

28. *Cassell's Movie Quotations.* Ed. Nigel Rees, 2000, p. 110.

29. *Ibid.,* p. 195.

30. *Hollywood Wit,* p. 69.

31. *Talking Pictures.* Arrow, 1987, p. 32.

32. *Lights, Camera, Action,* p. 218.

33. *Forbidden Films.* Dawn B. Sova, Checkmark Books, 2001, p. 273.

34. *The Whole Equation.* David Thomson, Little Brown & Co., 2005, p. 154.

35. *Ecstacy and Me.* Hedy Lamarr. W.H. Allen. 1967, p. 138.

36. *Censored Hollywood.* Turner Publishing, 1994, p. 63.

37. *The Hollywood History of the World,* p. 124.

38. *Ibid.,* p. xiii.

39. *Hollywood in the Thirties.* John Baxter, Tantivy Press, 1968, p. 35.

40. *Guinness Dictionary of Poisonous Quotations.* Ed. Colin Jarman, 1991, p. 114.

41. *Hollywood Wit,* p. 69.

42. *Movies: A Crash Course.* John Naughton and Adam Smith, Simon & Schuster, 1998, p. 20.

43. *An Empire of Their Own: How the Jews Invented Hollywood.* W.H. Allen, 1989, p. 205.

44. *The DeMilles: An American Family,* p. 122.

45. *Hollywood Censored,* p. 66.

46. *Ibid.*

47. Daniel Lord to Cecil B DeMille, April 10, 1932, DeMille Collection.

48. *Swanson on Swanson,* p. 345.

49. *Cecil B. DeMille.* Charles Higham, p. 166.

50. *Sin and Censorship.* Frank Walsh, University Press, 1996, p. 80.

51. *People on People,* p. 104.

52. *TheDeMilles: An American Family,* p. 83.

53. *Ibid.,* p. 123.

54. *True Confessions.* Ed. Jon Winokur, Victor Gollancz, 1992, p. 75.

55. *Celluloid Saints: Images of Sanctity in Film.* Mercer University Press, 2002, p. 39.

56. *Ibid.*

57. *Guinness Book of Humorous Anecdotes.* Nigel Rees, 1994, p. 132.

58. *The Movie Brats.* Michael Pye and Lynda Myles, Faber, 1979, p. 19.

59. *Pan Book of Contemporary Quotations.* Compiled by Jonathon Green, 1989, p. 183.

60. *Take Two: A Life in the Movies and Politics,* McGraw-Hill, p. 250.

61. *Ibid.,* p. 252.

62. *The Epic Film.* Routledge & Kegan Paul, 1984, p. 47.

63. *Rita Hayworth: Portrait of a Love Goddess.* John Kobal, Berkley Books, 1982, p. 247.

64. *The Hollywood History of the World,* p. 29.

65. *Divine Images,* p. 84.

66. *The Bad and the Beautiful.* Sam Kashner and Jennifer MacNair, Little Brown & Co., 2002, p. 129.

67. *Ibid.,* p. 130.

68. *The Dilys Powell Film Reader.* Ed. Christopher Cook, Carcanet, 1991, p. 302.

69. *The Epic Film,* p. 128.

70. *Take Two,* p. 255.

71. *The Worst Movies of All Time.* Michael Sauter, Citadel, 1999, p. 54.

72. *Paul Newman.* Daniel O'Brien, Faber, 2004, p. 24.

73. *Ibid.*

74. *Ibid.,* p. 26.

75. *Ibid.,* p. 28.

76. *Paul Newman.* Elena Oumano, Robert Hale, 1990, p. 47.

77. *The Epic Film,* p. 42.

78. *The Hollywood History of the World,* p. xii.

79. *True Confessions,* p. 102.

80. *Hollywood Wit,* p. 69.

81. *Ibid.,* p. 20.

82. *Adventures in the Screen Trade.* Futura, 1990, p. 103.

83. *People on People,* p. 103.

84. *The DeMilles: An American Family,* p. 207.

85. *Charlton Heston: A Biography,* p. 63.

86. *The DeMilles,* pp. 207–208.

87. *In the Arena,* p. 131.

88. *The Dilys Powell Film Reader,* p. 305.

89. *Charlton Heston: A Biography,* p. 71.

90. *Religion in Film.* University of Tennessee Press, 1982, p. 28.

91. *Movies: A Crash Course,* p. 74.

92. *Take Two,* p. 256.

93. *Oxford Dictionary of Humorous Quotations.* Ed. Ned Sherrin, 2001, p. 120.

94. *Hollywood Wit,* p. 70.

95. *Ibid.,* p. 69.

96. *People on People,* p. 103.

97. *In the Arena,* p. 205.

98. *Guinness Dictionary of Poisonous Quotations,* p. 134.

99. *Photoplay.* January, 1975.

100. *The Movies: An Illustrated History of Cinema.* Adrian Turner, Orbis, 1980, p. 814.

101. *Palimpsest: A Memoir.* Gore Vidal. Andre Deutsch, 1995, p. 303.

102. *Ibid.,* p. 305.

103. *In the Arena,* p. 206.

104. *Faith and Film.* Chalice Press, 2000, p. 70.

105. *Ibid.*

106. *Ibid.,* p. 71.

107. *Charlton Heston: A Biography,* p. 115.

108. *Videohound Epics,* p. 62.

109. *In the Arena,* p. 299.

110. *An Open Book.* John Huston, Da Capo, 1994, p. 321.

111. *Ibid.,* p. 320.

112. *The Hollywood History of the World,* p. 5.

113. *Hollywood and After.* Jerzy Toeplitz, Allen & Unwin, 1974, p. 49.

114. *Take Two,* p. 247.

115. *Ibid.,* pp. 249–250.

CHAPTER 2

1. *The DeMilles: An American Family,* p. 104.

2. *Ibid.*

3. *Explorations in Theology and Film.* Blackwell, 1997, p. 129.

4. *Hollywood Wit.*

5. *The Dilys Powell Film Reader,* p. 309.

6. *Sin and Censorship: The Catholic Church and the Motion Picture Industry.* Frank Walsh, Yale University Press, 1996, p. 295.

7. P. 46.

8. *Imaging the Divine: Jesus and Christ Figures in Film.* Lloyd Baugh, Sheed & Ward, 1997, p. 52.

9. *Divine Images,* p. 131.

10. *Reading the Gospels in the Dark,* p. 133.

11. *Biblical Epics: Sacred Narratives in the Hollywood Cinema.* Bruce Babington and Peter William Evans, Manchester University Press, 1993, p. 133.

12. *Divine Images,* p. 132.

13. *Ibid.*

14. *Ibid.*

15. *Lights, Camera, Action.* John Gau and Tony Bilboa. Little Brown, 1995, pp. 190–191.

16. *The Epic Film,* p. 44.

17. *Images of the Passion*, p. 68.

18. *Saviour on the Silver Screen*. Richard C. Stern, Clayton N. Jefford, Guerric DeBona, Paulist Press, 1999, p. 112.

19. *Reading the Gospels in the Dark*, p. 171.

20. *Ibid.*, p. 154.

21. *The Word Made Flesh*. Scarecrow Press, 1998, p. 91.

22. *Divine Images*, p. 161.

23. *Explorations in Theology and Film*, p. 236.

24. *Imaging the Divine.*

25. *Photoplay*. July, 1987.

26. *Saviour on the Silver Screen*, p. 180.

27. *Reading the Gospels in the Dark*, p. 35.

28. *Ibid.*, p. 36.

29. *Ibid.*, p. 5.

30. *Divine Images*, p. 189.

31. *Imaging the Divine*, p. 83.

32. *Empire*. March 2003, p. 146.

33. *Ibid.*

34. *Playboy*. November, 1979, p. 216.

35. *New York Times*. 17 August, 1979.

36. *Divine Images*, p. 146.

37. *Easy Riders, Raging Bulls*. Peter Biskind, Bloomsbury, 1998, p. 406.

38. *Ibid.*

39. *Forbidden Films*, p. 174.

40. *Reading the Gospels in the Dark*, p. 34.

41. *Alien Sex*, p. 258.

42. *Schrader on Schrader and Other Writings*. Kevin Jackson, Faber, 1990, pp. 135–140.

43. *Film, Faith and Cultural Conflict*. Robin Riley, Praeger, 2003, p. 88.

44. *Divine Images*, p. 207.

45. *Ibid.*

46. *Martin Scorsese: A Journey*. Mary Pat Kelly, Thunder's Mouth Press, 1991, p. 6.

47. *The Word Made Flesh*. Scarecrow Press, 1998, p. 91.

48. *Ibid.*

49. *New York Times*. August 13, 1998.

50. *Film, Faith and Cultural Conflict*, p. 129.

51. *Ibid.*, p. 21.

52. *Ibid.*, p. 124.

53. *Schrader on Schrader*, p. 135.

54. *Faith and Film: Theological Themes of the Cinema*. Chalice Press, 2000, p. 54.

55. *Images of the Passion: The Sacramental Mode in Film.* Peter Fraser, Praeger, 1998, p. 103.

56. *Ibid.,* p. 106.

57. *Newsweek.* February 18, 2004, pp. 54–55.

58. *Mel Gibson: Man on a Mission.* Wensley Clarkson, Blake, 2004, p. 232.

59. *Newsweek.* February 18, 2004, p. 55.

60. *Ibid.*

61. *The Times.* 25 March, 2004, p. 3.

62. *Ibid.*

63. *Ibid.,* p. 2.

64. *Mel Gibson: Man on a Mission,* p. 330.

65. *March 11, 2004.*

66. *Ibid.*

67. *Mel Gibson: Man on a Mission,* p. 340.

68. *Newsweek.* February 18, 2004, p. 54.

69. *Sunday Independent.* April 4, 2004.

70. *Ibid.*

71. *Eyes Wide Open: Looking for God in Popular Culture.* William Romanovski. Brazos Press, p. 133.

72. *Newsweek.* February 18, 2004, p. 15.

73. *Sight and Sound.* 4, 2004, p. 15.

74. *Irish Times.* October 11, 2003.

75. *Ibid.*

CHAPTER 3

1. *Caught in the Act.* David Shipman. Elm Tree Books, 1985, p. 108.

2. *Notorious: The Life of Ingrid Bergman.* HarperCollins, 1997, p. 180.

3. *Ibid.*

4. *Ibid.*

5. *Magic Hour.* Jack Cardiff, Faber, 1996, p. 88.

6. *Fred Zinnemann: An Autobiography.* Charles Scribner, 1992, p. 157.

7. *Ibid.,* p. 155.

8. *Ibid.*

9. *This Week: Audrey Lives a Nun's Life.* April 6, 1958, pp. 36–37.

10. *Good Housekeeping: Audrey Hepburn.* August 1959, p. 119.

11. *Ibid.*

12. *Fred Zinnemann: An Autobiography,* p. 167.

13. *Audrey.* Charles Higham. Hodder & Stoughton, 1984, p. 136.

14. *Ibid.*

15. *Ibid.,* p. 171.

16. *Audrey Hepburn.* Ian Woodward. St. Martin's Press, 1984, p. 116.

17. *Baby I Don't Care*. Lee Server, Faber, 2001, p. 309.

18. *Solid, Dad, Crazy*. Damien Love, Batsford, 2002, p. 116.

19. *Baby I Don't Care,* p. 310.

20. *Ibid.,* p. 117.

21. *Julie Andrews*. Robert Windeler. Comet, 1984, p. 106.

22. *Ibid.*

23. *Ibid.,* p. 100.

24. *Sean Penn: A Biography*. Nick Johnstone. Omnibus Press, 2000, p. 137.

25. *Sean Penn: His Life and Times*. Richard T. Kelly. Faber, 2004, pp. 298–299.

26. *Faith and Film*. Bryan Stone. Chalice Press, 2000, p. 173.

27. *Dead Man Walking*. Helen Prejean. HarperCollins, p. 47.

28. *Ibid.,* p. 48.

29. *Ibid.,* p. 189.

30. *Ibid.,* p. 41.

31. *Empire*. March 2003, p. 144.

32. *Ibid.,* p. 147.

33. *Sin and Censorship,* p. 229.

34. *Ibid.*

35. *Hollywood and the Catholic Church: The Image of Roman Catholicism in the American Movies*. Les and Barbara Keyser. Loyola University Press, 1984, p. 93.

36. *Starspeak: Hollywood on Everything*. Ed. Doug McClelland. Faber, 1987, p. 265.

37. *The Wind At My Back*. Pat O'Brien. Doubleday, 1964, p. 298.

38. *Gregory Peck*. Michael Freedland, Coronet, 1980, p. 66.

39. *Ibid.*

40. *The Films of Gregory Peck*. John Griggs. Columbus, 1984, p. 38.

41. *Gregory Peck*. Michael Freedland, p. 67.

42. *Ibid.*

43. *Gregory Peck: A Charmed Life*. Lynn Haney. Robson, 2003, p. 106.

44. *Ibid.,* pp. 105–106.

45. *Diary of a Country Priest*. Fontana, 1965, p. 5.

46. *Images of the Passion: The Sacramental Mode in Film*. Praeger, 1998, p. 13.

47. *Horizons 8*. No. 1, 1981, p. 93.

48. *The Films of Robert Bresson*. Ed. Ian Cameron. Praeger, 1969, p. 46.

49. *Robert Bresson: A Spiritual Style in Film*. Continuum, 2003, p. 52.

50. *Afterimage*. Richard A. Blake. Loyola Press, 2000, p. 52.

51. *Hitch: The Life and Times of Alfred Hitchcock*. John Russell Taylor. Da Capo, 1996.

52. *The Illustrated Who's Who of Hollywood Directors*. Farrar, Strauss and Giroux. New York, 1995, p. 203.

53. *It's Only a Movie.* Charlotte Chandler. Simon & Schuster, 2005, p. 205.

54. *Alfred Hitchcock: A Life in Darkness and Light.* Patrick McGilligan. Wiley, 2003, p. 461.

55. *Hitchcock: The First Forty Four Films.* Eric Rohmer and Claude Chabrol. Translated by Stanley Hochman. Ungar, 1979, p. 113.

56. *Sin and Censorship,* p. 220.

57. *Alfred Hitchcock: A Life in Darkness and Light,* p. 466.

58. *Ibid.,* p. 441.

59. *Ibid.,* p. 457–458.

60. *Ibid.,* p. 466.

61. *The Complete Hitchcock.* Paul Condon and Jim Sangster. Virgin, 1999, p. 178.

62. *Daily Variety.* November 1986, p. 116.

63. *Solid, Dad, Crazy,* p. 129.

64. *Robert Mitchum.* George Eels. Robson, 1984, p. 187.

65. *Cult Movies.* Danny Peary. Sidgwick & Jackson, 1989, p. 157.

66. *Ibid.,* p. 158.

67. *Bogart: A Life in Hollywood.* Jeffrey Meyers. Andre Deutsch, 1997, pp. 295–296.

68. *Rex Harrison.* Allen Eyles. W.H. Allen, 1985, p. 130.

69. *Ibid.,* p. 132.

70. *Ibid.*

71. *Take Two,* p. 316.

72. *Ibid.*

73. *Ibid.*

74. *Trevor Howard: A Personal Biography.* Terence Pettigrew. Peter Owen, 2001, p. 139.

75. *Trevor Howard: The Man and His Films.* Michael Munn. Robson, 1989, p. 131.

76. *Ibid.*

77. *Deeper Into Movies.* Pauline Kael. Little Brown, 1973, p. 191.

78. *Trevor Howard: A Personal Biography,* p. 198.

79. *Ibid.*

80. *The Big Book of Noir.* Jon L. Breen, p. 150.

81. *Robert De Niro: The Hero Behind the Masks.* Keith McKay. St. Martin's Press, 1986, p. 104.

82. *Robert De Niro.* Patrick Agan. Robert Hale, 1989, p. 102.

83. *Robert De Niro: The Hero Behind the Masks,* p. 105.

84. *Ibid.*

85. *Untouchable.* Andy Dougan. Thunder's Mouth Press, 1996, p. 136.

86. *Robert De Niro.* John Baxter. HarperCollins, 2002, p. 212.

87. *Ibid.,* p. 213.

88. *Robert De Niro: The Hero Behind the Masks,* p. 109.

89. *Some Like It Cool*. Michael Freedland, Robson, 2002, p. 207.

90. *Jack Lemmon: His Films and Career*. John Baltake. Citadel, 1986, p. 262.

91. *Ibid.*, p. 264.

92. *What's Eating Johnny Depp*. Nigel Goodall. Blake, 1999, p. 208.

93. *Ibid.*

94. *Ibid.*, p. 209.

95. *Irish Times*. May 12, 2006.

96. *RTE Guide*. May 13–19, 2006.

97. *Irish Times*. May 12, 2006.

CHAPTER 4

1. *Starring Roles*. Ron Base. Little Brown, 1994, p. xiv.

2. *Eyes Wide Open: Looking for God in Popular Culture*. William D. Romanowski. Brazos Press, 2001, p. 78.

3. *Ibid.*, p. 23.

4. *Celluloid Saints*. Theresa Sanders. Mercer University Press, 2002, p. xi.

5. *Hollywood Cameramen:* Sources of Light. Charles Higham. Thames & Hudson, pp. 143–149.

6. *Videohound Epics,* p. 184.

7. *Naked Hollywood*. Nicolas Kent. BBC Books, 1991, p. 144.

8. *Cult Movies*. Danny Peary. Vermilion, 1982, p. 162.

9. *Frank Capra: The Name Above the Title*. Macmillan, 1971, p. 383.

10. *James Stewart: A Biography*. Donald Dewey. Turner Publishing, 1996, p. 266.

11. *James Stewart: The Hollywood Years*. Roy Pickard. Robert Hale, 1992, p. 70.

12. *Ibid.*, p. 72.

13. *Ibid.*

14. *James Stewart*. Donald Dewey, p. 271.

15. *The Complete Films of Frank Capra*. Victor Scherle and William Turner Levy. Citadel, 1992, p. 229.

16. *Cary Grant: A Biography*. Marc Eliot. Aurum Press, 2005.

17. *The Movies: An Illustrated History of Cinema*. Orbis Publishing, 1980, p. 701.

18. *The Ghost and Mrs. Muir*. Frieda Grafe. British Film Institute, 1995, p. 17.

19. *Take Two,* p. 186.

20. *Fallen Angels*. Kirk Crivello. Futura, 1998, p. 164.

21. *Forever Young: Untimely Deaths in the Screen World*. Rona Wheaton. Warner, 1994, pp. 234–235.

22. *Chamber's Film Quotes*. Ed. Tony Crawley. W&R Chambers, 1991, p. 13.

23. *Movies of the Fifties*. Ed. Ann Lloyd. Orbis Publishing, 1982, p. 120.

24. *Faith and Film: Theological Themes at the Cinema.* Chalice Press, 2000, p. 28.

25. *Warren Beatty.* John Kercher. Proteus Publishing, 1984, p. 115.

26. *Warren Beatty: A Life and a Story.* David Thomson. Secker & Warburg, 1987, p. 383.

27. *Religion in Film,* p. 208.

28. *Ibid.*

29. *Ibid.*

30. *God in the Movies.* Albert J. Bergeson and Andrew W. Greeley. Transaction, 2003, p. 40.

31. *Ibid.*

32. *Steven Spielberg.* Andrew Yule. Little Brown, p. 241.

33. *New Yorker.* January 8, 1990, p. 92.

34. *The Films of Steven Spielberg.* Citadel Publishing, 1995, p. 193.

35. *Ibid.,* p. 194.

36. *Rochester Democrat and Chronicle: Audrey Hepburn Is a Class Act.* Angela Fox Dunn. December 21, 1989.

37. *Steven Spielberg.* Andrew Yule. p. 241.

38. *Ibid.*

39. *Screening the Sacred.* Joel Martin. Westview Press, 1995, p. 70.

40. *God Goes to Hollywood: A Movie Guide for the Modern Mystic.* Ben Frost and Mary Kay Mueller. Writer's Club Press, 2000, p. 84.

41. *Faith and Film.* Bryan P. Stone, p. 125.

42. *New York Post.* February 12, 1993, p. 31.

43. *Time.* August 15, 1993.

44. *Shooting Stars.* Harry Shapiro. Serpent's Tail, 2003, p. 231.

45. *Abel Ferrara: The King of New York.* N. Johnstone. Omnibus Press, 1999, p. 124.

46. *Rolling Stone.* November 26, 1992.

47. *God in the Movies,* p. 115.

48. *Ibid.*

49. *Ibid.,* p. 118.

50. *Nicolas Cage: Hollywood's Wild Talent.* Brian J. Robb. Plexus, p. 149.

51. *Ibid.*

52. *San Francisco Sunday Examiner and Chronicle.* October 31, 1999, p. 50.

53. *Empire.* March 2003, p. 147.

54. *Celluloid Saints.* Theresa Sanders, Mercer University Press, p. xi.

55. *Reel Spirituality: Theology and Film in Dialogue.* Baker Academic Press, 2000, p. 73.

56. *Cinema, Religion and the Romantic Legacy,* p. 184.

57. *Ibid.*

58. *Film as Religion: Myth, Morals and Religion,* p. 249.

59. *Ibid.*

CHAPTER 5

1. *Chambers Film Quotes,* p. 218.
2. *Blessings in Disguise.* Alec Guinness, Fontana, p. 64.
3. *Ibid.,* p. 75.
4. *Ibid.,* p. 61.
5. *Tubridy Tonight.* RTE, March 25, 2006.
6. *The Sheens.* Lee Riley and David Schumacher. Robson, 1991, p. 28.
7. *Ibid.*
8. *Ibid.,* p. 31.
9. *Ibid.*
10. *Afterimage,* p. 61.
11. *Ibid.*
12. *Hitchcock: The First Forty Four Films,* p. 113.
13. *Flesh and Fantasy,* p. 143.
14. *James Dean in His Own Words.* Ed. Chris Charlesworth. Omnibus, 1989, p. 77.
15. *Woody Allen.* Eric Lax. Jonathan Cape, 1991, p. 41.
16. *Ibid.*
17. *American Film-Makers Today.* Dian G. Smith. Blandford Press, 1984. p. 116.
18. *Scorsese on Scorsese.* Faber, p. 118.
19. *Hollywood Migraine.* Ray Greene. Merlin, 2000, p. 253.
20. *Martin Scorsese: A Journey.* Mary Pat Kelly. Thunder's Mouth Press, 1991, p. 11.
21. *Explorations in Theology and Film,* frontispiece.
22. *Hollywood Renaissance.* Diane Jacobs. A.S. Barnes, 1997, p. 129.
23. *American Film-Makers Today,* p. 117.
24. *Once a Catholic.* Ed. Peter Occhiogrosso. Houghton Mifflin, 1987, pp. 98–99.
25. *Easy Riders, Raging Bulls.* Peter Biskind. Bloomsbury, 1998, p. 251.
26. *Martin Scorsese.* Andy Dougan. Orion, 1997, p. 14.
27. *Afterimage,* p. 46.
28. *An Open Book.* John Huston. Da Capo. 1994, p. 329.
29. *Ibid.*
30. *Bob Dylan: In His Own Words.* Omnibus Press, 1993.
31. *Ibid.*
32. *Ibid.*
33. *Ibid.*
34. *Ibid.*
35. *Ibid.*
36. *Ibid.*
37. *Ibid.*

CHAPTER 6

1. *Screening the Sacred*, p. 6.
2. *The Science Fiction Film Source Book,* p. 54.
3. *Illuminating Shadows: The Mythic Power of Film.* Geoffrey Hill. Shambala Publications, 1992, p. 3.
4. *Image and Likeness.* Ed. John R. May. Paulist Press, 1992, p. 121.
5. *Ibid.,* p. 55.
6. *Ibid.,* p. 64.
7. *Ibid.*
8. *Ibid.,* p. 62.
9. *Ibid.*
10. *Ibid.*
11. *George Stevens: An American Romantic.* Donald Richie. Museum of Modern Art, 1970, p. 62.
12. *Explorations in Theology and Film,* p. 236.
13. *Reading the Gospels in the Dark,* p. 162.
14. *Explorations in Theology and Film,* p. 241.
15. *Ibid.*
16. *Ibid.,* p. 61.
17. *Ibid.,* p. 63.
18. *Hollywood in the Fifties.* Gordon Gow. A.S. Barnes & Co. International Film Guide Series, 1971, p. 125.
19. *Religion in Film,* p. 120.
20. *Paul Newman.* Robert Hale, 1989, p. 109.
21. *Paul Newman.* Daniel O'Brien. Faber, 2000, p. 131.
22. *Ibid.*
23. *Ibid.,* p. 132.
24. *Religion in Film,* p. 71.
25. *Going Steady.* Pauline Kael. Atlantic Monthly Press, 1970, p. 122.
26. *The Primal Screen.* John Brosnan. Orbit, 1991, p. 145.
27. *Alien Sex.* Gerard Loughlin. Blackwell, 2004, p. 69.
28. *Stanley Kubrick: A Biography.* Vincent LoBrutto. Faber, 1997, p. 302.
29. *Kubrick.* Michel Ciment. Rinehart & Winston, 1983, p. 131.
30. *Ibid.,* p. 128.
31. *Kubrick.* Michael Herr. Picador, 2000, p. 4.
32. *The Primal Screen,* p. 145.
33. *The Making of Kubrick's 2001.* Ed. Jerome Agel. Signet, 1970.
34. *Stanley Kubrick: A Biography.* John Baxter. HarperCollins, 1997, p. 210.
35. *The Epic Film: Myth and History.* Derek Elley. Routledge & Kegan Paul. 1994, p. 166.
36. *Stanley Kubrick: A Biography.* Vincent LoBrutto, p. 268.
37. *Ibid.,* p. 314.

38. *Cult Movies*, p. 370.

39. *Ibid.*, p. 371.

40. *Stanley Kubrick: A Biography*. Vincent LoBrutto, p. 313.

41. *Films Illustrated*. October, 1979.

42. *Crime Movies: An Illustrated History*. Carlos Clarens. Secker & Warburg, 1980, pp. 287–288.

43. *Afterimage*, p. 211.

44. *Image and Likeness*, p. 147.

45. *On Finding the Cuckoo's Nest*. The Christian Century. August 4, 1976, p. 688.

46. *Image and Likeness*, p. 151.

47. *Faith and Film*, p. 99.

48. *American Filmmakers Today*, p. 123.

49. *The Scorsese Connection*. British Film Institute, 1995, p. 48.

50. *Martin Scorsese*. Marie Connolly, McFarland, 1993, p. 42.

51. *The Movie Brats: How the Film Generation Took Over Hollywood*. Michael Pye and Lynda Myles, Faber, 1979, p. 213.

52. *Ibid.*, p. 212.

53. *Eyes Wide Open: Looking for God in Popular Culture*. William D. Romanowski. 2001, p. 66.

54. *Time*. April 26, 1999, p. 92.

55. *The Primal Screen*, p. 181.

56. *Ibid.*

57. *The Steven Spielberg Story*. Tony Crawley. Zomba Books, 1983, p. 59.

58. *Ibid.*, pp. 60–61.

59. *The Science Fiction Film Source Book*, p. 15.

60. *The Steven Spielberg Story*, p. 111.

61. *Steven Spielberg*. Philip Taylor. Batsford, 1994, p. 41.

62. *Ibid.*, p. 95.

63. *Ibid.* p. 63.

64. *The Steven Spielberg Story*, p. 115.

65. *Steven Spielberg*. Philip Taylor, p. 55.

66. *Steven Spielberg: Father of the Man*. Andrew Yule, Little Brown, 1996, p. 82.

67. *Ibid.*

68. *Ibid.*, p. 133.

69. *The Films of Steven Spielberg*. Douglas Brode. Citadel, 1995, p. 127.

70. *Ibid.*

71. *The Films of Steven Spielberg*. Neil Sinyard. Hamlyn, 1987, pp. 83–84.

72. *This Month: Jesus at the Movies*. December 1994, p. 494.

73. *Ibid.*

74. *The Primal Screen*, p. 260.

75. *The Science Fiction Film Source Book*, p. 89.

76. *Film as Religion.* New York University Press, 2003, p. 199.

77. *Steven Spielberg.* Philip Taylor, p. 131.

78. *Steven Spielberg: Father of the Man,* p. 134.

79. *Ibid.,* p. 135.

80. *Schrader on Schrader.* Ed. Kevin Jackson. Faber, 1990, p. 133.

81. *Ibid.,* pp. 131–133.

82. *Partisan Review.* December 20, 1993.

83. *The Word Made Flesh.* Michael Bliss. Scarecrow Press, 1998, p. 71.

84. *Flesh and Blood.* Ed. Peter Keough. Mercury House, 1995, p. 282.

85. *Using Film to Teach the New Testament.* Marc C. Boyer. University Press of America, 2002, p. 81.

86. *The Big Picture: Finding the Spiritual Messages in Movies.* J. John and Mark Stibbe. Authentic Lifestyle, 2002, p. 92.

CHAPTER 7

1. *The Satanic Screen.* Nikolas Schreck. Creation Books, 2000, pp. 5–6.

2. *Ibid.,* p. 192.

3. *Ibid.,* p. 10.

4. Celluloid Saints, p. 64.

5. *Roman: By Polanski.* Pan, 1985, p. 262.

6. *Polanski: A Biography.* Barbara Leaming. Simon & Schuster, 1981, p. 288.

7. *Ibid.*

8. *Mia Farrow.* Sam Rubin and Richard Taylor. Robson, 1990, p. 49.

9. *Mia.* Edward Z. Epstein and Joe Morella. Robert Hale, 1992, p. 131.

10. *Roman: By Polanski,* p. 312.

11. *Ken Russell: An Appalling Talent.* John Baxter. Michael Joseph. 1973, p. 210.

12. *Film Censorship.* Guy Phelps. Victor Gollancz, 1975.

13. *Evil Spirits: The Life of Oliver Reed.* Cliff Goodwin. Virgin, 2000, p. 150.

14. *An Appalling Talent,* p. 202.

15. *Reed: All About Me.* Oliver Reed. W.H. Allen, p. 35.

16. *Evil Spirits,* p. 149.

17. *Fallen Stars.* Julian Upton. Headpress, 2004, p. 26.

18. *Rich.* Melvyn Bragg. Hodder & Stoughton, 1988, p. 356.

19. *Ibid.*

20. *Easy Riders, Raging Bulls,* p. 200.

21. *Ibid.,* p. 197.

22. *The Exorcist and Legion: Classic Screenplays.* William Peter Blatty. Faber, 1998, p. vii.

23. *Ibid.,* p. viii.

24. *Ibid.*

25. *Easy Riders, Raging Bulls,* p. 199.

26. *Ibid.,* p. 223.

27. *New York Times.* December 27, 1973.

28. *Alien Sex,* p. 40.

29. *The Satanic Screen,* p. 168.

30. *Religion in Film,* pp. 84–85.

31. *The Satanic Screen,* p. 170.

32. *The Horror People.* John Brosnan. Macdonald and Jane's, 1976, p. 261.

33. *Ibid.*

34. *Adventures of a Suburban Boy.* John Boorman. Faber, 2003, p. 204.

35. *Ibid.*

36. *Ibid.,* p. 229.

37. *Gregory Peck: A Charmed Life.* Lynn Haney. Robson, 2003, p. 366.

38. *Gregory Peck.* Robert Hale, p. 201.

39. *Gregory Peck: A Charmed Life,* p. 367.

40. *Ibid.,* p. 366.

41. *The Films of Gregory Peck.* John Griggs, Columbus, 1984, p. 224.

42. *Ibid.*

43. *The Films of Jack Nicholson.* Douglas Brode. Citadel, 1987, p. 208.

44. *Jack Nicholson: The Life and Times of an Actor on the Edge.* Peter Thompson, Mainstream, 1997, p. 182.

45. *Jack's Life.* Patrick McGilligan. HarperCollins, 1995, p. 340.

46. *Flesh and Blood,* p. 145.

47. *Jack's Life,* p. 387.

48. *Jack Nicholson: The Life and Times of an Actor on the Edge,* p. 66.

49. *Jack Nicholson: An Unauthorised Biography.* Donald Shepherd, Robson, 1991, p. 154.

50. *Ibid.,* p. 155.

51. *The Films of Jack Nicholson,* p. 253.

52. *Mickey Rourke.* Bart Mills. Sidgwick & Jackson, 1988, p. 63.

53. *Robert De Niro.* Patrick Agan. Robert Hale, 1989, p. 141.

54. *Untouchable.* Andy Dougan. Thunder's Mouth Press. 1996, p. 288.

55. *Robert De Niro.* John Baxter. HarperCollins, 2002, pp. 261–262.

56. *Ibid.,* p. 261.

57. *In the Arena.* Charlton Heston. HarperCollins, 1995, p. 300.

Bibliography

Agan, Patrick. "Robert de Niro." Robert Hale, 1989.

Agel, Jerome. Ed., "The Making of Kubrick's 2001." Signet, 1970.

Anger, Kenneth. "Hollywood Babylon." Arrow, 1986.

Babington, Bruce. "Biblical Epics." Manchester University Press, 1993.

Baltlake, Joe. "Jack Lemmon: His Films and Career." Citadel, 1986.

Base, Ron. "Starring Roles." Little Brown, 1994.

Baugh, Lloyd. "Imaging the Divine." Sheed and Ward, 1997.

Baxter, John. "Hollywood in the Thirties." Tantivy Press, 1968.

———— "Ken Russell: An Appalling Talent." Michael Joseph, 1973.

———— "Robert de Niro." HarperCollins, 2002.

Behlmer, Audrey. "Behind the Scenes." Samuel French, 1990.

Bergeson, Albert J. "God in the Movies." Transaction, 2003.

Biskind, Peter. "Seeing Is Believing." Pluto Press, 1983.

———— "Easy Riders, Raging Bulls." Bloomsbury, 1998.

Blake, Richard A. "After-Image." Loyola Press, 2000.

Blatty, William Peter. "The Exorcist and Legion: Classic Screenplays." 1998.

Bliss, Michael. "The Word Made Flesh." Scarecrow Press, 1998.

Boyar, Mark C. "Using Film to Teach the New Testament." University Press of America, 2002.

Bragg, Melvyn. "Rich." Hodder & Stoughton, 1988.

Brode, Douglas. "The Films of Jack Nicholson." Citadel, 1987.

———— "The Films of Steven Spielberg." Citadel, 1995.

Brosnan, John. "The Primal Screen." Orbit, 1999.

———— "The Horror People." McDonald and Janes, 1976.

Brown, Michele. "Hammer and Tongues." Grafton Books, 1988.

Buford, Kate. "Burt Lancaster: An American Life." Aurum Press, 2008.

Cameron, Ian. Ed., "The Films of Robert Bresson." Praeger, 1969.

Capra, Frank. "The Name Above the Title: An Autobiography." Macmillan, 1971.

Cardiff, Jack. "The Magic Hour." Faber, 1996.

Chandler, Charlotte. "I, Fellini." Bloomsbury, 1994.

———— "It's Only a Movie." Simon & Schuster, 2005.

Charlesworth, Chris. Ed., "James Dean in His Own Words." Omnibus, 1989.

Ciment, Michel. "Kazan on Kazan." Secker & Warburg, 1973.

———— "Kubrick." Rinehart & Winston, 1983.

Clarkson, Wensley. "Mel Gibson: Man on a Mission." Blake, 2004.

Clemens, Carlos. "Crime Movies: An Illustrated History." Secker & Warburg, 1954.

Coates, Paul. "Cinema, Religion and the Romantic Legacy." Ashgate, 2003.

Connolly, Marie. "Martin Scorsese." McFarland, 1993.

Cook, Christopher. Ed., "The Dilys Powell Film Reader." Carcanet, 1991.

Crawley, Tony. "The Steven Spielberg Story." Zomba Books, 1983.

Crivello, Kirk. "Fallen Angels." Futura, 1998.

Cunneen, Joseph. "Robert Bresson: A Spiritual Style." Continuum, 2003.

Davis, Ronald L. "Hollywood Anecdotes." Macmillan, 1987.

Dewey, Donald. "James Stewart: A Biography." Turner Publishing, 1994.

Dougan, Andy. "Untouchable." Thunder's Mouth Press, 1996.

———— "Martin Scorsese." Orion, 1997.

Edwards, Ann. "The DeMilles: An American Family." Collins, 1988.

Eels, George. "Robert Mitchum." Robson, 1984.

Eliot, Marc. "Cary Grant: An Autobiography." Aurum, 2005.

Elley, Derek. "The Epic Film: Myth and History." Routledge & Kegan Paul, 1994.

Epstein, Edward Z. "Mia." Robert Hale, 1992.

Essoe, Peter Gabe. "Cecil B. DeMille: The Man and His Pictures." Castle Books, 1970.

Eyles, Allen. "Rex Harrison." WH Allen, 1985.

Fishgall, Gary. "Against Type: The Biography of Burt Lancaster." Scribner, 1995.

Fraser, Peter. "Reading the Gospels in the Dark." Trinity Press, 2003.

———— "Images of the Passion." Praeger, 1998.

Freedland, Michael. "Gregory Peck." Coronet, 1980.

———— "Some Like It Cool." Robson, 2002.

Frost, Ben. "God Goes to Hollywood." Writer's Club Press, 2000.

Gau, John. "Lights, Camera, Action." Little Brown, 1995.

Goodall, Nigel. "What's Eating Johnny Depp?" Blake, 1999.

Goodwin, Cliff. "Evil Spirits: The Life of Oliver Reed." Virgin, 2000.

Gow, Gordon. "Hollywood in the Fifties." A.S. Barnes & Co., 1971.

Grafe, Frieda. "The Ghost and Mrs. Muir." British Film Institute, 1995.

Greene, Graham. "The Pleasure Dome." Oxford University Press, 1980.

Greene, Ray. "Hollywood Migraine." Merlin, 2000.

Griggs, John. "The Films of Gregory Peck." Columbus, 1984.

Goldman, William. "Adventures in the Screen Trade." Futura, 1990.

Guinness, Alec. "Blessings in Disguise." Penguin, 1997.

Hadleigh, Boze. "Hollywood Babble On." Birch Lane Press, 1994.

Haney, Lynn. "Gregory Peck: A Charmed Life." Robson, 2003.

Hays, Will H. "The Memoirs of Will H. Hays." Doubleday, 1955.

Heston, Charlton. "In the Arena." HarperCollins, 1995.

Higham, Charles. "Hollywood Cameramen." Thames & Hudson, 1970.

——— "Cecil B. DeMille." Scribner, 1973.

——— "Audrey." Hodder & Stoughton, 1984.

Hill, Geoffrey. "Illuminating Shadows." Shambala Publications, 1992.

Hogg, James. "Religion and Film." Wallflower, 2008.

Hopp, Glenn. "Videohound Epics." Gale, 1998.

Huston, John. "An Open Book." Da Capo, 1994.

Jackson, Kevin. Ed., "Schrader on Schrader." Faber, 1990.

Jacobs, Diane. "Hollywood Renaissance." A.S. Barnes, 1997.

Johnston, Robert K. "Reel Spirituality: Theology and Film in Dialogue." Baker Academic, 2000.

Johnstone, Nick. "Abel Ferrara." Omnibus, 1999.

——— "Sean Penn: A Biography." Omnibus, 2000.

Kael, Pauline. "Deeper Into Movies." Little Brown, 1973.

Kardish, Laurence, "Reel Plastic Magic." Little Brown, 1972.

Kashner, Sam. "The Bad and the Beautiful." Little Brown, 2002.

Kelly, Mary Pat. "Martin Scorsese: A Journey." Thunder's Mouth Press, 1991.

Kelly, Richard T. "Sean Penn: His Life and Times." Faber, 2004.

Kent, Nicolas. "Naked Hollywood." BBC Books, 1991.

Keough, Peter. Ed., "Flesh and Blood." Mercury House, 1995.

Kercher, John. "Warren Beatty." Proteus Publishing, 1984.

Kinnear, Roy. "Divine Images." Citadel, 1992.

Kobal, John. "Rita Hayworth: Portrait of a Love Goddess." Berkley Books, 1982.

Kovary, Phil A. "Yes, Mr. DeMille." Putnam, 1959.

Lax, Eric. "Woody Allen." Jonathan Cape, 1991.

Leaming, Barbara. "Polanski: A Biography." Simon & Schuster, 1981.

Lobrutto, Vincent. "Stanley Kubrick: A Biography." Faber, 1997.

Loughlin, Gerard. "Alien Sex." Blackwell, 2004.

Love, Damien. "Solid, Dad, Crazy." Batsford, 2002.

Lyden, John C. "Film as Religion." New York University Press, 2003.

Marsh, Clive. "Cinema and Sentiment." Paternoster Press, 2004.

Martin, Joel. "Screening the Sacred." Westview Press, 1995.

Marx, Samuel. "Mayer and Thalberg: The Make-Believe Saints." WH Allen, 1976.

May, John R. "Image and Likeness." Paulist Press, 1992.

Mayer, Arthur. "Merely Colossal." Simon & Schuster, 1953.

McBride, Joseph. "Hawks on Hawks." University of California Press, 1982.

McClelland, Doug. Ed., "Starspeak." Faber, 1987.

McGilligan, Patrick. "Alfred Hitchcock: A Life in Darkness and Light." Wiley, 2003.

McKay, Keith. "Robert de Niro: The Man Behind the Masks." St. Martin's Press, 1986.

Meyers, Jeffrey. "Bogart: A Life in Hollywood." Andre Deutsch, 1997.

Morecambe, Gary. "Cary Grant: In Name Only." Robson, 2001.

Munn, Michael. "Charlton Heston: A Biography." Robson, 1986.

————— "Trevor Howard: The Man and His Films." Robson, 1989.

————— "Burt Lancaster." Robson, 1995.

Naughton, John. "Movies: A Crash Course." Simon & Schuster, 1998.

Neve, Brian. "Film and Politics: A Social Tradition." Routledge, 1992.

Nicolosi, Barbara. "Behind the Screen: Hollywood Insiders on Faith, Film and Culture." Baker Books, 2005.

Norman, Barry. "Talking Pictures." Hodder & Stoughton, 1987.

O'Brien, Daniel. "Paul Newman." Faber, 2004.

O'Brien, Pat. "The Wind at My Back." Doubleday, 1964.

Ortiz, Gaye. "Explorations in Theology and Film." Blackwell, 1998.

Oumano, Elena. "Paul Newman." Robert Hale, 1990.

Parish, James Robert. "The Hollywood Book of Scandals." McGraw-Hill, 2004.

Peary, Danny. "Cult Movies." Sidgwick & Jackson, 1989.

Pettigrew, Terence. "Trevor Howard: A Personal Biography." Peter Owen, 2001.

Pickard, Roy. "James Stewart: The Hollywood Years." Robert Hale, 1992.

Powdermaker, Hortense. "Hollywood: The Dream Factory." Secker & Warburg, 1951.

Prejean, Helen. "Dead Man Walking." HarperCollins, 1994.

Pye, Michael. "The Movie Brats." Faber, 1979.

Reed, Oliver. "All About Me." WH Allen, 1979.

Richie, Ronald. "George Stevens: An American Romantic." Museum of Modern Art, 1970.

Riley, Lee. "The Sheens." Robson, 1991.

Riley, Robin. "Film, Faith and Cultural Conflict." Praeger, 2003.

Robb, Brian J. "Nicolas Cage: Hollywood's Wild Talent." Plexus, 1998.

Romanowski, William. "Eyes Wide Open." Brazos Press, 2003.

Rubin, Sam. "Mia Farrow." Robson, 1990.

Sanders, Theresa. "Celluloid Saints." Mercer University Press, 2002.

Sauter, Michael. "The Worst Movies of All Time." Citadel, 1999.

Scherle, Victor. "The Complete Films of Frank Capra." Citadel, 1992.

Schiach, Don. "The Movie Book." Acropolis, 1992.

Schreck, Nicolas. "The Satanic Screen." Creation Books, 2000.

Server, Lee. Ed., "The Big Book of Noir." Carroll & Graf, 1998.

———— "Baby I Don't Care." Faber, 2001.

Shapiro, Harry. "Shooting Stars." Serpent's Tail, 2003.

Shepherd, Donald. "Jack Nicholson: An Unauthorized Biography." Robson, 1991.

Sinyard, Neil. "Directors: The All-Time Greats." Gallery Books, 1985.

Smith, Dian G. "American Film-Makers Today." Blandford Press, 1984.

Spelling, Cass Warner. "Hollywood Be Thy Name." University Press of Kentucky, 1998.

Stallings, Penny. "Flesh and Fantasy." Harper & Row, 1978.

Stern, Richard. "Saviour on the Silver Screen." Paulist Press, 1999.

Stibbe, Mark. "The Big Picture: Finding the Spiritual Message in Movies." Authentic Lifestyle, 2002.

Stone, Bryan. "Faith and Film." Chalice Press, 2000.

Thompson, Peter. "Jack Nicholson: The Life and Times of an Actor on the Edge." Mainstream, 1997.

Thomson, David. "The Whole Equation." Little Brown, 2005.

Toeplitz, Jerzy. "Hollywood and After." Unwin, 1974.

Turner, Adrian. "The Movies: An Illustrated History." Orbis, 1980.

Upton, Julian. "Fallen Stars." Headpress, 2004.

Vidal, Gore. "Palimpsest." Andre Deutsch, 1995.

"Warren Beatty: A Life and a Story." Secker & Warburg, 1987.

Wheaton, Rona. "Forever Young." Warner, 1994.

Windeler, Robert. "Julie Andrews." Comet, 1984.

Winokur, Jon. "True Confessions." Victor Gollancz, 1992.

Woodward, Ian. "Audrey Hepburn." St. Martin's Press, 1984.

Wright, Melanie J. "Religion and Film: An Introduction." I.B. Tauris, 2006.

Young, Jeff. "Kazan: The Master Discusses His Films." Newmarket Press, 1999.

Yule, Andrew. "Steven Spielberg: Father to the Man." Little Brown, 1996.

Zinnemann, Fred. "An Autobiography." Scribner, 1992.

Filmography

Birth of a Nation (D.W. Griffith, 1915).
The Ten Commandments (Cecil B. DeMille, 1923).
Ben-Hur (Fred Niblo, 1926).
The King of Kings (Cecil B. DeMille, 1927).
Rain (Lewis Milestone, 1932).
Sign of the Cross (Cecil B. DeMille, 1932).
Death Takes a Holiday (Henry Travers, 1934).
Topper (Norman MacLeod, 1937).
Angels With Dirty Faces (Michael Curtiz, 1938).
Boy's Town (Norman Taurog, 1938).
Topper Takes a Trip (Norman MacLeod, 1940).
All That Money Can Buy (William Dieterle, 1941).
The Devil and Daniel Webster (William Dieterle, 1941).
Here Comes Mr. Jordan (Alexander Hall, 1941).
Heaven Can Wait (Ernest Lubitsch, 1943).
Song of Bernadette (Henry King, 1943).
Going My Way (Leo McCarey, 1944).
A Guy Named Joe (Victor Fleming, 1944).
Keys of the Kingdom (John M. Stahl, 1944).
Bells of St. Mary's (Leo McCarey, 1945).
Blithe Spirit (David Lean, 1945).
The Picture of Dorian Gray (Albert Lewin, 1945).
Yolanda and the Thief (Vincent Minnelli, 1945).
Angel on My Shoulder (John Berry, 1946).
It's a Wonderful Life (Frank Capra, 1946).
A Matter of Life and Death (William Powell, 1946).

The Bishop's Wife (Henry Koster, 1947).
Black Narcissus (Michael Powell, 1947).
The Fugitive (John Ford, 1947).
The Ghost and Mrs. Muir (Joseph L. Manciewicz, 1947).
Joan of Arc (Victor Fleming, 1948).
Samson and Delilah (Cecil B. DeMille, 1949).
Diary of a Country Priest (Robert Bresson, 1950).
Angels in the Outfield (Clarence Brown, 1951).
David and Bathsheba (Henry King, 1951).
Quo Vadis? (Mervin LeRoy, 1951).
A Streetcar Named Desire (Elia Kazan, 1951).
The Miracle of Our Lady of Fatima (John Brahm, 1952).
I Confess (Alfred Hitchcock, 1953).
The Robe (Henry Koster, 1953).
Salome (William Dieterle, 1953).
Shane (George Stevens, 1953).
On the Waterfront (Elia Kazan, 1954).
The Silver Chalice (Victor Saville, 1954).
The Left Hand of God (Edward Dmytryk, 1955).
The Night of the Hunter (Charles Laughton, 1955).
The Prodigal (Richard Thorpe, 1955).
We're No Angels (Michael Curtiz, 1955).
The Ten Commandments (Cecil B. DeMille, 1956).
Heaven Knows, Mr. Allison (John Huston, 1957).
Saint Joan (Otto Preminger, 1957).
The Seventh Seal (Ingmar Bergman, 1957).
Bell, Book and Candle (Richard Quine, 1958).
Damn Yankees (Stanley Donen, 1958).
The Old Man and the Sea (John Sturges, 1958).
Ben-Hur (William Wyler, 1959).
Say One For Me (Frank Tashlin, 1959).
Conspiracy of Hearts (Ralph Thomas, 1960).
The Devil's Eye (Ingmar Bergman, 1960).
Elmer Gantry (Richard Brooks, 1960).
Spartacus (Stanley Kubrick, 1960).
Barabbas (Richard Fleischer, 1961).
The Hoodlum Priest (Irwin Kershner, 1961).
King of Kings (Nicholas Ray, 1961).
The Singer Not the Song (Roy Baker, 1961).
The Cardinal (Otto Preminger, 1963).
Hud (Martin Ritt, 1963).
The Agony and the Ecstacy (Carol Reed, 1965).
The Greatest Story Ever Told (George Stevens, 1965).

Simon of the Desert (Luis Bunuel, 1965).

The Sound of Music (Robert Wise, 1965).

The Gospel According to St. Matthew (Pier Paolo Pasolini, 1966).

The Singing Nun (Henry Koster, 1966).

Cool Hand Luke (Stuart Rosenberg, 1967).

Dr. Faustus (Richard Burton, 1968).

The Milky Way (Luis Bunuel, 1968).

Rosemary's Baby (Roman Polanski, 1968).

Ryan's Daughter (David Lean, 1968).

2001: A Space Odyssey (Stanley Kubrick, 1968).

Change of Heart (William Graham, 1969).

The Devils (Ken Russell, 1971).

The Godfather (Francis Ford Coppola, 1972).

Hammersmith Is Out (Peter Ustinov, 1972).

The Poseidon Adventure (Ronald Neame, 1972).

The Ruling Class (Peter Medak, 1972).

Godspell (David Greene, 1973).

The Exorcist (William Friedkin, 1973).

Jesus Christ Superstar (Norman Jewison, 1973).

Mean Streets (Martin Scorsese, 1973).

One Flew Over the Cuckoo's Nest (Milos Forman, 1975).

The Omen (Richard Donner, 1976).

Damien: Omen II (Don Taylor, 1976).

Taxi Driver (Martin Scorsese, 1976).

Close Encounters of the Third Kind (Steven Spielberg, 1977).

The Heretic (John Boorman, 1977).

Jesus of Nazareth (Franco Zeffirelli, 1977).

Oh God (Carl Reiner, 1977).

Heaven Can Wait (Buck Henry, 1978).

The Manitou (William Girdler, 1978).

Superman (Richard Donner, 1978).

Apocalypse Now (Francis Ford Coppola, 1979).

Being There (Hal Ashby, 1979).

The Life of Brian (Terry Jones, 1979).

All That Jazz (Bob Fosse, 1980).

Altered States (Ken Russell, 1980).

The Devil and Max Devlin (Steven Hilliard Stern, 1980).

Raging Bull (Martin Scorsese, 1980).

The Shining (Stanley Kubrick, 1980).

History of the World: Part 1 (Mel Brooks, 1981).

True Confessions (Ulu Grosbard, 1981).

E.T. (Steven Spielberg, 1982).

Poltergeist (Steven Spielberg, 1982).

Mass Appeal (Glenn Jordan, 1984).
Oh God You Devil (Paul Bogart, 1984).
Agnes of God (Norman Jewison, 1985).
Hail Mary (Jean-Luc Godard, 1985).
Crossroads (Walter Hill, 1986).
Hannah and Her Sisters (Woody Allen, 1986).
The Mission (Roland Joffe, 1986).
Angel Heart (Alan Parker, 1987).
Wings of Desire (Wim Wenders, 1987).
The Witches of Eastwick (George Miller, 1987).
The Last Temptation of Christ (Martin Scorsese, 1988).
Sextette (Ken Hughes, 1988).
Always (Steven Spielberg, 1989).
Dead Poet's Society (Peter Weir, 1989).
Field of Dreams (Phil Robinson, 1989).
Jesus of Montreal (Denys Arcand, 1989).
Sinners (Charles Kanganis, 1989).
Almost an Angel (John Cornell, 1990).
Flatliners (Joel Schumacher, 1990).
Ghost (Jerry Zucker, 1990).
Heart Condition (James D. Parriott, 1990).
Jacob's Ladder (Adrian Lyne, 1990).
Nuns on the Run (Jonathan Lynn, 1990).
Dead Again (Kenneth Branagh, 1991).
Truly, Madly, Deeply (Anthony Minghella, 1991).
Bad Lieutenant (Abel Ferrara, 1992).
Basic Instinct (Paul Verhoeven, 1992).
Leap of Faith (Richard Pearce, 1992).
Sister Act (Emile Ardolino, 1992).
Fearless (Peter Weir, 1993).
Groundhog Day (Harold Ramis, 1993).
Needful Things (Fraser Heston, 1993).
Natural Born Killers (Oliver Stone, 1994).
The Shawshank Redemption (Frank Darabont, 1994).
The Basketball Diaries (Scott Kalvert, 1995).
Dead Man Walking (Tim Robbins, 1995).
Priest (Antonia Bird, 1995).
Seven (David Fincher, 1995).
Michael (Nora Ephron, 1996).
Phenomenon (Richard Kiley, 1996).
Sleepers (Barry Levinson, 1996).
Contact (Robert Zemeckis, 1997).
The Devil's Advocate (Taylor Hackford, 1997).

Kundun (Martin Scorsese, 1997).
Meet Joe Black (Martin Brest, 1998).
The Truman Show (Peter Weir, 1998).
This Is My Father (Paul Quinn, 1998).
What Dreams May Come (Vincent Ward, 1998).
Dogma (Kevin Smith, 1999).
A Love Divided (Sydney Macartney, 1999).
End of Days (Peter Hyams, 1999).
The Matrix (Andy Wachowski, 1999).
The Ninth Gate (Roman Polanski, 1999).
The Sixth Sense (M. Night Shyamalan, 1999).
Stigmata (Rupert Wainright, 1999).
The Third Miracle (Agnieszka Holland, 1999).
Keeping the Faith (Edward Norton, 2000).
Little Nicky (Steven Brill, 2000).
Unbreakable (M. Night Shyamalan, 2000).
The Man Who Sued God (Mark Joffe, 2001).
Dragonfly (Tom Shadyac, 2002).
Life or Something Like It (Stephen Herek, 2002).
The Magdalene Sisters (Peter Mullan, 2002).
Signs (M. Night Shyamalan, 2002).
Song for a Raggy Boy (Aisling Walsh, 2002).
The Good Thief (Neil Jordan, 2003).
Phone Booth (Joel Schumacher, 2003).
Big Fish (Tim Burton, 2004).
The Passion of the Christ (Mel Gibson, 2004).
The Village (M. Night Shyamalan, 2004).
The Da Vinci Code (Ron Howard, 2006).
Angels & Demons (Ron Howard, 2009).

Index

About the Author

AUBREY MALONE was born in the west of Ireland in 1953. He has been a film critic with various Irish magazines and newspapers since the early 1970s. He has published a number of books on movies: *Hollyweird* (Michael O'Mara) in 1996, *I Was a Fugitive from a Hollywood Trivia Factory* (Prion) in 1998, *On the Edge* (Solar) in 1999, *The Rise and Fall and Rise of Elvis* (Greenaway) in 2003, etc. He has also written biographies of Ernest Hemingway, Brendan Behan, Charles Bukowski and Tom Jones as well as a number of humor books and some fiction. He lives in Dublin.